Climber's Paradise

THE UNIVERSITY OF ALBERTA PRESS

Climber's Paradise

Making Canada's Mountain Parks, 1906-1974

PEARLANN REICHWEIN

Published by

The University of Alberta Press
Ring House 2
Edmonton, Alberta, Canada T6G 2E1
www.uap.ualberta.ca

MOUNTAIN CAIRNS ▲ A series on the history
and culture of the Canadian Rocky Mountains.

Copyright © 2014 PearlAnn Reichwein

LIBRARY AND ARCHIVES CANADA
CATALOGUING IN PUBLICATION

Reichwein, PearlAnn, 1966–, author
     Climber's paradise : making Canada's
     mountain parks, 1906–1974
     / PearlAnn Reichwein.

(Mountain cairns)
Includes bibliographical references and index.
Issued in print and electronic formats.
ISBN 978-0-88864-674-3 (pbk.).—
ISBN 978-0-88864-828-0 (epub).—
ISBN 978-0-88864-829-7 (Amazon kindle).—
ISBN 978-0-88864-830-3 (pdf)

     1. National parks and reserves—Rocky
Mountains, Canadian (B.C. and Alta.)—
History—20th century. 2. Mountaineering—
Rocky Mountains, Canadian (B.C. and Alta.)—
History—20th century. 3. Outdoor recreation—
Rocky Mountains, Canadian (B.C. and Alta.)—
History—20th century. 4. Rocky Mountains,
Canadian (B.C. and Alta.)—History—20th
century. 5. Alpine Club of Canada—History—
20th century. I. Title. II. Series: Mountain
cairns

FC219.R42 2014   333.78'3097110904
C2014-902313-8
C2014-902314-6

Index available in print and PDF editions.

First edition, first printing, 2014.
Printed and bound in Canada by Houghton
Boston Printers, Saskatoon, Saskatchewan.
Copyediting and proofreading by
Meaghan Craven.
Map by Wendy Johnson.
Indexing by Adrian Mather.

The University of Alberta Press is committed
to protecting our natural environment. As part
of our efforts, this book is printed on Cougar
Natural Opaque Smooth, which is 10% post-
consumer waste, process chlorine free and
elemental chlorine free.

The University of Alberta Press gratefully
acknowledges the support received for its
publishing program from The Canada Council
for the Arts. The University of Alberta Press
also gratefully acknowledges the financial
support of the Government of Canada
through the Canada Book Fund (CBF) and the
Government of Alberta through the Alberta
Multimedia Development Fund (AMDF) for its
publishing activities.

*Title page photograph: Three climbers traverse
on ascent of Mount Robson during ACC Mount
Robson Camp, 1924. Harry Pollard photograph.
[WMCR, V14/AC192P/011]*

To my parents

Each one of us dreams dreams and sees visions. The peaks we climb in our reveries are nobler than any we can hope to ascend in real life, but it is our visionary mountains which govern our actual accomplishments.

—ACC PRESIDENT CYRIL WATES
The Gazette, October 1938

Contents

Preface

AS I LOOK DOWN from the snowcapped ridge of Mount Victoria, dawn pours into Banff National Park on my right while shadows still linger in Yoho on my left. Many mountaineers have come to know this place as the roof of the Rockies on the Great Divide. The horn of Mount Assiniboine juts up to the south, the Wapta Icefields spread out to the north, the Sawback Range to the east, and, far out on the western horizon, forest-fire haze clings to the distant peaks of the Selkirks. I spot fresh tracks in the snow far below as I climb down from the ridge. They run up and over Abbot Pass near the refuge hut and lead in various directions to Mount Lefroy, to Mount Victoria, and to a watering spot on the lower Victoria Glacier. Tracks streak down through the scree to Lake Oesa. Mountaineers have been here. The historical footsteps, trails, and ascents of mountaineers point south, east, west, and farther north to other parks and other mountains. And to other stories.

The history of Canada's mountain parks and the Alpine Club of Canada (ACC) is the focus of this volume, and the narrative that follows is situated in the mountain national parks of Alberta, British Columbia, and the Yukon Territory. Banff, Yoho, Jasper, and Kootenay national parks in the main ranges of the Rocky Mountains in Alberta and British Columbia figure prominently in the history of the ACC. Other points of interest include Glacier and Mount Revelstoke national parks in the Columbia Mountains of British Columbia and Waterton Lakes National Park in the southern Alberta Rockies.[1] The term "Rockies" is often applied in popular usage to include all these areas, but technically the Rocky Mountain Trench separates the Rocky Mountains from the Columbia Mountains to the west. These areas are also linked in the popular imagination as Canadian mountain parks.

Living and working in the mountain national parks in Alberta and British Columbia in the 1990s grounded my research and enriched my attachment to these places, but it also highlighted their contradictions. New subdivisions outraced the mountain pine beetle up the slopes of Banff town. Elk and caribou appeared on the local menu as often as they did on the traffic signs in Jasper that warned drivers to slow down.

Semi-trailers and SUVs pushed 120 km/h in 90 km/h park zones on the Yellowhead and TransCanada highways. Every year wild bears in Banff congregated on the railways tracks to eat grain spilled from boxcars, and tourists congregated to watch.

Parks Canada wanted the public to learn about the mountain parks, but, in the midst of the recessionary 1990s, it went in the opposite direction when it raised the entry fees at the park gate and introduced cost-recovery user fees for its guided public interpretive hikes. During those same years, affordable housing for residents and transient workers was scarce. I began to notice that marginal incomes and poverty are often masked as "lifestyle" in national parks and seasonal mountain tourism towns. The federal Banff–Bow Valley Study (1996) was struck to investigate such environmental, social, cultural, and economic concerns, but it excluded major related issues from its terms of reference, such as the twinning of the TransCanada Highway and the future of Lake Louise. At the same time, my reading at the archives made clear that the national parks in the Canadian Rockies had never been an unpeopled landscape, despite the powerful cultural mythologies of pristine wilderness that veil the historical presence of women, men, and children in a landscape that has a human history of class, gender, and ancestry as much as it has mountains. The present function and politics of parks affect the history we assign to these places; I realized I had to peel back layers of memory to better understand parks as historical landscapes.

Studying the ACC led me to view mountaineering as a way of understanding the people, places, and politics of mountain parks. I went to the places I had read about in one of Canada's longest running periodicals, the *Canadian Alpine Journal* (*CAJ*), published by the ACC since 1907. In a 2009 editorial responding to criticism of its emphasis on elite climbing performance, Sean Isaac writes, "The purpose of the *CAJ* is to record the history of Canadian climbing, year by year. Like it or not, much of what makes climbing history is cutting-edge ascents. In fact, that is the definition of history: a chronological timeline punctuated by important events."[2] His observation that "[a]lpine journals are time capsules" is enticing but ignores how such capsules were filled, by whom and for what purposes, what was left out, and how the contents are read and interpreted. Although the masculinist nationalist approach to mountaineering history is commonly reasserted through the representations of Canada's "hard men" (and hard women) of climbing on the covers and inside pages of climbing publications, the *Canadian Alpine Journal* provides an archive of a broad range of mountaineering culture and club life. The social and cultural history of mountaineering can go far beyond the simple understanding of history as a fixed chronology of great ascents in a progressive evolution of "important events"; indeed, such a teleological orientation to historiography was characteristic of an earlier tradition of writing political history and of the nascent field of Canadian sport history in the 1960s. This approach tends "to detach sports from their economic, political, and social context," as Bruce Kidd comments, and ignores factors of class, gender, and ethnicity.[3] A broader, contested, and more human history of mountaineering and the ACC is both possible and promising, and the field of sport and leisure scholarship related to physical cultures generally has moved in this direction.[4] Academics must attend to enduring sport narratives and popular conceptions of history, and how they serve to entrench or challenge power. These debates also prevail among climbers and in the pages of the *CAJ*. The history of mountaineering in Canada is not a unilinear process of sport "progress" or a "coming of age," but a diverse and contested field of ongoing social relations interacting in specific times and places as a dynamic site of culture.

The history of leisure and sport can be brought together productively with environmental history and philosophy. Literary scholar Jeffrey McCarthy identifies mountaineering as "a conflicted site for symbolic configurations of human interaction with the environment."[5] The stories of mountaineering, he argues from an implicitly Western worldview, encompass three primary modes of conceptualizing nature: as objects to conquer, as picturesque settings to admire, and (his main focus) as a site for "the interpenetration of the human and the natural."[6] These modes are neither chronological nor teleological but coexist across time. He reads climbing literature as a means of deconstructing the dualism of nature and culture in order "to reimagine the ways human beings understand their connection to the natural world."[7]

Mountains often mark boundaries, forming and falling into borderlands both real and imagined.[8] The history of the Alpine Club of Canada in the twentieth century, as it was written by mountaineers and inscribed on mountainous landscapes from Canada's south to its north, provides apt commentary on such borderlands. How did the ACC's actions form and reform these landscapes, create and recreate mountain parks? What impact did the ACC have on the ways in which Canadians imagine and know wild places?

Acknowledgements

MANY PEOPLE SUPPORTED MY WORK on Canada's mountain parks and my ventures as I wrote this book. I would like to express my appreciation and thanks all of them, if not all by name as there are so many.

My research relied on the expertise of archives and library professionals. Lena Goon, Elizabeth Kundert-Cameron, Jennifer Rutkair, former archivist Don Burdon, and their practicum students at the Whyte Museum of the Canadian Rockies assisted my work over the course of many years. I would like to gratefully acknowledge their collegial assistance. Access to books and collections facilitated by the excellent professional staff at British Columbia Archives, Canadian Pacific Railway Archives, City of Edmonton Archives, Library and Archives Canada, local and regional Parks Canada libraries, the Royal Alberta Museum, University of Alberta Archives, Yukon Archives, and other institutions was also vital to my research. Parks Canada offices and other agencies across the country offered helpful service in response to my research inquiries. Many thanks to the ACC members and families I was pleased to meet—as well as ACC staff and volunteers. I extend sincere thanks to those who kindly shared photos. Thank you, also, to the excellent ACMG guides, ACC crews, and all my travel companions.

The University of Alberta Press formed a talented team around my book as they prepared it to become part of the *Mountain Cairns* series. Special thanks are due to editors Meaghan Craven and Mary Lou Roy, and to designer Alan Brownoff. Thank you, Linda Cameron, Peter Midgley, and Sharon Wilson. My early work on this subject germinated at Carleton University and grew to a comprehensive study. Earlier versions of parts of the book were published in *The Canadian Historical Review* and *Journal of the Canadian Historical Association*. I am grateful to David Mills, Graeme Wynn, and anonymous reviewers who offered valuable comments. Past graduate assistants Paulina Retamales and Yanan Lin provided valued technical support. Diverse professors and students joined many discussions of history and mountain scholarship during my teaching and research, especially in the History of Nature, Parks, and Travel seminars, as did those in the Canadian Mountain

Studies Initiative. I thank them, along with other past and present colleagues at University of Alberta, for thoughtful conversation. Various members of the Alberta Recreation and Parks Association, Canadian Historical Association, Canadian Studies Network, International Society for the History of Physical Education and Sport, North American Society for the History of Sport, NiCHE, and others, also fostered valuable interactions. In the end, of course, the views expressed in this book are my own.

I would like to acknowledge with sincere appreciation the generous contributions made to support publishing this book, with special thanks to Jennifer Wheeler Crompton and David Crompton, and other gracious donors. I also gratefully acknowledge grants to support the book's publication: Alberta Historical Resources Foundation, Heritage Preservation Partnership Program; Alberta Sports, Recreation, Parks and Wildlife Foundation; University of Calgary Parks and Protected Spaces Research Group; and University of Alberta Endowment Fund for the Future.

Above all, the spirit and good company of friends and family enriched the time I dedicated to writing this book. I thank you all warmly. Of course, Marcus and Maya deserve a special mention. My wonderful parents Ronalda and Baldwin followed the project as we shared our lives together. I am grateful for your dedication, conviction, and infinite belief. I dedicate the book with love to you and the memories that light my way. *Sic itur ad astra.*

Abbreviations

AAC	American Alpine Club
ACC	Alpine Club of Canada
BNP	Banff National Park
CAJ	*Canadian Alpine Journal*
CNPA	Canadian National Parks Association
CNR	Canadian Northern/National Railway
CPAWS	Canadian Parks and Wilderness Society
CPR	Canadian Pacific Railway
CPRA	Canadian Pacific Railway Archives
EA	City of Edmonton Archives
GA	Glenbow Archives
GCAR	Government of Canada Annual Reports
GMC	General Mountaineering Camp
NFB	National Film Board of Canada
NFTSA	National Film, Television and Sound Archives
NPPAC	National and Provincial Parks Association of Canada
RG	Record Group
UFA	United Farmers of Alberta
UNESCO	United Nations Educational, Scientific, and Cultural Organization
WMCR	Whyte Museum of the Canadian Rockies
YACE	Yukon Alpine Centennial Expedition

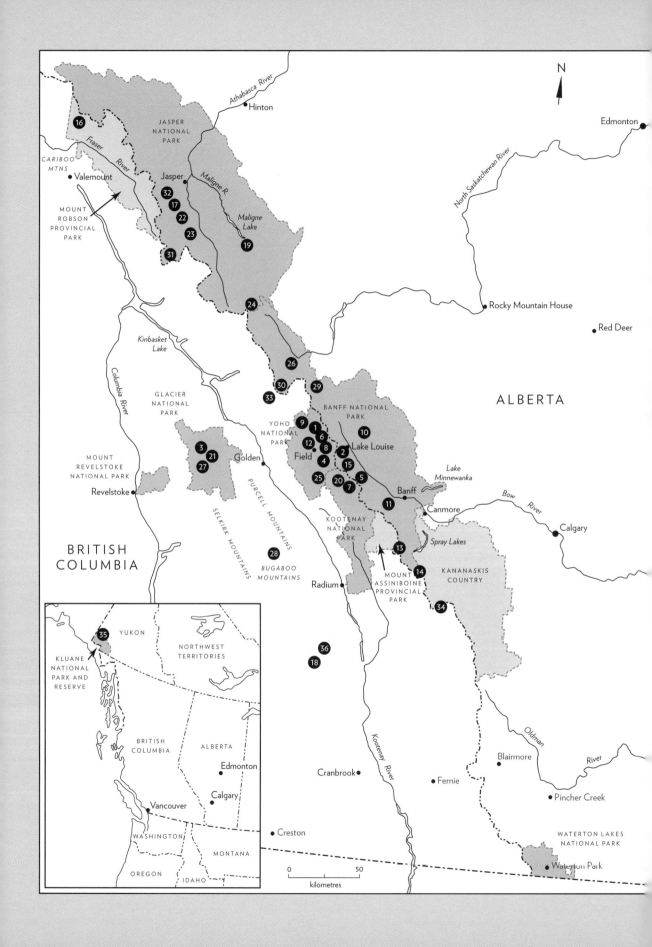

N

JASPER
NATIONAL
PARK

Athabasca River

Hinton

Edmonton

CARIBOO
MTNS

Fraser River

Valemount

MOUNT
ROBSON
PROVINCIAL
PARK

16

Jasper

32
17
22
23
31

Maligne R.

Maligne
Lake

19

24

North Saskatchewan River

Rocky Mountain House

Red Deer

Kinbasket
Lake

Columbia River

GLACIER
NATIONAL
PARK

MOUNT
REVELSTOKE
NATIONAL PARK

Revelstoke

3
21
27

Golden

PURCELL MOUNTAINS

SELKIRK MOUNTAINS

26

30
33

29

BANFF NATIONAL
PARK

YOHO
NATIONAL
PARK

9
1
6
12
8
4
15
25
20
7
5
11

Field

2

10

Lake Louise

Lake
Minnewanka

Banff

Canmore

Bow River

Calgary

ALBERTA

BRITISH
COLUMBIA

28

BUGABOO
MOUNTAINS

Radium

KOOTENAY
NATIONAL
PARK

MOUNT
ASSINIBOINE
PROVINCIAL
PARK

13

Spray Lakes

14

KANANASKIS
COUNTRY

34

35

YUKON

KLUANE
NATIONAL
PARK AND
RESERVE

NORTHWEST
TERRITORIES

BRITISH
COLUMBIA

ALBERTA

Edmonton

Calgary

Vancouver

WASHINGTON

MONTANA

OREGON

IDAHO

36
18

Kootenay River

Cranbrook

Fernie

Oldman River

Blairmore

Pincher Creek

WATERTON LAKES
NATIONAL PARK

Waterton Park

Creston

0   50

kilometres

ACC General Mountaineering Camps, 1906–1974

1   Yoho Pass, 1906, 1919

2   Paradise Valley, 1907, 1918, 1933, 1944

3   Rogers Pass, 1908, 1929

4   Lake O'Hara, 1909, 1921, 1925, 1951, 1968

5   Consolation [Lakes] Valley, 1910, 1942

6   Sherbrooke Lake, 1911

7   Vermilion Pass, 1912

8   Cathedral Mountain, 1913

9   Upper [Little] Yoho Valley, 1914, 1927, 1937, 1943

10   Ptarmigan [Lake] Valley, 1915

11   Bow Valley [Healy Creek], 1916

12   Cataract Valley, 1917

13   Mount Assiniboine, 1920, 1935, 1952, 1966

14   Palliser Pass, 1922

15   Larch Valley, 1923

16   Mount Robson, 1924, 1955, 1974

17   Tonquin Valley, 1926

18   Lake of the Hanging Glacier, 1928

19   Maligne Lake, 1930, 1950, 1962

20   Prospectors Valley, 1931

21   Mount Sir Donald, 1932

22   Chrome Lake (Eremite Valley), 1934, 1945, 1963

23   Fryatt [Creek] Valley, 1936, 1960, 1972

24   Columbia Icefields, 1938

25   Goodsirs, 1939, 1954, 1961

26   Glacier Lake, 1940, 1965, 1973

27   Glacier, BC, 1941, 1947, 1956

28   Bugaboo Creek, 1946, 1959

29   Peyto Lake, 1948

30   Freshfields, 1949, 1969

31   Hooker Icefield (Whirlpool Valley), 1953

32   Moat Lake, Tonquin Valley, 1957, 1970

33   Mummery, Blaeberry River, 1958

34   French Military Group, 1964

35   YACE [Steele Glacier], 1967

36   Farnham Creek, 1971

Imagining
Canada's
Mountain
Parks

1

Where the sounds of music and dancing on the veranda once drifted out into the cool night air, it is now quiet, a grassy plateau in the trees near the traffic grinding up the town's Mountain Avenue.

For decades the "Club House at Banff" was a popular gathering place for the ACC. Climbers slept in tent cabins on the hillside (left, out of view). Calgary Section members with friends on the way to Palliser Pass Camp in 1922. N. Hendrie, Mr. Mumm, Mr. F. Green, H. Walsh, M. Hendrie with Mr. McGeary (atop pillar), unidentified, Malcolm Geddes (ice axe), and Tom Porter (stairs). Harry Pollard photograph. [WMCR, V14/AC29P/3/1]

FORGOTTEN IN THE FOREST, the site of the once-grand Alpine Club of Canada (ACC) Banff Clubhouse is on Sulphur Mountain adjacent to the town of Banff, Alberta. Hundreds of pairs of leather boots once crossed the gravel driveway and clattered up the clubhouse stairs. Where the sounds of music and dancing on the veranda once drifted out into the cool night air, it is now quiet, a grassy plateau in the trees near the traffic grinding up the town's Mountain Avenue. From this vantage point, the national ACC clubhouse overlooked Banff, the Parks Administration Building, and the Banff Springs Hotel: major landmarks of administration and commerce. Until it was demolished in 1974, the clubhouse was an abiding landmark of the ACC and a symbolic cornerstone of the Canadian national park idea.

The Alpine Club of Canada, formed in Winnipeg in 1906, shaped many visions of Canada's mountain parks as a climber's paradise. Examining the club's history fosters a critical understanding of key interactions between mountaineering and national parks. The club became a leading proponent of recreation, conservation, and tourism in the Rocky Mountain parks, and its history sheds light on the culture of alpinism and the history of the Canadian national park idea. The ACC and the federal government forged a close relationship that promoted the goals of public enjoyment, conservation, and commercial tourism. The club's effect on public policy reveals its enduring role in creating and transforming the visions of three of Canada's key nation-building organizations: the Geological Survey of Canada (GSC), the national railways, and Dominion Parks, especially mountain parks.

Unlike many other national sport organizations existing in Canada at the beginning of the twentieth century, the ACC started in western Canada and was strongly oriented westward. It operated through club sections in larger cities across the country, as well as internationally. A broad-based pyramid of recreational interests and members supported the club's elite mountaineering endeavours and expeditions. Membership was strongly grounded in Alberta and British Columbia, but club sections radiated across the country and abroad with their own regional characters and activities. The national character and structure of the club, however, allowed it to gain official status and close alignment with national parks and government officials.

The making of national parks and the making of Canada's national mountaineering club were closely connected, and much of the history of Canadian mountaineering is suspended between them. As Canadian historian Bruce Kidd suggests, national sport organizations like the ACC "shaped the dominant practices and coined the very language with which Canadians discussed what sports should mean."[1] And as sport historian Colin Howell writes, wherever it was produced, Canadian sport history was made on the ground.[2] In this case, the ground was Canada's mountain parks: contested spaces subject to many interpretations, political, social, and cultural.

The idea of national parks in Canada's mountains was generated through the politics of conservation, recreation, tourism, and resources on public lands. The ACC helped to reshape the mountain park idea throughout the twentieth century through a continuous process of social, cultural, and political invention. A voluntary organization peopled by diverse stakeholders, the club was central to changes emerging from land-use and resource-management policies. The shifting idea of Canada's mountain parks over time both reflected meanings made outside the realm of leisure and sport and also was a product of that realm. However, even as ideas about the parks changed, mountaineering—people interacting with the mountains in a specific way—was and continues to be an ongoing attribute, perpetuated through the institutional work and presence of the ACC. From the beginning, the ACC has highlighted the presence of people in parks, especially in the Canadian Rockies, where the meaning of "park" has shifted greatly since the early days of the ACC until now.

National parks in the Rockies are vast and rugged, especially so when the ACC was instituted; they were the first, the biggest, wildest, and the most spectacular, according to standard assumptions that now warrant closer inspection. In his influential history of Canada's national parks published in 1970, R.C. Brown assesses the parks as an outgrowth of John A. Macdonald's National Policy and economics, in keeping with a "doctrine of usefulness." The first national mountain parks offered patrons mountain scenery, hot springs, timber, and minerals useful for nation-building.[3] Brown's work can be read as an indication of how closely mountain parks in the West were aligned with the historiography of an earlier, centralist, national, political, and economic history. More recently, historians of national parks in Canada have reacted against centralizing narratives of western parks, much as earlier proponents of regional history in Canada once challenged nationalist narratives of Canadian history focused on central Canada. Today's national parks histories highlight regional and bioregional interests, the social and cultural histories (and stories) of people, the environment, and the state.[4] The histories of Banff, Yoho, Glacier, Mount Revelstoke, Waterton, Jasper, and Kootenay national parks are regional histories of borderlands in Alberta and British Columbia, as is Kluane in the Yukon. Mountain regions are productive places to think about diverse problems, such as social relations, resource use, and climate change: mountains and parks are landscapes with local, regional, national, and international stories.[5]

In 1885 a federal reserve was designated around the Cave and Basin Hot Spring on Sulphur Mountain, and legislation two years later declared it Rocky Mountains Park. When a railway was built through Kicking Horse Pass, the Canadian Pacific Railway (CPR) saw potential for commercial tourism and encouraged Ottawa to establish national parks in the mountains. The first Dominion parks were situated all along the CPR: Rocky Mountains Park, and Yoho and Glacier (1886). Waterton and other parks were established in what is now Alberta before the end of the century. The Grand Trunk Pacific and Canadian Northern rail lines later passed through Yellowhead Pass to the north, prompting the establishment of Jasper Park in 1907. Mountaineers, attracted to the parks, radiated from the railways in search of new climbs and unnamed peaks, prompting Canada's golden age of mountaineering from the 1890s to 1920.

Railway tourism brought the Canadian Rockies to a world stage. During the era of luxury train travel, corporate rail lines promoted travel to CPR hotels in Canada's Rockies in campaigns promising "Fifty Switzerlands in One" and "The Challenge of the Mountains."[6] Under the patronage of the CPR and the Canadian National Railway (CNR), artists known as the Canadian railway school emerged to produce works that promoted tourism.[7] Parks in the Canadian Rockies became iconic landscapes synonymous with Canada, as did the act of mountaineering.

In the increasingly urbanized Victorian era, travellers with a yearning for outdoor holidays were attracted to the idea of a grand alpine playground. Framed by the windows of elegant CPR dining cars and studded with citadels like the Banff Springs Hotel, Chateau Lake Louise, and Mount Stephen House, the mountains were considered an exotic landscape, perceived by the Victorian mind not as sublime terror but sublime majesty.[8] Adventurous guests took to the peaks. Glacier House in Glacier National Park, British Columbia, was a CPR hotel in the Selkirk Range visited by international tourists, scientists, surveyors, mountaineers, and various leading lights in the late nineteenth century, some of whom explored the mountains with Swiss mountain guides, employed by the CPR to lead guests on nearby climbs and ascents.[9] The experience of the Vaux family—Quakers from the Philadelphia Academy of Natural Science who frequented Glacier House—is representative of the sense of discovery that moved natural history enthusiasts to travel the Canadian Rockies. Glaciologist George Vaux, Jr. (1863–1927) commented on "the consciousness that so little exploration has been carried out that each visitor is practically a new discoverer."[10] His sister Mary Vaux (1860–1940), a botanical painter and photographer, spent more than forty summer seasons studying plants in the Canadian mountain parks: "Sometimes I feel that I can hardly wait till the time comes to escape to the free air of the everlasting hills. I sometimes wonder how it is that those who love the out of doors so much, seem always to have their lots cast in the manmade town."[11] The convergence of geographic exploration, inventory sciences, and romanticism in Victorian tourism in the late nineteenth century formed a crucial intellectual juncture from which flowed twentieth-century ideas about national parks and Canadian alpinism[12]—ideas that were then fleshed out by the Alpine Club of Canada's directorship and members during its seasons of work and play in the mountain parks.

The ACC's first and perennial campgrounds and climbing areas were typically located in the Canadian Rockies east and west of the

Continental Divide, although the St. Elias Range in the Yukon Territory and other northern ranges also hosted the club's mountaineering ventures and were important sites to the growth of national parks. As well, some provincial mountain parks, particularly those contiguous with the Canadian Rocky Mountain parks, such as Mount Robson and Mount Assiniboine, as well as Bugaboo Provincial Park in British Columbia, and Kananaskis Provincial Park in Alberta, figure in the club's social and environmental history. Within these bounds, the ACC contributed to the construction of the "idea" of national parks; and how we think about this idea affects how it works.

Of course, mountain parks are and were not simply spaces that can be taken for granted as "nature" or "wilderness," because these terms are mutable and anchored in specific contexts of time and place in a given society and language. The parks, as well, are not just ideas but also material entities with implications for land, resources, and living organisms, including people. In response to certain environmental history debates that render nature simply as a discourse and cultural construct, Canadian environmental historian Claire Campbell underscores the impossibility of writing "environmental history without paying a great deal of attention to the environment in question; and it is irresponsible to imply that this environment does not have either an independent reality or a tangible effect on the course of human history."[13] However, if the idea of national parks in Canada is mutable, so, too, is their physical materiality. In the end, it is through a dialectic of landscape as idea and landscape as material that people interact with mountains to make the meanings of place, and to affect other ideas related to mountainous places: tourism, conservation, and nationalisms.

The mountaineers who made up the initial membership of the ACC had both a sense of place and a land ethic that figured in early conservation and environmentalism in Canada. They were invested in the mountains, developing seasonal affiliations to them and having a stake in knowing them. Interplay between people and mountains helped to form landscapes and created a sense of place through time and familiarity.[14] The club and its members also produced and reproduced themselves by inventing traditions through change and reconsolidation, adding to the geographic imagination of place by learning through embodied knowledge and the experiences of "being there." As mountaineering historian Peter Donnelly suggests, "the meanings of spaces are socially constructed...such meanings vary by time and place, and...changing social and material conditions can result in the social reconstruction of such meanings."[15]

Perhaps the most powerful thing the ACC did in its process of meaning-making and space construction was to claim the mountain parks as home. When the club did this, it gave itself a privileged distinction in a climber's paradise. "The heritage of home is particularly powerful from both personal and collective perspectives," sport heritage analyst Gregory Ramshaw observes, "as the sites, artefacts, rituals and traditions associated with home construct notions of continuity and identity."[16] But the club did not claim the parks as its home to the exclusion of others; ACC members promoted "Canada's mountain heritage" and taught Canadians in general to be at home in the mountains. As a result, mountain parks emerged from being merely faceless spaces in a rationalized regime of controls and also became places where people could invent and change how they saw and engaged mountains, how they were at home there. Through the production and consumption of places and experiences, the club's members made concrete their dreams of wilderness, the freedom of the hills, and a climber's paradise. Much like the modernist architect Le Corbusier's rationalized designs for spaces as "machines for sport," mountain parks in turn regulated the spaces and people of mountaineering even as they gave rise to strong place affiliations among mountaineers who felt they belonged there.

In order to understand how the ACC related to the mountain parks and created meaning there, one must consider its human history and organizational culture. For example, at the club's annual summer camps, conversations between humans and landscapes were spoken, meanings made, homes found. "Old camp friends" developed their own collective identity as a distinct class of visitors to the national mountain parks and participated in creating the ACC social culture. On the rope, in the tea tent, around the campfire, the club rediscovered, instilled, and perpetuated its values with each generation of alpinists: the beauty of the mountains; nature's role in physical and moral health as a corrective to mechanized urban life; the significance of the national parks as spiritual and recreational escapes from daily life in a modern technological age; the uplift of well-used leisure and organized physical sport with one's class peers; the nationalist dimension of Canadian participation on the world stage of mountaineering. The ACC's position in Canadian mountain cultural circles ensured its elite leadership role in defining the key priorities of Canada's national parks in both public policy and popular opinion. The annual mountaineering camps framed the structures of common experience that united women and men of the

Alpine Club of Canada as a distinct, middle-class subculture organized around the ideals of alpinism.

Through storytelling, and famously, its journal, *The Canadian Alpine Journal* (CAJ), the ACC spread its vision of the mountains. Mountaineering narratives, both oral and written, offer a possible epistemology of place predicated on a unity between mountaineers and the environment, rather than their separation. This sense of unity between people and mountains dissolves the disassociation of subject and object positioning typical of Cartesian paradigms that divide the human and non-human. The knowledge of place combines people with a physical space, creating a "subjective connection to landscape"[17] that points toward connections and oneness of being, however fleeting, rather than alienation. In other words, an ontology and epistemology of place can be constituted by the stories, images, and human history of mountaineering that speaks to being in and of nature. The ACC's role in this ongoing narrative is vital because understanding the connections between people and nature is important when we confront the environmental problems of thinking about nature as Other and to the "estrangement from the natural world"[18] that climber and environmental studies professor Jeffrey McCarthy contends is a fundamental issue current in contemporary North American society. Mountains have been heavily invested with meanings, as English scholar Reuben Ellis observes, and "it would be shortsighted to discount their significance and vitality as symbolic landscapes."[19]

One way to investigate the history of outdoor recreation and camping, and thereby trace human relationships to the natural world by methodologically following "the hiking trails," is proposed by environmental historian James Morton Turner, who juxtaposes the American woodcraft movement with the later, twentieth-century "Leave No Trace" movement in the United States. "Opening the backpacks, leafing through the guidebooks, and revisiting the campsites reveals more than just changes in the ways people have returned to nature. Indeed, it reveals the historical pliability of the very ideals to which wilderness travelers have aspired," Turner contends.[20] Wilderness recreationists have been "some of America's most ardent environmentalists," yet the ideals of the wilderness movement were historically contingent and contested with regard to trends in the capitalist market for commodified wilderness experiences. Both movements were implicated in social changes and critiques played out around leisure. Likewise, mountaineers in the ACC who were active in the Canadian mountain parks were implicated in social changes and critiques that played out through leisure within civil society. They participated in making the ideologies and political economies of outdoor recreation, sport, tourism, and conservation. They were buyers in the capitalist market for commodified wilderness experiences, yet they were also party to contingent historical ideals of nature and the wilderness movement.

Mountaineering provides an amalgam of recreational practices that opens a way of knowing people and place as an integrated entity and offers a site to investigate the shifting ideals of parks. The history of the ACC and its long-standing regional presence demonstrates that mountaineers and mountain parks in Canada are closely connected. These connections have both absorbed and constituted philosophies of being and knowing that played into larger systems of political economy and environmental politics in civil society. Following the history of the ACC along hiking trails and climbing routes to its gatherings and destinations—not to mention following its members' thoughts and deeds by tracing actions at political meetings, and the ideas expressed in the club's many letters and journal articles, stories, maps, and photographs—helps us better understand the integration of nature and culture in Canada.

What is the future of mountain parks in Canada, and where might a history of the present lead? What is the power of imaginary landscapes and imagined worlds? In an era that laments what American journalist Richard Louv terms the "nature deficit" in North American life and childhood as the end of a frontier, discourses of risk, moral panic, and nationalistic pride may affect the way we justify and encourage nature-based leisure.[21] In this respect, themes in the antimodernist culture of nature that prompted Canadian mountaineering in the early 1900s deserve to be revisited. Yet first-hand outdoor interactions with nature remain fundamental to a philosophy and epistemology of oneness that may be transformative and lead to environmental awareness and stewardship. Clearly, concerns about land, water, and parks do not go away. These concerns can also reconnect living worlds through outdoor interactions that inspire a politics of environmental advocacy for the places we know and love. What is the role of civil society in such a political culture? How might we lead and how might we follow in a reflexive pedagogy that unites nature and culture? Is knowing nature as our home place, backyard, and part of who we are central to this transformation? The answer to these questions may return us to the roof of the Rockies.

More than a century after its creation, the ACC has more than ten thousand members. The once proud Banff Alpine Clubhouse no longer looks out from Sulphur Mountain in Banff National Park, and, like the clubhouse, the old view from the veranda is gone, blocked by the growth of trees and town. Only the mountains remain seemingly unchanged, slowly aging in geophysical time while people come and go. On this backdrop flicker visions of the Alpine Club of Canada and its ideas of a climber's paradise.

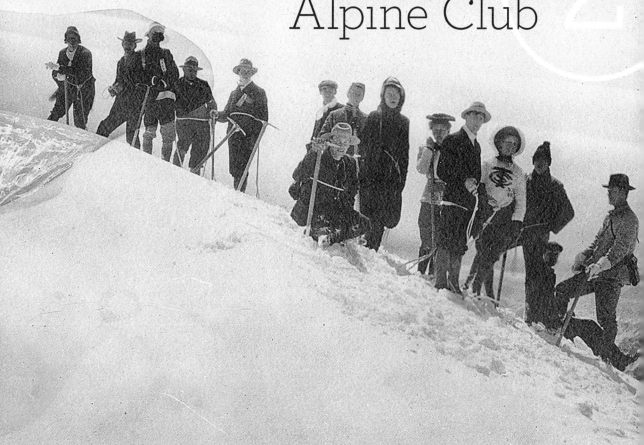

Canada's Alpine Club

No doubt in the next hundred or two hundred years...a great many mountaineering clubs will flourish...for mountaineering is going to be more and more a Canadian sport...

But the Alpine Club of Canada will still be the national mountaineering club, and will have gathered to itself a noble succession of Canada's good men in every high and useful vocation in life...will have added a worthy somewhat to Canadian literature, art and science.

—ELIZABETH PARKER, 1908[1]

∧ *"Alpiners on Peak of Temple." ACC ascent from Paradise Valley Camp, 1907. George Kinney photograph.* [WMCR. V14/AC14P/26]

CLIMBING MOUNTAINS was part of the job for Arthur Oliver Wheeler when he was sent to the Selkirk Mountains to conduct a photo-topographic survey in British Columbia for the Dominion Land Survey. While staying at Glacier House in 1901, he took climbing instruction from the resident Swiss mountain guides of the CPR hotel recommended by the matronly Scottish manager Mrs. J.M. Young. Six guides accompanied Wheeler up Mount Overlook, "all keen to impart information" and ready to offer their expertise to a new climber, but they had a difficult client as Wheeler was a man keener to lead than to follow. He soon dismissed the professional guides and confidently asserted by the end of the season that he and his survey team were "quite their equals" climbing.[2] The world of the Selkirks and its social encounters converted Wheeler to mountaineering, as he later recalled: "the climbs, the nightly gatherings around the fire and the yarns, in which the summits were always reached, soon had the usual effect and I became a devoted enthusiast of climbing in the delightful, devilish Selkirks…"[3]

At the time, vast ranges of mountains in western Canada were unmapped and officially unclimbed; there was no national alpine club, and few Canadians pursued mountaineering. "The climbs, the nightly gatherings around the fire and the yarns" were experiences central to the culture of climbing in the Selkirks and Rockies, but interest in these practices was generally limited to foreign travellers visiting the parks. The establishment of the ACC in 1906, in which Wheeler played a key role, opened the outdoors for more converts to climbing in Canada.

When Wheeler visited Glacier House in 1901 and 1902, he met a small but extremely active international community of climbers, adventurers, scientists, and artists, all bent on illuminating the mysteries of mountain wilderness. Glacier House was a popular summer resort for travellers belonging to various learned societies and sports organizations, such as the Academy of Natural Sciences of Philadelphia, the Appalachian Mountain Club, and The Alpine Club (London). The first recorded mountaineering ascents near Glacier House had been made in 1888 by the Irish minister William Spotswood Green, a member of The Alpine Club (London), who drew and published the first maps of the Selkirk Range based on his explorations.[4] Non-Canadian mountaineers and European guides made the recorded first ascents of Canadian peaks in the Rockies and Columbia Mountains before Canadians caught on to the late-Victorian vogue for mountaineering. The CPR carried mountain-hungry visitors through the Rockies and Columbia ranges and offered comfortable accommodations. Built near the summit of Rogers Pass and below the ice sheet of the Illecillewaet Glacier, Glacier House was a particular favourite among prosperous Americans from the northeastern United States who returned annually to escape the humidity and stifling heat of the city and enjoy a temperate alpine summer committed to amateur scientific, artistic, and literary pursuits characteristic of their belief in Victorian rational recreation. Among these regulars were many of the leading natural history experts studying the region: the Vaux family of Philadelphia, who produced extensive glaciological measurements and photographic records; Mary (Sharples) Schäffer and Charles Schäffer, who studied wildflower botany; and Charles Doolittle Walcott of the United States Geological Survey, later secretary of the Washington Smithsonian Institute, who discovered the Burgess Shale fossil bed in 1909. William Vaux, Jr., referred to this league of tourists as a "decidedly Rocky Mountain cult."[5]

Among the mountaineers at Glacier House in 1901, Arthur Wheeler met the tall, leggy, literature professor Dr. Charles E. Fay from Massachusetts. Fay was then the president of the Appalachian Mountain Club, which originated in the early 1870s as a group devoted to the appreciation of the New England hills. An enthusiast of climbing trips to the Canadian Rockies and Columbia Mountains, he was instrumental in

Arthur Oliver Wheeler (1860–1945)

Land Surveyor and Mapmaker to Western Canada

ARTHUR OLIVER WHEELER was born May 1, 1860, at his father's estate in Kilkenny, Ireland, the eldest son of Captain Edward Oliver Wheeler and Josephine Helsham, members of the landed Anglo-Irish gentry. He attended a Dublin private school, then Ballinasloe and Dulwich colleges. In 1876 diminishing financial circumstances forced the Wheeler family to emigrate. They settled in Collingwood, Ontario, joining like-minded Anglicans and Conservatives. Captain Wheeler became harbourmaster and his son, Arthur, entered a land survey apprenticeship.[6]

In 1877 Wheeler joined a field survey party that journeyed across the Great Lakes into the bush north of Bruce Mines, Ontario. His first summer of rough-country survey work set a pattern for the years to come, with most summers devoted to cross-country travel and drawing survey lines through the West. His life was a personal and professional nexus for developments in topographic science, alpine exploration, and westward expansion. In 1878 he made his first trip west of the Great Lakes while assisting Elihu Stewart survey Indian reserves near the Prince Albert Settlement in the North-West Territories, walking from Winnipeg to Prince Albert and back. On other expeditions to the West early in the 1880s, he surveyed timber berths in Manitoba and prairie townships in the North-West Territories that became part of Saskatchewan. After completing his studies, he qualified as an Ontario land surveyor (1881) and a Dominion land surveyor (1882), followed by professional accreditation in Manitoba (1882), British Columbia (1891), and Alberta (1911). By the age of thirty-one,

< *A.O. Wheeler demonstrates camera and tripod for mountain survey mapping. Canada's pre-eminent mountain surveyor committed to lifelong leadership in the ACC.*
[WMCR, V465/PD/3/374]

Wheeler held professional credentials as a surveyor across Canada.

The federal Department of the Interior engaged Wheeler as a technical officer in its Ottawa Topographical Surveys Branch in 1885, where he was introduced to a specialized branch of topography. The Surveyor General of Canada, Dr. Edouard Gaston Deville, taught Wheeler photogrammetry, an innovative method of using high mountain stations to photograph and survey mountainous areas. Training in photogrammetry allowed Wheeler to forge his reputation as a specialized surveyor and alpine topographer. Meanwhile, western expansionism sent crisis into action on the prairies.

During the 1885 Métis Uprising, Wheeler served as a lieutenant in the Dominion Land Surveyors' Intelligence Corps, which joined forces against supporters of Louis Riel in Saskatchewan. Surveyors in the vanguard of Canadian nation-building in the North-West Territories knew the lay of the land and the economic and strategic implications of resettlement in the region. He applied his geographic expertise to moving General Frederick Dobson Middleton's men over rough terrain and took a shoulder wound in crossfire during conflicts at Batoche. He was awarded the Saskatchewan Medal and Clasp for service in the conflict.

When he returned to Ottawa, Wheeler befriended the family of Dominion Botanist John Macoun, an early explorer and notable proponent of western settlement who worked for the Geological Survey of Canada (GSC), and his wife Ellen Terrill. On June 6, 1888, Wheeler married the Macouns' daughter, Clara (1864–1923). Clara was a capable organizer with "a faculty for detail that amounted to genius." When she was just seventeen, she and her sister had assisted their father by compiling and organizing the research material for his first book, the classic *Manitoba and the Great Northwest* (1882). Family life for Arthur and Clara was marked by seasonal separations, but she held a strong research interest in western exploration and was accustomed to the annual field work cycle associated with survey life. A friend once commented: "Her sympathy for her husband's pursuits was based on real knowledge."[7] Their only child, Edward Oliver (1890–1962), was born in Ottawa and educated at Kingston's Royal Military College. Following his father's lead, Oliver Wheeler became a mountain surveyor and gained renown for the laborious survey reconnaissance of approaches to Mount Everest in 1921. Serving the British Empire as the Surveyor General of India, he was knighted Brigadier Sir Oliver Wheeler in 1943.[8]

Encouraged by John Macoun's enthusiasm for the western frontier and opportunities for survey work in British Columbia, Arthur Wheeler and family moved in 1890 from Ottawa to New Westminster, where he went into private business. Through the economic depression of the early 1890s, he was hired to survey timber berths and mining sites in the mountainous British Columbia interior and to outline townships and subdivisions between Edmonton and Calgary. He returned to the federal civil service from 1893 until 1910, working again in the Topographical Survey Branch of the Department of the Interior, where his work concentrated primarily on surveying the vicinity of the Continental Divide. Increasingly challenging mountain terrain brought his skills as a photo-topographer into full play. As a toponymist, he named more than fifty-five mountains, passes, lakes, and other features during his career.

Working in the Rockies and the Selkirk Range led Wheeler to develop a reputation for mountain surveys. In 1900 he surveyed and mapped the coal-mining region in the Crowsnest Pass. In 1901–02 his surveys of the Selkirk Mountains defined Wheeler's professional reputation as an alpine surveyor. These trips laid the groundwork for *The Selkirk Range* (1905), a comprehensive geography and mountaineering history of the region, accompanied by photo illustrations and a map folio. The book was well reviewed. The literary editor of the *Manitoba Free Press*, Elizabeth Parker, wrote, "Mr. Wheeler has reason to be proud of his really great achievement in Canadian mountain literature."[9]

Together, Parker and Wheeler would create another achievement before long.

As a pioneer surveyor advancing new technical methods, Wheeler emerged as an authority in the field of alpine photo-topography. By 1902 he was admitted to the Royal Geographical Society sponsored by Sir Sandford Fleming. Rising professional status and international exposure took him farther afield to a 1904 meeting of the International Geographic Congress in Washington, DC, and the St. Louis World's Fair, where his alpine photos and maps were exhibited in the Canadian Pavilion. He worked on surveys in British Columbia from 1910 to 1913. In 1913 he was appointed British Columbia Commissioner for the Alberta–British Columbia Boundary Commission, overseeing the surveys and mapping that would officially demarcate the provincial boundaries along the Continental Great Divide. The watershed line of the Rocky Mountains, running from the 49th parallel nearly a thousand kilometres north to its intersection with the 120th meridian near the Yellowhead Pass, is today the boundary between southern British Columbia and Alberta, and among several mountain park jurisdictions. Three atlases of Wheeler's contoured maps accompanied the final interprovincial boundary report. It was a monumental achievement for the commission and its staff. On the report's completion in 1925, Wheeler retired from active professional surveying at age sixty-five. The Dominion Land Surveyors' Association recognized his work by electing him honorary member in 1929.[10] He continued to play a role in his profession, presenting research in 1931 as Canada's representative on the International Commission on Glaciers. His professional accomplishments went far beyond those of the average land surveyor. From Ontario to British Columbia, his career spanned a groundbreaking period of geographic expansion and methodological development in Canadian surveying and topography central to the definition of modern Canada. He was also party to laying the institutional foundations of a Canadian alpine movement, and the Alpine Club of Canada.

turning wider attention to terrain in western Canada, as did sumptuous new travel and adventure chronicles by American and British authors, such as W.D. Wilcox's *Camping in the Rockies* (1900) and H.C.M. Stutfield and J.N. Collie's *Climbs and Explorations in the Canadian Rockies* (1903). Fay hoped to see the formation of a national alpine club in the United States like The Alpine Club (London); Wheeler was contemplating the same for Canada, and they talked together. Inspired by these dreams at Glacier House, Wheeler talked up the idea of starting a club in Canada, but with the exception of a few select mountaineers, response to the idea fell flat. When Wheeler corresponded with others about the feasibility of forming a club, "I met with scepticism and indifference and found only one enthusiastic supporter, the Rev. Dr. J.C. Herdman, pastor of the Presbyterian church at Calgary, who was an enthusiastic lover of the mountains and an ardent climber."[11]

Most Canadians were reluctant to embrace what was often considered a risky sport, if not a foolhardy passion. By the following summer, Fay, however, was making headway organizing what would become the American Alpine Club in 1903. Hearing of the difficulties Wheeler was having drumming up support for a Canadian club, Fay suggested Wheeler try forming a Canadian branch of the American Alpine Club.[12] The suggestion propelled nationalists to renew the drive for Canadians to establish an independent club.

At the time, American, European, and British climbers dominated mountaineering in Canada. Few lamented the loss of national prestige occasioned by Canadian indifference to achievement in mountaineering, and Canadian records for first alpine ascents on domestic soil remained sparse. Canadian journalist Elizabeth Parker called attention to this situation, "How many first ascents have been made by Canadians? It is simply amazing that we leave the hardships and the triumphs of first ascents to foreigners. Even a Hindoo [sic] Swami has climbed one of the highest peaks in this region. Canada has not even an Alpine organisation...Is the mountaineering prestige gained by climbing our high mountains to be held by Americans and Englishmen?"[13]

In a 1905 column in the *Manitoba Free Press,* Parker urged the Winnipeg Canadian Club to initiate a national alpine club responsible for encouraging Canadian mountaineering and the appreciation of Canada's "mountain heritage." She was against amalgamating Canadian mountaineering interests within the structure of an American alpine club and linked nationalism to mountaineering. "We owe it to our own young nationhood in simple self-respect, to begin an organized system of mountaineering on an independent basis. Surely, between Halifax and Victoria, there can be found at least a dozen persons who are made of the stuff, and care enough about our mountain heritage to redeem Canadian apathy and indifference."[14]

Arthur Wheeler had found an ally. As he later recalled, Parker's reaction took him "roundly to task, declaimed my action as unpatriotic, chided my lack of imperialism and generally gave me a pen-lashing in words sharper than a sword."[15] Parker was an energetic journalist and intellectual. Her literary columns in the *Manitoba Free Press* were widely read from 1904 through the interwar period, and her book reviews and editorials provided a frequent forum for her strong views on Canadian subjects. And so it was with style, grace, and a wry sense of humour that she set in motion the formation of a Canadian alpine club.

Parker and Wheeler joined forces in 1905 to organize the ACC, but reports of how they did that vary. According to Wheeler, Parker's review of his book, *The Selkirk Range,* played "right into [his] mitt," and he promptly replied: "If you will give me your assistance and can open the columns of the *Free Press* to our support, I shall be very glad to go ahead on patriotic and imperial lines." Addressing his letter to the reviewer as "Dear Sir," he soon discovered the author to be Elizabeth Parker writing under one of her pen names, "M.T." Then, with the support of editor J.W. Dafoe, Parker began to publicize the formation of a Canadian alpine club through the *Free Press*. In Calgary, Rev. J.C. Herdman launched a similar publicity campaign in the *Calgary Herald.* Their "propaganda" was highly successful in bringing the cause to public attention, according to Wheeler, in that it "made other papers sit up and take notice" and prepared the ground for organizing the club.[16]

Parker recalled things differently. After her review of the book, she says that Wheeler approached her to join his efforts to form a Canadian branch of the American Alpine Club: "Would I help? I would, but only for an independent club. He was dubious about success in organizing on our own basis, and argued for his proposed branch of the older, active club." Correspondence between Wheeler and Fay ensued, wherein Fay contended that the "American" in the club's name could stand for all of North America. Parker opined that "the word had a national not a geographical significance." When Fay and Wheeler proposed to change the name of the American Alpine Club to the "Alpine Club of North America," Parker queried, "What about the significant national symbol, the Eagle, on their crest?" In the meantime, she gained the support of her editor, the Canadian nationalist J.W. Dafoe, "who said that though

Elizabeth Parker (1856–1944)

Journalist, Nationalist, and the ACC's Great Champion

ELIZABETH PARKER was born in Colchester County, Nova Scotia, on December 19, 1856, to Mary Tupper and George Fulton. Mary Tupper died when her daughter was only two years old, and in later years, the girl's lifelong appreciation of literature was nurtured by an invalid stepmother. Educated in Nova Scotia public school, Elizabeth Fulton continued her studies at the Truro Normal School, obtaining a first-class teaching certificate. She worked as a teacher for one year before marrying Henry J. Parker when she was eighteen. She began married life in Halifax and raised three children—Henry S.F., James Glen, and daughter Jean. She was interested in literature, and she pursued it through several literary organizations and by attending lectures at

Dalhousie University.[17] The family moved to Winnipeg in 1892, where her husband was employed as a railway clerk and remained a longtime employee of the Canadian Pacific Railway, working as an abstracts clerk and a chief forwarding clerk in the local freight department until roughly 1915, when he became an accountant.[18] Elizabeth's growing independence prior to Henry's death in 1920 may have been partly due to a troubled marriage. A neighbour later commented that Parker's husband "was incapacitated mentally."[19]

Parker became actively involved in the community, charitable projects, and church work in Winnipeg, much in keeping with the voluntary service roles, social reform impulses, and activist leadership characteristic of contemporary Anglo-Protestant women in Canada, such as Lady Aberdeen and Nellie McClung. She served as the first secretary of the Winnipeg Traveller's Aid Society, founded the Winnipeg branch of the Women's Canadian Club (1907), and was regarded as an "instrumental" organizer of the Young Women's Christian Association. Several organizations, including the Alpine Club of Canada, the University Women's Club, and the Poetry Society in Winnipeg, recognized Parker as an honorary member during her lifetime.[20]

In 1904 Parker formed a circle of friends who met to study poetry at her home during the long Winnipeg winters. Her affinity for the works of Robert Browning led unexpectedly to a career as a professional writer and contributor to the *Manitoba Free Press*, a pro-Liberal prairie daily known after 1931 as the *Winnipeg Free Press*.[21] Its staff included several independent women writers, most notably the crusty, indomitable, agricultural editor and women's activist Ella Cora Hind (1861–1942). At the turn of the century, the *Free Press* championed Sir Wilfrid Laurier's vision of Canada and effectively promoted many of the causes of the day, including women's suffrage and Canadian nationalism.

When Parker complained that a Winnipeg recital of Browning's works was not covered in the *Free Press*, she was invited to write a review, which was published on January 13, 1904. That review led to a regular weekly column entitled *Literary Causerie* and articles in 1905 about her holidays in the Rockies. *A Reader's Notes* began to appear on the editorial page in 1912 as her daily feature under the pen name, The Bookman. Avoiding the pretension of so-called "highbrow" literary critics, Parker preferred to present her column as a personal review of books and literature.

Toronto's *Saturday Night* remarked on the acuity of Parker's reviews and their place in Canadian journalism: "'A Reader's Notes' has won a unique place in Canadian journalism not only as the one daily column in the dominion, but particularly for the special flavor, the individuality and keen literary perception born of sound judgment which have all these years gleamed unfailingly through it."[22] Having started a career in journalism in her late forties, Parker continued writing her popular column until she was eighty-four.

Strengthening an awareness of Canada's mountain heritage became one of Parker's passionate concerns in the early 1900s. She had first travelled through the mountains in the late 1880s and 1890s.[23] In 1904 she went with her three children to Banff for an eighteen-month sojourn, apparently intending to restore her health in the fresh mountain air and take the waters at the therapeutic hot springs; her daughter Jean's reported susceptibility to tuberculosis, along with tensions involving Henry's mental health, may have also contributed to their journey.[24] Their stay included side trips to Lake Louise, Field, and Glacier House, which she featured in a series of articles she wrote for the *Free Press* about holiday attractions in the Rockies. She highlighted the potential for mountain climbing as a key attraction in "The Canadian Rockies: A Joy to Mountaineers."[25] Although foreign publications had begun by the early 1900s to reveal the secrets of the Canadian Rockies to travellers, Parker was one of the first Canadians to write about the attractions of the mountain west for readers in Canada. Her prolonged stay in Banff had a profound effect, as her obituary in the *Free Press* emphasized: "She lived there with her children for 18 months and during that time formed a love for the Rocky Mountains which lasted all her life."[26]

Parker expressed her love for the Rockies in her articles and her work for the ACC. She imbued her writings with nineteenth-century romanticism and mysticism, referring to hikers as "mountain pilgrims," as if they were party to a spiritual quest for the sublime that could inspire renewal and personal transformation among the high hills:

> The rambler secretes physical energy and goes in the strength of that energy for many a long, monotonous day of grinding and commonplace. Then he gets some dawning sense of infinitude and of the immensity and mystery of the creation.... He learns unspeakable things about himself. No man standing in the wet sunshine of the summer morning, lifting his eyes unto the hills and making his vows can do other afterwards than fight the fight of life with higher might and with greater gentleness to his fellow fighters, all too ill equipped for such fighting.[27]

For Parker, contact with nature's mysteries brought one closer to the divine. Many twentieth-century men and women chained to the secular monotony of modern urban existence craved this "restorative power" of nature.

Parker's affinity for the English Romantic poets shaped her literary sensibilities, as well as her perception of the mountain environment. With repeated visits to the Canadian Rockies, she trained her inward eye—in the style of Wordsworth—to see the transcendental insights of nature's beauty.[28] As Parker reflected in the first issue of the *Canadian Alpine Journal*:

There comes to the mountaineer of pure mind and willing spirit the sense of which Wordsworth tells, of the presence interfused in Nature; the presence that dwells among the sheer peaks and in the living air and the blue sky and in the mind of man; the motion and the spirit that rolls through all things. Browning sums it in his swift way: "which fools call Nature and I call God." To this climber is given a key to many an utterance of the Masters, which else remained for him unlocked.[29]

Being in the mountains also moved her, as Wheeler observed, "...she seemed deeply impressed by the feeling of being in touch with the Almighty Creator whose presence was inspired by the solemn beauties of the snow-clad heights and flower-strewn valleys all around."[30]

A strong vein of middle-class Anglo-Canadian nationalism flowed through Parker's admiration for the Rockies and Columbia Mountains. She saw them as a magnificent natural heritage to be treasured by all Canadians and connected them to Canadian nationalism. She would not accept the indifference of Canadians to their own mountains or to mountaineering, and she believed the mountain wilderness had lasting value: "The Canadian Rocky Mountain system, with its unnumbered and unknown natural sanctuaries for generations yet unborn, is a national asset. In time we ought to become a nation of mountaineers, loving our mountains with the patriot's passion."[31] Her beliefs in the mountains as a "national asset" and in the importance of "natural sanctuaries" informed the origins of the ACC and its vision of the early federal parks system.

lacking personal mountaineering ambition, if an alpine club was formed, he would favour decidedly a Canadian club." Parker and Wheeler corresponded with "university men" and other interested parties to ascertain which direction to follow. "There was only one answer," she insisted, and they proceeded with a Canadian club.[32]

The club promoted a distinct combination of alpinism and Anglo-Canadian nationalism made in western Canada, and regard for the idea of a Canadian club grew in circles of those interested in the Rockies. This group included Mr. R. Marpole, general superintendent of the western division of the CPR, as well as a number of regional outfitters and trail guides. For Dr. Arthur Philemon Coleman, University of Toronto geologist in the School of Practical Science, and Mrs. Julia Henshaw, author of a book about Rocky Mountain wildflower botany, science prompted an interest in creating the club. For climbers who already frequented the Rockies for recreation and sport, such as Calgary's Reverend Dean Paget, the appeal of mountaineering was obvious, and a club offered many attractions.[33]

At a western division conference of railway officers held at Mount Stephen House in Field, British Columbia, on February 14, 1906, Marpole arranged for Wheeler to meet William Whyte, the CPR's second vice-president and company czar. Wheeler boldly approached Whyte for twenty return railway passes to Winnipeg, from anywhere in Canada, to transport delegates to a conference where they would found the club. Whyte's response was as dramatic as it was canny, according to Wheeler's account: "He looked astounded, then incredulous, then scornful, as much as to say 'What confounded cheek.' Then he roared, 'Twenty passes to Winnipeg from any part of the Railway!'"[34] Even before the formal genesis of a club, the Canadian alpine movement had secured the CPR as a major corporate donor, initiating a recurring pattern of sponsorship through railway tourism.

The Winnipeg Meeting

Situated on the flat windswept flood plains of the Red River, Winnipeg is no mountaineering mecca. Although it is an unlikely place for alpine sports, Winnipeg was the turn-of-the-century railway hub of Canada and the geographic midpoint of the country. And so, the "Chicago of the North" was the gathering point for the founders of the ACC.

Delegates steamed into Winnipeg on the CPR in March 1906. Through the offices of Elizabeth Parker, the inaugural conference was held at the YMCA, where the delegates stayed overnight during the meetings. Wheeler and Herdman arrived together by train on March 26 and met informally with Parker at her home to finalize the conference agenda. Twenty-six delegates met for their first session on the afternoon of March 27. This session was chaired by Arthur Coleman, who rapidly appointed committees responsible for electing club officers, establishing a constitution, and carrying out business. In the evening, Wheeler and Herdman presented a lecture with a magic lantern slide show before an enthusiastic public audience. *The Wonderland of Canada* showed "many high peaks, ice and snow features, lakes, waterfalls and torrents, fauna, flora and climbing scenes in the mountain regions along the Canadian Pacific Railway," outstanding panoramas shot from "lofty peaks" looking fifty to one hundred miles in all directions, and even a peek inside the Cave of Cheops discovered near the summit of Rogers Pass.[35] The slide show was typical of an imperialist gaze, complete with an exotic frame around the mountains based on turn-of-the-century tourism constructs of geographic wonder and exploration that sensationalized the sublime, curious, and bizarre. To viewers in the crowd who may never have seen a mountain rising on the horizon or a glacier serac, these images were as far removed from everyday life as the Egyptian pyramids; the wonderland of Canada appeared as an unpeopled landscape, a *tabula rasa* open for conquest.

Events on the second day began with a constitution committee, which drafted the principles of the club. Next, several delegates attended a luncheon of the Winnipeg Canadian Club addressed by Arthur Wheeler, whose speech about Canada's mountain heritage and aims of the proposed Alpine Club of Canada was met with the support of clergyman Dr. Charles W. Gordon and E.L. Drewry, who each paid $25 to become associate members of the nascent organization. That afternoon, the delegates adopted the club constitution, elected the club officers for a two-year term, and decided on three important matters. First, the temporary headquarters and library of the club would be at the Parker family home in Winnipeg, 160 Furby Street. Next, the club would hold its first annual camp in Yoho Pass, British Columbia, in July 1906, only four months later. The annual camp would be the vehicle to teach and promote mountaineering in Canada. Last, the club decided to publish an annual periodical, the *Canadian Alpine Journal* (*CAJ*), as an enduring record of the club's activities and a representation of Canadian mountaineering to the world at large.[36]

The conference closed at Manitoba Hall with what would be the first of a series of annual dinners held by each section of the club. An

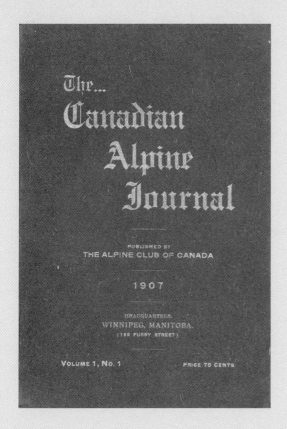

The *Canadian Alpine Journal*

Sic Itur Ad Astra

THE *CANADIAN ALPINE JOURNAL* premiered in 1907 as the club's annual publication. It was edited by Arthur Wheeler from 1907 to 1927, with initial assistance from Elizabeth Parker and later from Stanley Mitchell. The first edition was a hefty volume filled with carefully crafted articles by prominent authors in various fields of mountain exploration, science, literature, and climbing, as well as black-and-white photographs, hand-drawn maps, and engraved prints. From its first issue, the CAJ served as the clarion of alpinism in Canada. With grand optimism, Parker rang out a rallying call for the club and mountaineering:

> For the Alpine Club of Canada will more than any national sport in the Dominion, weld together the provinces in the bonds of brotherhood; and furnish training in the more Spartan virtues in times of

peace. It will not be many years before it will have entrenched itself deep in every province between the two oceans, when its membership will be in the thousands, and each and every Canadian mountaineer make the Club's motto his own—"sic itur, ad astra."[37]

The 1907 issue, priced at 75 cents including postage, was 196 pages. It was printed by the Herald Company in Calgary on cream-coloured, heavy, bond paper with a forest-green cover. The frontispiece beamed with a beatific portrait of honorary patron Sir Sandford Fleming, and the journal opened with greetings from William Whyte, CPR vice-president, and an introduction to the club by Elizabeth Parker. Several articles were accounts of mountain reminiscences written by well-known figures like Sandford Fleming, Charles W. Gordon, and Mary Vaux. Arthur Wheeler legitimized the Canadian Rockies as a vast and formidable alpine region for mountaineering, calling for more extensive exploration.

The journal was and continues to be a forum wherein mountaineers discuss and debate the conventions and ethics of mountain pursuits. "Writing was part of the mountaineering experience because it provided individuals with an opportunity for reflection and sharing," geographer Caralyn Kelly explains in her study of Canadian climbing narratives. "These communications also helped to reinscribe the beliefs that mountaineers valued and to socialize readers into the norms of the mountaineering community."[38] In addition, to write about an ascent was to make a public claim.

The mountaineering section of the first journal included accounts of no fewer than eleven mountain ascents in Canada. Contributors such as Dr. Charles Fay of the American Alpine Club, American scientist Dr. Herschel C. Parker, and international climber Gertrude E. Benham, as well as six clergymen, all wrote concise accounts of their climbing ascents in the Rockies and Selkirks. Photos of route lines tracked across the summits of Mounts Goodsir and Hungabee, the snow-covered

CANADIAN ALPINE JOURNAL

The Publishing Committee is not responsible for statements made by contributors to the Canadian Alpine Journal.

CONTENTS—VOLUME I.

< The first cover (see page 27) and contents page of the 1907 Canadian Alpine Journal, an institution and archive of mountain pursuits in Canada and beyond. Published today as an annual magazine.

Wapta Icefields, craggy routes on Crow's Nest Mountain, and the elegant horn of Mount Assiniboine punctuated the text. A glossary of mountaineering terms was also included, compiled by Wheeler, to instruct readers in proper terminology, from aiguille to talus, tongue to watershed.

Three articles appeared in the first journal's scientific section dealing with botany and glaciology. "The Mountain Wildflowers of Western Canada," by Julia Henshaw, discussed and showcased with photographs the regional plant species found in Banff and Glacier national parks. George and William Vaux elaborated on their scientific observations of glaciers in the Selkirk and Rocky Mountains with measurements, a foldout map, tables, and photos, pointing to the importance of documenting glacial change. In the service of its scientific mandate, the club had embarked on "yearly observations of the more prominent and accessible ice-cascades of the Canadian Rockies," as Arthur Wheeler reported in

an article detailing the status of the Yoho Glacier, based on study undertaken in 1906 at the first ACC camp.

Finally, the official section detailed club business and presented reports by the secretary, treasurer, librarian, and chief mountaineer, illustrating a high degree of delegation and organizational management even in the club's first year.

The annual publication of the *Canadian Alpine Journal* was rarely interrupted through the course of the twentieth century, despite war, depression, and changing circumstances. Its format was redesigned in 1970 as a magazine, but it continues as an annual club periodical to document the history and development of the club, climbing, and mountain life.

elated atmosphere, high spirits, and toasts capped off the proceedings that night, as Parker noted: "some stirring speeches were made born of experiences in rare altitudes, and the healths of the King (God bless him!), the Club and its officers, were drunk with all the enthusiasm of a young mountaineering organization."[39]

Twenty-six delegates attended the founding meeting[40] from six provinces: British Columbia sent five, Alberta nine, Manitoba eight, Ontario two, Quebec one, and Nova Scotia one. Clearly the greatest numbers were from the western provinces; the Canadian alpine sport movement was concentrated in the West. Elizabeth Parker and her daughter Jean were the only two women registered. The well-known Banff outfitters Tom Wilson and Bill Brewster attended, along with the magazine editor of *Rod and Gun,* W.S. Taylor, and Presbyterian social reformer Rev. Charles W. Gordon (also known as novelist Ralph O'Connor). The presence of academics, such as Dr. Coleman from the University of Toronto, and members of the Dominion Land Survey indicated an emphasis on science and exploration. The mountain outfitters and guides from Alberta and British Columbia, along with CPR representatives from Winnipeg and Montreal, held a direct commercial interest in the potential of the ACC to boost mountain tourism. Significantly, Protestant ministers were a strong presence, drawn to the divine proximity of the summits and the redeeming social benefits associated with outdoor recreation and exercise. What did this seemingly disparate group have in common? The ambition to organize mountaineering in Canada.

The ACC defined a national framework for mountaineering based on its institutional mandate, structure, and social practices, as well as its distinctive ideological understanding of Canadian alpinism. The homegrown club was, in Elizabeth Parker's words, "an organized system of mountaineering" that emulated other clubs. First among them was The Alpine Club. Formed in London, England, in 1857, The Alpine Club (as if there could be any other) was the world's first national alpine club, modelled after a scientific institution like the Royal Geographic Society. With typical British clubbishness and imperial breadth, its purpose was "the promotion of good fellowship among mountaineers, of mountain climbing and mountain exploration throughout the world, and better knowledge of the mountains through literature, science and art."[41] The broad imperialist vision of the British club served as a model for the constitution adopted by the ACC, entrenching the principles of a national alpine organization that was, by design, much more than a simple athletic

club for climbers. The club sought to foster broad cultural objectives that
were far-reaching in scope, such as:

a. The promotion of scientific study and exploration of Canadian
   alpine and glacial regions.
b. The cultivation of art in relation to mountain scenery.
c. The education of Canadians to an appreciation of their
   mountain heritage.
d. The encouragement of the mountain craft and the opening of
   new regions as a national playground.
e. The preservation of the natural beauties of the mountain places
   and of the fauna and flora in their habitat.
f. The interchange of literature with other alpine and geographical
   organisations.[42]

In short, the club sought to promote knowledge—through science, art,
literature, or sport—and instill respect for nature, looking to mountains
as a medium for nationalistic aspirations and the construction of
Canadian identity.

A major distinguishing feature of the ACC objectives was the "preservation of the natural beauties of the mountain places," along with
their biota and habitat. By 1906 conservation was important to many
Canadians, especially those with an interest in the outdoors or natural
history. Preservation, however, was in many ways at odds with "the
opening of new regions as a national playground."[43] The potential for
conflict would soon become evident in Canada's national parks. The
ACC constitution in effect duplicated the dual mandate of national parks
legislation and its inherent conflicts between use and preservation, even
as it brought the ACC in line with the goals and aspirations of the
national parks.[44]

The club's mission to foster Canadian alpine pursuits played out
through an organizational and management structure that functioned
on two levels. At the national level, the ACC headquarters acted as a
central organizing body for the club, while club sections formed in major
cities across Canada and abroad at the local level. ACC officers initially
included a president, eastern vice-president, western vice-president,
secretary, treasurer, librarian, and patron. This group, plus a three-
member advisory board, constituted the executive board of the ACC. As
the club grew, the executive expanded to include new positions: director
(1910–26), American vice-president (1948), and central vice-president

(1966).[45] At the section level, a chairman and secretary performed executive duties. The number and location of the ACC's various sections changed over time in accordance with changes in membership. Soon after the Winnipeg meeting, sections sprang up in Victoria, Vancouver, Calgary, Winnipeg, Toronto, New York, and London, England. As the activities of the club expanded, several committees replaced the advisory board to oversee issues related to management, the clubhouse, skiing, glaciers, alpine huts, and the *CAJ*.[46] The ACC instituted and adapted a national and a local management organization that reflected a well-ordered hierarchy common to many management structures of its day, not unlike the national parks administration that functioned through its Ottawa headquarters at the national level and through its superintendents in each park.

At the Winnipeg meeting, the first ACC executive officers were elected for a two-year term. Arthur Wheeler accepted the position of active president, which he fulfilled until 1910. Canada's pioneer of railway surveys, Sir Sandford Fleming, KCMG, was appointed club patron as honorary president. Two vice-presidents, Arthur Coleman and J.C. Herdman, were elected to represent eastern and western Canada respectively. Winnipeg became a centre of club organization based around National Club Secretary Elizabeth Parker, Assistant Secretary Stanley Mitchell, Librarian Jean Parker, and Treasurer David L. Laird, who was also a lawyer. In addition to the club's officers, an advisory board consisted of Banff outfitter Tom Wilson, Vancouver mechanical engineer E.A. Haggan, and Revelstoke Dominion Land Surveyor J.A. Kirk. Together they served as the club's executive board and managed the business of running a volunteer national organization.[47]

The ACC's national business was conducted at an annual general meeting usually held outdoors or in a tent during the summer camp. The club's constitution called for an annual camp where members could gather to climb, explore, study, and appreciate the mountains together. During the rest of the year, club life was animated at local meetings and outings, and business operated via a sustained correspondence among members of the national and local executives.

Five grades of membership in the ACC were established at the 1906 Winnipeg meeting. Membership grades and the associated annual dues, as defined in the ACC constitution published in 1907, were: subscribing members ($2), graduating members ($2.50), active members ($5), associate members ($25), and a special life membership for active members who paid a one-time sum of $50. Subscribing members, though "unable to take an active part in the outdoor work of the Club," could subscribe to ACC publications and exchanges, such as the *CAJ*. These memberships also facilitated journal exchanges and sharing publications with other organizations, such as international alpine clubs, government departments, and libraries. Among long-term subscribers, Canada's national parks department and the Toronto Public Library started collections of the journal beginning in 1907. Graduating members required training and accreditation. Inexperienced climbers were allowed a maximum of two years to fulfill the qualifications for active membership. This requirement was usually achieved with a "graduating" climb at the annual camp, where mountaineering techniques were taught on guided ascents.[48]

Active members were also evaluated in order to receive such standing. They had to have: made an ascent of not less than 10,000 feet (3,048 metres) above sea level in some recognized mountain region; or, for eight years prior to the date of organization been annual visitors to Canada's mountain regions and contributed to the knowledge of the same by means of scientific or artistic publication.[49] These eligibility standards for active members compassed early trailblazers, travellers, and researchers, who, in some cases, were not mountaineers at all but who had nonetheless made a significant contribution to understanding Canada's mountain regions. Active membership automatically carried with it the right to vote on club business.[50]

The category for associate members accommodated club sponsors and patrons who were unable to qualify as active members. ACC supporters could be affiliated with the club and "lend a helping hand towards its maintenance."[51] In the first year of the ACC's existence, this class of membership included several prestigious patrons, such as Mrs. Pat Burns, the wife of Calgary's cattle king, as well as Chancellor of Queen's University Sir Sandford Fleming, Toronto President of the Canadian Bank of Commerce Byron E. Walker, and Winnipeg's powerful CPR executive William Whyte.[52] The participation of these social worthies lent legitimacy and organizational prowess to the fledgling institution.[53]

Finally, the ACC associated itself with various leaders in the mountain world by granting honorary memberships to those who had "pre-eminently distinguished themselves in mountaineering, exploration or research and in the sacrifice of their own interests to the interests of the Club." Honorary members were elected by a two-thirds majority of recorded club votes.[54] Along with Elizabeth Parker, others elected to honorary status included British alpinists Dr. J. Norman Collie, FRS, and Edward Whymper of London; Irish mountaineer Rev. W. Spotswood Green, MA, FRGS, of Dublin; Surveyor General of Canada Dr. Edouard Deville, LLD, FRSC, of Ottawa; the father of photogrammetry, Col. A. Laussedat, of the Institute of France of Yzeure; and President of the American Alpine Club, Prof. Charles E. Fay, LITT. D., of Tufts College, Massachusetts.[55]

Initial enrolment in the club grew rapidly, from 79 in the first year to 200 early in 1907, 400 in 1908, and more than 650 in 1911. There were 599 in 1922, and 652 in 1930. Growth in the membership rolls was generally steady until the Depression, which caused a sharp drop in the early 1930s, reaching a low of 402 in 1934 before rebounding to 510 in 1939. Membership declined again during the Second World War as numbers fell due to military enlistment and wartime pressures. The return of peace and renewed prosperity improved club registration, which rose to 472 in 1946 and 871 by 1956.[56] Though membership fluctuated, the ACC remained modest in size when compared to other contemporary amateur national sporting organizations in Canada. Amateur Athletic Union of Canada, for example, served more than 18,000 men paid as senior members in 1936; the socialist Worker's Sports Association of Canada served 5,000 men, women, and children across Canada in 1933 in the midst of the Depression.[57] By these measures, the ACC was small, a specialist niche for mountaineering pursued by a club with fewer than a thousand people a year through most of the first half of the twentieth century.

The ACC was an English-speaking organization dominated by members who were urban, well-educated, leisured, and drawn largely from professionals and business people of British ancestry in the middle to upper classes. This social profile was characteristic of most national amateur sporting organizations emerging in Canada around the turn of the century.[58] About half of the membership was urban prior to the First World War, living in rapidly expanding Canadian cities.[59] White-collar professionals, such as engineers, barristers, and schoolteachers joined, as did celebrated summiteers, explorers, scientists, luminaries, and literati.[60] The occupational characteristics of the Canadian club were not unlike those of The Alpine Club (London), which at the time and during the mid-Victorian decades was marked by a predominance of "the genteel professions, including bankers, barristers, civil servants, clergymen, country gentlemen, university dons, and public schoolmasters," and by the late century, doctors and businessmen. However, the British club also fostered an elite membership of gentlemen based on "de facto social

qualification," according to Peter Hansen, thereby ensuring lower numbers but a "somewhat higher" social profile than many mountaineering clubs established in Europe.[61] In contrast, Canada's national alpine club leaned more toward a broadly middle-class membership, and it admitted both sexes.

Like Wheeler and Parker—forty-six and fifty years old respectively when they started the club—the first generation of ACC participants was generally middle-aged. As a result, "many of the ACC were themselves raised in the heyday of Victoria's reign," as LaForce indicates,[62] and were grounded in the imperial Victorian outlook on exploration, science, nature, and sport as a means to greatness and empire.

In 1907 Canadians were 85 per cent of the total number of ACC members. Among foreign nationals, Britons and Americans were 12 per cent. Belonging to more than one club was common practice in the international world of mountaineering, and a fair share of committed climbers in the ACC also belonged to British and American alpine clubs.[63] Various clubs were represented at the ACC camps, including The

∧ *Members in the Calgary Section with their families, 1921. Mountaineering in the ACC attracted urban professionals, particularly in western Canada. Harry Pollard photograph.*
[WMCR, V14/AC192P/1]

Alpine Club of England, the American Alpine Club, the Appalachian Mountain Club, the Mazamas, the Seattle Mountaineers, and the Swiss Alpine Club. The Alpine Club (London) affiliated with the ACC in 1920.[64]

However, in the beginning the majority of ACC members were from western Canada. Representation from Quebec and Atlantic Canada was noticeably absent from the ACC. Over time, the regional distribution shifted, but the club retained a critical mass of western interest throughout its first fifty years.[65] Selected membership samples through the period show that almost half the membership was concentrated in British Columbia and Alberta.[66] The western Canadian sections were particularly predominant from 1935, with the demise of the Toronto Section, to the end of the Second World War. In effect, the Alpine Club of Canada was largely a western-based national sport organization and a voice of Canadian sport nationalism.

Gender and Mountaineering
Women in the ACC

Among the middle classes, education and organized physical pursuits were commonly segregated by sex in the early twentieth century; likewise, gender shaped how Canadians looked at the outdoor pursuits of men and women in the field of leisure and sport, and how climbers lived a gendered experience in the ACC. Western philosophy emerging with the Enlightenment defined males as rational persons ruled by the mind and females as emotional beings who were closer to "nature." Women were also seen by the Victorians as a civilizing influence on "wild" colonial landscapes, bringing culture, domesticity, and morality into the frontier lives of men.[67] These essentialist assumptions about the sexes drew polarized gender frames and dualistic expectations around the lives of men and women, and inhabited mountaineering as a cultural phenomenon.

In an era of rising urbanization and modernization, the outdoors was construed as a fortifying environment for building a strong Canadian manhood. Living and exercising in the open air, as well as practicing sports, was believed to combat the perceived pitfalls of sedentary occupations and soft city life that might feminize men. Outdoor activities like climbing, canoeing, and camping were seen to enhance the development of good health and virility in men and boys. Sport, in the tradition of the British games ethic, was believed to encourage boys and men to cultivate the manly virtues of strength, discipline, courage, fair play, and team work; these qualities assisted the modern man to fulfill his station in life and his duty to the empire in times of war.[68] Suffering pains of deprivation and agony with courageous fortitude, a common theme of mountaineering literature, was likewise celebrated. Boys' stories were populated by men of action embodying heroic masculinity, frontier figures such as explorers, voyageurs, scouts, soldiers, and warriors.[69] The antimodernist representations of such heroes—painter Tom Thomson who guided in Algonquin Park or Yukon Mountie Sam Steele of the North West Mounted Police—were personified as strong and self-reliant men of the Canadian North; they knew how to explore, endure, and survive in the wilderness, even though they were also modern professional men.[70]

Anglo-Canadians drew on the British heritage of mountaineering imbued with nationalistic sentiments that conferred heroic masculinity on climbers who claimed summits for nation and empire. Male mountaineers were lionized, and climbing was seen as a rigorous physical pursuit that cleansed a man of urbane trappings and restored pure mind and body. "Bring me men to match my mountains," the ACC resounded at its first dinner, as Elizabeth Parker reiterated in the *CAJ*, calling on Canadian men to meet the challenge of a noble landscape.[71] Mountaineering was not simply sport but a thinking man's physical enterprise. Climbing for men would counteract everyday modern existence through the physical expression of rugged frontier masculinity in the mountains.

Women began climbing in western Canada as an outgrowth of Victorian tourism. Englishman Alfred F. Mummery lamented in 1896 that "all mountains pass through three stages—An inaccessible peak—The hardest climb in the Alps—An easy day for a lady."[72] Mountaineering did not have to take the form of competitive sport when it was viewed as a nature outing, and the standard of "a lady's climb" in the Alps was suited to a modest female effort rather than a strenuous male ascent, notwithstanding that many, such as Mount Blanc, were by the standards of the time substantial ascents and that both men and women usually climbed with mountain guides. By the time the ACC was formed, contemporary ideals of Canadian womanhood were shifting as several currents of social reform ran toward the ideal of the "New Woman." The gendered social horizons of Canadian women were beginning to expand beyond the traditional domestic sphere, even into the domain of mountaineering. Climbing was a site where new ideals of physically active womanhood and femininity were tried and constituted by pushing the boundaries of middle-class social acceptability, removed from city life.

Unlike The Alpine Club, or many European clubs formed in the 1860s and 1870s, from the outset, the ACC admitted women as members. Women in England and on the continent formed their own climbing clubs, such as the Ladies Alpine Club (UK) in 1907, the Ladies Scottish Climbing Club (1908), and the Swiss Women's Alpine Club (1918), upholding sexually segregated notions of physical culture and organizations for sports like golf. Among national European alpine clubs, the French alone admitted women. However, most climbing clubs in the United States admitted both sexes, among them the Appalachian Mountain Club, the American Alpine Club, and the Seattle Mountaineers.[73]

The Victorian medical and scientific establishment frowned on physical exercise for women and girls. The prevalence of male-dominated Western science exerting theories of vitalism, moralistic physiology, and biological determinism represented female bodies as weak, invalid, and, in the words of historian Patricia Vertinsky, "eternally wounded." The female body was inferior by comparison with the male. However, some doctors on the margins joined with social reformers in promoting the cause of female health through modest exercise and "rational dress." By the 1890s, medical progressives advocated mild physical activities, such as walking (not running), to improve the health and reproductivity of women.[74]

Nature retreats were seen as a particularly therapeutic holiday for affluent women who suffered nerves and were diagnosed with illnesses "peculiar" to their sex: hysteria, female neurasthenia, or anxiety. Going to the Muskokas for a "rest cure in a canoe" or staying in Banff at the hot springs sanatorium was often a ticket to escape from ennui, and the limiting conventions of the female domestic sphere in modern urban life.[75]

Outdoor pursuits appropriate for females—swimming, paddling, and camps for girls—were seen to develop the body beautiful, good health, and fertility, in order to help women in their roles as wives and mothers. Professional women, generally assumed to be single, stood to benefit by becoming more productive in their work. Sport in general would help all women and girls develop the "womanly virtues": grace, agility, co-ordination, sociability, and self-expression. At the turn of the century, competition, strenuous exertion, and perspiration were not considered ladylike, and yet university women and progressive teachers were beginning to encourage women and girls to practice "manly" sports, such as ice hockey, baseball, and basketball.[76] Young women who belonged to the ACC and who participated in Canadian mountaineering at this time were typically university educated and therefore exposed to physical education.

Sporty ideals of healthy young women gained social currency in the 1900s. The weekly outdoor magazine *Rod and Gun* featured articles about women camping, fishing, and canoeing in Canada's great outdoors, and in 1904 it published an account of Gertrude Benham's ascents on Mounts Lefroy and Victoria in the Rockies, written by Mary Schäffer.[77] Adventure stories for girls featured imperial heroines, such as missionaries, nurses, and frontier wives, and real-life Canadian women like widow Mina Hubbard, who canoed to the northern frontiers of Labrador to complete her late husband's scientific agenda. Self-sacrifice while caring for others, serving god, or in pursuit of science was considered high adventure for females. Many also believed that women drew on heightened sensitivities in the wilderness when seeking the romantic sublime as an experience of landscape, emotion, and pleasure that transcended modernity.

American feminist Fanny Workman literally carried a "Votes for Women" banner to the summits of the Karakorams in 1912, when movements for women's suffrage were calling for political emancipation, yet not all female adventurers self-identified as feminists. As Mary Russell suggests in her work on women travellers, others like British explorer Mary Kingsley were conservative in their outlook and rejected feminism and the New Woman, even though Kingsley's own solo expeditions in turn-of-the-century Africa were highly independent for an Englishwoman and seemed to contradict the gender standards of her day.[78] Climbing opened up new possibilities for self-construal and a sense of social place for women. Quaker precepts encouraging sexual egalitarianism and education encouraged Mary Vaux and Mary Schäffer, both members of the Philadelphia Academy of Natural Sciences, to venture into the Canadian mountains as scientific explorers. Vaux climbed Mount Stephen in 1900, making the first major ascent by a woman of a peak over 3,050 metres in the Rockies, and Schäffer scrambled in the Rockies during summer-long horse trips as a widow. Both were in their forties. These women often described camping as making a home in the outdoors, and their affluence allowed them to hire male staff to serve domestic needs while on the trail.

Explorer Phyllis Munday's adventures on Mount Waddington after the First World War exemplify strenuous mountaineering ascents by an elite Canadian climber during the interwar period. Munday was among a small league of highly skilled women in mountaineering. She travelled with her husband, climber Don Munday, on wilderness expeditions without compromising her social status as a respectable woman because she was a wife. She played a major role in the domestic work, altruism, and interpersonal dialogue needed to support her expeditions, as well as in the physicality of climbing. Karen Routledge argues that Munday played two sides of a gender game as both a woman and a climber, ultimately positioning herself as an exceptional woman, reasserting the dominant view that mountaineering was a man's world yet finding a loophole through which to pursue her passion for climbing with pride while bringing "elements of traditional femininity into the mountaineering identity—elements as important to survival in the mountains as the more masculine ones of strength and daring."[79]

Even though their gender still constrained female mountaineers, most women seeking mountain adventures pursued degrees of independent self-determination on the cusp of redefining the place of the modern twentieth-century woman. Elizabeth Parker saw climbing as a fine sport for women as well as men. Many Canadian mothers might have paled at the thought of their daughters venturing out as mountain climbers, yet Parker proudly referred to her daughter Jean as "my climber" and encouraged her to pursue mountaineering as a health-giving fresh-air pursuit.[80] When the ACC was formed in 1906, Elizabeth Parker was fifty and in marginal health, which deterred her from active climbing; still, she considered herself a climber "who scales the rock and cuts the ice-stairway in imagination only."[81] So, while Jean Parker climbed actively with guides and joined three alpine clubs, her mother threw her energy into building a Canadian alpine club open to both sexes. The rules were as yet unwritten, but Elizabeth Parker did her fair share in creating them.

A camp circular issued by the ACC in 1907 insisted ladies wear practical sports attire for climbing: "No lady climbing, who wears skirts, will be allowed to take a place on a rope, as they are a distinct source of danger to the entire party. Knickerbockers or bloomers with puttees or gaiters and sweater will be found serviceable and safe."[82] The guidebook Parker co-authored with Arthur Wheeler advised, "What applies to one sex applies to the other in all matters of clothing for actual climbing."[83] However, an unwritten dress code applied in camp. Women were expected to wear skirts, especially at the campfire, as considered befitting a lady's modesty before the First World War. Parker, for one, wore a skirt when climbing Cascade Mountain and wears a full-length skirt in extant photos taken at later ACC camps. Accounts of early climbers suggest that "the vast majority of women happily wore long skirts and felt comfortable, as females, to do so." Historian Kate Strasdin suggests that wearing skirts was a strategy "to maintain a level of femininity that they enjoyed as women whilst participating in the sport of their choice."[84] What individual ACC women preferred or chose to wear for sport and camp attire was an area of potential contestation fraught with issues of gender, modesty, and sexuality that men typically did not have to manage to the same extent, although the presence of ladies at the club's camps implied higher expectations for respectable grooming and decorum among gentlemen than on all-male trips.

A female medical doctor in the ACC justified the practice of mountaineering for women by setting it in the context of therapeutic exercise. In the 1909 edition of the *Canadian Alpine Journal,* Dr. Mary E. Crawford wrote an illustrated article entitled "Mountain Climbing for Women," in which she argued that the question "Should women climb mountains?" was a century "behind the times." Crawford pointed to the history of female European climbers active in the Alps, Andes, and Himalayas to make the point that women had been climbing mountains since the nineteenth century (that she did not refer to Andean or Himalayan women as climbers suggests how she defined both climbing and women climbers in Eurocentric and imperialistic terms). Because women, like men, were making alpine history, she encouraged more women to take up the sport of mountaineering. She emphasized the "therapeutic value of climbing": "There is no recreation which, in all its aspects of surrounding and exercise, will bring about a quicker rejuvenation of worn out nerves, tired brains and flabby muscles than mountaineering."[85]

Alpine clubs that admitted women as members provided affordable equipment and put "the summits within reach of all." Crawford insisted that the lack of sports literature on women's climbing should not deter women from setting forth. She went on to explain that mountain sickness was of no concern to the average woman, whose ambitions would likely take her to "the more easily obtainable ascents" under 12,000 feet (3,658 metres); indeed, "climbing was for the stout woman as well as the thin." Ultimately, the rewards of mountaineering contributed to a woman's ordinary life as she resumed her work, performing better than ever:

> And so the woman goes back to her tasks revivified. For the teacher new lights have been thrown upon history, literature, geography or mathematics. The artist and writer have found a mighty inspiration. The student of natural history has fresh specimens to classify. The nurse need not rack her tired brain for material to while away the heavy hours of pain for her patient—she has a fund of thrilling and amusing anecdotes to give out of her own experiences.[86]

The end goal of leisure for professional career women, in utilitarian terms, was better productivity in service to others. Still, mountaineering risks were assumed to be too great for women with young children, as mothers were not mentioned in Crawford's description. In the style of popular turn-of-the-century women's magazines, she concluded that a woman mountaineer "knows she is the happy possessor of the beauty of health gained from her sojourn among the heights."[87] Although Dr. Crawford's article has often been assessed as an indication of her support for women in mountaineering, she also admonished a twenty-eight-year-old teacher from Winnipeg for climbing too much when Margaret Fleming attended her first club camp in 1929 and did ten climbs within a month, including the spire of Mount Louis near Banff.[88]

The ACC was one of many organizations wherein the new and expanding roles of turn-of-the-century Canadian women became evident during an era of active social reform and rapid modernization. Women of the ACC tended to be well-educated, Protestant, middle- and upper-class, urban Anglos from western Canada and the northeastern United States. They were joiners who believed in organized activity, and as exemplified by the Parkers, women were club organizers in the ACC. The majority of ACC members were men, yet women formed a large part of the membership. In 1907 women made up 31.3 per cent and men 68.7 per cent of the total 201 members: about one woman to every two men. In 1917 women comprised over 40 per cent of the membership, and from 1922 into the post–Second World War era, the number of women members comprised 41 per cent of the club membership. However, this number dropped to 32.4 per cent in 1967. By 1994 1,586 of 5,298 members (30 per cent) were women.[89]

A quick glance at the ACC's roster of national leaders fails to impart a full historical picture of gendered leadership within the club, because men were highly visible at the national level, whereas women most often served as leaders at the local section level or behind the scenes. Miss E. Valens, Miss Margaret D. Fleming, Miss M.E. Nickell, and Miss A.C. Dalgleish, for example, served repeatedly as local secretaries through the 1930s, most often working with chairmen.[90] The secretaries of the local club sections were typically women. Women emerged as ACC section chairs only after the First World War. Dr. Cora Best, an internationally renowned American conservationist and adventurer, was the first. In 1922 Best founded the club's Minneapolis Section and served as its chair through 1926 with Mrs. M.J. Nero as her secretary. The Calgary Section chair in 1932 was Miss Margaret C. Wylie, a teacher and school principal who was a graduate of the University of Toronto and held a Master of Arts degree from Columbia University. In 1938 Dorothy Gladys Bell, a painter married to the ACC's former eastern vice-president and national president Dr. Fred Bell, was the first "lady chairman" of the Vancouver Section. For five years running from 1949, women chaired the Edmonton Section.[91] Having climbed with the club since they were young Vassar University graduates in the 1920s, Lillian Gest and Polly Prescott each volunteered as ACC American vice-president during the 1950s and brought a long institutional memory to their work. Stripping back the predominantly male national level of ACC executives, it becomes clear that women not only were active members in the club but also contributed considerable skills to its leadership and facilitation.

Women were also involved as editors of the *Canadian Alpine Journal.* Elizabeth Parker and Arthur Wheeler co-edited the first issues of the annual journal. When editor Alexander McCoubrey died suddenly in 1942, the club sought a man to replace him. Unable to find a man for the job, the ACC reluctantly appointed assistant editor Margaret Fleming, based on what they viewed as her knowledge of McCoubrey's methods. She volunteered as editor for ten years until retiring in 1952. Her sustained intellectual labour shaped the journal even as she remained in the background, showcasing the work of other mountaineers; her own personal stories of a lifetime of mountain leisure seldom entered the public forum.[92] Phyllis Munday, who organized the club's photo competitions and cross-Canada exhibits while volunteering as the club's honorary photographic secretary during the 1930s, also acted as editor of the *CAJ* from 1953 to 1969. The journal was thus in the hands of female editors for twenty-seven years, but its pages were primarily given over to masculinist mountaineering literature, suggesting the constraints of gender and literary genre at work through the operations of the club.

Like Fleming, the majority of ACC women in Red Book samples between 1907 and 1956 were single, although on average roughly a third were listed as "Mrs." and often belonged to the club with their husbands, as did Phyllis Munday.[93] These women worked as college instructors, schoolteachers, office workers, nurses, occupational therapists, missionaries, doctors, social workers, writers, and artists, as well as mothers and women who worked in the home, reflecting the expanding occupational horizons of women in Canada. While women were actively involved in club life, most women, married or single, still had to attend to the demands of the home and family, whether homemaking on a small scale or managing large household operations, such as the Philadelphia residence and Llysyfran dairy farm Mary Vaux operated for her family. Vaux noted her perplexing feelings of being caught by domestic responsibilities in Pennsylvania: "Sometimes I feel that I can hardly wait till the time comes to escape from city life, to the free air of the everlasting hills."[94]

Democracy or Discrimination?

More than a simple desire to find freedom in the hills was required to enter the ACC. Elizabeth Parker believed the ACC to be "as democratic as the Church itself" and willing to admit "any man of good character who fulfils the conditions of active membership."[95] However, the ACC membership selection process was neither open nor ideally democratic. According to the ACC constitution, new members were subject to

Phyllis Munday (1894–1990)

Mountaineer and Mother

COMBINING PARENTHOOD and mountaineering posed its own rewards and strains, as seen in the case of Phyllis and Don Munday. It seemed natural to exceptional mountaineers like Phyl and Don to lead family life outdoors after having a baby in 1921. "Our daughter Edith grew up, right from the start, in the mountains. We had her on the top of Crown [1,503 metres] when she was eleven weeks old," Phyl Munday recounted. She also described her husband's active parenting: "we carried her in a hammock strung around Don's shoulder...and she used to hum with the rhythm of him walking." Later that summer, they took her with them to a camp organized by the British Columbia Mountaineering Club (BCMC) in the Selkirks, some distance away from Glacier House. Family life at a mountaineering camp was the last thing hotel guests anticipated as, according to Phyl, "the people there wouldn't believe there was a baby at camp up the valley."[96] The Mundays were completely at home in the mountains, and, to the intrepid mountaineering couple, the comforts of camp were as suitable as home. On their longer explorations, baby Edith stayed behind; Phyl carried her photo inside a diary but missed her young daughter terribly. The Mundays played a critical role in the exploration of the Mount Waddington district of the British Columbia Coast Mountains, starting in 1925 when their daughter was four years old.

Climbers who were the mothers of young children were expected to avoid objective dangers; fathers were not subjected to the same social expectations to factor parenthood into issues of risk related to their climbing plans. Phyl described her many journeys to the area as an all-consuming quest for knowledge. When she was older, Edith Munday also climbed but did not stay with it.

Phyllis Munday ascended about a hundred peaks in her lifetime, a third of which were claimed as first ascents and many of which were first female ascents. Her great strength exceeded that of her husband, who said of their climbing partnership that "she and I formed a climbing unit something more than the sum of our worth apart."[97] In her later years, Phyl Munday's reflections on women in mountaineering focused on equal enjoyment, physical capability, and skill: "If a person enjoys it, and you are strong enough, and well enough to do it, and you can hold your own with a party...then there is no reason in the world why a woman can't do it."[98] As Karen Routledge has argued, Phyllis Munday "did whatever was necessary in order to climb, successfully combining and manipulating gendered stereotypes to fit into a place that had its own exigencies and rules for survival. In so doing, she demonstrated the inconsistencies of the stereotypes themselves, and the reluctance of even extraordinary people to reject them completely."[99] She was ultimately awarded the ACC's Silver Rope for leadership. Munday's support for nature appreciation, first aid education, and safety in outdoor recreation extended to volunteer leadership in the Girl Guides, St. John Ambulance Brigade, and her mountaineering clubs—pursuits more characteristic of conventional gender roles played by women in service organizations.

nomination and election by registered club members. Candidates for membership first had to be proposed to the executive board by a minimum of three ACC members acting as sponsors. The board created a ballot bearing the names and mountaineering qualifications of approved candidates. Ballots were then circulated by the club secretary to all active members for the election of nominees; six weeks were allowed for their return.[100]

In practice, the nomination and election of candidates for membership acted as an exclusionary process that reinforced a socially homogenous group character and could screen out "undesirables." ACC records reveal instances in which religion and ancestry also figured into determining acceptance. While references to such instances are few, they appear repeatedly in the written record over a prolonged period, suggesting that social screening was conducted based on factors of class, sex, ancestry, and religion. The social character of the early ACC raises important implications related to the profile of recreationists enabled by the club to be active in the mountain national parks and those who were silently precluded. Discrimination in Canada's national parks took place by various means. In the Maritimes, Jewish guests were excluded from certain hotels in Prince Edward Island National Park in the 1940s, and even Martin Luther King, Jr., and his wife were discouraged from visiting Fundy Park in 1960, leading historian Alan MacEachern to question "if the exclusivity of the national parks often permitted or even fostered such acts of exclusion."[101]

Specific cases of anti-Semitic discrimination arise in the executive correspondence of the ACC. Jewish applicants were quietly refused membership in more than one documented case in the 1920s and 1930s. An American schoolteacher named Miss Mendelson was nominated by ACC members Crosby and Harmon in September 1928, with Secretary Mitchell serving as a third "on request." Mendelson was then blackballed by the ballots of several "good members" of the New York ACC, including Helen Buck, Miss H.M. Smith, Miss Merrill, and Dr. Mary Potter, as Mitchell reported to the club's president T.B. Moffat:

She is a Brooklyn school teacher, in [the] same school as Miss H.M. Smith. There is nothing of serious import against her but she is a Jewess and such of her friends and relations as the New York members know are very "sheeny." They are blackballing her. I have already four adverse votes and understand more are on the way. They declare she would be most uncongenial. The Jewish subject is a sore one in New York. They are of course quite within their rights in every way and there is nothing to be done in the matter...The Constitution is quite plain and no reasons have to be given.[102]

President Moffat did not want Jews to intrude on membership in the club: "if a few of them were to get into the membership it might create a good deal of unpleasantness."[103]

By September 26, Mendelson's candidacy had been effectively blackballed, as Mitchell wrote: "So far I have received eleven votes against Miss Mendelson, which is of course more than enough, five only being necessary. The Constitution is quite plain on this matter."[104] When asked if the matter should be raised before the executive or management committee, Moffat replied, "I suppose the only thing to do will be to notify Miss M. that her application has not been supported by all of our members and therefore she cannot be accepted as a member."[105] The final message from the club to Miss Mendelson was clearly social rejection.

As this example suggests, the official rules of membership in the ACC sanctioned exclusion and allowed club executives to assert a role in decision-making while masking the personal and systemic prejudices actively played out through private bureaucratic procedures and formalities. At the centre of the national ACC executive, Mitchell and Moffat policed the social boundaries around club membership. Born in Glasgow and raised as an Anglican, Mitchell's categorical religious prejudices also decried Roman Catholics for the overemotionality of their "race" among southern Europeans and the Irish, but, unlike Jews, Catholic climbers were admitted as members in the ACC.[106]

Executive correspondence between President Wates and Secretary-treasurer Tweedy from 1939 to 1940 demonstrates the enduring organizational prevalence of anti-Semitic discrimination in the club. In this case, Tweedy, a native Englishman and military veteran, stated that Jews were unwanted in the club, "We do not want that type of person as a rule and it will be hard to keep out our Jewish friends if we once start."[107] Despite the restrictions inherent in the nomination and election process, he expressed concern that the ACC was still porous and did not have entirely sufficient control over ensuring its membership was exclusive.[108] He opposed wide circulation of ACC publicity pamphlets for just this reason. Key Canadian leaders in the ACC executive actively worked to exclude Jews from the club. Anti-Semitism was prevalent in Canada through the interwar era.[109] Sentiments expressed by Tweedy were more than a mirror of attitudes fostering anti-Semitism in Canada

> *Shozo Kitada and Cyril Wates at ACC camp.*
[EA-41-50]

and its larger global politics at the outset of the Second World War; they acted to constitute them through sport and leisure. Other examples of exclusionism include the story of Shozo Kitada.

Only four years after the stunning first ascent claimed by Yuko Maki's Japanese team on Mount Alberta in Jasper Park in 1925, a Japanese man applied to join the ACC. Shozo Kitada's application to join the club in 1929 illustrates the influence of senior ACC members in gaining approval for his admission based on the connections of class privilege. When Kitada applied for membership, after attending the 1928 ACC summer camp as a guest, Secretary Mitchell proceeded to flag the file with racial cautions:

> *As you know he was a very pleasant, well behaved young man but there is a strong feeling amongst many members against the Yellow*

race. Privately I think Mr. Wheeler is rather strong on that point but I am not sure. It would be unfortunate if Mr. Kitada's name were put up for ballot and then...blackballed.[110]

Moffat advised that there was little danger of being "swamped with Japanese members" and suggested that Mitchell find out Wheeler's views on the matter. Kitada's application entertained them and led Mitchell, a bachelor, to make a sexualized racial joke: "I also was amused at Kitada's letter regarding my wife and wondered if he thought I was a polygamist and was married to my two office helpers!"[111]

As it turned out, Wheeler thought it was a good idea to accept Shozo Kitada, an executive member of *Nihon Aruko Kwai* (Japan Walking Club). Adventurer Dr. Cora Best, the former chair of the ACC Minneapolis Section, had been on a climb of the Aso-Zan led by Kitada while visiting Japan. Wheeler offered to nominate him and suggested Colonel Foster and President Moffat add the weight of their names as sponsors to ensure Kitada's application passed the vote of the general members. Conscious of British standards of class and respectability, Wheeler further advised Mitchell, "If anyone protests we should mention a Japanese is Hon. Member of the English Alpine Club which is particular and generally considered pretty respectable."[112] That Kitada's nomination had to be backed by three of the ACC's prominent leaders to overcome any objections indicates that the prevailing norms in the club were anti-Asian but could be countervailed.[113] In this particular case, international fraternity and class privilege among mountaineers who hobnobbed together through sport diplomatically opened club doors.

Because the ACC enabled members to gain access to prime areas in the mountain parks, it also prevented others from attending its camps, huts, and clubhouse there. ACC membership practices were private and fell outside the scope of the Parks Branch, yet the branch sanctioned the club as the pre-eminent mountaineering organization operating inside park jurisdictions. The ACC's interwar social outlook was summed up in Mitchell's appraisal of British aristocrat Lady Rosemary Baring's involvement with the club. When she arrived at the 1930 ACC camp, he remarked that Lady Baring was "the right sort for us."[114] Likewise, the Parks Branch approved of the club as bringing the right sort of visitor to the mountains.

Early Exploration and the Expedition to Mount Logan

Science and exploration in the mountains were important dimensions of the ACC mandate, as was the protection of wildlife and habitat. In 1911 the ACC prepared to strike out on an extensive exploratory expedition to Jasper National Park through Yellowhead Pass to the Mount Robson region. In conjunction with members of the Smithsonian Institute of Washington, DC, Wheeler led a party into the northern Rockies to map the territory and undertake a survey of the area's geological and biological forms. Collecting specimens for the Smithsonian was another aspect of the expedition.[115] A separate survey in 1911 conducted by Mary Schäffer, a prominent ACC member recruited by federal officials, contributed to advocacy of park protection around Maligne Lake by producing the first published map of the area. Wheeler's 1911 expedition also surveyed the lake. Schäffer and Wheeler each subsequently urged the federal government of Canada to include the area within the boundaries of Jasper Park.[116]

In 1912 ACC members fought through bad devil's club on the approach to climbs in the Coast Range during an expedition to Strathcona Park on Vancouver Island. This trip was made with the help of the province of British Columbia in order to reconnoiter alpine features of the park, and CAJ published articles and papers detailing the region's flora, fauna, and geography. The expedition resulted in A.O. Wheeler and the chair of the Vancouver Section, William W. Foster, (who was also minister of BC Public Works), forging an alliance between the club and the province to promote the park, preserve its natural heritage, and make it accessible to the public by building trails and expanding boundaries.[117]

The Strathcona expedition was a great undertaking, as was the 1913 summit of Mount Robson, which happened during the ACC's annual camp. William W. Foster, Albert H. MacCarthy, and Austrian guide Conrad Kain made the first recognized ascent to the summit of Mount Robson, the highest mountain in the Canadian Rockies. An earlier ascent of the mountain by Reverend George Kinney and Donald "Curly" Philips in 1909 was discredited as fraudulent, and, on the strength of the club's growing authority, the 1913 party asserted claim to *bona fide* first-ascent status, as the *Canadian Alpine Journal* legitimated soon afterward.[118]

However, the ACC's crowning achievement during its early years was the Mount Logan Expedition in 1925. Mount Logan (5,959 metres), at 60 degrees north in southwestern Yukon, is the highest mountain in Canada and the second highest elevation in North America after Alaska's Mount

McKinley (Denali). Named after the nineteenth-century founder of the GSC, Sir William Logan, it is one of the most immense massifs in the world. Many peaks rise from a domain of perpetual snow to Logan's glacial tiara, yet, despite its massive size, the remote mountain remained unsighted by modern explorers until 1890.[119] Public attention, captivated by the series of British attempts on Mount Everest through the early 1920s, envisioned Mount Logan as "Canada's Everest."[120] Immediately following the ascent of Mount Robson, the highest peak in the Canadian Rockies, Wheeler spoke enthusiastically to climbers at the club's 1913 annual camp, urging, "And now for Canada's highest, Mt. Logan!"[121] The outbreak of the First World War, however, delayed efforts.

The groundwork for the expedition commenced at the 1923 annual summer camp, held in Rocky Mountains (Banff) Park near Lake Louise.

A group of senior leaders convened in November 1923 as the Mount Logan Executive Committee with hopes of launching an attempt in 1924. Albert H. MacCarthy, a former banker and retired American naval captain who ranched in British Columbia's Windermere Valley, was chosen to lead the trip. A skilled mountaineer, he belonged to no fewer than three mountain clubs: the Alpine Club of Canada, the American Alpine Club, and The Alpine Club (London).[122] All three clubs backed the expedition, which was officially organized under the auspices of the ACC. The AAC contributed directly to funding the expedition and sent climbers. An advisory committee was also established with experts Belmore Browne, the American climber of Mount McKinley in 1912, and Edward Oliver Wheeler, the Canadian surveyor with the British Everest reconnaissance in 1921. The overall logistics and climbing methods adopted for the Logan expedition were similar to those used on Mount McKinley by Browne and Hershel Parker in 1912.[123] It soon became apparent that more reconnaissance and resources were needed, however, and the expedition was postponed to 1925.

Leaders in the club looked to the Government of Canada to support the venture, requesting that H.F. Lambart from the Geodetic Survey and his assistant be assigned to join the expedition in the interests of conducting a photographic survey of Mount Logan. Having worked on the 1913 Alaska–Yukon boundary survey, Fred Lambart had mountaineering experience in the North and privileged access to crucial federal maps and photographs of the region; he was also a member of the ACC and served as a club vice-president (1924–26). Wheeler campaigned to persuade Ottawa officials to offer assistance to the expedition. In a letter to Deputy Minister W.W. Cory, who was familiar with the ACC, Wheeler identified the trip as a matter of "national concern" and drew attention to the international reputation of the ACC and its work promoting the Rockies in his justification for Crown assistance for the expedition, expressing his feeling that the club could "look to our own Government with the expectation of the assistance we ask for in this our biggest undertaking, and that our Government will not turn us down."[124]

Canada's director general of surveys, Dr. Edouard Gaston Deville in the Department of the Interior, supported the initiative.[125] A mentor in Wheeler's early survey work with the Interior, Deville was one of the alpine club's first honorary members and a patron of the club. Lambart contacted J.W. Craig, another senior department official, to ascertain what assistance would be made available. Craig agreed with Deville that the ascent would be "an important undertaking of considerable magnitude and the publicity already given to it has made it a matter of international interest and importance." Both Deville and Craig likened the Logan expedition to the Mount Everest one, which Craig noted had "received assistance from many sources and the progress of which has been followed with marked attention throughout the world." Further, Craig reminded the deputy minister, "We are indebted to Mr. Wheeler and Mr. Lambart for preventing the attempt from becoming a purely United States undertaking and I am strongly of the opinion that the Government should aid to the fullest possible extent."[126]

Ottawa was thus prompted to assist the expedition based on the international profile of a summit likened to Everest and the potential to lay Canada's claim to a significant first ascent before another nation took the peak, especially with the spectre of American imperialism looming in the northern borderlands. The Alaska–Canada boundary dispute had already challenged Canadian sovereignty in the region. Deputy Minister Cory decided to approve Crown assistance, and two civil servants were assigned to participate in the expedition. Fred Lambart acted as the deputy leader and chief of topography on the trip; Hamilton M. Laing, a federal biologist with the Department of Mines, was stationed in Chitina Valley for the summer of 1925 as a field naturalist to inventory flora and fauna, collect representative specimens, and shoot footage for a film documentary intended for the public.[127] The Physical Testing Laboratory in Ottawa provided the climbing team with instruments, in particular an aneroid barometer for high altitude.[128] After cobbling together support from Ottawa, alpine clubs, private donors, and corporate sponsors, the ACC-led expedition moved ahead in 1925.

It elicited dramatic press coverage across Canada and the United States. The press described the expedition in militaristic terms with headlines extolling "Mount Logan: The Attack Begins on Canada's Mighty Peak," "The Assault on 'The Canadian Everest' Mount Logan," and "Off to Attack King of Canadian Peaks."[129] In many ways, the "conquest" of Canada's highest peak proved a turning point in the history of the ACC, as well as a newsroom example of summit nationalism. The national parks department followed the story intently, as is evidenced by newspaper clippings on file.

Where the Pacific seacoast curves to meet the Alaskan panhandle, the land folds, buckles, and turns upward, stretching east into Canada's Yukon along the St. Elias Mountains. Today most climbers approach Mount Logan, in Kluane National Park, by small aircraft from Haines Junction in the Yukon, but in May 1925 the expedition team went by sea from Seattle up the Inside Passage to Cordova Bay and by rail to McCarthy, Alaska, before heading inland to Canada. Albert MacCarthy and hired outfitters had already spent two arduous months preparing for the arrival of the climbing team by hauling a supply cache up the Ogilvie Glacier, despite punishing subarctic temperatures. MacCarthy met naturalist Hamilton Laing and climbers Fred Lambart, William Foster, Allen Carpé, Henry S. Hall, Robert Morgan, and Norman Read—the latter four from the United States—on the dock at Cordova Bay. Once assembled in McCarthy, they set out together on May 12 with the assistance of a pack train; the climbers would not reunite in McCarthy until two months later on July 15. A 50-mile (80-kilometre) backpacking trip over rough moraines preceded sled-pulling across icefields to the base of Mount Logan. The mountaineers hauled four thousand pounds (1,814 kilograms) of equipment, supplies, and provisions 308 miles (496 kilometres), by relay to base camp, and camped on ice and snow for forty-four consecutive days. The climb was a classic alpine mountaineering ascent (non-technical), hampered by heavy snowstorms, cold temperatures, altitude, and frostbite. A combination of snowshoes and crampons were used for travel as skis were not yet in fashion for snow travel in mountaineering ascents in Canada. Moving to take up a position ready for the summit bid and running low on rations, MacCarthy relentlessly drove the men to continue ferrying supplies up the mountain during a blinding snowstorm. As a result, Morgan froze his feet and turned home the next day with Hall. The rest of the team reached the two summits of Mount Logan late on June 23, 1925, during a thirty-four-hour final episode, during which they spent a night in misery, and one rope lost the route down from the top and suffered prolonged exposure to the elements. Most of the climbers suffered frostbite to fingers and toes; Lambart shed the flesh of his toes down to the bone during the return to McCarthy by foot and raft down the Chitina River. MacCarthy later suggested that high altitude may have affected his rational judgement and leadership: "If sometimes while above that level, I was harsh and disagreeable, I ask that my companions please forgive me."[130] Even by the standards of high-altitude expeditions of the time, it was an extremely difficult journey, inducing popular historian Chic Scott to conclude, "In the annals of mountaineering no mountain has ever extracted more sweat, suffering and hard work than this one."[131]

"Mount Logan, the highest peak in Canada, has been conquered by an expedition of the Canadian Alpine Club composed entirely of amateur members," reported *The Globe*'s front page on July 15, once the team had reported back from the wilderness.[132] The amateur status of the climbers was considered a worthy highlight in the news; there were no professional mountain guides among the group (although Lambart was paid as a surveyor on the expedition and Andy Taylor was a hired packer). The American press tended to portray the expedition as an international effort led by Americans, although it was organized under the auspices of the ACC, whereas the Canadian press sought out its own heroes to attest to Canada's newfound sense of autonomous nationhood after the First World War, emphasizing "Mt. Logan Conquered! An Epic of Canadian Heroism—Victory Over Fearful Odds."[133] The language of conquest actively forged the story as a heroic narrative of epic human triumph over wild nature represented symbolically by the mountain, the elements, the altitude, and the North. Surviving the extreme subarctic environment to ascend the mountain was understood in a modernist sense as a remarkable act of manly courage that pushed the limits, contributed to the adventurous spirit and ingenuity of humankind, and opened the frontiers of knowledge, rather than as a private exploit of an elite few sportsmen, a suffering episode of masculinist brutality inflicted to the body, or the colonialist occupation of Aboriginal homelands in Kluane.[134]

The *Canadian Alpine Journal* devoted 126 pages of the 1925 issue to recounting the saga, illustrated with photos and maps, and published various reports with scientific observations of geography, topography, geology, weather, wildlife, plants, and high-altitude human physiology.[135] The ACC was clearly impressed by its own achievement and sought to publicize it, effectively legitimating its claim to the first ascent, as well as discovery. William Foster drew attention to the achievements of the expedition in terms of expanding "the store of human knowledge" about the Mount Logan district through exploration and research.[136]

The groundwork entailed in this approach to mapping and describing the land—alike in many ways to contemporaneous federal initiatives related to geographical surveys, wildlife conservation, and national parks—fostered the identity of Mount Logan as a Canadian wilderness known through the natural sciences, biological inventories, and visual documentation that promoted ideals of scenic beauty, as well as progress through mountaineering lore.

Despite contemporary acclaim, various historians have suggested that the ACC pursued an outdated style of mountaineering on this expedition more characteristic of pre-war expeditions to Mount McKinley than other international climbing emerging after the First

World War. For example, Chris Jones and Gina LaForce argue that the classic style of the Mount Logan ascent was outmoded compared to the 1925 ascent of Mount Alberta in the Rockies by a Japanese team with local Swiss guides, judging the latter more difficult and innovative due to sections of vertical incline and technical rock work.[137] As Jones writes, "Mount Logan summarized the achievements of the past: stoic heroism in the face of brute nature. Mount Alberta looked to the future: New skills learned in Europe were applied to a technically demanding route. The turn-of-the-century mountaineers would have had an excellent chance on Logan; they would have had no chance on Alberta."[138]

Further, in 1976, Jones remarked that the MacCarthy team may have exaggerated its difficulties on Mount Logan: "Perhaps the suffering was as much due to the slow pace and the party's state of mind as to the intrinsic difficulties of the mountain. The nub of the problem may be that the climbers approached Mount Logan as if it were a Mount Everest. Difficulties are sometimes as much a creation of man's imagination as a creation of nature."[139] But even his assessment reinscribed Mount Logan as Canada's Everest.

Although the two ascents did differ in style, these critiques rely on a modernistic premise of teleological progress, underpinned by a belief in sport modernization, and assume that mountaineering followed one developmental trajectory evolving to more difficult forms and styles of climbing, rather than probe cultural tensions in sport as a contested terrain wherein multiple forms and styles have been practiced in specific cultural and historical contexts, often simultaneously.[140] Classic siege assaults and expeditions were not simply relegated to the dustbin of the nineteenth century in favour of emergent technical climbing during the interwar era, as later Himalayan official first ascents by the French on Annapurna (1951), the Germans on Nanga Parbat (1953), and the British on Everest (1953) would exemplify. Moreover, three innovations introduced by the Mount Logan expedition—the single-pole Logan tent, willow wands for route marking, and nutritious Logan bread—were adopted by other expeditions in decades to follow.[141]

Diverse forms of climbing proliferated, and, through the interwar era, the ACC, like most North American mountain clubs, continued to practice in a conservative mode, whereas technical climbing typically emerged in other contexts as change that was contested as either unethical or the "leading" edge of the sport.[142] The Mount Logan trip was slow, and laboured through various delays and errors, but how else could a team have reached the summit of Mount Logan in 1925? The mountain was large, glaciated, and very remote. The exact route to the base of the mountain and to the summit was unknown, necessitating an expeditionary style of approach, with heavy gear, in new terrain where there was no hope of outsider rescue from the hinterland. The route was a classic non-technical line, walking over icefields to and from the summit, complicated by the rigours of high altitude and storm-ridden weather. Aside from equipping the expedition with professional guides, using skis for glacier travel, or building a larger support pyramid—which would have necessitated greater cost and resources—there were few other viable options for these climbers to improvise a wilderness ascent on the mountain, given their skills and resources in 1925.

The ascents of Mount Robson in 1913 and Mount Logan in 1925 were emblematic of the organized national system of mountaineering ushered in by the ACC. Whether or not Canadians would have laid claim to first ascents on these peaks by 1925 without the backing of a national club is speculative. Personnel, funding, logistics, promotion, and organizational partnerships were highly dependent on a club structure as the framework for mounting a large expedition in the case of Mount Logan in the 1920s. Celebrated ascents boosted the domestic and international currency of Canada's national mountaineering club. Consolidating a sense of nationhood around such events spurred the ACC to promote summit nationalism and assert claims that high mountain peaks were Canadian landscapes invested with special cultural significations. Mountaineers stood on the highest point in Canada and made Mount Logan a meaningful place. Its cultural status was then heralded internationally as a trophy summit and emblazoned as an overpowering landscape of pristine wilderness and scenic beauty in the sovereign Canadian North, meanings later regenerated through its nationalization as Canada's first national park in the northern territories. Following the 1925 ascent, the Department of the Interior was pleased to salute the ACC and stake a claim in the venture and the advance of Canadian geographical knowledge by acknowledging federal assistance to the expedition.[143] Although Mount Logan was still far from the reach of most travellers in 1925, and no one attempted the ascent again until 1950, the expedition delivered on the club's mission to open and publicize new mountain regions.

Following the success on Mount Logan, the inaugural series of first ascents on Canada's highest mountains was complete. First ascents on monumental peaks in Canada became increasingly difficult to find. Of course, there were still many unascended peaks across Canada, but the Rockies and Columbia Mountains were no longer the vastly uncharted wilderness conceived by earlier colonial outsiders. Climbers had summitted the highest peaks in the country. By these standards, Canada's "golden age" of climbing was over.[144] If Canadian mountaineers were no longer limited by the country's highest mountain, they would have to seek out different challenges to test their sport on rock, snow, and ice.

▲ Following the fanfare of triumph on Mount Logan, Arthur Wheeler retired as the ACC's managing director. An ACC management committee replaced the director's post in 1926, and Wheeler was named honorary president for life. He had given more than twenty years service to encouraging Canadian alpinism as the club's first president (1906–10), director (1910–26), and editor of the *Canadian Alpine Journal* (1907–27). Renowned British climber Arnold Louis Mumm, of champagne fame, expressed high praise for Wheeler: "I can't think of anyone who has accomplished quite such a bit of constructive work in the cause of mountaineering as you have done."[145] Considering Wheeler's autocratic leadership style and strong personality, others may have toasted the advent of management by committee and the club's next generation.

By the time Wheeler retired, the first generation of the ACC had succeeded in raising the profile of Canadian mountaineering from obscurity to international recognition, and, as Elizabeth Parker had predicted in 1908, mountaineering was becoming "more and more a Canadian sport," or, at least, more Canadians were participants. Wheeler had succeeded in "his keenest desire—to spread the gospel of the mountains," and, during the interwar period, the club would continue to convey these tidings and prepare the way for the popularization of mass tourism in the mountain parks.[146] The club's emerging tradition of annual summer camps held in enticing mountain places shaped both. Elite expeditions basked in glory, but the ACC's annual summer camps continuously generated a unique culture that informed mountain sport, recreation, and conservation in Canada.

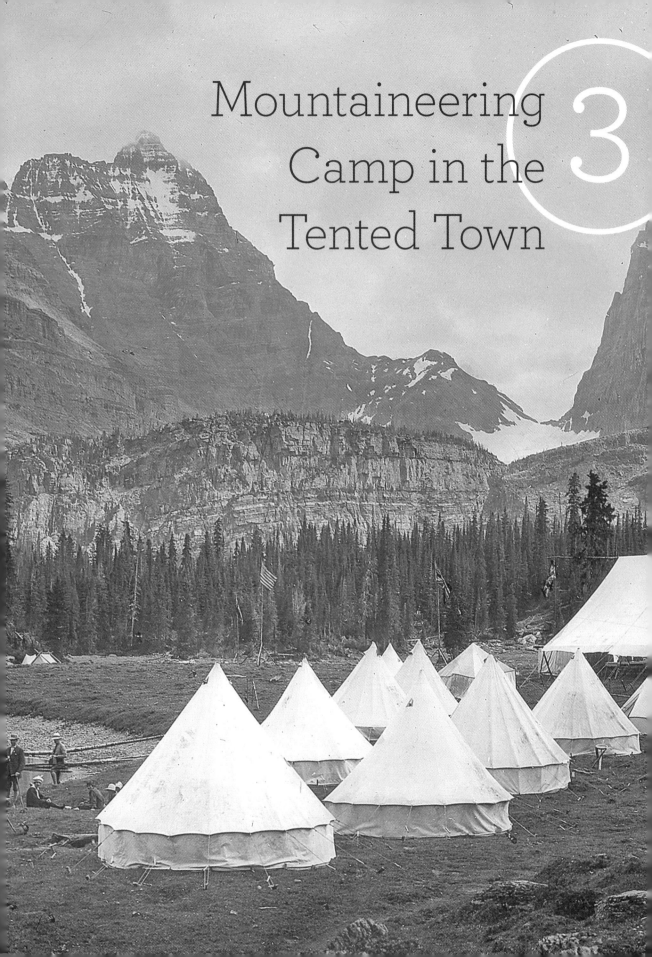

Mountaineering Camp in the Tented Town

3

Yoho, Yo-ho
We are the people who climb, you know;
Up the mountain through snow and cloud
And then, returning, we shout aloud
Yo-ho, YO-HO.

—E.O. WHEELER, "Golden Jubilee," 1956[1]

∧ "Alpine Club Camp in
O'Hara Lake Valley." Peaks
surround Lake O'Hara near
the Great Divide in Yoho
National Park, 1919. Harry
Pollard photograph, hand-
tinted lantern slide.

[WMCR, V14/AC176P/7]

THE FIRST ALPINE CLUB OF CANADA CAMP, held in the Yoho Pass
in 1906, made a lasting impression on Toronto writer Frank Yeigh. He
left his home at 667 Spadina Avenue and crossed the prairies by
passenger train to Field, British Columbia, a CPR town west of Kicking
Horse Pass on the Great Divide, where alpinists bearing ice axes, alpen-
stocks, and umbrellas—"laden with impedimentia"—gathered to wait in
anticipation for the next morning's trek into camp in Yoho National Park.
"No wonder we were excited!" he recounted, "for once in our blessed
lives we all saw the sun rise and flood the awesome canyon of the
Kicking Horse as the dark shadows of the night were dispelled."[2] The
rose-hued dawn on a mountain skyline was an exhilarating sight,
followed by the hike into camp. Whenever the Alpine Club pitched its
tents at summer mountaineering camps in Canada, throughout the next
hundred years, climbers like Frank felt a sense of excitement.

Annie Louise Laird and her brother David, who was at the inaugural
Winnipeg meeting, also attended that first camp at Summit Lake. The
two were Elizabeth Parker's friends from a well-known Winnipeg family.
Annie taught at a girls' private school after studies in social work at
Queen's, and her brother was an alumnus in law.[3] They were keen to qualify

as active ACC members by making a graduating climb on Mount Vice President in a party guided by M.P. Bridgland and H.G. Wheeler on July 13. Brigland gauged it a worthy feat for beginners, and he aimed as chief mountaineer "to graduate as many as possible as safely as possible."[4] Frank, Annie, and David were among the forty-two who qualified.

Frank and Annie met at that camp, and then again in 1907 at the next ACC camp. Frank (a widower) married Annie a year later.[5] In Toronto, he authored a book about his westward travel adventures even as he managed publicity for acclaimed poet Pauline Johnson. Annie remained an ACC member until she was eighty-one. Although Frank and Annie never again attended an ACC camp, like many ACC climbers who formed lifelong bonds and long-standing social relations at camp, Frank and Annie discovered that alpinism was more than a hobby. It was a spirit and shared experience that could bring together the lives of mountaineers.

Year after year, alpinists migrated to Canada's mountain national parks and shared the "incomparable scene" that Frank recalled from his first idyllic look at the Alpine Club of Canada's tented town. The practice of holding an annual club mountaineering camp was decreed in the club's first constitution, and the summer camp became the club's main annual event, central to social and cultural life in the national organization. Winter camps were later added to the club's activities, but the national summer mountaineering camp functioned as the central hub of club tradition and established a substantial continuity ritualized throughout its first seven decades. Large annual mountaineering camps were not held by all alpine clubs; the ACC's tradition was inventive.

A closer look at the camps reveals the basis of collective identity, leisure practices, and ideological impulses at work within the club, all of which are integral to understanding how the club functioned, what its values were, its goals. ACC members developed their own organizational, social, material, and physical culture, a backcountry blend of western mountain sport and outdoorsy camp life amid polite society. The annual summer camp was a site for inventing tradition in a middle-class club culture of Canadian climbing that institutionalized summer holidays in the mountain parks for the purpose of alpine recreation and sport, which in turn influenced a culture of mountain tourism and conservation in places known as Canada's parks today.[6]

∧ *"The Happy Throng,"* ACC
Palliser Pass Camp, 1922.
Harry Pollard photograph.
[WMCR, V14/AC29P/3/14]

Old Friends and New

An Alpine Club of Canada songbook called *Songs of Canadian Climbers*, edited by Edmonton's Cyril Wates, was published in 1922. "The Call of the Alpine," lyrics by Malcolm Geddes, opens the volume, set to the regimental tune of "Bonnie Dundee." It suggests the tension in Canadian climbing culture in the 1920s: of living in two worlds, asserting that real life is lived not at work (ten months of the year "slaving away") but on holidays, as a climber, following the call of the alpine:

> *Far away in the mountains where bigness abounds*
> *Man's worth is not rated in dollars and pounds;*
> *The gold of our friendships is sifted from dross;*
> *Our friendships are real, without tarnish or gloss;*
> *There we live as our Maker intended we should,*
> *Each thought building truly for one common good;*
> *Thus while Mountains abide or true love doth endure,*
> *There is nothing can equal the Alpine Club's lure.*[7]

> Songs of Canadian Climbers, *(1922), cover with song lyrics.*

> Songs of Canadian Climbers, *(1922), cover with song lyrics.*

Seeking alpine adventure was in many ways an expression of antimodernist longings for authenticity, fulfillment, and moral uplift. In an era of modern industrial capitalism and intensified urbanization in Canada, which gave rise to a dehumanizing sense of alienation and the obliteration of nature decried by poets and patriots, the mountains were positioned as a virtuous space, where salaried urban men and women—like Calgary journalist and mountaineer Malcolm Geddes—could find temporary reprieve from the city. Mountain life, they believed, stripped away excess and imparted higher values as a restorative to urban existence. A sizable contingent of middle-class urban Canadians sought their summer escape at the ACC camps in Canada's national mountain parks.

The early 1900s was an era of exclusive luxury travel, which largely restricted tourism in the Canadian Rockies to affluent travellers. However, Arthur Wheeler made it clear that the ACC attracted middle-class tourists to the mountains, "those whose means prevented their visiting the mountain regions under existing tourist conditions, which are only for the wealthy."[8] They were, nonetheless, people of sufficient means and privilege to invest in travel and club pursuits. University of Toronto professor A.P. Coleman, New Westminster schoolteacher Emmie Brooks, Calgary clergyman Rev. Dean Paget, and Toronto artist Fred Brigden were typical of the class of visitor who attended the camps.[9]

In some ways, the early ACC camps resembled Thomas Cook's tours that opened the Swiss Alps to middle-class British tourism in the 1860s.[10] Cook's success reflected his ability to deliver scenery, safety, and social security to his clientele; a Cook tour took the "right" people to the "right" destinations, fed and exercised them well, and was presumed to build their character and ideals. Similarly, Wheeler's camps exerted a democratizing influence on the tourist market operating in the national parks of the "Canadian Alps." The club existed to bring people to the Rockies; unlike commercial interests, such as outfitters and the CPR, it did not labour to raise its profit margin through tourism. The club "furnishes for from three to four dollars a day opportunities that would otherwise cost from ten to fifteen dollars a day. Not only that, but it furnishes facilities for mountain climbing, recreation and study that could not otherwise be obtained, even at the highest prices charged."[11] As a result, the camps spurred the growth of tourism in the Rockies. As Arthur Wheeler wrote to National Parks Commissioner J.B. Harkin in 1921, "Canadians of moderate means who desire to travel in the hills have as much right to enjoy the privileges and beauties of their mountain heritage as wealthy outsiders, or wealthy motorists."[12] Wheeler's argument was in line with Harkin's own democratic vision of national parks open to the Canadian public.

Inspired by a nationalistic dedication to share the Canadian "mountain heritage" by promoting climbing and tourism in the Rockies, the ACC camps were the club's principal means of broadening mountaineering. This inclusive approach stood in contrast to other clubs, such as the New Zealand Alpine Club (NZAC), founded in Christchurch in 1891, which acted chiefly as a national fraternity for the experienced elite of New Zealand climbers. NZAC maintained that "the role of the club was to publicise and promote mountain activities. It was not to teach newcomers how to climb. That task was to be accomplished by professional guides." However, in response to concerns about "needless deaths," NZAC camps started in 1931 to indoctrinate newcomers to mountaineering with the "proper attitude to safe climbing."[13] The ACC camps described to New Zealanders by Conrad Kain—an Austrian mountaineering guide regularly employed by the ACC—subsequently served

James Bernard Harkin (1875–1955)

JAMES HARKIN was Canada's first commissioner of national parks and an inspiration behind the federal parks administration from 1911 until his retirement in 1936.[14] He began his career as a journalist in Montreal and Ottawa and was appointed to the public service of Canada in 1901. From 1904 to 1911, he served as a private secretary to Minister of the Interior Clifford Sifton and his successor Frank Oliver. Informed of the minister's intention to create a distinct department to oversee national parks in 1911, Harkin readily accepted a position as commissioner of the newly created Dominion Parks Branch. During his twenty-five-year term, Harkin guided the development of parks from a handful of jurisdictions in the Rockies to a larger family of nationally protected natural areas and historic sites across Canada. He saw "the great principle of Conservation" as "the duty of a nation to guard its treasures of art, natural beauty, or natural wonders for generations to come." Central to this philosophy was Harkin's belief in "the right of the people to share in the use and enjoyment of the noblest regions in their own land."[15] The ACC espoused a similarly democratic vision, and in it Harkin would find a steady ally.

> *National Parks Commissioner J.B. Harkin at* ACC *Larch Valley Camp, 1923. Harry Pollard photograph. [WMCR, V14/AC192P/1]*

as the model for NZAC's instructional camps. Its annual climbing camp persists and welcomes members, guests, and climbers from overseas clubs to explore and enjoy New Zealand's many mountains.

The ACC's camps were attended by many newcomers to hiking and mountaineering, but the club did not consider its members' inexperience in the mountains an obstacle to participation. On the contrary, the camps were a venue for instruction in "mountain craft" and served to channel newcomers into the culture of alpinism, in keeping with the club mandate.[16] The club's constitution specifically called for an annual summer camp to teach new climbers and revitalize the work of the ACC. A "graduating climb" was required to certify new climbers as active members. Each camp produced a fresh graduating class of mountaineers ready to explore Canada's mountain parks and revitalize the rituals and values at the heart of the club. ACC administration, outfitters and packers, mountain guides, cooks and volunteer tea ladies, the requisite members (young and old), and others attended the camps. Of course, camp was more ideal for some than it was for others.

THE CAMP OFFICE AND ADMINISTRATION

From their first moments in camp, guests fell into the administrative hands of the ACC national secretary-treasurer and a team of office assistants. Co-founder Elizabeth Parker first held the job, followed by two long-standing secretaries, Stanley Hamilton Mitchell from 1908 to 1928 and Wharton Richard Tweedy, "The Major," from 1929 to 1943.[17] These secretary-treasurers were, to a large degree, the managers of national club business and operations. Their long service provided much continuity within the club.

Secretaries Mitchell and Tweedy brought their organizational talents to bear on the ACC camps and year-round club operations. They did not run business alone; they built an administrative structure to support and operate the camps. The fresh mountain air may have invigorated the club's idealism, but the club bureaucracy, administrators, and volunteers did the work that ensured members could engage in the summer activities that brought the club together annually.

Each year, an office tent was set up for conducting ACC business at camp. A staff of clerical assistants enlisted by the secretary-treasurer handled registrations, fee payments, paperwork, and mail. Miss Erma Arneson was a frequent figure on Tweedy's staff in the 1930s. She received a free stay at camp in exchange for her capable clerical work that held much in common with her professional duties as the assistant

Stanley Hamilton Mitchell (1863–1940)

BORN IN GLASGOW, Stanley Mitchell attended
public school in England and lived in Switzerland as a
child, where his "love of high mountains was born in both
mind and heart."[18] Mitchell served as the ACC secretary
through twenty-one formative years of the club's history.
As a young man, he had emigrated from Scotland to
Canada, where he joined his brother, Henry Bucknall
Mitchell, in the lumber trade. Stanley was forty-three
when the ACC was founded and was one of its original
members, working as Elizabeth Parker's secretarial assistant while the club was getting off the ground. He acted
as assistant editor of the *Canadian Alpine Journal* from
1907 to 1926 under Arthur Wheeler. Although held back
from sports since childhood by weak health, he loved the
mountains and adopted the ACC "alpine idea" whole-
heartedly. A lifelong bachelor, he made the ACC his
lifetime vocation.[19]

For a time, Mitchell operated the club from his stark
bachelor apartment, storing part of the voluminous club
library on shelves in the bathroom due to a lack of space.
In a letter to President Bell in 1926 outlining his plan to
install shelves there, he mused with good humour about
the collection of back issues of the *CAJ*, "I wonder if
bath steam would damage them. I should not think there
would be enough to make any difference. I do not plan a
Turkish bath arrangement!"[20]

By 1927 a bookcase—8 feet high by 9 feet long
(2.4 by 2.7 metres)—was installed in Mitchell's residence
to hold "over 700 journals" along with club files and
records.[21] Managing records and library collections,
however improvised, were instrumental tasks in building
the club. Other furnishings in the two-room bed-sitter
were minimal, but Mitchell offered the use of his rooms
for meetings of the Vancouver Section.[22] Middle-class
frugality, the modest means of the club, and making do
among mountaineers marked Mitchell's attitude toward
the use of his personal living space for club events. His
was a generous and overwhelming commitment to the
club. During Mitchell's tenure, he was based in Calgary,
Banff, Vancouver, and Sidney on Vancouver Island,
British Columbia. Through the terms of seven national
ACC presidents—A.O. Wheeler (1906), A.P. Coleman
(1910), J.D. Patterson (1914), W.W. Foster (1920), J.W.
Hickson (1924), F.C. Bell (1926), and T.B. Moffat (1928)—
Mitchell's life was woven through the club's first decades.[23]

Mitchell excelled at tending to the needs of guests
at the annual camps. Most of his summers were spent in
the Rockies, where he was well known at the Banff clubhouse on Sulphur Mountain. His obituary noted that
"he had the gift of creating lasting friendships and was
well adapted to meeting and looking after the enter-
tainment of visitors to the Alpine Club House at Banff,
where he spent his summers, and of members and visitors attending the Club's annual camps."[24] Arthur
Wheeler recalled Mitchell's "warm-hearted solicitude for
the comfort of our guests that would lend them the half
of his own camp-bedding sooner than have them sleep
cold." Year after year, although the walk to the Banff
post office and back uphill along Mountain Avenue to
the clubhouse taxed his weak heart, Mitchell persisted
in "his own austere sense of a secretary's duty." Despite
his Spartan nature, however, he understood middle-class
refinement and took great pride in his club, delighting
that the Royal Alexandra Hotel in Winnipeg had laid out
"the best Spode china and solid silver as used by royalty
and vice-royalty" on the occasion of the ACC's tenth
anniversary dinner in 1916.[25]

In addition to his many camp experiences, Mitchell
enjoyed reading mountain literature and maps and,
in this respect, outpaced many active climbers. Club
members thought of him as "a reading gentleman" who
walked the Rockies, Himalayas, and other great ranges
through literature.[26] In many respects, he was a Scot
with Victorian sensibilities, living in twentieth-century
Canada, regarding his duty to the club as much like his
duty to king and country.

In his sixties, Mitchell began to feel cardiac stress due to altitude when he travelled to the Rockies in the summer. He subsequently retired to a nursing home in Victoria, British Columbia. He suffered from impaired hearing, and a weak heart forced him to avoid higher altitudes, but, despite confinement in later life, he continued to serve the club in an honorary role. Even in his reduced capacity, Mitchell was active. As Cyril Wates observed, "His finger was constantly on the pulse of the Club, and, in view of his necessarily restricted outlook, his accurate knowledge of Club affairs was nothing short of amazing."[27]

Mitchell's ability to follow club affairs was always based on his large number of correspondents among various sections of the ACC and extensive letter writing to keep up social ties among friends and acquaintances. His strong sense of fraternity held fast during old age when, according to Wheeler, "he maintained a correspondence with very many of his old mountain friends, which seemed to be his chief remaining interest in life." Mitchell's "chatty and humorous letters" transported him from confinement back to the Rockies and "kept alive the memories of happy days spent at camps in the mountains he loved so well"; likewise, his annual messages read at camp renewed the memory of Mitchell as one of the club's founders. He died in 1940, and his funeral was held in Victoria after which his ashes were taken to Banff, where he had spent so many summers, to be buried in the local cemetery as he desired.[28] Club President Cyril Wates remarked, "here was a mountaineer and a man, in the finest sense of the words...he cherished ideals for the Club which cannot fail to inspire us for all future time."[29]

to the University of Saskatchewan's registrar. Women volunteered at the camp office in exchange for free fees for each day worked.[30] Single professional women, such as Miss Henley, the 1931 camp stenographer, were engaged as clerks in exchange for their expenses attending camp and making some climbs, along with the occasional bonus.[31] In 1931 and 1932, camp clerk Miss Valens was responsible for taking minutes at the club's annual general meeting and typing them.[32] Mitchell generally required two clerks and a camp boy to run the office. Tweedy initially tried to reduce the size of the office staff, but after he had a few camps under his belt, the office staff returned to more or less Mitchell's original system.[33] The success of the club relied on such volunteerism and quid pro quo for professional skills and labour.

SUPPORT TEAMS
Outfitters and Packers, Mountain Guides, and Cooks at Camp

Outfitters and packers, mountain guides, and cooks were always present at ACC annual camps. Cowboy outfitters and packers built the tented town occupied by the ACC in the mountains each summer. Taking over one hundred visitors camping in the national parks required the services of commercial outfitters experienced in guiding parties through the mountains, transporting people and goods, wrangling horses, supplying expeditions, pitching tents, preparing meals, and organizing a comfortable home away from home in camp. At least six outfitters and trail guides attended the ACC's inaugural meeting in Winnipeg in 1906. Largely due to the donation of free services by trail guides from Laggan, Banff, Field, and Glacier, the ACC was able to stage its first camp less than four months later.[34]

The club augmented the local tourist traffic and increased outfitting business in the Rockies; it was not long before the camps became a lucrative venture for outfitters. Ultimately, contracts for the annual ACC summer camps and spin-off private parties became an important part of the business on which regional independent outfitters relied for their own financial success.[35]

The western cowboy image of sinuous hard-working frontiersmen, much popularized in turn-of-the-century wild west shows, rodeos, dime-store novels, Baden Powell's Scout movement, and *Boys Own* tales of imperial adventure,[36] took shape before the very eyes of Rocky Mountain tourists. They embellished the cowboys at camp as the "men in buckskin."[37] Fringed jackets, neckerchiefs, handlebar moustaches, and plug

Wharton Richard Tweedy, "The Major" (1889–1965)

MITCHELL WAS SUCCEEDED as club secretary in 1929 by "The Major," another key figure in ACC camp life. Wharton Richard Tweedy, a tall, well-groomed, ex-military man, was the second-longest-serving ACC secretary and "a devoted servant of the Club" for over fifteen years.[38] Born and educated in England, Tweedy travelled to British Columbia as a young man and settled in the Okanagan Valley, where he had a business running pack trains for survey parties until the outbreak of the Great War. He rose to the rank of major in the Royal Army Service Corps and served as a horse master in France and Greece. Returning to British Columbia, he married and became a father. Later, Tweedy ran an orchard with his wife at West Summerland.[39]

Tweedy was considered "a consummate horseman and leader of men" possessed of "an uncanny knowledge of the mountain country." He combined these qualities with energetic efficiency in his management as ACC secretary. Dissenters suggested Tweedy had a rigid hard-nosed manner that hurt the club more than helped it, but an empathetic club obituary suggested there was more than one side to his personality:

> On first acquaintance the Major appeared somewhat unapproachable...His gruff demeanour and military bearing may have caused some apprehension to the uninitiated. But behind this stiff facade dwelt a kindly gentleman and generous soul who would go to any length to help others in time of need and trouble. Many a time weary and benighted climbers have been cheered on their way back to camp by the timely appearance of the Major, who could always produce a "wee drop," a saddle pony and an encouraging word.[40]

Major Tweedy benefitted from past secretary Stanley Mitchell's experience, and the two became good friends

∧ *H.E. Sampson and Major Tweedy keep business going at ACC camp in Jasper National Park in 1930. Tweedy was adept with equine and field operations. [EA-41-28]*

during the course of Tweedy's work despite an age difference of twenty-six years. When Tweedy was absent, Mitchell took charge of operating the ACC national office and its reams of correspondence. Tweedy illustrated both sides of his capable yet caring nature when Mitchell was nearing death in 1940, writing, "I fear he will not last long and I was really horrified to see how he had sunk...I feel he will just slip off quietly very shortly; and he wished me to take charge of things for him."[41]

During Tweedy's appointment as secretary-treasurer from 1929 to 1943, he was associated with six ACC presidents: T.B. Moffat (1928), H.E. Sampson (1930), A.A. McCoubrey (1932), A.S. Sibbald (1934), C.G. Wates (1938), and E.C. Brooks (1941). Unlike Stanley Mitchell's friendly banter, Tweedy's correspondence was brisk and to the point, much like the economical management style he practiced through a period marked by the Depression and war.

In 1933 he proposed running the outfitting of the ACC camps himself. Eventually, he took over their operations with the collaboration of Banff's Swedish guide and outfitter Ralph Rink.[42] As camp manager, Tweedy responded readily to emergencies, including evacuating an injured mountaineer rescued from a crevasse off the Columbia Icefields by horse in 1938, and relocating the Glacier Lake Camp in a "round-the-clock effort" to avoid a devastating forest fire and ensure the camp opened on time as expected in 1940. Tweedy, then about fifty, was rejected due to age when he wanted to re-enlist for active military duty during the Second World War,[43] but he served the war effort by outfitting the club's July 1943 military training camp in the Little Yoho Valley.[44]

The Major also compiled the first index to the *Canadian Alpine Journal*, which lacked an effective reference aid for finding articles, maps, routes, descriptions, photographs, and other data. President McCoubrey applauded the progress on this project, never before attempted.[45] The demanding project extended past Tweedy's retirement from the ACC, circa 1944 until 1963, when he had to cease work on the index because of his health. By then, the index covered the volumes from 1907 to 1958. Major Tweedy died in 1965.[46]

hats did much to enhance the effect of the local cowboys on the tourist trade. The majority of these cowboys had drifted to the Rockies from Ontario, the northern United States, England, and Ireland, and found a life in the saddle.[47] Some, like William Warren, were English veterans of the Boer War who, rather than go home, hankered for adventure in distant corners of the empire; others, like Jimmy Simpson, were remittance men sent away to Canada by their families. Ones like Edward Moberly were guides and hunters descended from Métis homesteading families evicted from the Athabasca Valley when Jasper Park was established.[48]

Just as the outfitters provided camp attendees with a taste of the cowboy lifestyle, the presence of foreign mountain guides at camp lent a European cachet to the club's camps and helped legitimate the Canadian alpine movement. Sun-bronzed faces, striped neckties, and handsome suits played up the sporty appeal of the guides, glamorized for their good looks, daring, and wit. The first professional mountain guides to live and work in Canada were Swiss Oberlanders who left the alpine districts near Interlaken to seek economic opportunity as CPR employees in mountain hotels.[49] Some were sent to camp "on loan" from the CPR and CNR.

Swiss guides, and the Austrian guide Conrad Kain who was hired by the club, introduced ACC climbers to the fundamentals of mountaineering and led them safely on routes. Edward Feuz, Jr., complained that "in 1906, the first year, I had to drag a lot of idiots to the top of Mount Whyte (now Vice President) in the Yoho just so they could qualify for Club membership." Great responsibility fell on the shoulders of the guides when dealing with such an inexperienced group, and they received little reward for the additional strain. Accustomed to leading mountaineering excursions for wealthy guests of the CPR hotels, Feuz expressed dismay with the middle-class ACC climbers and the club's constraining regime:

> *Those people at the camps were the cheapest skinflints I ever had. They took all my time when I could have been with rich Americans and Englishmen who were regular clients and knew me well. Those tips at the camps were nothing—maybe $10 for two weeks. I had to work night and day, and again listen to a damned [wake-up] bell, the way I did when I was fifteen years old. Most of the people didn't know a thing about climbing. I had to teach them how to use their feet.*[50]

The Brewsters and the ACC

Not All Cowboys were Honest Men

AT THE OUTSET, commercial outfitting in the Canadian Rockies was largely a matter of small independent businesses run by various regional operators; the exception was the growing influence of the Brewster clan. Arthur Wheeler was a strong proponent of the independents and sought to defeat the monopolistic tendencies of Banff's Brewster family dynasty in the local transportation business.[51] In 1909 the Otto brothers were appointed as "Official Outfitters to the Alpine Club of Canada," but this position was short-lived as the Brewster Transfer Company soon took over their business in the Field–Leanchoil district of Yoho National Park, British Columbia. The change bedeviled Wheeler, who was forced at the last minute to accept the services of the Brewsters for the 1910 camp in Consolation Valley: "It is much to be regretted that here the mountain transport is handled by a monopoly, which can only result in poor service. The individuality of the old-time outfitters has gone and a lot of cheap hirelings have been substituted."[52]

Only days after returning to Banff from the ACC founding meeting where they had promised "to give the proposed [1906] Yoho camp all possible assistance," Bill Brewster, one of the brothers, and their partner and brother-in-law, Philip A. Moore, resigned from the ACC without explanation. Wheeler contended that the Brewsters' change in plans came at a cost to the newly formed ACC: "Unfortunately, the day of loaves and fishes is past and when 100 people come out of the train at Field they will expect to be transported with their baggage to the Camp and when there to be fed, tented and provided with plenty of diversion. All this means money or its equivalent and the Brewsters' withdrawal represents in hard cash, something over $200.00."[53] The total cost for the 1906 camp was estimated at $1,500, with half the amount payable by those in attendance.

Again, in advance of the 1909 Lake O'Hara camp, the Brewsters attempted to beleaguer the club. Wheeler recounted the incident to William Whyte, vice-president of the CPR:

To carry out his contract with the Alpine Club, Otto Bros. had to employ Jimmy Simpson and his outfit of horses, some ten in number. After the camp was over J.W. Otto told me that Brewster had offered $300.00 to lose his horses so that they would not be available for the Camp, but that Simpson had declined to break faith with Otto. Otto told me this in confidence, but a few days later I was told the same story at Glacier, and found that it was current gossip. Had the scheme been successful we should have been badly left in the lurch with a number of distinguished English alpine people on our hands, and naturally, I felt rather indignant.[54]

Club officials became wary of the Brewster clan for various reasons because, as Stanley Mitchell explained, "for the first years...the Brewsters were always covertly opposing the Club."[55] This mercenary scramble illustrates the club's brush with the realities of Rocky Mountain business. The purest alpine ideals unavoidably provoked commercial considerations that could lead to skulduggery, greed, and petty corruption in a small regional market. The mountains were not removed from capitalist competition, nor were all cowboys honest men.

As the ACC gained prominence and offered commercial outfitters associated with the club a competitive advantage in a regional market, the Brewsters and Moore sought to align themselves with the club on more favourable terms. Moore joined as a new member in 1927, "nothing being said about bygones as it was

∧ *Outfitter Jack Hargreaves packs a horse with dunnage for an ACC camp in Jasper. Camps relied on cowboys and pack trains for transportation.* [EA-41-84]

considered he had never really been a member," and the Brewsters managed to work their way back in as honorary members, publicly parading themselves as founders of the ACC once memories had faded. Secretary Mitchell suffered no memory lapse, however, and privately objected to admitting the Brewsters based on his reading of the ACC constitution. "I can not see the slightest justification in admitting them as Charter members," he wrote, "or as we call them Original members....It of course was not intended to apply to people who resigned within less than a calendar month."[56]

Feuz felt stuck with this duty at the early camps, year after year, and
eventually called on the railway to alternate the assigned mountain
guides.[57] Still, Swiss guides were waged company men with little choice
about working "on loan" at the camps and assisted for decades. Tips
from clients were a valuable supplement for guides subject to seasonal
employment, work shortages, and layoffs. During the Depression, the
CNR laid off its entire staff of Swiss guides;[58] theirs was not an easy
profession, and it was fraught with dangers inherent to climbing.

Still, climbers were expected to heed the authority of their guides.
One exception was Arthur Wheeler. He refused to rope up for safety
when requested, rebuked his guide, and nearly sailed off a thousand-foot

cliff once when he slipped, only to be saved by Edward Feuz. The guide leapt on him to halt the fall and later claimed, "if anybody was reckless, it was Wheeler." Feuz claimed Wheeler never went on a rope. When leading another party back late into the club camp one night to Wheeler's dismay, Feuz told Wheeler, "when I'm on a climb as guide, I'm the boss, not you."[59] In later years, Wheeler conceded that he had been "a novice in much conceit of his physical power...who knew everything of the art that he did not."[60]

Swiss guides working for the CPR had an impeccable safety record through fifty years of service. When climbing accidents happened, mountain guides were called to lead search and rescue efforts. One outstanding case involved American ACC members Dr. W.E. Stone and his wife Margaret Stone on Mount Eon in 1921. Winthrop Stone was a chemist and the president of Purdue University in Indiana. Both were experienced mountaineers who sought a first ascent on Mount Eon before heading to the ACC's camp at Lake O'Hara in late July. They embarked from the Banff clubhouse to the Mount Assiniboine Walking Tour main camp, then started for Mount Eon on July 15. When they were late returning, a search party led by guide Rudolph Aemmer found Margaret Stone alive, after eight days of exposure on a ledge, following her husband's fatal fall near the summit point on July 17. Aemmer looped Margaret in a sling and carried her tied to his back for four and a half hours on the way to a bivouac where she was attended by the club's Dr. Fred Bell and made comfortable by Mrs. Bell and Miss Brown at Trail Centre Camp; within days, Aemmer, Feuz, Conrad Kain, and two ACC men recovered the remains of Dr. Stone.[61] The incident was documented extensively in the *Canadian Alpine Journal* and reported in the *New York Times*.

Without the guides, the early ACC would have lacked a knowledgeable group of mountaineering leaders and instructors at a time when there were few skilled Canadian mountaineers. In some cases, guides were well known to club members and built guide-client rapport through the years at successive camps. They also transmitted the practices and ethics of mountain craft to club climbers, thereby creating continuity in climber education and regulation of camp physical culture. Key Swiss guides served club camps in ongoing professional relationships that lasted throughout their long careers. Three were officially acknowledged for serving the club through its first forty years when President Eric Brooks conferred honorary life memberships on Rudolph Aemmer and brothers Ernest and Edward Feuz at the 1947 Glacier Camp. Presenting

Volunteer Guides and Instructors

IN ADDITION TO the professional guides, the ACC also recruited volunteer instructors and guides—most of them male—from among its members. Skilled volunteers, like Canmore coal miner Lawrence Grassi and Edmonton district farmer Rex Gibson, led ropes and assisted the professional mountain guides at camp. Emmie Brooks, Polly Prescott, and Phyl Munday—all exceptional climbers—were among the women who led climbs from the 1920s onward. In 1945 the club ran the annual camp in Eremite Valley solely with amateur guides, nineteen men (including Rex Gibson and Bob Hind) and six women (among them Phyllis Munday and Elizabeth Brett).[62] The club devised of the Silver Rope award for its amateur guides to encourage leadership in the ACC, and, in 1940, it debated and approved the principle of granting the award to men and women on the same basis, which came as late recognition for the leadership of Phyllis Munday and Polly Prescott.[63] In effect, the annual camps allowed the club to develop a corps of experienced leaders who assisted professional guides and kept the club's climbing program going.

< *Andy Drinnan and Lawrence Grassi volunteer ready to lead ropes at camp, c. 1928. [WMCR, V14/AC192P/7]*

∧ Head cook Jim Pong
(right) was known for his wry
sense of humour. He poses
here with Chinese CPR cook
staff at the Vermilion Pass
Camp, 1912. Byron Harmon
photograph.
[WMCR, V263/NA/0051]

each with an illuminated certificate and "a small purse," the president
noted that the guides "had come to be regarded by countless members of
the Club with ever increasing affection and respect" and thanked them
"for their unselfish services and friendship towards the Club."[64]

Even with stellar outfitters, packers, and professional guides, a cook
could make or break an ACC camp's success. There was "no more fatal
mistake," one ACC organizer observed, than changing the grub expected
at camp.[65] Oven-fresh bread, bacon and eggs, hotcakes, and all manner
of hearty camp fare were expected. The first cooks at the ACC camps,
provided from the capable staff of the CPR, laboured over woodstoves in
the canvas cook tent. In the early years, they were Chinese railway men.
Jim Pong was the head cook between 1906 and 1911, known to campers
by the nickname "Ping-Pong."[66] Pong knew how to run a camp kitchen.
Taskmaster Wheeler called "Jim and his assistants...the perfection of
camp machinery, and the surest token was the fact that there were always
plenty of good things to eat just when they were wanted."[67]

Liquor and heavy drinking were commonly condoned among kitchen
staff and cowboys, in keeping with frontier masculinity in the mountain

backcountry, whereas the early ACC camps were assumed to be respectably dry, particularly in the presence of women, in keeping with the middle-class temperance movement. The cook was reputed to keep his own supply of spirits on hand. Swiss guide Edward Feuz, Jr., claimed this stock came in handy when the chance arose for staff to sip a drink unseen by their clients. According to Feuz, the cook tent burned down on a few occasions when the cook was drinking and staff failed to extinguish the flames, despite "frantic efforts."[68] Covert behaviours of frontier masculinity and "working-class" conduct among cooks, guides, and cowboys indicate that the well-oiled "camp machinery" could resist the dominant class expectations of orderly regulation. Even Wheeler overlooked typical transgressions and enjoyed his own Scotch.

An assorted crew succeeded the Chinese railway cooks. In Secretary Mitchell's review of the 1927 camp, he noted to the club president that "there were white cooks but they were not overwhelmingly a success." When a woman applied for the job in 1929, she was rejected by Mitchell, who stated, "Privately I do not think a woman cook would fit in." Presumptions about the frontier masculinity of the camp staff and the sensibilities of a respectable woman (the only kind for the club) likely precluded the possibility. Mitchell preferred to retain a man named Gillespie, who had cooked at the previous camp, even though he had relied on dry goods and failed to offer much in the way of fresh food.[69]

For thirty years, beginning in 1935, a perennial figure in the cook tent was Ken Jones, a Canadian-born mountain guide, packer, and jack-of-all-trades from Golden, British Columbia, who liked to combine cooking with leading some climbs for the club, whether as a paid staff member or a volunteer. Jones and a group of about six women from Victoria all volunteered to cook under Eileen Maurice in 1946. Cooking for a record 185 people at the camp in the Bugaboos was an enormous task for inexperienced volunteers, according to Jones, and he helped to organize their efforts. He even managed to climb every other day. "When we were going to make an alpine start, I would get up early, say three a.m., and make breakfast for the climbers."[70] Scenes of these women working as volunteer cooks and dishwashers were recorded in the silent film *Alpine Climbers in Canada*.[71]

YOUNG ACC CAMPERS

Minors were officially discouraged from attending the early ACC camps even though youth camping movements brought young people into the wilderness in Ontario and elsewhere during the same period.[72] In 1928

The Tea Tent

A Haven for Climbers

CLIMBERS COMING INTO CAMP, often wet and tired, found warm refuge inside the tea tent. Under the flaps, a woolly steam rising from climbers, clothing, and gear drying around the wood stove hovered over conversation about the day's exploits, humour, routes, and snow conditions, over a mug of tea and a bite to eat. Tea was not simply a sustaining fluid; it was the beverage of hospitality and social exchange.

Ladies in the club customarily ran the tea tent, although male outfitters were known to take on the job. Although the club was progressive in its practice of admitting women as members, women did not escape the supportive domestic gender roles ascribed to them by the middle-class social standards of the day, even in the backcountry. Clara Wheeler, who was raised in

comfortable Ottawa society, was a "capable collaborator," whose "guiding hand was on the cooks, the commissariat, and on all other arrangements for the comfort of large mountaineering parties" at the early ACC camps organized by her husband. At camp, she presided with genteel hospitality in the tea tent. Although delicate and considered too frail for the exertion of climbing, she managed to fulfill the demanding club social duties that befell the president's spouse as a volunteer: "She presided as hostess, and at any time of day or evening she had the indispensable tea ready for tired climbers and listened with keen interest to their experiences of the day."[73] Miss Edna Caroline Kelley, a member of the Edmonton ACC Section, also acted as "Tea Hostess" on several occasions, winning campers'

∧ Assembly line produces camp lunches in the tea tent at Maligne Lake Camp, 1930. [EA-41-32]

approval for her "gracious and thoughtful solicitation." Although an enthusiastic skier and golfer, her health was not strong enough for climbing, and she focused instead on "camp life, the friends she met there, the Alpine flowers, animals, and the comradeship of the camp fires."[74] These matronly women enjoyed interacting as campers and took pride in playing a support role as social facilitators, much in keeping with the function of a voluntary ladies' auxiliary. Even while seeking the wilderness in the alpine backcountry, the club transported familiar social patterns, civility, and class structures to its tented town.

Other women found duty in the tea tent onerous. As late as July 1936, Tweedy remarked there was a shortage of help in the tea tent except for Miss Rita Rushworth, "the only lady I have managed to get so far for the tea tent."[75] By the following year, Rushworth was no longer available: "Miss Rushworth is marrying Heb Dickson in the summer and [I] do not think they will be in camp; in any case I do not suppose she would care to honeymoon in the office or tea tent!"[76] By 1939 the tea tent was "run by a committee of ladies" who traded shifts with the main volunteer.

Preparing lunches for more than a hundred campers was part of the job in the tea tent. This was a chore for some volunteers. Tweedy argued to President Cyril Wates that he must have an experienced volunteer in the tent. "I do not agree with a change each year, it takes about a year to train one up properly, and is much easier for all concerned (cooks, girl, guests and myself) to have someone who knows the ropes."[77] This argument led Wates to respond sarcastically that Tweedy ought to go ahead and enlist Edna Kelley from Edmonton into "Tea Tent Slavery" as "Chamber Maid in Chief and Sandwich Slasher." Despite the heavy workload, Wates was concerned that giving the position to one of his section members might result in charges of favouritism, a hint that suggests social tensions operating between club sections on matters of minor privilege as well as those involved in gendered volunteer labour.[78]

Stanley Mitchell wrote that he thought it "unwise to admit young people under age except under very exceptional circumstances,"[79] and the ACC camps were mainly adult events until the Depression brought about a change in practice and policy.

Following inquiries in 1933 about the attendance of two sixteen-year-olds—the son and the nephew of a member—Tweedy recommended creating a junior section at camp to accommodate teenaged campers. President McCoubrey dissuaded him, arguing that it was simpler to accept the teens at camp and benefit from the added revenue they would bring to the club.[80] Following a similar request in 1934, Tweedy reminded McCoubrey that it was against the club constitution to allow families with children at camp. (Tweedy wrote that breaching the rules might risk tension between the members,[81] as even he was constrained by the policy—his own children did not attend camp.) Still, President McCoubrey accepted the teenagers in 1934, reasoning that they "would not be in the way," and he advised that the club could ill afford to be "too choosy" under tight financial circumstances. Thus, financial considerations combined with repeated requests eroded the policy against younger participants.

Although long excluded from attending as campers, children had a role working at the camps. "Camp boys" were recruited as workers to haul members' luggage from train platforms to trucks, tote dunnage bags to the tents, fetch mail, and run errands. However, in 1934, "the usual camp boys" were cut from the camp staff.[82] Banff outfitter Ralph Rink was "glad to get rid of the boys," but Tweedy prepared to enlist "some local Boy-Scouts" to replace them if necessary.[83] Certain camp boys were so impressed by their experiences that they aspired to join the ranks of mountaineers and served the organization in later life, like Bob Hind, who started as a camp boy, was elected an active member around 1933, and ultimately served as ACC western vice-president (1954–56) and national president (1964–66).[84]

By 1937 younger people were officially admitted to camp for the first time. Although Tweedy complained that they ate twice as much as adults, the general consensus was that the younger participants "proved a valuable addition to all camp activities, including the camp fires."[85] Family participation was, in effect, a significant means of transmitting the club's ideals and traditions from generation to generation. The club also factored the issue of age into liability and group safety because rope members had to be prepared to share the risks of climbing and to respond in case of emergency or rescue.[86]

INTERNATIONAL TRAVELLERS

Mountaineering formed an international network of travellers and clubs attracted to ACC camps. The *Canadian Alpine Journal* enumerated country of origin, club, and other affiliations at camp. Travellers commonly came from the United States, Britain, New Zealand, and countries in the European Alps, along with India and Hong Kong among those farther afield. Englishmen Arnold Louis Mumm, Himalayan climber and heir to a family fortune in champagne, and Leopold S. Amery, journalist and British imperialist, were among social notables at camp. Noel Odell and Lord Hunt of Llanfair, members of the 1924 and 1954 British Everest expeditions respectively, were also welcomed at camp. American photographer Georgia Engelhard (Alfred Stieglitz's niece) bagged nine peaks in nine days at a camp. Experienced American mountaineers Albert and Beth MacCarthy often attended camps. The Alpine Club (London), American Alpine Club, Scottish Mountaineering Club, Fell and Rock Climbing Club, French Alpine Club, Swiss Alpine Club, Mazamas, Mountaineers, Harvard Mountaineers, Pinnacle Club, Appalachian Mountain Club, B.C. Mountaineering Club, and various "Ladies" alpine clubs were represented throughout the years. Climbers belonging to learned societies, such as the Royal Geographical Society and Royal Meteorological Society, were also represented at camp.

So it was that the complement of camp attendees was set: a mix of participants from children to outfitters, packers to international travellers, cooks and kitchen helpers and tea tent ladies to office staff

and administration. Within this mix formed a community within the tented town that established a pattern of social interaction through sport and recreation, not to mention the culture and identity that arose from the gear and other material "things" needed for the camps.

Living in a Material World
Gear, Sites, and Expansionism

> *Hail! Hail! the Gang's all here;*
> *Boots and Ropes and Rucksacks,*
> *Dunnage Bags and Iceaxe;*
> *Hail! Hail! the Gang's all here;*
> *What the heck do we care now?* [87]

All campers and their "stuff" took part in a process that created identity through a certain material culture associated with mountaineering in Canada.[88] The material campers needed to participate in ACC camps thus became a means to identity. The production of camps as material artifacts also underscores Andrew Garner's premise that "identity is 'made' in the process of making 'things,'" in this case the making of an entire mountaineering camp with its own logic, form, and underlying order.[89] Although there were logistical adaptations to meet new circumstances, the overall material culture, equipment, and spatial organization of ACC camps was remarkably enduring, even as the camps began to take part in imperial expansion—reaching farther into uncharted territory and "opening up" terrain to mountaineering.

At first, camps were staged in beauty spots within relatively close reach of the railway corridors; later, they moved beyond what is today considered the frontcountry into more remote areas. Outfitting for such camps was no picnic for the commercial operators, such as Ralph Rink. The camp at Mount Assiniboine Provincial Park in 1935, for example, required Rink to hire a staff of cooks and packers, transport all supplies, equipment, and dunnage by pack train from Banff, Alberta, into the British Columbia backcountry, and provide about forty horses for club members who wished to ride to or from the campsite. The crew packed the horses and set off to Assiniboine in the last week of June, about a week prior to the start of the camp. "We had a devil of a time getting the pack train into Assiniboine that trip," recalled Ken Jones. Making progress from Banff was difficult due to an unruly horse train and snow clogging Allenby Pass, over the top of which the packers had to shovel a pathway. On arrival at Lake Magog, their work was just beginning to prepare for 250 campers. According to Jones: "First we unloaded the pack train and looked after the horses. Then we started shovelling out areas for the tents. The Alpine Club was using these World War One bell tents. They got them cheap, as war surplus. These tents had a pole in the centre, then spread out in a circular manner like a teepee. They would sleep eight or ten people. People slept with their heads out and their feet toward the centre."[90]

Extensive operations conducted by packers and outfitters ensured that the camp opened and closed like clockwork, and ran smoothly, despite variables of weather and site location. When the flags were finally raised over the campsite, the ACC could typically accommodate about one to two hundred people in canvas tents for up to two weeks during the brief mountain summer period in July and August. The camp layout was planned around a large campfire. Official tents, including a huge dining pavilion, offices, cook tent, and tea tent were positioned on a main square in militaristic fashion. Campers dined in the open air sitting at rough-hewn tables and benches under a canvas marquee suspended high

overhead on log support poles and ropes. Sleeping tents, often clumped in a stand of trees, meadow, or near running water, were segregated into men's and women's quarters, with the addition of a few "married tents" for couples. Latrines were situated out of sight.[91] Paraphernalia of all kinds were transported to service the camp, including wood stoves, water buckets, a notice board, national flags, club standards, medical supplies, and a variety of bells, horns, and alarm clocks to help rouse early climbing teams and camp cooks in the hours before dawn.

Camp life centred on a large fire that burned continuously, consuming huge quantities of wood cut from nearby sources. In 1906 Frank Yeigh found that this fire "burned unceasingly, brightening up for the evening hours, when it was surrounded by as many fire worshippers as there were occupants of the tents, and where were heard more Demosthenian eloquence and oratory, more jokes and quips and antique chestnuts, and more accomplished entertainers than ever gathered on a mountain summit before."[92]

The layout of the camp within an official square bore certain similarities to military parades in long-standing designs for camps and town planning, and, for at least sixty years, the overall plan and appearance of the camps differed little. Film and photographs hint at some of the small changes evident over time, but they also underscore the strong continuity in camp appearance and material culture with the white bell-shaped and A-frame tents adjoining the official square in striking mountain locations. In a 1911 photo taken by Banff's Byron Harmon, the official ACC photographer in its early years, a row of five young men pose "asleep" in their canvas tent, like peas in a pod, lying under plaid quilts and woollen blankets. That 1911 Harmon photo is similar to the image of camp portrayed in a 1950 National Film Board of Canada feature film, wherein several women relax in the sun on air mattresses lined up outside a large dining tent with flaps rolled up, while other campers in the main square relax, coil ropes, and prepare for climbing.[93] And, it didn't seem to matter where the camp was located: it looked the same. For example, in 1967, the entire camp outfitted by the Harrisons was flown into the St. Elias Mountains in the Yukon. With the exception of gas stoves instead of wood fires, the overall appearance and material culture of the camp followed the format used for years in the South. And this culture, in turn, took its cues from its members.

Club members were part of a sporting movement that was both national and international. The ACC had a national infrastructure, mirroring other national entities like the railways, the postal system, and national parks, but it was also tied to a sphere of ethnic and class cohesion, and to British and European sensibilities. Its international heritage could easily be seen in the climbing equipment and accoutrements used at the camps, which came from Britain and Europe. Supplies of the "English Alpine Club rope" were ordered from Beale in England; boot nails were sent from Hungary; snowglasses and rucksacks came from Switzerland (and were sold at camp).[94] In the 1930s, club badges and brooches bearing the ACC insignia and ice-axe symbol were ordered from G. Durouvenoz-Duvernay of Geneva, at a wholesale cost of 3.25 and 4.50 francs respectively, for sale to members for $2.50 and $3.50.[95] Imported goods, not unlike the Swiss and Austrian mountain guides who used them, emphasized the foreign origins of mountaineering and added an old-country mystique to climbing in the Canadian Rockies.

Boot nails, snow glasses, and smaller imported items were gradually phased out as they lost popularity or were replaced by more easily obtained goods. The supply of three-sided Tricouni boot nails was a concern that exposed the poor climbing skills or lack of training among some ACC members. Tweedy wrote, "the Tricouni seem most popular, though they are hard on the ropes: far more damage results from standing on the rope with Tricouni as against the edge nail. (Of course they should not stand on the rope BUT they do.)"[96] Gradually the club considered replacing some of the less-specialized, imported, European mountaineering items with Canadian-made items, such as club badges from Birks-Dingwall of Winnipeg. As this change came about, the *Canadian Alpine Journal,* which began by advertising predominantly British and European climbing gear, increasingly featured a mix of Canadian and foreign goods in its ads during the 1920s and 1930s. Camel hair sweaters and sleeping bags by Jaegar Company of Montreal were advertised to mountaineers, along with climbing boots "Made in Canada" by C.A. Vanzant of Banff and "worn and recommended by members of the Alpine Club of Canada." Dave White and Sons Ltd. in Banff, which served tourists, advertised "climbers' sundries" that included "Austrian Akademiker Ice-axes, English-made Mountain Boots," "the famous Norwegian Bergansmeis" backpack used by the army and polar expeditions, woollen Hudson's Bay blankets, and specially crafted mountaineers' rucksacks "hand-made by Wenman of Golden, British Columbia." Goods produced by Vanzant and Wenman indicate the emergence of local European-born craftsmen who made specialty alpine gear catering to climbers in the Rockies. However, by 1941 Canadian-made gear still lacked the most important piece of safety equipment, as Tweedy averred "there does not seem to be a decent Canadian rope made."[97] This, too, emerged later with wartime and the advent of nylon.

In today's era of ultralight outdoor gear, it is easy to forget that gear transported to the ACC camps weighed thousands of pounds. For instance, in 1937, 7,066 pounds (3,205 kilograms) of freight was hauled by truck from the Banff clubhouse east to Calgary, then shipped by rail north to Edmonton, and by the CNR west to Jasper National Park, where it was then packed by horse into Maligne Lake.[98] A large portion of the ACC freight consisted of heavy canvas tents and tarpaulins. Supplying and managing the camps was no easy task: "Thirty or forty tents, enormous amounts of food (each day's meals consumed fifteen sides of bacon, four hams, eighty loaves of bread, innumerable tins of produce and jams), and tools and utensils had to be hauled in by pack train."[99]

For many climbers, desire for material gear was matched by the pursuit of new terrain. Having the right stuff and occupying the right places came together in ambitions for mountaineering camps in exciting new playgrounds.

Alpinism, as it originated in the European Alps in the eighteenth and nineteenth centuries, was by definition an expansionist form of

imperialistic conquest pursued for the goals of nation, science, or romanticism.[100] Canadian alpinism was also an expansionist activity that
advanced the national project of territorial claims through the discovery,
occupation, and naming of spaces. Mountaineering pushed back the
frontiers, always in search of new climbs and ostensibly unnamed and
unclimbed peaks, as it radiated out from the railway lines and reached
farther into the backcountry.[101] The frontiers of mountain sport in Canada
were a geography of shared imagination among climbers. Within the
context of promoting climbing in the mountain wilderness and parks,
the club contributed to modern expansionism and forged ahead with the
internal colonization project of opening the Canadian West.

The ACC operated primarily along the CPR line through Rocky
Mountains, Yoho, and Glacier national parks until the end of the First
World War. The 1916 camp, for example, was held relatively close Banff
near the CPR, as Arthur Wheeler estimated "the locality is very fine and
well deserves advertising."[102] But by 1922, Thomas Moffat, leader of the
ACC Calgary Section, warned the superintendent of Rocky Mountains
Park that the club had exhausted nearby places, and, without continued
federal sanction and support for Wheeler's ACC-affiliated backcountry
tour operation, the club would have to take its business elsewhere: "We
as a Club, have exhausted the near-in points such as Yoho, O'Hara,
Paradise, etc., and we must reach out to points further in the heart of
the Rockies...failing this we will have to transfer our activities to the
Mt. Robson district."[103] In other words, the club wished to expand, to open
"new" recreational terrain.[104] Starting in the 1920s, the club turned its
sights northward to the draws of climbing country in Jasper National
Park and the Yellowhead district, including Mount Robson, British
Columbia. Whereas the 1913 Mount Robson Camp was the only ACC
camp held in the northern region from 1906 to 1923, one third of the
camps between 1924 and 1945 were conducted there. This trend began
with a camp at Mount Robson in 1924 and was followed by more frequent
camps in the Jasper country, such as Tonquin Valley in 1926, Maligne
Lake in 1930, Chrome Lake in 1934, Fryatt Valley in 1936, the Columbia
Icefield in 1938, Glacier Lake in 1940, and Chrome Lake in 1945.

Returning to camps in familiar places in the mountain national parks
bored some ACC campers after the Second World War. As the club president Oliver Wheeler—Arthur Wheeler's son—explained in 1951 to James
Smart of the National Parks Branch headquarters, "there is a great urge,
particularly from our younger members, for new ground." For the 1953
ACC camp, Wheeler advised Ottawa to open up the "virtually unknown"

Fortress Lake region in Hamber Provincial Park, established in 1941, by laying a road from Sunwapta Falls in Jasper National Park to the wilderness headwaters of the Chaba River in British Columbia. His rationale hinged on promoting the growth of mass tourism and sport in scenic backcountry areas, as he contended, "the Alpine Club of Canada could popularize one of the finest scenic and climbing areas in the main Rockies..."[105]

ACC presidents often repeated the refrain that "tourists bring the large money, but the Alpine Climber opens up the region for the tourist."[106] Clearly setting itself apart from "tourists," the ACC cast itself in an imperialist role by promoting recreational mountaineering as the exploration and discovery that preceded mass tourism and regional economic development in the mountain parks. In many cases, the club's campsites were the precursors of twentieth-century mass tourism in the mountain parks, as the auto age placed parks within easier reach of a growing population of leisure seekers after the First World War. Material culture was part and parcel of how the ACC camps produced identities and social relations that were likewise acquired through camp practices and rituals.

Four ACC mountaineering camps were staged in Paradise Valley prior to 1945.[107] In 1907 the club extolled the valley's remote wilderness virtues; now it can be accessed from the Moraine Lake Road near Lake Louise, one of Canada's most visited landmarks. Parks Canada regulates how and when hikers travel in the area, not only to enhance public safety in bear country but to protect the grizzly population from humans. At the nearby Moraine Lake Lodge, early images of ACC members standing on the Giant Steps and the club's tents collapsed in snow have become tourism icons of an earlier Paradise Valley, a time when the club popularized public access and broke the ground for greater tourism traffic in the mountain parks. These images speak to a longing for the physical and spiritual experience of imagined pasts, such as club camps that no longer take place in Paradise Valley.[108]

Camp Rituals

Bluebird skies were clear over Larch Valley Camp in Rocky Mountains National Park as Arthur Wheeler rolled out of his tent on July 28, 1923, to ensure the first climbing party had begun for Mount Neptuak in the Valley of Ten Peaks. It was a "lazy morning," with many climbers relaxing, as he noted in his diary:

> *Men don crampons for the ascent of Mount Huber from ACC Lake O'Hara Camp, 1909. Byron Harmon photograph.*

[WMCR, V263/NA168]

Glorious day. Windy but hot and bright in the morning. Up at 4.45 a.m. but on going to the fly found the Neptuak Party had gone. Turned in and had another snooze. Up again at 6 a.m. and had breakfast. At 7 a.m. sent off Pinnacle Party and Temple Party. Wenkchemna and Opabin Party on tryout. Lazy morning in camp. Some seventy in camp. Clouding over. Party came in at 3.30 p.m. arriving therein Osborne Scott. Camp fire gathering. Calgary party came in over Sentinal Pass. With them J.B. Hutchings. Several cloud showers. Nothing of account.[109]

Wheeler's diaries record the overall social rhythms of the ACC summer camps—comings and goings, climbing days and rest days, campfires and changing faces. Once ensconced in the "tented town," campers turned their attention to the events ahead of them for the next one or two weeks. These events stressed certain practices of physical culture, recreation, mealtimes, worship, and business, as communal rituals within camp that accentuated the club's social culture and collective identity.

TRADITIONAL "MOUNTAIN CRAFT"

Clearly mountain sport and the art of climbing were the major foci of physical culture in the tented town. Organized club climbs formed the backbone of the annual camp program. Here the ACC fostered a long-standing tradition of classic alpine mountaineering, much in keeping with its nineteenth-century origins, whereby a guide led a party on ascents assisted with basic equipment: ice axes, hobnailed boots, and ropes. A climbing committee at the camps planned and determined the leaders and composition of climbing parties for designated ascents.

Daily guided climbs and hikes were posted on the camp bulletin board. Mountain guides filed out of camp, trailing large multi-rope groups of up to about twenty climbers to ascend the routes on surrounding peaks. Fly camps—smaller camps put up beyond base camp—were sometimes provided for excursions venturing out to surrounding climbs. Many participants began without climbing experience and were introduced to "mountain craft" in preparation for climbing on rock and ice. Considerable emphasis was placed on teaching and supervised practical training, such as exercises for skills on rock, ice, and snow, and graduating climbs.

Guided group climbs in classic alpine mountaineering style were a shared rite of ACC physical culture. At the 1934 Chrome Lake Camp in Tonquin Valley, for example, various climbs were organized, including

the first ascents of Anchorite (2,880 metres), Angle (2,910 metres), and
Needle Peaks (2,970 metres), and the Pinnacles at the head of Eremite
Pass in Jasper National Park.[110] R.J. Cuthbertson, a manager of the
Royal Bank in Shaunavon, Saskatchewan, published his account of the
Anchorite climb in the widely circulated *Royal Bank Magazine*. His story
sketched an exciting picture of outdoor sport that his employer sought to
promote among its professional bank men, in keeping with its Canadian
corporate image, but it also records an essential conservatism in the
physical culture of sport in Canada's alpine club at this time.[111]

> *The climbing party in each case was limited to one rope of five expe-
> rienced mountaineers, the writer being a member of the Anchorite
> party. This party—Capt. E.R. Gibson, Winterburn, Alta. (leader), R.T.
> Zillmer, Milwaukee, U.S.A., Miss P. Prescott, Cleveland, Ohio, U.S.A.,
> Henry J. France, London, England, and the writer—left Camp at 8
> a.m. The route taken was up the Eremite Creek, through a beautiful
> evergreen bluff and over a meadow alpland. Then over a very rough
> morain[e] to Eremite Glacier on the extreme right, leading up to the*

*very steep snow slopes from which we followed a rock ridge to the
summit of the mountain.*

*The steep snow slopes and the rock ridge proved quite interesting
and we reached the summit about 12.30, where we erected a cairn.
A record of the climb, consisting of the names of the members of the
party, the route followed, etc., was left. Owing to the extremely cold
wind and sleet storm we remained on the summit only a few minutes
and dropped down to a lower level where we had a hurried lunch.*

*No difficulty was encountered in the descent of the mountain,
which was varied to a considerable extent by glissading down some
of the steep snow slopes. We arrived back in Camp at 4 o'clock, in
time for afternoon tea, with a feeling of satisfaction at having added
another peak to the long list of mountaineering exploits, and in also
having had the privilege and real thrill of making a first ascent—a
thrill which is now left to comparatively few mountaineers.*[112]

This ascent of Anchorite illustrates the general trend of ACC
mountaineering and indicates the style, form, and ethics of climbing
commonly practiced at the camps from their inception. The line of
the route, along accessible snow slopes and a ridge to the summit,
and climbing without mechanical aids indicate the club's preference
for a traditionalist style of mountaineering. Gibson's designation as
the guide demonstrates the growing acceptance of amateur leaders in
the ACC by the 1930s, but it is clear that only "experienced mountaineers" were selected for the privilege of making an increasingly rare first
ascent, groups were dominated by men, and a male leader was considered normative even when a highly skilled female leader was present.
Anchorite's currency as a first ascent rested on colonial assumptions and
sporting claims based on conservative sport ethics. Published climbing
accounts, such as this one, laid claim to first ascents and publicized the
"mountaineering exploits" of the ACC, however, the emphasis on making
first ascents in classic alpine form and style in 1934 underscores the
conservative ethics of climbing promoted by the amateur club.

The last of the highest summits in the Canadian Rockies was ascended
by a Japanese team in 1925, but ACC members were still keen to gain
first ascents on lower peaks in the back valleys of the mountain parks,
reflecting the dominant traditionalist ethics within the club.[113] In Europe
the sport of climbing was redefined after the First World War as the
ethics of the game moved beyond simple peak bagging to rediscov-
ering known summits by embracing increasingly difficult vertical routes,

such as the sheer faces of the Dolomites, and new variations, including verglassed north faces, *direttissima* routes, and winter ascents. As well, female first ascents were increasing in number. Although classic alpine mountaineering persisted, the introduction of technical climbing styles that employed artificial aids—carabiners, pitons, double ropes, and hammers, for example—expanded the boundaries of the sport into new forms of increasingly popular rock climbing, ice climbing, and ski mountaineering. In the ACC, however, many club members continued to practice classic mountaineering traditions, especially at summer camps.[114]

Adherence to an earlier tradition of climbing at its annual mountaineering camps does not deny innovative moments or challenging routes put up by the club's elite climbers, such as Conrad Kain, Emmie Brooks, Bob Hind, or Roger Neave. Rock climbing was an emerging trend among an avant-garde, such as the young climbers in the ACC Winnipeg Section who called themselves the Dolomite Club and practiced, without technical aids, on the "walls" of the Gunton rock quarries near Winnipeg in the 1920s and 1930s.[115] Nonetheless, the ACC's large guided group climbs in classic alpine style, typically walking up ridge routes to the summit, persisted as the predominant form of the sport embodied through the physical culture of ACC camps. Old school tradition suited the group well, in many respects, considering the leanings of new recruits, older mountaineers, multi-rope parties, and Swiss guides; it was also a direction reinforced by its camp traditions whereby climbers enjoyed alpine classics and could still pursue first ascents in the northern Rockies and farther afield.

CAMP RECREATION AND RITUALS
From Holiday to Imperial Pursuits

Along with mountain craft, the club's 1906 constitution instilled a comprehensive outlook on mountain recreation and appreciation that encouraged myriad leisure pursuits in the open air, and not just climbing, hiking, and walking. An inclination toward science, art, and literature encouraged diverse field studies of natural history. Longtime curator of the Banff Park Museum Norman Sanson used the camps as a base for collecting museum specimens, and club members Mary Schäffer and Julia Henshaw were wildflower experts noted for their botanical guides on regional species. Landscape painting *en plein air* was enjoyed by professional artists like Fred Brigden and amateurs like Dr. H.E. Bulyea, a University of Alberta dean of dentistry whose work hangs at the

∧ *Climbers enjoy a*
swimming party at Marion
Lake in 1932. Margaret
Fleming from Winnipeg
shared the high spirits.
Lillian Gest photograph.
[WMCR, V225 PD9]

Wates-Gibson Hut, in the Tonquin Valley, Jasper National Park. Fishing and swimming were also a part of camp recreation. Margaret Fleming returned from a climbing attempt on Mount Abbott and reached Marion Lake to find "a picnic and swimming party in progress...I had a most enjoyable swim in the almost warm waters of the lake...a delicious cup of tea and numerous sandwiches before five."[116] Camera enthusiasts were keen on taking mountain photographs, and, under the leadership of Phyllis Munday, a photography competition was assembled for display at camp each year. Watching other climbers as they attempted routes or practiced techniques was also a long-standing pastime integral to the social dimension of climbing. These diverse activities were all a regular part of ongoing social recreation at the camps; formal and informal recreation programming spanned various levels of interest, skill, and exertion, in keeping with its broad age span and membership.

Sharing the table was another key aspect of ritualized social life at camp. Even in the backcountry, long log tables and rustic benches seated visiting campers together under the dining fly to enjoy an outdoor banquet hall. Club dinners commonly accommodated a hundred or more campers at tables laden with dishware and cutlery. Meals were communal, served with attention to collective manners, meal schedules, and menu planning. In 1934 outfitter Jack Hargreaves offered the following menu plan "to be sure of giving satisfaction to the Alpiners":

Breakfast
orange, grapefruit
oatmeal, wheatlets, whole wheat
grape nuts, cornflakes, etc.
ham or bacon and eggs
jam, marmalade, toast, hotcakes, syrup and honey
tea, coffee

Trail Lunch
meat sandwiches, sardines
sweet sandwiches, cookies
fruits

Dinner
soups, meat or fish, vegetables
cheese and crackers
pie, pudding, fruit and cake
cocoa, tea, coffee
fresh lettuce and celery

Evening "Lunch"
canned fish, smoked fish, meat
vegetables (fresh and canned)
pudding, pie, fruit
bread or biscuits
coffee, tea[117]

On a hilarious note, a campfire skit in 1914 played up the typical demands climbers made on the camp cook at breakfast time:

> *Four other climbers followed them,*
> *And yet another four;*
> *And thick and fast they came at last*
> *And more and more and more,*
> *And called for tea and toast and jam,*
> *Till Jim Pong nearly swore.*[118]

> A.O. Wheeler bestows an award on British mountaineer Noel Odell at ACC Maligne Lake Camp in 1930. Odell was the last to witness climbers George Mallory and Sandy Irvine on Mount Everest. News of the tragedy soon reached the ACC at its Mount Robson meeting in 1924. [EA-41-73]

Here the repetition of tea and toast are emblematic of both the Anglo-Canadian profile of the climbers and the labour of Chinese cooks baking endless loaves of bread. A camp's success depended on the quality of camp grub as much as on the weather, and, although the weather was beyond control, an agreeable review of the food went a long way toward a good review of the camp.

At night, as the sun receded on the peaks after a long day and the air grew chill, climbers came together around the blazing logs of the campfire—the centre of storytelling, mythmaking, and institutional nightlife. Around the campfire, the social network of the club was woven between campers on an interpersonal level, and the ideologies of the club were re-instilled in a collective culture. In 1910 Elizabeth Parker recounted the words of one climber who compared the campfire symbolically to "the altar and hearthstone of the Club."[119] ACC members, mugs of hot cocoa in hand, gathered around it to listen to speakers, play music, sing songs, tell stories, and amuse themselves. Speakers touched on the exploration,

∧ *The Welcome Home Camp, 1920. Campfire and dining fly at Mount Assiniboine, British Columbia. Songs, stories, and ritual marked annual campfires.*
[WMCR, V14/AC29P/14]

geology, history, art, botany, and philosophy of the mountains. Climbers regaled listeners with stories of adventures on challenging peaks, and outfitters entertained with chilling bear stories and well-received tall tales of life in the bush. Edward Feuz commented that he doubted the verity of many tales even when they were told by ACC dignitaries about their early days in the wilderness.[120]

A rapt crowd of climbers gathered about the campfire to listen as famed mountaineers recounted stories of their ascents. Sir Edward Whymper, that old lion of English climbing whose conquest of the Matterhorn in 1865 was marred by the tragic loss of four comrades in a fall, spent three days at the 1909 ACC camp and delivered a campfire address in which he "read passages of letters from British alpinists, talked about the beauties of the Rockies and the inspiration to be found in mountaineering." Whymper then auctioned off his ice axe and articles of climbing gear, at Arthur Wheeler's request, to raise funds for the ACC; his axe resides at the ACC clubhouse in Canmore to this day.[121] Other campfires featured talks given by the likes of Albert H. MacCarthy, who made the 1913 ascent of Mount Robson with William Foster and Conrad Kain; Sir Noel Odell, who saw Irvine and Mallory disappear into the mist during the 1924 British Everest expedition; and Toronto artist Fred H. Brigden, who gave a talk about Canadian art.[122] Campfire stories reiterated not only the climbing story that improved with every telling but the club's underlying beliefs in the power of mountain wilderness to test and transform the muscular body through epic adventure, heroic manhood, summit nationalism, imperial conquest, and the artistic inward eye. It was a strong narrative combination that underwrote the ACC's culture of nature expressed through outdoor recreation.

The ambiance of the Alpine Club campfire drew together members of the 1910 camp in Consolation Valley, Banff National Park, evoking a romantic appreciation for transcendent nature melded with a consummate vision of civil society; it was not unlike an "at home" parlour gathering for the fashionable outdoor set. Arthur Wheeler recalls the evening:

> The camp fire was as usual the evening centre of attraction. There is something peculiarly fascinating in watching the flames lick up towards the black, star-strewn sky, surrounded by the tall spruce trees overtopped by mighty precipices of rock crowned with stained snow. The sing-songs varied in excellence. L.S. Amery's camp fire song, inspired by last year's experiences at Lake O'Hara was rendered several times. Miss Chevrier's recitations were greatly appreciated. The audience was most enthralled, however, when Dr. Longstaff could be induced to related some of his Indian experiences. It is perhaps making much of little, but it is such intercourse as this that makes fellow subjects from different parts of the Empire understand each other and tends to bring about a most beneficial solidarity.[123]

Englishman L.S. Amery, an avid mountaineer and proponent of the British Empire, had penned alpine lyrics to his old school song from days at Harrow with young Winston Churchill. The Dr. Longstaff in question was Thomas Longstaff, the physiologist and climber, who had explored the frozen Arctic and the Himalayas in India. Wheeler's imperialist overtones suggest the ACC campfire was an international forum for alpine clubs worldwide, and, particularly, for the Anglo-imperial mountaineering brethren joined around the fire. As a national mountaineering

∧ A new world luminous by firelight. ACC mountaineers attend campfire night dressed as "Indians" at Sherbrooke Lake, 1911. Camps performed a Euro-Canadian worldview. C.H. Mitchell photograph. Harry Pollard album. [WMCR, V14/AC24P/6]

club inspired by British example, the ACC placed Canada in the ranks of the world's great mountaineering nations and generated a nationalistic "sense of power" for Canadians.[124] Even campfire songs like "Call of the Alpine" underscored Wheeler's "most beneficial solidarity" that captivated the hearts of many club members, as the lyrics affirmed: "There we live as our Maker intended we should, / Each thought building truly for one common good; / Thus while Mountains abide or true love doth endure, / There is nothing can equal the Alpine Club's lure." But there was an underside to these aspirations.

While sharing the company of like-minded people, the normally buttoned-down professional had a chance to unwind in playful fantasies. "Playing Indian" was a popular example, and the 1910 camp aroused much excitement and gaiety on this score, as Wheeler described. A mock "Indian pow-wow" threw the crowd into childlike camp revelry around the campfire: "One night blankets and quilts were purloined from the tents, the ladies dressed their hair in braids and an Indian pow-wow was held, the big dish-pan forming an effective tom-tom. This all sounds very childish, but to enjoy camp life thoroughly one must revert to the child-like spirit. The fact remains that to the healthy mind it is singularly attractive, and to the wearied brainworker, singularly restful."[125]

In the fresh mountain air, it was believed that childlike games allowed the "wearied brainworker" to relax the standards of adult professionalism demanded by bloodless modernism while getting back to nature. Such antics were thought to inspire workers to return to city life renewed.

Nature proponent Ernest Thompson Seton and militarist Lord Baden Powell both promoted Indian themes in recreation for boys, as did the Girl Guides and the YWCA for girls, varsity clubs, popular children's literature, and stage shows such as *Peter Pan*.[126] Summer camps for many boys and girls also elaborated on Indian motifs and ritualized pseudo-traditions. "Playing Indian is the history of whites and of white middle-class culture," historian Sharon Wall argues, concluding that, ultimately, "going Native" at children's camps was a shallow critique of both modernism and whiteness.[127] In the case of the ACC, the vast majority of alpinists did not radically abandon the privileges of city living, racial identity, or their professions to live in the wilderness. They merely went on holiday.

Other racial playacting also took place at camp. Regina club members performed "A Minstrel around the Campfire" (circa 1923–24) dressed in blackface. In doing so they reproduced dominant notions of black identity commonly presented in popular culture through vaudeville theatre, music, and early cinema.[128] Overall, these campfire theme nights underscored the white, professional, middle-class character of the club and offer insight into the racialized construction of civil society as a mirror of Anglo-Canadian white identities; for example, club members marked the national parks as white recreational space, a territory where real Aboriginal people were conspicuously absent much of the time due to colonialism and the combined regulatory force of federal statutes and policies.[129]

When the antics were over and Sunday morning rolled in, members reaffirmed their roles in society as Anglo-Canadians by taking part in common worship. There was no shortage of Protestant clerics among the climbers to lead the club in outdoor devotional services on Sunday mornings around the campfire. Wheeler claimed to feel his strongest sense of divine presence amid the hills, as did many campers. Frank Yeigh, a devout Presbyterian, wrote of his 1906 experience in British Columbia's Yoho Valley: "One stood entranced among the scenic grandeur: the wonderful colouring, the titanic peaks guarding the vale, and the distant views of other alpine giants....We had sped across God's plains to reach the Rockies, now we were living amid God's hills."[130]

To believers among the ACC, the "revelation of Nature" showed the hand of a divine creator at work. Spiritual communion in the mountains merged the meanings of climbing and nature with Christian religious precepts. The symbolism of mountains put divinity and human life into a larger religious framework familiar to readers of the Old and New Testaments. Scriptures and hymns rich with alpine allusions were quoted by climbers, as Yeigh noted, "'I to the hills will lift mine eyes.' Often rang out the words of the grand old psalm, as hillward and mountainward the eyes of all were instinctively lifted in solemn worship and in admiring praise."[131]

Religious services continued through the 1950s. Many Sunday sermons were led by Major Rex Gibson, a club leader and devout Christian. In a campfire clearing in the forest, about a mile below Peyto Glacier, Gibson conducted "in these ideal surroundings, on a beautiful Sunday morning, a service of inspiration and praise" at the 1948 Peyto Lake Camp, where a special memorial service was led by H.E. Sampson to commemorate lost comrades.[132] A camp service held in an old cabin adorned with alpine flowers and evergreens at Mount Robson in 1955 began with singing the hymn "Go Tell It on the Mountain."[133] Although it was often difficult to achieve in Canadian churches before the Second World War, an ecumenical level of Protestant religious expression arose at club gatherings in mountain splendour that may have fostered an overall sense of community among some climbers as transcending the divine through nature and physicality informed their common worship.

Rituals and annual events in the tented town generated a shared ACC culture of Canadian mountaineering written through the physicality, narratives, belief structures, and community orchestration involved in making collective identities among climbers. Early alpine starts, communal meals, Sunday sermons—social recreation at the annual ACC summer camp built a framework of rituals and a shared identity that united members collectively as Anglo, white, urban, middle-class mountaineers and carried them back to their home club sections, until they could meet again around the big annual campfire or, at least, read about it in the club journal. Although they ostensibly sought to escape on holidays in the mountains, their social practices at summer camp tended to reconstitute the larger social identities and power relations of class, gender, ancestry, and nation familiar every day in modern urban life; creating the "beneficial solidarity" of climbers asserted elements of communal culture that they felt were increasingly lost in the bustle of

Muscular Christianity in the ACC

IN ADDITION TO the explicit Christianity of Sunday worship, religion also informed the physical culture of mountaineering in the ACC in the early 1900s. Club members such as Rev. Doctor Charles W. Gordon, a well-known Canadian novelist by the pen name Ralph Connor, carried the ideology of muscular Christianity into the ACC. Gordon was an enthusiastic climber, pastor of the Presbyterian church in Canmore, Alberta, and famous author of *The Man from Glengarry* (1901), *Sky Pilot* (1901), and other novels, later made into Hollywood movies, that exerted the values of whole-some outdoor exercise and the bible in forming rugged Christian manhood. Calgary clergyman and ACC founding member Rev. J.C. Herdman also empha-sized these values in the club. Climbing built discipline, strength, teamwork, and moral character, in the eyes of its proponents, fostering muscular Christianity, just as the YMCA did through its sport programs for boys and men. Teaching bible classes for boys at Bloor Street Church and his philanthropic work as a member of the central Toronto branch of the YMCA board of direc-tors made Frank Yeigh no stranger to this philosophy.[134] Building stronger Christian men through physical exer-cise and sport fit well with the organizational impulse behind the ACC and the nationalistic leanings of the club.[135] Mountaineering was understood as training for good citizenship, and putting men on mountaintops embodied popular beliefs in muscular Christianity and nationalism.

> *Calgary clergyman Rev. J.C. Herdman, 1906.*
[WMCR, V14/AC00P/77]

capitalist modernity, the "delving for gold" satirized in club campfire songs.[136] Although the call of the alpine fell short of a cure to the problems of a modern era, the ongoing desire to escape to ACC summer camp and the long continuity of camp rituals among these climbers attest to their beliefs in the relaxation and benefits of sociable mountain recreation as an agreeable antidote.

Climbing Partners
The ACC, Business, and Government

Paramount to the ACC's long record of successful annual camps were the enduring partnerships it developed. Staging a large camp in a new location every summer required remarkable co-operation between private and public partners. If cowboys and guides made the camps possible logistically, railways, distant politicians, and bureaucrats made them possible strategically. Railways—already heavily invested in mountain tourism—were the largest private operators with an interest in the ACC camps. The CPR ran through Banff, Yoho, Glacier, and Mount Revelstoke national parks; the CNR went through Jasper National Park and British Columbia's Mount Robson. Smaller operators, such as guide-outfitters, hoteliers, and suppliers, also assisted the ACC. The private sector built relationships with the ACC because the club promoted tourism in the Rockies and stimulated the regional economy with its annual camps, spin-off tours, and publicity for the mountain parks. Public partners backing the camps included the federal government, through the national parks administration, and the provincial governments of Alberta and British Columbia.

A PARTNERSHIP WITH RAILWAYS

The ACC brought tourist business to the Rockies, directly through their summer camps and indirectly by promoting the region as a destination for holiday-goers. William Whyte, CPR second vice-president, donated free rail tickets to the 1906 Winnipeg meeting and continued to be a club supporter. His greetings opened the first volume of the *Canadian Alpine Journal* in 1907 and confidently underscored the patriotic value of the club and its camps: "[O]ne cannot help but prophesy that the Camp this year will be a great success, and I cannot too strongly urge all of our young Canadians to attend, when the opportunity will be afforded them of climbing their own mountains and thus securing an appreciation of some of the beauties of their own country."[137]

The railways offered the ACC camps assistance in the form of preferential passenger fares, financial grants, and the loan of Swiss guides, cooks, and equipment. In turn, the club offered a commercial opportunity to market the Canadian Rockies to a broad range of visitors who advertised or stayed at the CPR's resorts. This tradeoff was crucial to the client–patron relationship between the club and the railway.

John Murray Gibbon served as the CPR's liaison with the ACC for many years, and he acted on various issues that involved the vested interests of the railway and the club, including the road and trail improvements to the Lake of the Hanging Glacier. In 1927 Gibbon prompted ACC President Fred Bell to lobby British Columbia politicians for these improvements to the Lake of the Hanging Glacier area, which would allow the ACC and the Trail Riders of the Canadian Rockies easy access to a 1928 summer camp held in the Purcell Mountains. British Columbia Lieutenant Governor Randolph R. Bruce, a tireless promoter of the Kootenays and Columbia Valley, was also a mountaineer and member of the ACC. He suggested the club's lobby should be directed toward W.H. Sutherland, the British Columbia minister of public works.[138] In correspondence with Bell, Speaker of the House J.A. Buckham, MLA for Columbia, agreed to improve the trail to Lake of the Hanging Glacier but objected to a motor road leading directly to the lake because it "would detract from the pleasure of the trip out there." He pursued appropriations for trail work but remarked, "I could never have the heart to ask for an Automobile Road to Hanging Glacier."[139] As far as ACC Secretary Mitchell was concerned, however, a road was linked to future tourism development in the district near Invermere, and he wanted "the road extended as far as possible, good enough for average cars, not Rolls Royce. The main object is to shorten the trail both for ponies and walkers."[140]

In April 1928, the annual ACC dinner in Victoria included a notable guest, John MacLean, the premier of British Columbia, giving the club a chance to communicate its desire for road access to the Lake of the Hanging Glacier.[141] Trail construction went ahead in 1928. Ultimately, an unusually lucrative ACC 1928 camp—a profit of $700—was held at the Lake of the Hanging Glacier, due largely to the profit the ACC made by accommodating the Trail Riders of the Canadian Rockies in camp, at a total charge of $822.[142] By working in tandem with J.M. Gibbon and the CPR Trail Riders, and by exercising the political influence of its members with British Columbia politicians, the ACC contributed to leveraging tourism expansion into the Lake of the Hanging Glacier.

John Murray Gibbon (1875–1952)

The CPR's Tourism Ringmaster

WRITER JOHN MURRAY GIBBON belonged to the ACC and enjoyed rambling in the Rockies by foot or on horseback. He made significant contributions to the promotion of Canadian arts and culture, and oversaw the CPR's assistance to ACC camps through the 1920s and 1930s. Born in Udewelle, Ceylon, in 1875 and educated at Oxford, Gibbon, the son of a tea planter, acted as the CPR's general publicity agent based at the company's Montreal headquarters in Windsor Station (1913–45). To promote CPR adventure packages on mountain trails, Gibbon founded the western horseback Trail Riders of the Canadian Rockies in 1924 and the Sky Line Trail Hikers of the Canadian Rockies in 1933. Author and founder of the Canadian Authors' Association, Gibbon's literary works included *Canadian Folksongs Old & New* (1927), five novels, and a history of the CPR entitled *Steel of Empire* (1935). His initial interest in ethno-culture led to organizing various CPR-sponsored folk festivals that celebrated Canada's ethnic heritage while promoting new tourism attractions at its railway hotels across the country. The French Canadian Folk Song and Handicraft Festival at the Chateau Frontenac in Quebec City, Banff's Highland Gathering at the Banff Springs Hotel, and similar events drew big crowds. Gibbon received the Order of Canada for his efforts in embracing ethnic cultures and folk arts within Canadian national identity. He died in 1952 and was buried in the Banff cemetery where his grave is marked by a bronze plaque of a riderless trail horse cast by Banff's cowboy sculptor Charles A. Beil.[143]

∧ *John Murray Gibbon, c. 1929. [GA, PB-163-1]*

In addition to helping the ACC open up new areas for camps, the CPR gave free advertising to the camps in the *Canadian Pacific Railway Bulletin* through the 1920s.[144] In 1927 Gibbon advised the ACC of the value of publicity and suggested the club should launch a campaign to increase its membership.[145] Secretary Mitchell met with Gibbon in August 1928 to plan the 1929 camp at Rogers Pass, and Gibbon promised the following assistance from the CPR:

1. Transport of outfit and supplies in one car from Banff to Glacier Station and return.
2. Haulage of [tent] poles from Donald to Glacier Station. The poles are to be selected and cut by our construction gang.
3. To supply water from Bear Creek to the Camp. Estimated 300 feet of 1-inch pipe will be sufficient.
4. To overhaul and put in shape the Rogers Pass Hut.[146]

"You understand that anything Mr. Gibbon guarantees will go," Mitchell explained to the club's incoming president, T.B. Moffat.[147] Through this type of assistance, along with an average subsidy of $200 a year, the CPR assisted the continuation of the ACC camps through the Depression.

The ACC's claim on assistance from the CPR, however, grew increasingly tenuous by the early 1940s. The company had a well-established international and domestic reputation for mountain tourism in Canada, due, in part, to successful tourist marketing campaigns for its grand hotels, such as the Banff Springs Hotel and the Chateau Lake Louise; moreover, by this time it had closed its mid-size hotels, such as Glacier House and the Mount Stephen Hotel, and opened automobile bungalow camps in a shifting trend toward mass automobile tourism. By this time, too, J.M. Gibbon had guided the CPR to develop its own backcountry camp excursion packages, in the form of the Trail Riders of the Canadian Rockies and the Sky Line Trail Hikers. In 1938 Tweedy noted to the ACC president that the CPR objected to affordable accommodations at the Banff clubhouse poaching potential customers from the railway's hotels.[148] And by 1940, Secretary Tweedy indicated to President Wates that the CPR was becoming "harder to deal with each year."[149] The CPR treated Rocky Mountain parks along its line as its own special territory. Enthusiasm between partners shifted with corporate strategy as well as changing regional tourism markets.

Just as the CPR was eager to partner with the ACC in its early years, its northern competitor, the Canadian National Railway, was also

Alexander Addison McCoubrey
(1885–1942)

Mountaineer on the Inside Track

ALEXANDER "MAC" MCCOUBREY was a Glasgow-born Winnipeg outdoorsman. Ski mountaineering in Yoho, trail blazing in the Purcells, and amassing mountain literature were among his many passions. After a start in surveys and drafting for the CPR, he rose to assistant engineer. McCoubrey helped organize University of Manitoba's Student Union and was its first president during Bachelor of Science studies in his thirties; later he belonged to many sport, nature, and geographical clubs. Congenial yet shy, he enjoyed spending time with brainy outdoor friends, such as fellow alumni in the Winnipeg ACC. In 1908 he joined the ACC, serving later as Winnipeg Section chair (1926–40), eastern vice-president (1928), national president (1932–34), and editor of the *Canadian Alpine Journal* (1930–42). He collaborated with his close friend Margaret Fleming (herself a University of Manitoba gold medalist in philosophy) to edit the *CAJ* for over a decade. McCoubrey taught many of his section members to ski on the Assiniboine River and to climb at the Dunton rock quarries. He was an active trip leader and frequented districts west of the Great Divide in summer and winter. At fifty-six, he died suddenly of a heart attack while working. Friends remembered well the backseat of Mac's car—any guest who avoided "the obvious danger of impalement on ski poles or ice-axes, was likely to land heavily on a volume of European history or release an avalanche of periodicals and phonograph records."[150]

As the CPR's chief draftsman and assistant engineer, McCoubrey was also a key broker for CPR assistance to the club's camps at Lake of the Hanging Glacier in 1928 and Paradise Valley in 1933. Swiss guides would be on loan for the duration of the 1933 camp, as McCoubrey wrote, "Owing to the fact that we have only three Guides on the payroll this year, I was very apprehensive about getting this, but the Company have been good

∧ *Winnipeg's Alexander McCoubrey (sitting, second from right) was an editor of the club journal. Here with the Dolomite Club, Margaret Fleming is sitting, far right. [Manitoba Archives, SIS12310]*

enough to promise them." In keeping with precedent, there would be a $200 grant toward camp expenses "on the usual condition that Mr. Wheeler write the publicity articles for the camp."[151] In the midst of the Depression, McCoubrey was also able to obtain second-hand equipment for the club at low cost from the CPR.[152]

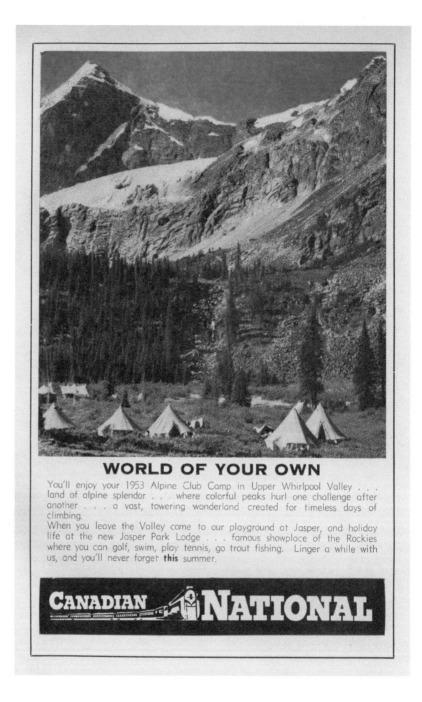

interested in supporting ACC camps in the 1920s and 1930s. At this time the CNR was advertising Jasper Park as a highlight destination on the northern trans-Canada line. The new Jasper Park Lodge opened in 1922, under the Grand Trunk Pacific Railway, and merged under the Canadian National Railway the following year.[153] Under the aggressive management of Sir Henry Worth Thornton (1871–1933), known as "the big man on the big horse," through the 1920s, the CNR developed an intense rivalry with the southerly CPR[154] and offered various enticements to the ACC to come to Jasper and the district of Mount Robson. "I think that it has been a good policy in the past," judged club President Fred Bell in 1927, "to visit the ground 'tributary' to the CNR occasionally, and still think so."[155] Alternating from the southern line to the northern stimulated business competition between railways to attract the ACC and helped stimulate the climbers' desire for new terrain.

The CNR warmly embraced business with the ACC during a crucial period of tourism development in Jasper National Park. To attract climbers to an ACC summer camp planned for the Tonquin Valley in 1925 (though held in 1926), for example, the CNR launched a series of advertisements in the pages of the annual *Canadian Alpine Journal*. The CNR began direct promotions featuring the destination and its attractions as early as 1923. "The Alpine Club will find in the Tonquin Valley Jasper National Park many peaks unexplored–unnamed" announced the railway's 1923 advertisement that rendered Jasper as unexplored territory for the much-beloved first ascents with "many peaks well over 10,000 feet unscaled." Photos of Mount Erebus, the Astoria Valley, Eremite Glacier, and the Ramparts whetted the appetite of climbers with scenes of what the Tonquin Valley held in store.[156] In 1924 ad copy depicted the Jasper Park Lodge as "one of the most inviting spots at which to spend a summer vacation." Readers were advised to contact Osborne Scott, general passenger agent in Winnipeg and a member of the ACC, for more information.

The CNR continued its strong support of the ACC, publicizing the Mount Logan expedition in 1925, the summer camp at Maligne Lake in Jasper National Park in 1930, and the Chrome Lake summer camp in 1934.[157] The CNR provided freight services for the 1934 camp equipment between Calgary and Jasper and contributed $200 toward the cost of transport. Osborne Scott promised the railway's support, stating "we will do everything in our power to make the attendance as large as possible."[158] Several first ascents were achieved by club climbers, such as banker R.J. Cuthbertson, during the 1934 camp. Ascents included Anchorite, Angle, Needle Peaks, and the Pinnacles.

In the same year, the CNR also agreed to transport without charge the club's alpine photography exhibit for display at the Hudson's Bay Company department stores across western Canada. The touring exhibit stopped in Edmonton, Calgary, Saskatoon, Regina, and Winnipeg, all cities with sizeable ACC constituencies and potential tourism markets linked by CNR to Jasper.[159] During this period, Hudson's Bay stores sought to cultivate shoppers by way of various gallery exhibits and entertainments that portrayed Canadian culture in discriminating good taste.[160] Artistic black-and-white photographs of alpine climbing and mountain landscapes, typically taken in Canada's national parks and composed by ACC members on holiday, depicted the exciting allure of adventure, travel, and national icons. Fashionable sportswear, passenger tickets, hotel rooms, and woollen camp blankets were part of the trade in vacation tourism. From the multiple perspectives of the railways, Hudson's Bay Company stores, national parks, and the ACC, furnishing the needs of the domestic market for Canadian mountain tourism required goods and services that played a part in larger econo- mies as bourgeois cultural capital transformed to middle-class consumer spending invested in outdoor recreation, sport, and tourism.

Without the cachet of Banff National Park, the CNR worked partner- ships to stimulate a northern market for Jasper. It was a newer park, farther from major cities and lacked a good highway. The CNR was quick to promote Jasper to climbers as an exclusive "World of Your Own" when the ACC camp at the Hooker Icefield in the upper Whirlpool Valley was planned for 1953. Exclusivity in the mountain backcountry was a keynote in marketing to the club and emphasized the appeal of "a vast, towering wonderland created for timeless days of climbing." The romanticized notion of nature as a timeless wonderland theme park for mountaineering in Jasper played well with the 1950s notion of national parks constructed as playgrounds for the growing postwar affluence of middle-class tourism. It appealed directly to ACC members, who were enticed to visit the CNR lodge resort to indulge in comfort after camp. Above a logo of a Canadian National passenger train, the ad copy concluded, "when you leave the Valley come to our playground at Jasper, and holiday life at the new Jasper Park Lodge...famous showplace of the Rockies where you can golf, swim, play tennis, go trout fishing. Linger a while with us, and you'll never forget **this** summer."[161] The campaign was a winning example of direct destination marketing that appealed to cultivated consumer tastes, fostered by a long-standing commercial relationship between the CNR and the ACC in the competitive regional tourism market in the Canadian Rockies. Promoters of Jasper could not afford to let down the friendly game of business.

Of all its partners, however, the ACC depended most on the federal government because it controlled the national parks in the Rockies and Columbia Mountains. Mountain districts in the British Columbia ranges outside of the national park boundaries, such as Mount Robson and Mount Assiniboine, were under the authority of the provincial government. Governments saw the club's activities as performing a dual role: increasing visitation to the mountains and improving general awareness of these regions. In an age when government surveys were still charting many districts, the ACC was an adjunct volunteer in geographic exploration and discovery in the Rockies. The ACC also sought to raise Canada's national profile on the world stage of mountaineering. For these reasons, it was in the interest of government to support the annual ACC camps. The division between the interests of park owners and park users was often difficult to discern.

The earliest ACC camps were subsidized by provincial and federal funding. In 1906 Alberta offered a $250 grant toward the first ACC camp, even though it was held in Yoho National Park, British Columbia. The 1910 camp in Consolation Valley, Banff National Park, Alberta, was supported by a $500 grant from Alberta and a $1,000 grant from British Columbia. Both provinces granted $500 in 1911 for the camp held at Sherbrooke Lake, British Columbia, near the border, and the club's expedition to explore the Mount Robson district that year.[162] Direct federal grants to the ACC were common from 1906 to 1930. As well, the Department of the Interior granted leave in the early years to federal survey crew workers A.O. Wheeler, Hector Wheeler, and M.P. Bridgland to set up, facilitate, and take down the ACC camps.[163] They also helped as guides.

From the outset, federal parks officials encouraged the ACC's activities. The club's role in publicizing the parks was continually highlighted as a rationale for close co-operation between the department and the club, as indicated, for example, by Howard Douglas, chief superintendent of Dominion Parks, in 1914: "the Alpine Club is doing splendid work in connection with the opening up and advertising of mountains within the Parks boundaries as well as outside and anything that we can do to facilitate their operations I think should be carried out."[164] In 1916 Dominion Parks Commissioner James Bernard Harkin stated that "it is the policy of the department to cooperate in every way possible with the Alpine Club."[165] Harkin and his senior officials personally visited many of the early ACC camps.[166] After Harkin's retirement in 1936, the department continued to support the ACC into the postwar period. As late as 1949, Roy A. Gibson, Ottawa director of the national parks, told his deputy minister that "the mountain parks receive splendid advertising from the activities of the Alpine Club. We have always considered this justification for special treatment."[167]

The ACC was a prominently placed, client-user group during the formative period of national park development. It explored and mapped many areas in the Rockies, circulated information about the parks, and for many years directly contributed a report of its camps and activities to the Dominion Parks section of the Department of the Interior Annual Report.[168] At a time when the whole Ottawa parks administration might have fit into a one-room office, the club proved an indispensable partner in park management.

A reciprocal relationship developed between the club and the parks administration, whereby the ACC called on the department for operational services, an annual federal grant to sponsor camps and activities, and access privileges within the parks. The national parks authorities, in turn, recognized the ACC as the national mountaineering authority, referred the public to the club for information, and relied on the ACC for expertise and free publicity. The two parties shared an interest in the aims of the national parks and generally encouraged each other's activities relating to mutual concerns of conservation, tourism, and mountaineering. From the club's perspective, the ACC was a selfless institution and first among groups deserving preferential treatment in the parks. This belief was passed from one club generation to the next as the ACC celebrated its achievements and sought to justify continued government support.

The national parks department was the prime player in the federal government's ongoing relationship with the ACC. The most effective ACC executives and parks administrators fostered this reciprocity to mutual advantage, frequently employing informal channels or internal collegial networks to carry on contacts. Arthur Wheeler and J.B. Harkin shared strong links from working in the Department of the Interior: Wheeler had worked for the Department of the Interior prior to Commissioner Harkin heading up the Dominion Parks office in Ottawa beginning in 1911. Throughout Harkin's term of office (1911–36), he interacted with Wheeler regarding matters of concern to the ACC and the parks. Harkin even used this conduit to spur the club's defence of the national parks against the incursion of resource developments.[169] This opportunity for dialogue opened communications and strengthened the partnership between the club and senior administration, although sometimes at the expense of park superintendents who found themselves circumvented by Wheeler's inclination to deal with top officials in Ottawa.

Generally, national park superintendents served the on-the-ground needs of the club in accordance with the daily operational demands of park management. Sending park wardens to assist at the ACC summer camps, installing telephone lines to the camps, loaning heaps of woollen blankets, getting the approach trails in better shape for hiking, and extending electrical power lines to the Banff clubhouse were among the many services national park superintendents offered. Some superintendents forged closer ties with the ACC, such as Jasper Superintendent Maynard Rogers, who encouraged ACC publicity for his park in the 1923 *Canadian Alpine Journal* and received invitations to informal gatherings of the Edmonton Section during the interwar period.[170] In the later 1940s, Homer Robinson, associate superintendent of Parks and Resources Information in Ottawa, reinforced liaisons with the club to profit from the promotion of mountaineering in park advertising and to monitor the inside workings of the organization as a subtle form of surveillance, particularly as related to park politics. Robinson made a graduating climb on Mount Trapper at the 1948 camp to qualify for active membership, but the club's camp report noted that, having welcomed the chief of the National Parks Department Personal Relations Branch, "there was universal regret that he sustained an injury to his foot through a falling rock which cut his visit short."[171]

The reciprocal relationship between the national parks administration and the club was also revealed in public policy formation. As the department coped with the daily realities of managing user demands, the ACC stimulated the making of parks policy, as related, for example, to regulation of public use of backcountry fire roads as access routes to ACC camps, licensing procedures for club huts, and mountaineering registration systems. By the early 1950s, ACC President Brigadier Sir Oliver Wheeler—retired from his post as India's surveyor general—instituted a system of advance planning to select sites for the annual camps two to three years ahead of time as the National Parks Branch required more lead time to prepare if the ACC wished to have trails and roads laid out to remote areas. While ACC president in the 1950s, Wheeler made a request to James Smart that Parks undertake long-range planning of trail projects to accommodate the club's advance selection of campsites. His request moved down the chain of command from Ottawa to park superintendents and wardens in the field, and back up the administrative ladder. This was how the national parks hierarchy set planning in action to co-ordinate ACC recreational demands within an overall policy framework for regular trail development.[172]

In other cases, the department approached the ACC for specialized input in the areas of safety, ski mountaineering, the training and regulation of mountain guides, and on-the-ground alpine expertise. Harkin noted, in 1933, with respect to the development of backcountry skiing that "it is considered that the Alpine Club being the pioneer organisation supporting such recreation throughout the Parks will be in a position to offer suggestions."[173] The easy assumption that the ACC was "the pioneer organisation" for backcountry skiing in the Rockies was an overstatement that neglected the early involvement of many local skiers and other skiing promoters[174] and magnified the influence of the ACC in park affairs into the 1950s. Such assumptions would be less convincing as recreational stakeholders proliferated.

Partnerships fostered between the club, railways, and governments illustrate the larger political economy of mountain national parks. In this scheme, the relations of the ACC, major corporate businesses, and the state were imbricated in tourism, trade, regional development, and public policy. To the extent that it was mutually beneficial, special status privileged the club as a key partner in these fluctuating commercial transactions and the business of nation-building.

▲ The tented towns erected annually each summer by the ACC with the help of its partners reveal much about the club, its upper- and middle-class members bound by the privileges and rules of polite society, escaping to the colonized mountains west for holidays away from the drudgery of modernist urban society, only to reproduce the same kind of society within a wild enclave. Through these camps, the national parks became peopled by Anglo-Canadians and were constructed as white, middle-class, touristic spaces. As a result, these places became part of a larger Canadian identity and came into the fore as objects worthy of policy, worthy of preservation, of conservation. In this way, the early tented town was supported by corporate and government sponsors, and yet the ACC and its members did not hesitate to take a public role in policy related to hydropower and national parks.

Advocacy
for Canada's
Hetch Hetchy

4

*The Alpine Club must make the
people realize that the mountains
are the heritage of all.*

—SIR JAMES OUTRAM, 1922[1]

KNOWLEDGE OF THE MOUNTAIN PARKS among mountaineers and
their advocacy for Canada's mountain heritage were reflected in conservation and recreation politics after the First World War. Mountain
heritage encompassed considerations that went beyond sport toward
activism. Water was a focal point for much ACC activism as the club
opposed proposals for irrigation and power dams infringing on national
park lands and waters throughout the 1920s and took a firm stand
against tampering with watersheds in the Rockies, which it feared would
ruin the natural environment and set a dangerous precedent for corporate encroachment on national park territory. During stormy conflicts
over dams proposed for Waterton Lakes and Rocky Mountains national
parks, the ACC and the Dominion Parks Branch enunciated the principles that later came to characterize public policy and legislation
governing Canada's national parks. Among these new tenets of management, national park inviolability emerged as a cardinal rule.

Environmental protection and wildlife preservation gained increasing
importance in national parks policy under Dominion Parks Commissioner
J.B. Harkin through the interwar period. Historian Barry Potyandi argues
that conflicts during the 1920s were crucial to the definition of conservationist philosophy in national parks policy.[2] In its opposition to water

development in the parks, the ACC played a critical role in promoting conservationist philosophy in public policy regarding the national parks, as club founder Arthur Wheeler signalled with his emphatic slogan "Hands Off Our National Parks."[3] However, before the club became a strong lobby group, it learned a few lessons in advocacy during a smaller debate about public access to national parks that took place in 1922. This debate, regarding federal subsidies to A.O. Wheeler's own enterprise— Mount Assiniboine Walking and Riding Tour—also drew the club closer to its allies in the national parks, sharpening its vision of what Canadian parks "should" be.

Warm-up for Debate
Advocacy for Public Access

Mount Assiniboine Walking and Riding Tour offered trips to the Mount Assiniboine district in British Columbia. Operated by A.O. Wheeler as a retirement venture from 1920 to 1927, the tours catered to middle-income tourists and were loosely affiliated with the ACC. The tour's clientele, many of whom were ACC members, sought an affordable way to see spectacular sights and landmarks accessible only by backcountry trails.[4] However, as early as fall 1921, some outfitters in Banff took exception to Wheeler's federally subsidized operation. They alleged that when Wheeler's tours offered side trips off the main Assiniboine route, they invaded the regional market for saddle outfitting.[5]

The concept of Wheeler's walking tour had the support of Commissioner Harkin as early as 1914. Like Wheeler, Harkin wished to extend the opportunities for middle-class urban Canadians to gain a first-hand appreciation of national parks, and thereby contribute to the health, education, and well-being of the nation. Wheeler emphasized to the federal Minister of the Interior the need for affordable travel and accommodations to permit "walking parties" of modest means to travel in the mountains: "The very high cost of hotels, and travel the moment you leave the railway, is now almost prohibitive except to the very wealthy and such a class is very largely in the minority of those who would visit the Rockies if accommodation could be placed within their means."[6] Replying on behalf of the minister, Harkin agreed.[7] Before the Great War unleashed new social and economic pressures on the policy landscape, there was an easy symmetry of federal administrators and alpine trekkers.

In concert with the economic arguments in favour of parks that filled the Department of the Interior's annual reports, Harkin admitted to a mystical belief that mountains had the power to inspire: "I devoutly believe that there are emanations from them, intangible but very real, which elevate the mind and purify the spirit."[8] Harkin offered a philosophical justification for the existence of the national parks that was rooted in a transcendental appreciation for the Rockies and informed by the principles of democratic citizenship:

> *National Parks are maintained for all the people—for the ill, that they may be restored, for the well that they may be fortified and inspired by the sunshine, the fresh air, the beauty, and all the healing, ennobling, and inspiring agencies of Nature. They exist in order that every citizen of Canada may satisfy his craving for Nature and Nature's beauty; that he may absorb the poise and restfulness of the forests; that he may steep his soul in the brilliance of the wild flowers and the sublimity of the mountain peaks; that he may develop in himself the buoyancy, the joy, and the activity he sees in the wild animals; that he may stock his mind with the raw material of intelligent optimism, great thoughts, noble ideals; that he may be made better, happier, and healthier.*[9]

Thus, affordable walking tours fit well with Harkin's democratic concept of national parks open, in principle, to "all the people." Although the citizens empowered to enjoy leisure in national parks were typically, though not exclusively, those privileged by disposable income and holiday time for travel, in contrast to the working classes, the poor, the urban masses, and regional Aboriginal groups, the philosophy proposed by Harkin framed parks as a democratic social asset for "every citizen of Canada" wherein publicly subsidized walking tours for the middle classes were a federal intervention to promote social equity in recreational tourism.[10]

Harkin assured Wheeler as early as 1914 that the department would welcome a private applicant interested in operating a walking tour.[11] In 1920 Wheeler thus began his "public walking tour" with the first economy-class commercial trips to the Mount Assiniboine district. The Parks Branch backed the idea and provided subsidies in the form of wage labour, camp equipment from surplus First World War military stores, and the construction of backcountry trails and bridges.

Wheeler advertised the irresistible benefits of his tours much as Harkin had described the national parks. He described the tours in romantic terms to those seeking out soulful respite and health in wild nature: "Here in this land of forest primeval, of lakes of exquisite blues and greens, of cascading torrents, flower-strewn alplands, wildly tumbling ice-falls, towering rock peaks and cloud-capped mountains massed with snow, one finds peace, health and happiness. Come and try it!"[12] He also organized a tour package and wide marketing campaign to target "Mountaineers, Hikers, Artists, Scientists, Photographers and Fishermen." As well, the CPR's publicity department accepted ten thousand walking-tour leaflets for distribution in 1921 and publicized the tour in its own promotional literature.[13]

Twice a week through July, August, and September, trips departed from Middle Springs Camp near Wheeler's summer residence—Claremount—on Sulphur Mountain, adjacent to the ACC Banff club-house, and headed toward Mount Assiniboine. A round trip of some 75 miles was fully supported by a circuit of multiple backcountry camps every 6 to 9 miles (9.7–14.5 kilometres) for the comfort and enjoyment of travellers who could opt to journey by foot or on horseback and were spared the burden of carrying heavy loads. The route typically ran from Banff's Middle Springs along the Spray River to the Spray Lakes, up Bryant Creek, and over Assiniboine Pass to Mount Assiniboine, with a return route via Sunshine Creek, Healy Creek, and the Bow River back to Middle Springs.[14] Although some of these areas are easily reached today via roads, helicopters, and gondolas, in the 1920s they were considered backcountry, as much as 20 miles (32 kilometres) beyond the CPR line.

When the Banff outfitters complained about the grants Wheeler was receiving to operate the tour, Wheeler was concerned that Parks might bow to the protests, and this concern grew into a struggle over the public right to national parks. Wheeler and ACC President W.W. Foster began to notify the chairmen of the regional club sections about the possibility that the tours might falter. Late in 1921, ACC chairmen sent out letters written on behalf of club sections in Vancouver, Victoria, Edmonton, Calgary, Winnipeg, and New York addressed to the Minister of the Interior—Calgary's Sir James Lougheed—under the government of Arthur Meighen. Considering James Lougheed served as a corporate solicitor—whose practice with R.B. Bennett represented accounts such as the CPR, Hudson's Bay Company, and the Bank of Montreal—and had substantial personal investments in real estate and industry, it is unlikely that the ACC's arguments fell on sympathetic ears.[15]

Without the affordable camps provided by Wheeler, they argued, the hidden beauties of the Rockies would remain inaccessible to the majority of Canadians. For example, the chairman of the ACC Vancouver Island Section, R.D. McCaul, advocated the continuation of the tour because it put "the Canadian Rockies within reach of all."[16] As he, and other chairs of sections, saw it, the principle of access to the public domain was at stake if participation in the national park system was based on wealth and limited in practice to those who could afford the CPR's luxury tourist resorts and the high-priced services of a small number of private operators.

As the letter-writing campaign was waged, Wheeler dramatized his conflict with local competitors to great effect. In an official 1922 New Year's greeting to members of the ACC, he claimed that "there is a cloud upon our horizon that not only threatens the freedom, but the very existence of the Club and its life work of opening up the mountain areas of the Canadian Rockies." Aligning his business interests with those of the club, Wheeler stressed the public right to access in the national parks as afforded by his tours for the middle class: "Our Club represents the large majority of those interested in such parts of the mountains as are yet little known. We people, who desire access to primitive Nature in the Great Hills of Canada for our revitalization...must be served. We look to a progressive Government to give us access in the way we want at a cost we can afford."[17] Throughout this battle for public access, Wheeler seemed unconcerned by complications inherent in his role as ACC director and as a private tour entrepreneur.

Wheeler's 1922 New Year's greeting to the ACC membership provoked a flurry of strongly worded letters from tour patrons to federal officials and Minister of the Interior Charles Stewart, newly appointed under William Lyon Mackenzie King's incoming Liberal government, late in December 1921.[18] The well-established recreational impulses and organizational structure of the club were easily redirected into a concerted attempt at lobbying public policymakers.

ACC members proved articulate, politically attuned, and reasonably well heeled; they had the will and the means to bend the ear of government. At a general meeting in Victoria the ACC passed a resolution supporting the tour, citing that it served the needs of middle-class travellers.[19] Dr. Cora Best, a longtime ACC member from Minneapolis, described this situation in a letter to the minister in which she decried price-gouging by private outfitters: "The charges at all times makes it prohibitive for many fine people to see the Rockies. Teachers, men and women in educational work, doctors, and other professional men and women have told me they have never gone because they could not afford it." She also claimed that several club "ladies" had been badly overcharged by the Brewsters for horse rentals.[20] In some ways, state subsidization of the Mount Assiniboine tour was a midpoint between two perspectives on the development of the national parks with unbridled commercialism on the one hand and controlled state development on the other. Some members of the American Alpine Club also forwarded letters. F.W. Waterman of the New York Section asserted, "it is the Club that brings us to the mountains," and B.F. Seaver, also of the New York Section, wrote that the "true future of the mountains is...to 'democratize' them."[21] Another letter was penned by noted climber and retired US naval commander Albert H. MacCarthy, who linked tourist travel with settlement and economic development when he wrote that he had camped with the ACC on his first trip to Canada in 1911, taken a pack-train trip, and, subsequently, decided to immigrate to the Lake Windermere district of British Columbia where he invested in ranching. "With the Walking Tours well established in various interesting sections beyond the railway zone by which travelers can make trips easily, safely, and at reasonable expense, public interest in this region will result in the upbuilding of homes and industry in its many beautiful valleys."[22]

As the campaign continued, Wheeler exerted further pressure on W.W. Cory, deputy minister of the Department of the Interior, when he said that the upcoming ACC summer camp at Palliser Pass would fail if it could not be supplied by the tour. He offered Cory a grim picture, saying that "if necessary, the matter will be carried to Parliament and to the newspapers of the country, for I do not think that...the country will stand for the loss of prestige, both at home and abroad, by the Alpine Club that would follow the necessity of calling off its annual camp."[23]

The lobby pressure hit its mark. By February 1922, Harkin reported to his superior W.W. Cory that Wheeler's "vigorous propaganda"—the letter-writing campaign—was "urging that this Department remove its objections to the operation of the service as conducted last season."[24] Harkin was aware Wheeler had steered the issue to his own advantage and he refuted several of what he believed to be misconceptions on Wheeler's part. Harkin challenged Wheeler for misrepresenting the fundamental question: "On reading over the [New Year's] Greeting, I am strongly of the opinion that not only does it cloud the issue but that it places this department in an unfair light....It is stated that the very existence of the Alpine Club of Canada is threatened. I do not see how this statement can be justified."[25] As Harkin pointed out in response to disgruntled alpine trekkers, the Department of the Interior was in sympathy with the goals of the tour and had subsidized their operation from the start. For example, he responded to Marcus Morton, Jr., a notable Boston judge, who had joined the ACC in 1921, that the department in fact, subsidized and supported the operation:

> *The Department has been very generous to date in the matter of assistance to the Walking Tours. The sum of some $3,300.00 has been paid out in wages and in the purchase of material by the Department since the commencement of the tours and in addition various equipment valued at $3,450.00 has been issued from stock in the Government stores....As I have already advised Mr. Wheeler I am strongly in favour of the continuance of the Walking Tours and am willing to recommend financial assistance for the 1922 operations as soon as the question of the saddle pony service is settled.*[26]

Within the Parks Branch, Harkin voiced a strong internal defence of the walking tour concept. In a letter to Rocky Mountains Park Superintendent R.S. Stronach, he wrote that he felt "convinced that it is my duty to persistently fight for the maintenance and extension of walking tours. If the Wheeler scheme by any chance failed to operate I would deem it my duty to make new arrangements which would ensure walking tours being available. The idea I want to drive home is that I do not think it right that the guides should look upon walking tours as necessarily inimical to their interests."[27]

Harkin and department officials sought to mediate the dispute at its source with the local outfitters and horse packers in Banff. At an open meeting on February 20, 1922, called by Superintendent Stronach, it became clear that local competitors objected specifically to Wheeler's federally subsidized tour running saddle and packing services off the main Mount Assiniboine circuit and allegedly cutting into their trade. The walking tour itself was acceptable, provided it did not compete with unsubsidized outfitters and packers in the regional saddle-tour market.[28] The location of the coming ACC camp at Palliser Pass, along with circuit trips via Citadel Pass and Simpson Pass, likely posed an aggravation to the outfitters.

In the end, the deputy minister concluded Wheeler possessed an unfair advantage over other private operators and would have to cease outfitting side trips from the main route of the Mount Assiniboine Tour. The department estimated that the tour brought only three hundred of 150,000 visitors to Banff from 1920 to 1921.[29] In 1922 Mount Assiniboine was declared a provincial park by British Columbia at the ACC's urging. Once Wheeler agreed to withdraw saddle services, the Department of the Interior continued to subsidize the tour, bringing an end to the tiny tempest. In 1925 Harkin continued to recommend support to the operation in the form of a $500 grant, saying that the tour had "been patronized by over five hundred people, representing seven countries." He argued that "considerable benefit and advertising" resulted to the department, and, moreover, "the object of the Walking Tours, namely to make accessible at reasonable cost the out-lying areas of our parks, is a worthy one and based on a sound principle."[30] The tour continued to operate subsidized until 1928. By that time it had become difficult to compete with well-established operators and the CPR in a regional market shifting toward automobile tourism. The controversy indicated how demand for backcountry recreation among the rising middle classes would bring greater numbers to frequent wild park areas. It also provided Wheeler and the ACC with a practice ground for advocacy.

The lessons the ACC gained from its 1922 foray into the realm of public policy proved valuable. The club emerged from its battle for public access as a highly motivated, broadly based, middle-class interest group committed to promoting its stake in the national parks. As club director, Arthur Wheeler manoeuvred a sizeable articulate membership of professional men and women accustomed to the machinery of politics and government. Notably, many of the most articulate ACC activists were from the United States and Britain and knew how to influence Canadian policymakers. Tour advocates employed various tactics with refined skill, such as lobbying through collegial networks, formal resolutions, and political correspondence campaigns. The ACC's two-tiered structure, with communication channels at the national and local levels, helped the club lobby for its objectives. Proponents of Wheeler's tour employed middle-class privilege and the rhetoric of civic populism effectively to achieve their own agendas; outdoor recreation for the middle class was their immediate goal—not recreation for all—but even that was a significant shift in terms of social opportunity given the existing means of tourism. As a self-conscious class of recreational park users, the club professed to stand on guard for the civic right to the public domain as embodied by Canada's national parks. Here, the club's vigilance merged with the concerns of Parks. These lessons were not lost as hydro-development proposals sprang up through the 1920s.

The Principle of Inviolability and the
Waterton Lakes Dam Proposal

As the Mount Assiniboine tour issue wound down in March 1922, the Alpine Club of Canada entered into a long drawn-out debate over the hydro-development potential of the eastern Rockies. The conflict created a divisive showdown between the friends of the national parks and the proponents of irrigation and hydropower. Not surprisingly, the ACC stood on the side of the national parks; in fact, it forged a co-operative alliance with Canada's National Parks Branch in the face of outside threats to Waterton Lakes National Park.

Following the First World War, Alberta's burgeoning population, urban growth, and economic development expanded the provincial market for electric power and stimulated irrigation projects on the dry southern prairies. Under the United Farmers of Alberta (UFA) government through the 1920s and into the 1930s, Alberta's political climate favoured agriculture. In southern regions, irrigation was increasingly instrumental in improving the viability of seed crops and cattle ranching because it reduced farmers' dependence on inconsistent rainfall.

Three years of severe drought gave rise in 1919 to an irrigation movement supported by farmers, UFA locals, and many small towns in southwest Alberta. The Lethbridge Board of Trade convened a meeting that launched the Irrigation Development Association, formalized in March, to rally public support for irrigation. In August pro-irrigationists at a mass meeting in Pincher Creek urged Ottawa to undertake studies relevant to the irrigation potential of the region. The momentum created by these meetings led to several proposed irrigation districts.[31] Federal control over western natural resources was a bone of contention in Alberta and Saskatchewan throughout the 1920s.

The Department of the Interior's Irrigation Branch had been conducting hydrometric surveys to assess the power and irrigation potential of rivers in southern Alberta since 1911 and readily came up with several irrigation proposals. During summer 1919, the Irrigation Branch surveyed the Narrows on Waterton Lakes in Waterton Lakes National Park. Subsequently, in 1920, Commissioner of Irrigation P.H. Peters recommended the area as an ideal site for a dam and water-storage reservoir as part of the proposed Lethbridge Southeast irrigation project. The project aimed to establish irrigation districts and supply water to farmers via private canal systems developed by the Canadian Pacific Railway and its subsidiary, the Alberta Railway and Irrigation Company.[32]

National Parks Commissioner J.B. Harkin found his branch of the Department of the Interior embroiled in an interdepartmental conflict with the Irrigation Branch. To counter Irrigation's claim to water rights in Waterton, Harkin's 1920–21 annual report restated the fundamental precepts of the national parks and enunciated for the first time the principle of inviolability:

> *The stand taken by the Parks Branch with regard to such applications is that the parks are the property of all the people of Canada and that consequently they should not be developed for the benefit of any one section of the country or of private interests; second, that such development constitutes an invasion of the fundamental principles upon which parks have been established, namely, the conservation of certain areas of primitive landscape with all their original conditions of plant and animal life and other natural features intact.*[33]

Meanwhile, irrigation was showcased in the Alberta press as the only answer to the dry lands question. "Farmers In Dry Belt Abandon Their Farms...Irrigation the Only Solution" headlined the *Western Farmer and Weekly Albertan* in early 1922. The Alberta press depicted irrigation as the panacea for Alberta's dry belt, "the only thing that will put it on its feet and transfer a barren waste into a Garden of Eden."[34] Irrigation was central to settlement and economic development in southern Alberta, as suggested by press coverage of the potential immigration of irrigation farmers from the western US, provincial legislation destined to facilitate more irrigation works, and Premier Greenfield's emphasis that "colonization must keep pace with construction of irrigation projects." In some quarters, the construction of dams for irrigation works was also seen as a legitimate means to create work for distressed farmers.[35] The Waterton Lakes dam and Lethbridge Southeast project characterized many irrigation projects proposed during this era, despite problems associated with finding markets for irrigation agriculture.[36]

Still, regional public opinion divided on the issue of constructing an irrigation dam in Waterton Lakes National Park. By January 7, 1922, the *Lethbridge Herald* reported that "little progress had been made" in the movement to block the Waterton dam. Several petitions were circulating and resolutions had been dispatched to Ottawa by opponents of the dam, reported the *Herald* without listing their names, requesting that the government preserve the Waterton townsite and "disallow any movement looking to the disfiguring of the national parks" by turning the lake into a reservoir. The *Herald* dismissed this opposition to the dam, insisting that generally southern Albertans believed that water was "needed more on the lands of the prairies in producing crops than in the mountains serving only a few."[37]

Pro-irrigationists mounted a strong offensive campaign to push the Waterton Lakes dam into existence. In February 1922, they paraded their local forces, including the Civic Council of Fort MacLeod, the Lethbridge City Council, the Southern Irrigation District, and the New Dayton Irrigation District, as well as the communities of Bow Island, Cardston, Grassy Lake, Lucky Strike, Macleod, Magrath, Milk River, New Dayton, Raymond, Taber, and Warner.[38] The organized irrigation lobby also included certain UFA locals in southern Alberta, the CPR, and the Western Canada Irrigation Association, which named the CPR's irrigation crusader William Pearce among its executive members. Pearce, a former public land surveyor with the Department of the Interior, was a longtime promoter of irrigation in the Canadian West and the "chief architect" of the western waters policy.[39] Southern Alberta papers the *Lethbridge Herald* and the *Weekly Albertan* took editorial positions in favour of irrigation. These forces insisted that the dam go ahead. Park proponents like the ACC faced formidable opposition as western agrarianism and eastern corporate capitalism formed a powerful coalition intent on irrigation.

One park proponent, although it had been at the centre of the 1919 irrigation movement, was the town of Pincher Creek, directly north of the national park. By January 1922, its town council had sent a resolution of protest to the Minister of the Interior.[40] The Pincher Creek UFA local also joined the protest and, in March, sent a resolution opposing the Waterton dam to the acting commissioner of Irrigation in Calgary. The commissioner responded that Waterton Lakes remained the "most economical and practically the only site available" and stated that "its use as a reservoir would not seriously affect the scenic approach to the park."[41]

At the time, federal Parks Commissioner Harkin was in the midst of the 1922 policy wrangle over the Mount Assiniboine Walking Tour. He drew Arthur Wheeler's attention to the irrigation proposals for Waterton Lakes National Park. Wheeler had been unaware of the issue, but he wanted to know more, as he wrote to Harkin: "If you will be so good as to put me wise, and let me know if the Alpine Club can help, I shall be glad to move in the matter. I think you know that our interests and sympathies lie with the parks."[42]

Harkin's summary of the Waterton dam proposal followed. A sixty-foot (18.3-metre) dam at the outlet of Upper Waterton Lake would block the Narrows between the lakes, submerge the existing Waterton townsite, and "almost entirely submerge Cameron Falls and do other damage to the lake which the Park Service considers will effectually destroy its beauty as a National Park."[43] The resulting reservoir was expected to supply irrigation to 75,000 acres (about 30,353 hectares) of drought-stricken Alberta land under the federal Reclamation Service's proposed Lethbridge Southeast project.[44] The federal Reclamation Service and the National Park Service, both part of the Department of the Interior, held divergent views of the proposal.

According to Harkin, the Reclamation Service held the advantage of an organized lobby in favour of the Waterton dam proposal. He lamented to Wheeler in spring 1922, there was "practically no publicity with respect to the Parks side" of the debate, and he was surprised that the alpinists of the club had not taken action "to present the other side publicly."[45] Harkin and Waterton's Superintendent Bevan wished to turn public opinion in favour of retaining the park in its natural state.[46] Here was an advocacy role for the ACC and the beginning of a larger, more persistent debate over national park protection.

Quick to pick up on the implications of the irrigation controversy, Sir James Outram—a renowned English mountaineer and senior ACC member—challenged the dam proposal in March 1922 during his address at the club's sixteenth-anniversary banquet in Calgary. He felt that water "could be secured from other parts for irrigation purposes [and]...should not be taken from places where such action would ruin the beauty spots of the country." Outram's speech, accompanied by lantern slides, was reported in the *Calgary Herald*. He recommended that "the Alpine Club must make the people realize that the mountains are the heritage of all."[47] The ACC subsequently acted on this philosophy.

At around the same time as Outram's speech, the international dimension to the Waterton Lakes controversy also came into play. Canada's Waterton Lakes National Park adjoins Glacier National Park, USA, along the Alberta–Montana border. The three interconnected Waterton Lakes cross the international boundary line. Canadian plans to dam a lake in this system became an international waters cross-border concern, and American parks officials and conservationists frowned on the proposal. When the US government refused entry to a Canadian irrigation survey crew in March 1922, it defied Canadian actions that might harm Glacier National Park. Prominent American conservationist George Bird

Grinnell opposed the Waterton dam; the Ecological Society of America offered its assistance to J.B. Harkin to fight it; and the US National Parks Association decried the project and the potential destruction that flooding could wreak on Glacier National Park.

The National Parks Association in the United States had been established in 1919 under Robert Yard with funding from Stephen Mather, the US National Park Service director and a member of the Sierra Club.[48] Harkin believed the Waterton issue would set a critical precedent and remarked that there was "the greatest need in Canada for an organization something along the lines of the American National Parks Association which, being independent of the Government, is free to actively carry on work in defence of National Parks."[49] As a case in point, the US National Parks Association opposed an irrigation dam similar to the Waterton proposal that was planned for St. Mary's Lake in Glacier National Park. The executive secretary of the American association sent Wheeler a circular letter in March 1922 regarding irrigation dams proposed for Waterton Lakes and St. Mary's Lake.[50] A well-defined coalition of American conservation interests actively opposed the dam proposals impinging on both national parks.

Meanwhile, the Alpine Club entered the fray over the dam proposal on the Canadian side of the border. At the ACC's annual general meeting on August 5, 1922, conducted at the Palliser Pass Camp in Rocky Mountains Park, the Waterton Lakes issue came before the club.[51] When opened to debate before the general membership, the Waterton issue revealed a fragmented range of opinions within the club.

Pincher Creek–area rancher Frederick W. Godsal of Cowley, Alberta, spoke of "the absolute necessity of the dam to keep the southern Alberta farmer from total ruin due to drought."[52] Godsal's view of Waterton Park had made a drastic reverse. In the 1890s, he had led a conservationist drive to reserve the Waterton area as a national park, concerned by the effects of increased human population already witnessed in fish and wildlife depletion, and the need to protect the Waterton Lakes headwaters. When lobbying for the creation of the Waterton Park reserve, Godsal had argued to the Minister of the Interior that it was "essential that the interest of the public should be properly safeguarded in this 'beauty spot.'" In 1895 Ottawa responded by creating the Waterton Park Reserve. Commenting on the park's 86-square-mile (139-square-kilometre) area in 1905, Godsal said, "I doubt the reserve is large enough for its purpose."[53] However, when it came to drought, Godsal the rancher took precedence over Godsal the conservationist.

James Outram rejoined that the Waterton Lakes "would be completely spoiled as a pleasure resort" if the dam went ahead. Wheeler agreed and dug even deeper, saying that a larger principle was at stake in the issue: "the point is, if the Mountain Parks are set aside for present and future generations they should be preserved untouched. The desire is to prevent the establishment of a precedent which will enable any corporation to go in and take away any part of the parks."[54] Like Harkin, Wheeler emphasized the principle of inviolability and believed the Waterton dam could set a dangerous precedent for public parks. T.B. Moffat, ACC Calgary Section chairman, echoed this theme, arguing, "The Government must not trespass upon the people's rights."[55] In the end, a resolution proposed by Fred Bell and seconded by James Outram, with a slight amendment suggested by F.N. Waterman, was passed to record the ACC's dissatisfaction with the irrigation proposal:

> With regard to the Waterton Lakes Irrigation Scheme, the Alpine Club of Canada, while it recognizes the undoubted economic value of the project, deplores the necessity of the action to be taken if it involves the destruction of the natural beauties of a park which the Government has already decided shall be set aside for the benefit of the public.
>
> The Club considers it a necessity to affirm its stand on a principle which involves such a precedent and desires that it may be kept fully informed by the Government of the details of the development of the scheme.[56]

With these words, the ACC asserted the primacy of protecting the public domain from corporate and state exploitation. Despite the club's acknowledgement of prairie agricultural economics, inviolability had emerged as a key principle in the protection of the public domain embodied by the mountain parks. Here the club was not alone, as G.G. Coote, Progressive Member of Parliament for Macleod, Alberta, indicated in the House of Commons: "I think just as many people are opposed to the using of Waterton Lakes as an irrigation reservoir as there are who are in favour of that proposition. I hope that the minister will see that the water-powers in our parks are preserved."[57]

By 1923 the Waterton Lakes dam proposal had died on the planning board. Washington's unyielding stance regarding Glacier National Park in Montana deterred Canada's Minister of the Interior from submitting the Waterton scheme to the International Waterways Commission. Under J.B. Harkin, the National Parks Branch summoned extensive arguments against dam construction. The branch contended that permitting the project within the park boundaries would create an open season on the national parks, setting a dangerous precedent for invasive commercial exploitation. Finally, just as debate over the dam culminated, the need for expensive irrigation works diminished due to a rise in average precipitation that produced bumper harvests in the southern Alberta districts by the mid-1920s.[58]

Historian Ian Getty attributes the victory over the Waterton dam scheme to the strength of American opposition to the proposal more than to the protests of Canadian park advocates. While the advanced state of American conservation advocacy certainly benefitted the Canadian national parks as far as the protection of Glacier National Park was concerned, the agency of Harkin and his staff in soliciting public support in Canada cannot be overlooked. That Parks administrators turned to the ACC in the face of the well-organized irrigation lobby suggests the department considered it to share a vision of the parks wherein the inviolability of the nation's natural heritage was paramount.

During the Waterton debate, the ACC voted to protect the public domain and made a clear stand for park protection, albeit with a pragmatic awareness of the need for economic growth in western Canada. Commissioner Harkin redirected its ire over the walking tour skirmish away from the department toward a common adversary. On the whole, the club had found its own advantage in being co-opted by Harkin and moved one step further as a political interest group defending the public domain. As a lobby group, the club expanded its tactics to include gala banquet speeches, press coverage, formal resolutions, internal contacts within the civil service, and collegial networks. ACC executives and leaders in various cities extended their networks to exert lobby pressure on Ottawa. It had learned the art of building alliances. Fundamentally, the ACC had enhanced its relationship with the Canadian National Parks Branch as a key stakeholder group with a kindred vision of the mountain parks. Again, accumulation of advocacy experience would help the ACC in its coming battle, also related to water: a protracted debate over the future of rivers and lakes in Rocky Mountains Park.

Hydropower in Rocky Mountains Park
The Beginnings of the Canadian National Parks Association

During the early 1900s, the Calgary Power Company extended a web of electrical power stations driven by rivers and waterfalls through the mountains and foothills west of Calgary. Here on the advancing technological frontiers of hydropower, the urban needs and corporate goals of prairie towns and cities clashed with a more abstract vision of the national mountain parks as a public trust.

In May 1911, Calgary Power's first hydroelectric plant went into operation on the Bow River's Horseshoe Falls, generating a total of 19,000 horsepower. Technology made it possible to combine the production of power from run-of-the-river systems with high-head hydro plants that generated energy as water dropped in elevation through a turbine system, as with the Horseshoe Falls installation. At a rate of $30 per horsepower, Calgary's electrical supply could now sustain the development of a street railway system, stimulate urban growth, and attract industrial investments, such as the CPR's regional repair centre. Horseshoe Falls was critical to the supply of inexpensive power to the city of Calgary, whose population soared from 4,398 in 1901 to 43,704 in 1911, and continued to grow to 63,305 by 1921.[59]

In 1912 the Calgary Power Company first dammed a storage reservoir on Lake Minnewanka in Rocky Mountains National Park. The company brought a dam and generating station at Kananaskis Falls into service in 1913, despite alleged infringements on the lands of the Stoney Indian Reserve and Rocky Mountains Park.[60] At this stage, the aggregate capacity of Calgary Power's hydroelectric plants totalled 32,000 horsepower and served Calgary, the Canada Cement Company at Exshaw, and the village of Cochrane west of Calgary.[61] During the peak of winter, however, flow rates on the Bow River dropped, causing the company's run-of-the-river hydro plants to operate at one-sixth their total capacity. For this reason, engineers turned to the idea of creating water storage reservoirs in the Rocky Mountains to augment the river's flow through high-head electrical plants and run-of-the-river generating stations.[62]

When Nova Scotia financier Izaak Walton Killam took control of Calgary Power in 1919, it was already a profitable monopoly. By this time, under the leadership of Max Aitken and Calgary lawyer and politician R.B. Bennett, the company had secured the contract to supply power to Calgary, along with franchises for Edmonton and Medicine Hat.[63] The company was eager to expand its power grid and increase its capabilities. As a result, Calgary Power doggedly pursued its interests in damming lakes in Rocky Mountains Park as storage reservoirs to boost the dry-season flows through its power plants.[64]

As the federal Water Power Branch of the Department of the Interior reported in 1920, harnessing the full potential of the Bow River promised to generate enough power for the ordinary needs of 300,000 people. With populations escalating across the Prairie provinces, manufacturing and industrial growth would "inevitably result in a rapidly increasing demand for cheap and dependable power." Along with transportation links, optimum reliable power capacity was a fundamental requirement in attracting this type of business diversification to prairie cities.[65] In 1923 Calgary Power negotiated a new contract with Calgary to combine the generating capacity of its municipally owned steam plants with the company's own hydroelectric stations, thus increasing output to carry a much higher load. Following the success of an experimental transmission line to supply smaller centres south of Calgary in 1926, Calgary Power launched a rapid expansion of urban and rural electrification.[66]

Through the 1920s, Calgary Power made repeated proposals to dam lakes in Rocky Mountains Park to generate more power to service Alberta's growing market for urban and rural electrification. The proximity of the national park did not deter its plans for developing hydropower dams on Lake Minnewanka, near the park resort town of Banff, and on the Spray Lakes, south of the coal-mining town of Canmore. In 1921 Charles Stewart, Minister of the Interior, was unreceptive to Calgary Power's request for permission to raise the water level of Lake Minnewanka beyond the height of an existing dam built in 1912.[67] The company claimed that the additional water storage capacity to be gained from a new dam would alleviate the problem of low winter-flow rates on the Bow River; supply power to nearby Canmore, Banff, and Bankhead; and improve the scrubby shoreline of the lake. On the other hand, federal Parks officials defended the public right to pristine national parks unspoiled by industrial landmarks. Although his ministry had responsibility for water-power resources in the West, Stewart remained unsympathetic to the proposed Minnewanka dam project and was receptive to advisors within the National Parks Branch.[68] As Stewart later explained in the House of Commons, he was "keen on scenic beauty" and felt that Lake Minnewanka would be marred by changing water levels.[69]

Stewart's response to the dam project was not out of line with federal policies on resource extraction in the national parks at the time, which had grown less permissive during this period. For example, controls on logging and mining were strengthened. In 1912 the Parks Branch had offered little resistance to the construction of dams at Kananaskis Falls and Lake Minnewanka, but by 1921, it strongly opposed further hydro plans for Minnewanka and sought to protect the environment from excessive resource extraction that might threaten the state of the park. Dam proposals in the 1920s thus became a rallying point for Canadian national parks advocates set on the conservation of "scenic beauty."

In 1922, hard on the heels of the Minnewanka proposal, Calgary Power renewed a 1920 request to dam the entire chain of Spray Lakes. The plan aimed to engineer a water-storage reservoir by flooding the Spray Lakes Valley between the Goat and Kananaskis ranges in southeastern Rocky Mountains Park. Squeezed by this corporate power play, the National Parks Branch suspected the spectre of the huge Spray project was designed to wrest approval of the Minnewanka application from the minister.[70]

A strong lobby of pro-conservation national parks supporters emerged to oppose the dam proposals. J.B. Harkin's office was flooded with letters and telegrams in 1922 and 1923 that protested hydro development in Rocky Mountains Park. Tourist groups such as the Calgary Automobile Club voiced concern that the mountain scenery would be marred, and the Banff Citizens' Council opposed "any attempt on [the] part of irrigation or water-power interests to invade national parks" and disrupt their natural beauty.[71]

The ACC voiced some of the strongest statements in favour of national park preservation. The club quickly sprang to the defence of the Spray Lakes. The Toronto ACC Section went on record: "We are of the opinion that the principle should be laid down and accepted once and for all that our national parks, which belong to the people of Canada, should be preserved for the whole people, and not destroyed or exploited for commercial purposes for the benefit of a few."[72] Again, the club was in harmony with J.B. Harkin's vision of the national parks as an inviolable public domain.

As in the case of the Waterton irrigation scheme, ACC Director Arthur Wheeler and Sir James Outram balked at the proposal to dam lakes in the national parks. At the Victoria Section's annual dinner in March 1923, Wheeler condemned the Spray Lakes plan, as reported in the *Daily Colonist*: "Such [a] scheme would, in his opinion, completely destroy the beautiful valley, which is a main thoroughfare to many of the most scenic centres of the Southern Canadian Rockies."[73] Because his Mount Assiniboine tour business passed through the area, Wheeler held a close interest and was well aware of the dam's potential impact on the environment and on tourism. At the Calgary Section's annual dinner in April

1923, Outram emphasized the duty of the club to oppose damming the Spray Lakes and uphold the preservation of the valley in its natural state, hoping "every single member would oppose to the last the proposed scheme of turning the Spray Lake district into a reservoir to generate electricity for Calgary, thus ruining a spot of wonderful beauty forever." His statements to a crowd of 125, including Parks administrator J.C. Campbell, emphasized that "National Parks were established for the people of Canada as a whole and for the world at large." The local club secretary T.O. West read an annual address from Wheeler "protesting the infraction of the rights of the Canadian people for the benefit of a small section, in the damming up of the Spray Lakes." Their stance was publicized in the club's national newsletter.[74]

Again southern Alberta rancher Frederick Godsal was one of the only recorded dam proponents in the ACC. He argued that the needs of the prairie farmer should take precedence over preserving the national parks in their natural state. Like many Canadians, Godsal believed in the superabundance of wilderness, and he did not approve of the club's advocacy, as he wrote candidly to CPR irrigation and hydropower proponent William Pearce: "I do not consider that it is the business of the Alpine Club...Considering the vast area of mountains and lakes in Alberta and B.C., it is positively hoggish to trouble about 2 or 3 lakes, or half a dozen, and thereby hinder the progress of the chief and main industry of the country, upon which all other wealth depends."[75] As in the case of the Waterton dam, Godsal urged the ACC "to think of the needs of the prairies, whether for water, or for power generated by water...and help Calgary and other towns to prosperity again...as intended by a wise Creator."

Godsal was convinced that ACC members had bowed to Wheeler on the matter of hydro development in the Rockies, a belief he disclosed privately to Pearce. His claim is unconvincing given the strong-minded individual leaders and members who made a concerted effort to oppose dams in the national parks, including William Foster, the deputy minister of British Columbia Public Works; Fred Bell, a Vancouver medical doctor; Selby Walker, a Calgary insurance broker; and Andrew Sibbald, a Saskatoon lawyer. The ACC was not Wheeler's puppet. It was an active interest group with an independent membership, and strong club leaders emerged as conservation activists and avid national parks defenders. Judging by the lack of other dissenters, it appears that Godsal's own efforts to persuade the Calgary and Edmonton ACC sections to oppose Wheeler met with little enthusiasm.[76]

Through spring and summer 1923, Arthur Wheeler devoted considerable energy to publicizing the dam controversy in western newspapers and club publications, as he laid the ground for the formation of a national parks advocacy association. In response to criticism from William Pearce, a former Department of the Interior colleague, Wheeler stated that his primary concern was to safeguard "the general principle that the mountain parks are reserved for the benefit of all the people and should not be subject to violation" by commercial ventures.[77] With prescient insight regarding Rocky Mountains Park, he warned Pearce against the erosion of the national parks through cumulative demands for development:

> As a club, we are opposed to commercial invasion of our National
> Parks, which are reserved for the people for their especial benefit.
> The Spray project is one particular case, as also the Waterton
> Lakes scheme and the Lake Minnewanka scheme, in which you are
> particularly interested. There will be assuredly, in the course of time,
> hundreds of other cases of varying types, all of which will have the
> same general grounds for argument as this particular one, and if
> not checked the ultimate result will be ruination to the National
> Parks of Canada. This has been amply proved by the experience
> of the United States, and the desperate fight that has been waged
> there for many years to save such public park reserves intact for
> the people.[78]

Wheeler also took issue with Pearce's letters to the *Calgary Daily Herald* in favour of development and refuted the case for the Spray Lakes dam, urging Canadians to guard against the erosion of the national parks by insisting on their inviolability.[79] It was at this time that Wheeler conceived of a public advocacy association that would work to prevent "commercial invasion" in the national parks. In the June 1923 edition of *The Gazette,* Wheeler primed club members to form the Canadian National Parks Association in order to play the watchdog role.

Wheeler thought a Canadian parks association would ensure that power companies could not violate national parks:

> In creating these reservations for the joy and lasting benefit of
> millions of people, the Government of Canada has followed a wise
> policy, not alone for the present generation but for generations to
> come. In the recent past commercial interests have endeavoured to
> encroach upon our park reserves, and utilize their scenic beauties

National Parks Association

An American Role Model

THE US NATIONAL PARKS ASSOCIATION was Arthur Wheeler's model for a non-government national parks advocacy group. It followed a tradition set by the Sierra Club, created in 1892 as the "guardian for the Yosemite." Proposals to construct a water reservoir for San Francisco by damming the Tuolumne River in Yosemite National Park's Hetch Hetchy Valley launched the Sierra Club's most famous conservation battle (1903–13). Faced with a divisive issue, Sierra Club leaders John Muir and William Colby created the Society for the Preservation of National Parks in 1909 to preserve national parks from "destructive invasion." This offshoot formed a national alliance with support from several alpine clubs from Seattle to Boston, walking clubs, women's clubs, and civic societies. Notably, it shared the Sierra Club's directors and San Francisco offices. Its successor, the National Parks Association, aimed "to defend the National Parks and National Monuments fearlessly against the assaults of private interests and aggressive commercialism" as irrigation and dam proposals continued to challenge US parks into the 1920s.[80]

to pay dividends to power companies. The greatest good to the greatest number is a universal law, and in this case particularly it applies. When one thinks of the undiluted joy and happiness that is given yearly by our scenic parks to thousands of workers of Canada and from other lands...interest in dividend paying stocks sinks into insignificance. The slogan "Hands Off Our National Parks" is a good one to adopt and to take measures to maintain.[81]

Wheeler proposed that the ACC form at its coming summer camp a Canadian association dedicated to parks advocacy. Wheeler's instinct to build a lobbying instrument and follow up with publicity campaigns and slogans showed a shrewd sense of political tactics. The ACC, meanwhile, would carry on with its main focus—promoting Canadian alpinism.

The club's annual general meeting at camp in Larch Valley, near Moraine Lake, Alberta, on August 2, 1923, devoted considerable time to the formation of a national parks advocacy organization. National Parks Commissioner J.B. Harkin—who had worked with Wheeler leading up to the camp to explore the idea of an advocacy body[82]—and Chief Park Engineer J.M. Wardle both attended.

At the AGM, the ACC stayed true to its origins, standing for Canadian mountain heritage. ACC President William Foster appealed to posterity in his call for the club to take action to protect the "scenic assets" of the Rocky Mountain Parks:

A big need of Canada at the present time was an organization responsible for the protection of these great domains. Science may someday solve the problem of utilities, but the great scenic assets can never be improved upon and must be preserved for all time. If the Club takes part in this conservation and resistance to encroachment, it will be doing something of real national value and will be known for its vision.[83]

Arthur Wheeler agreed with Foster and officially proposed that the ACC form the Canadian National Parks Association, as the club was "vitally interested in defending the entire system of national parks from commercial encroachment and despoliation of their beautiful scenery."[84] He called on Commissioner Harkin to explain the government's policy on national parks at the meeting, as was summarized in the club's 1923 *Gazette*:

Mr. Harkin said the policy of the parks was the policy of the Alpine
Club of Canada, the preservation of the natural beauties of Canada
for the people of Canada, free from all monopolies and special privi-
leges. The general opinion was that the parks were a sort of frill, of
no especial value. From a commercial standpoint, however, they were
a great asset to the nation, bringing enormous amounts of money
into the country and paying a huge dividend on the outlay. In 1921
the revenue that the National Parks brought into Canada was at
least $15,000,000. The output that year was $850,000...There were
also the human dividends to be considered...greater mental, phys-
ical and spiritual efficiency.[85]

Harkin's statements allied Parks bureaucrats and alpinists in support of
mutual goals. Clearly, in Harkin's eyes, the economic and "human dividends" of national parks contributed to Canadian development and
nation-building.

ACC section representatives from Vancouver Island, Calgary,
Saskatoon, Winnipeg, and Toronto proceeded to speak out "against the
spoliation of the parks," which they saw inherent in the Spray Lakes
hydro proposals, and they threw their support behind the motion to form
a national parks conservation body. Andrew Sibbald moved the proposal
be accepted, and Fred Bell seconded, thereby creating the Canadian
National Parks Association (CNPA).

During its early years, the ACC fostered development of the nascent
CNPA behind the scenes while maintaining its own formal role as
Canada's national mountaineering group. The ACC's executive and
membership overlapped with that of the CNPA, and the ACC offered the
CNPA organizational and financial assistance during the Spray Lakes
and Minnewanka controversies. All but one of the five CNPA officers
in 1924 were also ACC leaders: William Foster was CNPA president;
Alexander McCoubrey, central vice-president; Selby Walker, western
vice-president; Arthur Wheeler, secretary; and Andrew Sibbald, treasurer. Charles Hanbury-Williams, CNPA eastern vice-president and a
prominent conservationist, was the only officer who did not belong to
the ACC. In 1924 the CNPA executive committee had nine members,
seven of whom also belonged to the ACC. By 1930 four members of the
CNPA executive were not members of the Alpine Club,[86] and in 1934 the
ACC was allowed five votes in the CNPA elections and ACC President
Alexander McCoubrey ran for the position of CNPA vice-president.[87]

∧ *Canadian National Parks Association founders at ACC Larch Valley Camp, 1923. Back row: Mr. Sibbald, possibly J.B. Hutchings, Sir James Outram, Col. W.W. Foster, J.B. Harkin, T.B. Moffat, Mr. A.O. Wheeler, Dr. F. Bell. Front row: James M. Wardle, Mr. Geddes, Dr. Cora Best, Mrs. Longstaff, H. Graves. Harry Pollard photograph.* [WMCR, V14/AC192P/1]

Because of these overlaps, it was practical for the ACC to host the first CNPA general meetings at the club's annual mountaineering camps.

The goals and constitution of the CNPA were set in 1923 by members of the ACC. The CNPA constitution set forth three major objectives:

a. *The preservation of the National Parks of Canada in their entirety for the use of the people of Canada and of the world, and the prevention of detriment to them through the invasion of commercial interests.*

b. *The spreading abroad of propaganda with the object of attracting people to them.*

c. *The preservation of their natural beauties for the benefit of mankind, and of the fauna and the flora intact, for educational, scientific, artistic and recreational purposes. To maintain them inviolate as symbols of the great heritage we possess in this wide-spreading Dominion of Canada.*[88]

The last two objectives bear a striking similarity to the objectives of the Alpine Club's 1906 constitution that reflected the all-embracing Edwardian philosophy of alpinism as envisioned by Elizabeth Parker, Arthur Wheeler, and other founders.

In contrast to the social focus on mountaineering in the ACC, the CNPA was dedicated to a politicized focus on national parks advocacy and preservation and brought this focus to bear on hydro-development controversies over the next twenty years. Following the 1923 ACC camp, the CNPA publicly announced its stand against the proposed power developments. Calgarians Selby Walker and Thomas Moffat proclaimed the creation of the CNPA and its principles in the Alberta press, saying, "There are those who look enviously upon our parks and who believe that any enterprise profitable to themselves should be allowed, while the members of the National Parks Association believe that when a park is once set aside for the recreation of the Canadian nation, the Park Act should not be tampered with and no individual or community should obtain rights within these parks to the detriment of the remainder of the people of Canada."[89]

Like Commissioner Harkin, the CNPA voiced a combination of economic arguments against the hydro proposals, stressing the tourism potential of the national parks. The CNPA advised that "the Dominion government has nothing to gain by granting a concession within one of

William James Selby Walker (1879–1952)

WILLIAM JAMES SELBY WALKER, a Calgary insurance broker born in Galt, Ontario, became the CNPA's long-standing leader, executive secretary, and most vocal member. Having joined the ACC in 1906, Walker held various leadership roles in the club, notably the honorary treasurership (1914–22), and a position on the Banff clubhouse management committee; he also donated the club's first medicine chest for first aid and replenished it through the years. The Walker family settled in Calgary when Selby's father, Colonel James Walker, was stationed with the local North West Mounted Police when Selby was two years old. Selby later served as a military paymaster during the First World War, holding the rank of major in the 15th Light Horse. His status among the first Calgary settler families led him to leadership as a vice-president of the Southern Alberta Pioneers and Old Timers Association. He attended Knox United Church, and he also served as an advisory council member during the formative years of the Canadian Youth Hostels Association, promoting outdoor recreation. He left a significant legacy in the city of Calgary by creating the Inglewood Bird Sanctuary, which he founded in 1929 on part of the family estate, in conjunction with CPR and federal defence lands, along the banks of the Bow River, where he lived with his wife and daughter. In recognition of his contribution to

∧ *Comraderie and fresh pie in the tea tent with a camp boy, in the early 1920s. Mr. Hogoboom, A.O. Wheeler, Jimmy Wilson, Selby Walker, N. Hendrie and M.P. Hendrie, Andy Drinnan, Major Longstaff (left to right). Harry Pollard photograph.* [WMCR, V14/AC192P/014]

wildlife conservation, he was admitted to the Audubon Society of America in 1939.[90]

Walker emerged as the dominant leadership figure in the ACC's offshoot, the CNPA. Conducting his volunteer work from home, with clerical assistance from his daughter Mary and his company's secretary, he wrote a series of periodical bulletins issued by the CNPA from the 1920s through the 1940s.[91] His outspoken editorials recommended that Canada adopt similar public policies to those of the US national parks and advocated an eclectic agenda of concerns related to automobile tourism, modern forestry, outdoor recreation, and health. Walker raised consistent opposition to industrial encroachments in Canadian national parks and was "the moving spirit" that kept the CNPA going through the Depression and war. As later remembered in the *Canadian Alpine Journal*: "He was unalterably opposed to the spoliation of the Parks by power development and to any other kind of encroachment on the Park areas by industry, and did an immense amount of work to bring his protests and those of the Association which he represented most forcibly to the notice of the authorities concerned."[92]

the National parks, which by the precedent established jeopardizes all of the parks."[93]

In August 1923 Andrew Sibbald notified the Minister of the Interior of the formation of the CNPA and corresponded with Commissioner Harkin as to how the new association could best assist the Parks Branch. A barrage of form letters to the minister from CNPA supporters followed, many from Sibbald's hometown of Saskatoon and all opposed to the Calgary Power application. Roughly half were written by ACC members.[94] For example, W.J. Campbell, a new club member who had joined the ACC in 1922, wanted to place himself on record as "opposed to all such concessions or franchises in the Canadian National Parks as are illustrated by the present application of the Montreal Engineering Co. for reservoir and power rights in the Spray Lakes Basin."[95]

The CNPA's battle against power development in Canada's national parks attracted the support of many other groups, including the Banff Citizens' Council, Calgary Good Roads Association, Edmonton Automobile and Good Roads Association, Women's Canadian Club, National Council of Women, Alberta Provincial Liberal Association, the American Association for the Advancement of Science, local boards of trade, and various clubs devoted to natural history, fishing, and community service.[96] Together they formed a broad-based coalition.

In June 1923 Ottawa rejected Calgary Power's Cascade Power project and application to raise the water level of Lake Minnewanka. Noting that the Water Powers Branch and the Parks Branch were "widely at variance" on this issue, Minister of the Interior Charles Stewart provided the following rationale for his decision:

Anybody who has been at Banff knows that Lake Minnewanka is within a few miles of the centre of the attractive portion of the park. The Calgary Power Company already have a concession on that lake, and they have increased the lake level, and their application...was for the purpose of raising it by another ten or fifteen feet. After looking it over I came to the conclusion that it would absolutely destroy the scenic properties of that particular lake. It was very close to where all sightseers of the park come, and obviously if we are to get any return for our investment in our national parks we must keep them attractive enough to draw tourists, and on these grounds, I refused the application of the company.[97]

At the same time, the Spray Lakes application remained before the department, and Stewart intended to visit the Spray Valley during the summer of 1923 in order to make his assessment. He noted the project's corporate profit margins were still outweighed by costs.[98] Robert Forke, Member of Parliament and leader of the Progressive Party, called the minister's attention to the fact that the issue of power applications affecting the national parks was a "very lively question in the prairie provinces," and he had received telegrams protesting against "granting any further power privileges."[99] Aware of the potential political fallout of seeming to cater to business tycoons in Calgary and Montreal in the face of scrutiny from the western Progressives, the federal Liberals continued to move carefully on the issue.

Although the Minnewanka proposal was turned down in June 1923, victory for the ACC, CNPA, and other conservationists opposed to the dams was short-lived. Calgary Power merely withdrew its proposals until a more opportune time. The company could afford to play a waiting game, knowing that the demand for power was growing just as certainly as political factors would shift with time. It was well aware that the federal–provincial negotiations over the transfer of natural resources to the western provinces had started anew in 1922, this time between Prime Minister King and Alberta's Premier Greenfield. The political context of decisions made by the Department of the Interior was coloured by these negotiations.[100] The Spray Lakes question was held in abeyance until the matter of resource allocation along the eastern slopes of the Rockies was determined. In any case, Calgary Power's application for the Spray Lakes project may well have been premature in the 1920s, considering market demands for power, slow industrial growth in the West, and competition with the flourishing oil and gas sector.

Following the Lake Minnewanka victory, Wheeler continued to promote the Canadian National Parks Association, even through press interviews about the club's Mount Logan expedition plans.[101] But gradually he succumbed to the belief that Calgary Power would win out in the long run. The long-term interests of big business were entrenched in the Spray Lakes Valley and augured the transfer of this area to the province. Minister Stewart visited the Spray Lakes in summer 1923, and, by April 1924, he seemed to view Calgary Power's need to supply power to Calgary in a more sympathetic light. The Progressive threat in Ottawa had eased by 1924 as the party began to disintegrate. At the same time, the national and regional economy began to accelerate. By now, the

Province of Alberta had also applied to develop the Spray Lakes as a storage basin and commenced hydrological studies, hoping to block private development of a key water-power resource.[102]

In April 1924, the Minister of the Interior stated in the House of Commons that he was keeping "a perfectly open mind" on the issue: "I do not think the development would interfere very materially with the park as such, in view of the fact that it comprises so many hundreds of thousands of acres."[103] Members of Parliament from Saskatoon and Vancouver cautioned the minister to deal with the issue carefully. In the House of Commons, Saskatoon Progressive John Evans expressed the disapproval of the ACC:

> *I should like to inform the minister that the whole Alpine Club of Canada is watching this application with jealous eyes. They believe there should be no interference with Spray river park such as would detract in any way from the attractive and pleasurable features which make these national parks so desirable as playgrounds for the people. I think the government should formulate a policy respecting the national parks so that no unfortunate precedent would be created for the future.*[104]

The minister stated it was an important issue that would not be dealt with hastily.[105] Meanwhile, intergovernmental negotiations over natural resource transfers continued.

As a good chess player and tactician, Arthur Wheeler read the board and knew when to change his game. In March 1925, Wheeler shifted direction and advised J.B. Harkin to withdraw territory from the park rather than risk setting a precedent for the commercial violation of the national parks. "I am in hopes that the franchise will not be given, but it is possible that the pressure may be too strong to overcome. Should it be decided to grant the franchise and withdraw the area from the Banff National Park, as I think would be wise to avoid the precedent, then, in such case also, a good road should be insisted upon in order to maintain access to the Assiniboine area."[106] His request for a road was likely pertinent for general access to the provincial park as well as to his walking tour business; as in the case of the 1922 Waterton debate, Wheeler was conscious of avoiding precedents for "commercial invasion" of the parks. He argued for a vision of parks based on the principle of inviolability, preserving the national parks unimpaired for present and future generations. In the end, Wheeler's idea to sacrifice some of Rocky Mountains Park for the sake of park inviolability was prescient.

Calgary Power's hydropower plans for the Rockies rekindled in 1928. The western economy was hitting a prosperous stride again with a boom in wheat sales. Urban and rural demand for power surged. Bolstered by opposition to dams in the national parks, from western cities as far away from the Rockies as Winnipeg, Saskatoon, and Vancouver, the Minister of the Interior refused to acquiesce to Calgary Power's pressure to allow a renewed proposal to dam the Spray Lakes. Harkin and the Parks Branch suspected as early as 1927 that the size of Rocky Mountains Park would ultimately have to be sacrificed to safeguard the principle of national park inviolability, as Wheeler had advised earlier.[107] Anticipating provincial demands for the excision of resource-rich areas from the national parks, the branch prepared for an alienation of lands. The 1929 R.W. Cautley Report suggested new boundaries for Rocky Mountains Park that included new territory around Malloch Mountain and Jasper National Park and excluded areas ripe for resource extraction, primarily the Spray Lakes, Kananaskis, Exshaw, and Canmore.[108]

In 1930 the natural resources transfer acts were decreed, along with the new National Parks Act. The new federal park legislation changed the name of Rocky Mountains Park to Banff National Park, formalized Banff's boundary changes, and enshrined the principle of national parks inviolability. The act stated specifically, "the Parks are hereby dedicated to the people of Canada for their benefit, education and enjoyment, subject to the provisions of this Act and Regulations, and such Parks shall be maintained and made use of so as to leave them unimpaired for the enjoyment of future generations."[109] The area of Rocky Mountains Park was reduced to 4,160 square miles (6,695 square kilometres).[110] Despite its Faustian quality, Harkin's boundary surgery proved effective in warding off immediate hydro-industrial encroachment on Banff National Park and placed the principle of inviolability firmly in legislation. In the long run, the principle of inviolability would prove to be a far more pragmatically defined concept than national parks supporters like the Alpine Club and the CNPA expected. Wheeler's tactical strategy for an alienation of lands to protect the core of the park ultimately played out in Harkin's hand.

▲ Following the 1920s dam conflicts, the ACC lost its federal funding. If it had friends in the Parks Branch, the ACC had also acquired enemies in Ottawa's higher corridors of power. In 1930 the federal Conservatives swept to power, led by the favourite son of Calgary capitalism, R.B. Bennett. Prime Minister Bennett was slow to forget the ACC's opposition to Calgary Power and purportedly had "no use for the Alpine Club."[111] To Bennett, the club was an impediment to corporations doing business in the Rockies, corporations in which he held substantial personal investments. Bennett was a friend of business, not of maverick conservationists who put obstacles in the path of "progress"; after he became prime minister, this reality was made clear to the ACC.

As a result of decreased government support (and the collegial network therein) and the downturn of the Depression, during the 1930s, the Alpine Club of Canada moved away from active national parks conservation advocacy toward a more narrowly defined focus on mountain recreation. The CNPA was now in place to take over the ACC's earlier role in political activism. As it looked ahead to expanding recreational tourism in the Rockies, the ACC seemed unaware that the forces of urbanization, commercial agriculture, industry, and technological change were inexorable and would return in other guises. In its own way, mass tourism would eventually jeopardize the inviolability of the public domain and park values, just as irrigation and dam projects had done in the 1920s and 1930s.

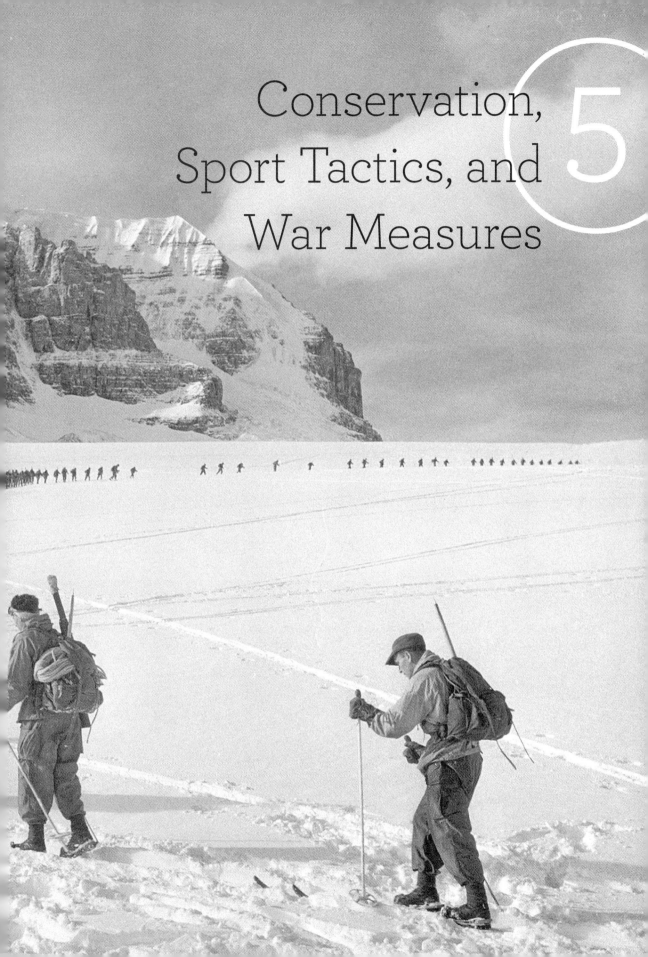

Conservation, Sport Tactics, and War Measures

...the park will not be a playground but a hive of industry in twenty or thirty years.

—*SASKATOON STAR PHOENIX*, August 20, 1930[1]

∧ *Led by John Brett, soldiers*
on a rope team walk up a
glacier using ice axes.
[LAC, e011061849]

LIKE MOUNTAINEERING, the world of conservation bridged beyond the Rockies and beyond borders. Arthur Wheeler made a winter visit to California in 1930, where he gave at least four talks related to the Canadian Rockies and ACC, including slide lectures to the Los Angeles Nature Club and the Sierra Club. His advocacy work for national parks continued on his return home; on May 31, 1930, only a day after the new National Parks Act passed into legislation in Ottawa, Selby Walker called Wheeler to discuss Canadian National Parks Association (CNPA) business. Wheeler swiftly set to drafting a letter to one of the club's prominent friends, the Honorable Randolph Bruce, Lieutenant Governor of British Columbia, with an invitation to join the membership of the CNPA. Bruce later paid a visit to the ACC summer camp on Maligne Lake and spoke at the campfire in Jasper on July 31, 1930, leaving Wheeler with a friendly "bottle of liquid gold" to remedy his cold when saying goodbye the next day.[2] A diplomatic touch allied wide advocacy networks.

The National Parks Act was Ottawa's response to calls to protect the public domain, and it strengthened the principle of inviolability in national parks legislation. Under the new legislation, several changes were highlighted: national park lands could be created or amended only by an act

155

of Parliament, wildlife was fully protected, and commercial mining and logging were to be phased out.[3] Although the national parks were better protected under this act, resolution came at the expense of alienating sizable tracts of park lands. Realistically, this resolution to resource-use conflicts was only one of the many tradeoffs that would continue to trouble Canada's national parks administration. Calgary Power's foothold in Banff National Park opened the way to future disputes over utilities, later seen in the ongoing case of the Lake Minnewanka dam project during the Second World War and the enduring TransAlta utilities right of way through Banff National Park that later resulted.[4]

Cuts to its federal grant under Prime Minister R.B. Bennett and a sharp decline in membership affected the ACC through the Depression years. After 1930 the ACC took its last stand to safeguard Lake Minnewanka, but its expanding emphasis on sport and infrastructure gradually eclipsed park inviolability as top priority. It receded from active conservation advocacy and refocused on a diverse sport and recreation agenda as it struggled for financial stability in hard times. Wartime posed new challenges: the landscapes of Canada's mountain national parks were redrawn for troop training, and the club's camps were converted to military duty. While the ACC redefined itself in terms of nationalistic military service in the 1940s, camps led by women and older men perpetuated civilian club traditions through times of upheaval. Mountaineering reproduced sites of sport in national parks as militarized areas in the 1940s—cultural landscapes that were later erased in peacetime and rewritten as holiday destinations occupied by Canada's postwar tourism economy.

Flooding Lake Minnewanka
The ACC's Last Stand against the Dam

The 1930 National Parks Act legislated that Canada's national parks were inviolable public domains to remain unimpaired for future generations, but the fight against hydro development and "commercial invasion" in the parks was far from over. The major challenge to the act came when Calgary Power wished to gain approval for its dam project on Lake Minnewanka in 1930. As the ACC and the CNPA discovered, inviolability was a principle subject to pragmatic definition. The ensuing fight for inviolability would prove to be the ACC's last for quite some time.

On December 19, 1929, Calgary Power resumed its campaign to gain approval of the Lake Minnewanka dam project just as its Ghost River power plant construction wound down. Since 1926 Calgary's power load had surged from 12,000 to 20,000 kilowatts. Just west of the Ghost River system, within the Banff National Park boundaries, Lake Minnewanka had long been a source of debate between those who sought to preserve it and those who wished to use it to produce hydropower on the Bow River. Federal parks officials saw the suggestion to excise Minnewanka from Banff National Park as an opportunistic propaganda campaign that took advantage of the worsening unemployment crisis of the early Depression.[5] The ACC, meanwhile, decried it as an assault on the new Banff National Park boundaries as determined by the National Parks Act. At the annual ACC summer camp in 1930, the membership passed a resolution led by Andrew Sibbald, protesting the Minnewanka dam proposal and any further reduction in national park lands, particularly petitioning the federal government not to take Lake Minnewanka out of Banff National Park.[6]

The resolution pointed out that the park boundaries had been revised as recently as 1929; the vicinity of Banff townsite was "the most congested Tourist district in the Park" and required more, not fewer, tourist facilities; and park conditions and public safety could be impaired near Banff town if Park authorities lost control over fire suppression, forestry, and game protection in the Minnewanka area. The resolution also suggested that there were means of "dealing with unemployment other than cutting down our Park areas," and that tourism statistics showed "the growing appreciation of thousands of people of the Canadian Rockies, and of the National Parks," which ought to have been Parliament's key priority, overriding "private interests and private applications."[7]

At the same ACC summer camp, the CNPA held an annual general meeting and also condemned the Minnewanka dam proposal in a resolution made available to all Members of Parliament. By 1930 the CNPA claimed to represent sixty other associations, clubs, and organizations representing 205,000 people across Canada. When representing the CNPA's stand on Minnewanka to the press on August 22, A.O. Wheeler recommended developing waste gas and coal as a superior means of economic diversification that would create year-round employment as illustrated in Europe.[8] Like the ACC, the CNPA argued that parks were "the property of all the people and belonged as much to Saskatchewan as to Alberta." In fact, ACC and CNPA leaders were closely integrated in lawyers H.E. Sampson and Andrew Sibbald.[9]

On August 20, 1930, the *Saskatoon Star Phoenix* published the ACC's resolution against removing Lake Minnewanka from Banff National Park, and sided with the club's stand against monopolistic power developments in the nation's parks: "There is only one way to preserve a national park from destruction, and that is to make a rigid rule for its protection and admit no exceptions whatever regardless of the exigencies. Several bites have already been taken out of the Banff park. If another bite is to be allowed every time a power company so desires, the park will not be a playground but a hive of industry in twenty or thirty years."[10] The article also suggested that Calgary Power was selling only "a fraction" of the energy it was producing, and it speculated that additional power would be sold to the American market if the dam went ahead.

Soon afterward, an editorial in the pro-irrigation farmers' newspaper the *Calgary Albertan* accused the ACC and the *Saskatoon Star Phoenix* of "Making Themselves Ridiculous" and showing an "appalling ignorance" when they revived "time-worn phrases as to the sanctity of the national public parks and other such platitudinous parallels." The paper suggested that Minnewanka had to be dammed. Because there was already a dam in place, the lake would not be spoiled and need not be removed from the park. The editorial condemned the ACC: "By their interference in this matter the Alpine Club, in the eyes of those who know the facts, has put itself into a perfectly ridiculous position. It has plunged into the affairs of Calgary and the district in a totally unjustifiable manner; it has made itself the butt of scorn and derision that will hang to it for years to come."[11] Furthermore, it decreed the *Star Phoenix*'s apprehensions about degrading the lake and power exports to the United States baseless and ridiculed the very idea of coal and gas power development. The *Calgary Albertan* also rebuked the Saskatoon paper for intervening in national park issues in Calgary's backyard: "Minnewanka is one of our chief resorts; it is a favored fishing ground for anglers, campers, [and] summer dwellers. We are far more interested in its reservation both in an aesthetic and practical sense than are the dwellers in the city on the South Saskatchewan. Calgary supports this scheme because, while not marring the lake, it will give an added security to our power supply and remove us from the fear of such a shortage as overtook Vancouver within the past two years."[12]

Interference in local Alberta affairs was, according to the *Calgary Albertan*, a transgression. The editorial provoked a vehement regionalist attempt to discredit conservation concerns about national parks by dismissing other Canadians as meddling outsiders when they raised critical concerns, even though CNPA leader Selby Walker and others were Calgarians.

The ACC responded quickly to this stinging attack. Within days, a delegation of Calgary Section members visited the offices of the *Calgary Albertan* to set the record straight by insisting that it was a serious alpine organization founded on broad-reaching aims related to Canadian alpinism and mountain heritage. The newspaper subsequently published the objectives from the club's formal constitution and clarified that the ACC had a wide mandate well beyond the Minnewanka issue. The newspaper also devoted another editorial to the Minnewanka question clarifying that the CNPA's resolution on the Minnewanka dam had been misconstrued as the ACC's resolution, a fact brought to their attention by then honorary treasurer Andrew Sibbald.[13] Of course, initially, the two bodies had met at the same time and place, shared many of the same members and executives, and exercised a similar style of conservation advocacy. However, for the first time, it seems the ACC did not wish to be connected too closely with the resolutions of its conservation offshoot, the CNPA, particularly if the ACC's authority as a national alpine club was put at jeopardy.

The CNPA had no such qualms. Selby Walker, CNPA executive secretary, did not let the *Calgary Albertan*'s biting criticism go unchallenged, retorting that the CNPA hoped many other clubs and newspapers would also "make themselves ridiculous" by standing up against monopolistic power development in the national parks, as he wrote in the local Banff *Crag and Canyon:* "Canada's natural resources have been exploited long enough for the enrichment of the few. It is high time they were developed for the best interests of the people." Walker argued that Calgary Power was not committed to an integrated Canadian energy policy or employment strategy. Walker stressed the importance of "agitating for an adequate parks system for Canada" while it could still be "procured free of cost and unspoiled."[14] In contrast to its parent organization, the CNPA put its strength into polemic arguments in resource-use debates stemming from national park issues.

Meanwhile, Calgary Power's formal application with the federal Department of Mines and Resources to proceed with the dam, filed on September 16, 1930, was set aside without action, and the company gave up its demands.[15] For the next decade, the Minnewanka scheme lay dormant. The company may have speculated that the Minnewanka application would gain momentum as layoffs at its Ghost River hydro location approached and the Spray Lakes were excised from the park as part of the 1930 natural resources transfers. If it failed to get through this window of opportunity, the company could afford to bide its time until its next chance to push Minnewanka ahead. That time would not come until the 1940s. The Depression would lower demand as Canada faced a power surplus, and the expense of the company's Ghost River location plunged it into the red at the outset of the crash.[16]

By the time Calgary Power was ready to push again for the dam on Minnewanka, the Second World War had begun and the ACC had changed its mandate. In October 1940, based on wartime exigency and the need to power the Alberta Nitrogen Company of Calgary operating under the British-Canadian Explosives Programme, Calgary Power applied for the authority to expand the Minnewanka hydro system under the War Measures Act. The federal emergency powers granted under the act provided a unique opportunity to override any law, including parks legislation. The dam was approved, supported by Munitions and Supply Minister C.D. Howe. Calgary Power's engineers diverted the Ghost River, constructed a new dam, raised the lake level by approximately 65 feet (19.8 metres), flooded the community at Minnewanka Landing, and, by 1942, had transformed the contour lines of the shores around the lake.[17] As a result, Minnewanka's depth sounded over 300 feet (91.4 metres); the reservoir was now the deepest lake in Banff National Park. Other than scrutinizing landscaping procedures, the Lands, Parks and Forests Branch was left without recourse for this serious infraction of national parks legislation. The Alberta Nitrogen Plant in southeast Calgary, meanwhile, consumed as much power as the entire city of Calgary, while producing anhydrous ammonia for explosives during the Second World War.[18]

The CNPA vehemently opposed the 1940 Minnewanka proposal, but the ACC failed to rise to the issue in either its gazette or journal. By this time, the ACC's prime mover in the 1920s and 1930s conservation debates had retired. A.O. Wheeler was in his eighties and no longer able to lead a fight against Calgary Power. Such a protest was perhaps also secondary to Wheeler's respect for Canadian patriotism and the wartime demands of British imperialism, as were most of the patriotic nationals among the ACC membership. In his 1940 address to the ACC, Wheeler admitted his mind was "totally preoccupied with the European situation" and freely emphasized his sympathy for the "British Empire in her fight for existence to maintain Christianity, civilization and freedom...against barbaric, inhuman hordes that seek to dominate the world."[19] Put into this context, the lake was one of many necessary sacrifices to wartime. Moreover, Wheeler's ally in the Parks Branch, Commissioner J.B. Harkin,

The CNPA's Fight for Minnewanka in 1940

EVEN THOUGH THE ACC WITHDREW from the hydro development debate in 1940 to concentrate on its mountaineering agenda, the Canadian National Parks Association entered the fray. Selby Walker's letters to western newspapers and federal officials in 1940 argued that Calgary Power should use Alberta's coal, oil, and natural gas reserves to generate power, rather than desecrate the national parks under the guise of wartime urgency.[20] (Calgary Power was controlled by the Montreal Engineering Company.) By April 1941, alienated by the ongoing conflicts over Minnewanka, Walker implied that Calgary Power was wringing natural resources out of the West, asking "how long must this suicidal exploitation of the natural resources of Western Canada for the benefit of the eastern capitalists and the votes of the eastern majority be carried on?"[21] His rhetorical question overlooked the fact that westerners were not exonerated from environmental responsibility. Many local Alberta interests had sided with the dam by 1940. Forces such as the Banff Town Advisory Council, the Calgary Board of Trade, *The Albertan* newspaper, and Member of Parliament for Calgary-West Manley Edwards all supported the dam.[22] In the case of the ACC, by fading out of active conservation advocacy during the recurrent hydro dilemmas, the western-based club had conceded the fight for the public domain.

had retired in 1936 at the age of sixty-one and was no longer active in national parks policy. The closely knit collegial network that had existed between Wheeler and Harkin no longer bonded the relationship between the club and the national parks administration in Ottawa when it came to conservation advocacy.

While the Minnewanka issue cooled down through the 1930s, the ACC had turned attention to promoting outdoor recreation and tourism, embracing the development of roads through the mountain parks. Despite the two organizations' hostile reaction toward hydro development in the 1920s, the CNPA and the ACC encouraged the trend toward commercial tourism in Canada's national parks. Additionally, the ACC may have remained silent on the Minnewanka project because the worldly politics of conservation advocacy were fraught with tension. Throughout the Depression, careful business management and a focus on sport prevailed after the club's finances were undermined by Bennett's new government as a result of the ACC's previous conservation actions.

Crunching Numbers
Taking Stock of Club Operations, Goals, and Membership

Economic decline brought on by the Great Depression, and economic upbraiding from the federal government, caused the ACC to rethink its organizational direction. The club had a predominantly western Canadian membership hit by a severe drop in personal disposable income. Falling membership combined with the end of federal grant funding affected many issues of club administration. Consequently, the ACC deliberately re-evaluated its function and the size of its membership to ensure the club's survival through hard and changing times.

Austerity policies under the Conservative government of Prime Minister R.B. Bennett shook the club's financial structure. As a regular recipient of an annual $1,000 federal grant from the Parks Branch since 1906, the ACC's finances were destabilized by the cancellation of funding in 1931. The grant from Ottawa had composed roughly 10 per cent of the club's annual income and half the cost of publishing the *CAJ*. In addressing the membership about the cancelled grant, President Herbert E. Sampson at first was hopeful that the grant could be reinstated the following year,[23] and that perhaps "influence brought to bear upon the Minister of the Interior," T.G. Murphy, would ensure the grant was reinstated that year.[24] However, efforts to smooth the grant back into place were unsuccessful.

The timing of the grant's cancellation coincided with R.B. Bennett's rise to power in Ottawa in 1930 and followed hard on the heels of ACC interventions against Calgary Power in hydro-development controversies in the Rockies. Funding allocated to the Department of the Interior for loans, subsidies, and grants actually increased from $134,255.75 in fiscal 1928 to $158,708.41 in 1931. While the ACC totally lost its grant, less than 1 per cent of the total 1928 grant budget, organizations such as the Canadian Forestry Association and the Dominion Land Surveyors' Association continued to receive funding.[25] It appears that the ACC was a specific target of funding cutbacks. Some club members, such as Secretary Mitchell, held that Bennett was penalizing the ACC for its political activism: "Mr. Bennett has told many people I believe that he has no use for the Alpine Club. We opposed the Calgary Power Co. in which he was and may still be interested."[26]

Bennett's alleged antagonism put the club's activism in a new light. The inviolability of the national parks was a divisive public-policy issue. Defending the parks from "commercial invasion" levied serious consequences on the ACC as a voluntary organization, relying in part on federal grants, when it contended against politically well-connected big-business and partisan interests. Bennett held a long-standing animosity toward ACC ally J.B. Harkin and the Parks Branch, following conflicts over national park boundaries and local issues while he was the Conservative Member of Parliament for the Banff region prior to 1917.[27]

The loss of federal grant funding combined with the deepening effects of economic depression caused the ACC to take stock of its position. In 1933 ACC President A.A. McCoubrey's annual address to the club focused on adapting to changing economic circumstances. Due to its astute management and loyal members, the ACC was reported to be surviving better than many clubs.[28] Still, as early as 1928, many loyal ACC members had to drop out as they found they could no longer afford their annual club fees, while the earliest older members began to pass away.[29] Despite efforts to economize, membership revenues declined as the club roster plummeted nearly 22 per cent during the 1930s, dropping from 652 to 510 members.[30] General belt-tightening measures—economizing on club publications, office operations, mailing, and camp costs—were introduced to streamline the club's operational budget.[31] However, careful economy ensured that the annual summer camps ran in the black (if with diminished profits) even during the worst years of the Depression.[32]

The ACC camp planners scaled down to plan for only seventy registrants in 1933 and consolidated the camp at a single accessible site in Paradise Valley, driving a hard bargain with outfitters, and came out $148 ahead. President Alexander McCoubrey noted, "Mr. Wheeler's thought was to have a large camp at O'Hara in addition to the Paradise Valley camp but this would nullify any thought of economy as well as hurt the Paradise camp."[33] By contrast, the Mount Assiniboine Camp in 1935 demonstrated calculated risk-taking. Higher costs related to a remote campsite raised expenditures to $6,030, more than double the norm, but a prime backcountry destination returned a $1,071 profit, with an exceptional turnout of 250 registrants due to an innovative business decision to accommodate the Skyline Hikers club at the ACC camp; 141 ACC members and 109 Skyline Hikers attended.[34] The size of this camp, set up in an alpine meadow on the shores of Lake Magog, led packer and cook Ken Jones to comment "you would never have known that there was a Depression."[35]

The Depression and loss of federal grants not only moved the ACC to take stock of operations but also to reconsider the club's goals, which in turn affected membership. President McCoubrey drew attention to two opposing lines of thought in 1933 on the issue of the club's future. He recounted that Arthur Wheeler had stated in 1911 that the ACC was a "mountain climbing organization" with educational, scientific, literary, and artistic goals, and "not a climbing club" strictly committed to sport, a distinction made clear in the objectives first listed in the ACC constitution. Younger members, along with a few old-timers, were critical of this assumption and preferred to implement more demanding climbing standards to promote a narrowly focused membership composed of athletic climbers keen on sport. Other members favoured a larger membership that admitted a wider range of climbers, hikers, trekkers, skiers, and mountain enthusiasts, in the general style of the Swiss and French alpine clubs, embracing wide membership and benefitting from extensive alpine hut systems. A larger membership, they argued, put more funds at the ACC's disposal for "alpine projects, including huts which are of assistance to those to whom climbing per se is the beginning and end of membership in a mountaineering club," and expensive expeditions, such as the 1925 trip to Mount Logan.[36]

McCoubrey invited the membership to express its views on the matter to the executive as part of the club's adaptation to economic and demographic change, concluding that "which viewpoint the Alpine Club of Canada will adopt in the future, is a matter for you, ladies and gentlemen, to settle."[37] A broad-based approach to membership in mountain recreation and sport ultimately prevailed, as is evidenced by the ACC's subsequent omnibus direction that left the doors open to as many members as possible.

At the same time that this internal debate ensued, greater emphasis was placed on the responsibility of local ACC sections to ensure that new recruits were trained and brought up to the class of active graduating membership according to the national club's standards for qualification. Membership in the club was categorized by several standards and fee rates, most notably active members, newly certified graduates, and subscribing members who received the club journal. Subscribing memberships, which were predominantly concentrated in British Columbia, had become a point of contention to the national club executive as revenues dwindled due to a drop in active membership fees. National club Secretary Stanley Mitchell was annoyed that some active climbers tried to get a cut rate by taking out subscribing memberships, saying, "this class was instituted for elderly and weakly people who were physically incapable of taking active part in the work of the Club."[38] President Moffat agreed. It is notable, however, that British Columbia sections also tended to allow participants without active ACC memberships to attend regional outings. Because they permitted greater flexibility, the British Columbia sections opened the door to more participants and did not suffer the loss of club enrolment common in the club's prairie sections at the time; in fact, the number and proportion of memberships west of the Rockies grew in 1930 compared to pre-Depression enrolments. Other income, age, and regional considerations may also have figured in the situation, given that British Columbia offered many local opportunities for mountaineering, apart from the ACC's annual summer camps, and that the British Columbia Mountaineering Club (BCMC) and varsity clubs in Vancouver were other venues for the regional climbing community. In this way, local sections and members could sometimes bend the rules to find openings to express their own agendas. The existence of the national club relied on its local sections.

Despite British Columbia's success, a resolution to encourage club sections to bring local members up to national standards of active membership was passed at the 1933 annual general meeting. The development of mountaineering skills through local climbing activities could not be neglected. As F.V. Longstaff of Victoria and C.A. Richardson of Calgary suggested, "it is up to each of us to try to do something extra, even at a sacrifice to ourselves. We must try to bring forward graduating

Local Sections and Club Vitality During the Depression

THE ECONOMIC DOWNTURN brought on by the Depression tested the vitality of the local ACC sections. Some sections simply fizzled out as problems related to leadership and membership were exacerbated by economic pressures. Sections could not operate without committed volunteers. As early as 1929, signs of weakness had started showing in the Toronto Section, and it was disbanded after 1935 due to lack of leadership, bringing a lull to ACC activity in Canada east of Manitoba.[39] Farther west, in 1930, the club scrambled to find someone willing to accept the chair of the Winnipeg Section after A.A. McCoubrey stepped down; during the interim between chairmen, the section was managed by a committee of young professional women, including teachers Margaret Fleming and Marjorie Macleod, and librarian Edna Greer.[40] Following the death of A.L. Mumm in 1928 and the demise of other Victorian leaders, the British Section of the ACC also went into decline. However, club sections in the United States did not fold. In fact, through the 1930s roughly a third of all

∧ *Dr. Cora Best (far right) and her gang from the Minneapolis Section at Lake of the Hanging Glacier Camp, 1928. A.W. Drinnan album. [WMCR, V14/AC192P/8]*

ACC members lived in the United States, and most of them were American citizens from urban areas. However, the Minneapolis Section membership faltered somewhat through the crisis years.[41]

Throughout the Depression, western Canada remained the heartland of the ACC. Alberta and British Columbia members together formed approximately 43 per cent of the club's total population in 1930 and almost 42 per cent in 1939. People living in these two provinces were geographically well situated to participate in mountain sport, and so, unlike most of Canada's national amateur sporting organizations, notably the Amateur Athletic Union of Canada, the Women's Amateur Athletic Federation, and the Canadian Intercollegiate Athletic Union, the ACC regional stronghold was strongly based in the western provinces.[42]

members who have been hardened up to a considerable extent through Section activities."[43] The resolution was closely tied to club finances and increasing the size of the membership, but one must bear in mind that the number of active members was at a standstill and skill development among beginners and the club climbing program would stall if the sections did not actively pursue the training essential to fulfilling the club's greater goals. Honorary Treasurer Andrew Sibbald, a lawyer from Saskatoon, threw his support behind it: "I think this Resolution is important...I am becoming a little concerned about our financial condition. If we can increase our membership 50% the financial problem of the Club would be automatically met."[44] The bottom line of club size was revenue.

To make matters worse, many members were slow to pay their club fees during the Depression. The club's annual fee for active and graduating members residing in North America was $7.50. Fred Lambart, the assistant leader of the club's 1925 Mount Logan expedition, for example, found it difficult to pay his fees when he was laid off from work as a federal surveyor with the Department of the Interior in 1933. However, McCoubrey decided to continue Lambart's journal subscription in recognition of "invaluable service to the club" and vouched to the club secretary that "as soon as he is on his feet he will pay up."[45] The total ACC dues charged in 1933 amounted to $3,285 but actual cash receipts from membership fees totalled only $2,551.50, resulting in a shortfall. The ACC's 1933 gross income totalled $10,109.95, but the club's main source of income, membership dues and entrance fees, had declined from 1931 to 1933, as 54 members had fallen off from a combined total of 526 active, graduating, and subscribing members in 1931 to 472 in 1933, amounting to a $330 decrease in potential annual gross income. A critical phase of this crisis mounted in 1933 to 1934. The annual auditor's report for 1933 recommended that the Banff clubhouse and annual camp "must" become self-supporting, considering the club's diminished membership revenues, and emphasized that the general operating expenses would have to be budgeted within the income from 1934 membership revenues.[46]

By the close of 1934, the club's finances showed considerable improvement over the preceding year but still drew attention to the declining membership base. The club's 1934 surplus of $1,168.71, compared to a 1933 deficit of $737.09, was achieved due to increased income from camp and clubhouse operations, and the executive's decision to collapse the publication of the 1933 and 1934 *Canadian Alpine Journal* into one issue rather than two. Revenues generated from the camp and clubhouse added credence to arguments in favour of a large membership.

Club properties involved expense but could also produce a revenue stream, and a small $391.20 profit from the 1934 camp helped, as did $800 realized from bonds. Skipping an issue of the annual journal, typically worth $2,000, also saved some money. Still, the auditor reported a slide in membership revenues, noting the loss of 70 more members, which reduced the club to only 402 in 1934.[47]

Club executives were acutely aware of the eroding membership base.[48] Consequently, Sibbald, who moved from the position of honorary treasurer to national president in 1934, redoubled his efforts to increase the club's membership and called for "a little missionary work by each member" to increase membership or at least conserve "our membership and hav[e] them indulge in paying their fees each year."[49] Aware of the bottom line, Sibbald argued that the annual camps like 1935 at Mount Assiniboine could attract more people.[50] He recommended each section and all members make contacts with other organizations interested in sport, adventure, travel, and exploration to "acquaint [them] with what we have to offer." He suggested making wider contacts by broadening the interests of the club to geology, botany, and whatever types of field research could be carried out at camp. And, in an unusual departure, Sibbald proposed youth members be recruited and admitted to the camps, which had until then been reserved for adults: "In a general way it has been considered before, and to a certain extent perhaps frowned upon...it is to the younger people that we have to look primarily for our recruits."[51]

In 1936 the club's nominating committee asked Andrew Sibbald to stand for a second two-year term as the ACC national president. Born in Owen Sound, Ontario, in 1888, Sibbald practiced law in Saskatoon, where he also lectured in the city's Faculty of Law. Herbert E. Sampson—a fellow Saskatoon lawyer—introduced him to the club, and he became a regular at annual camps beginning in 1917 with his graduating climb. As a boy he was injured in a farm accident, but he found that mountain exercise allowed him to "overcome the handicap of extreme lameness" that affected his walking to "become both a competent and safe climber and one of the Club's most dependable leaders." Members of the club recognized his perceptive judgement and "quick wit in good natured banter."[52]

Sibbald emphasized that expanding ACC membership would be the cornerstone of his re-election agenda in 1936, noting, "I would feel it to be my chief work for the Club during the next two years to put the membership on a much broader basis."[53] One of the results of Sibbald's policies was that the 1937 Yoho Camp officially admitted youth campers for the first time, although candidates for club membership were still required to be at least eighteen years old.[54]

The club's financial status had stabilized by the end of 1937, but Honorary Treasurer R.J. Cuthbertson noted that the ACC was still "handicapped" by the lack of the federal grant. Cuthbertson had conducted an ongoing lobby with Ottawa parks officials since 1934 to have the $1,000 grant to the ACC renewed, reiterating the rationale that the club brought a "desirable class of tourists" to Canada and opened up "new territories in the National Parks...in the mountains." J.B. Harkin supported the ACC requests and argued to his assistant deputy minister in 1935 that an annual grant was "a good business investment" because the club's promotion of the national parks had "greater publicity value than paid advertising."[55] Harkin's was an early variation on marketing and branding. However, the government continued to withhold funding.

Despite the continued lack of federal funding, however, the 1938 audit at the end of Sibbald's second term as president revealed a "very satisfactory financial condition" and a small membership gain from 501 in March 1937 to 521 by December 1938.[56] Careful management yielded modest gains toward recovery. Sibbald's initiative had nearly restored the membership total to the 1931 level.

Arthur Wheeler credited Sibbald in 1934 for doing "much to keep the Club solvent and progressive during the hard times that have depressed everyone more or less."[57] In 1938 the incoming club president, Cyril G. Wates, observed, "Mr. Sibbald took over the leadership at a very critical time. The depression had seriously depleted our membership roll; from the same cause, our finances were at low ebb, and there were pessimists who believed that it would be impossible for the Club to carry on all its activities."[58] Throughout the economic crunch, one of the most valuable assets to the club proved to be national leaders like Sibbald, accountant Walter Read, and banker R.J. Cuthbertson, all careful business managers and competent organization men.

Managing the books, membership, and logistics shored up the club's other goals and emergent aspirations for year-round mountain sports and recreation. Time and club resources shifted toward these directions during the 1930s and beyond.

Skiing, Rock Climbing, and Mountain Huts
The Recession Brings a Focus on Sport

As the club retrenched and re-envisioned itself for financial survival, it moved away from active conservation advocacy and park protection, focusing on seeing Canada's national parks primarily as public spaces for recreation use and sport tourism, particularly in the context of operating annual club camps and mountaineering trips. Meanwhile, changing tourism patterns and a lack of public funding for operations and maintenance led to overall slowdowns in the mountain national parks.[59] In Banff National Park, visitation fell 20 per cent from 236,801 in 1928–29 to 188,443 in 1930–31; although it retained the highest total visitation rate among national parks in Canada.[60] Bird watching, swimming, hiking, and camping were relatively inexpensive outdoor recreations when pursued near home; travelling across Canada to an ACC mountaineering camp in the Rockies involved a substantially larger expense.

Prime Minister W.L. Mackenzie King's government, elected in 1935, invested in national parks spending as one of the first cautious attempts to bring Canada out of the Depression. Capital projects worth $7.84 million were initiated in national parks as federal unemployment relief works to build roads, highways, buildings, and campgrounds. In the large western parks, this infrastructure development provided for greater access and recreation in the mountains. The construction of the first road between Banff and Jasper and a highway from Golden to Revelstoke, under the direction of the national parks Engineering Service, proved pivotal to public access.[61] Through the 1930s, the ACC did not speak out against development and resist these trends. It, too, was subject to constraints of suppressed means and growing recreational desires. The club drove hard toward a strong sport and recreation agenda.

Climbing in Europe underwent a metamorphosis in the 1920s and 1930s. Vertical ascents by German, Austrian, Italian, French, and eastern European climbers made startling innovations. Engineering difficult routes with the assistance of artificial aids was a new trend termed "technical climbing." It became popular among climbers bent on solving the last of the great problems posed by the Alps. The icy north faces of the Matterhorn, the Grandes Jorasses, and the Eiger were subject to daring first ascents in the 1930s undertaken by Germans and Austrians. While gentlemen among mountaineers trained in the classic British school of mountaineering ethics saw the use of carabiners, pitons, and other aids as an unsporting assault on impossible mountain routes, the death-or-glory approach of the Munich school and certain Italians active in the Dolomites and western Alps devised technical climbing as a new standard of achievement.

The sport of climbing had predominantly middle- and upper-class origins, but increasing numbers of the working class began walking and climbing for recreation in the hills of Britain and Europe following the First World War, leading to a new spirit of competition and higher standards of climbing difficulty. Rock climbing, which British alpinists had considered a second-rate gymnastic compared to classic mountaineering, gained new adherents among working-class climbers in the United Kingdom, such as men in the Glasgow climbing clubs. The existence of working-class climbers indicated a dramatic social shift, although they remained a minority next to the "university men" of The Alpine Club (London). In France, meanwhile, men and women of the French Groupe de Haute Montagne (GHM), formed after the First World War, created their own stylized aesthetic of elegant free climbing, without aids.[62]

It was at this time that climbers began to seek new challenges around the globe. Nations contended to lay claims to specific high-altitude mountains drawn within the postwar sphere of colonial politics circulating around sport achievement. Britain's Alpine Club and the Royal Geographical Society launched a series of expeditions to reach Everest during the 1920s, siphoning off much of its mountaineering talent and energy to the Himalayan enclave of the British Empire. Similarly, German climbers pursued Nanga Parbat.[63] The international climbing fraternity was also attracted to the Caucasus Range, the Andes, Norway, New Zealand, Africa, and the many North American ranges.

Between the wars in Canada and the United States, climbing was evolving in two main directions. First, great unclaimed alpine ascents were still possible in remote places, demonstrated by the first ascents of Mounts Logan (1925) and Steele (1935) in the Yukon, Mount Waddington in British Columbia (1936), Mounts Bona (1930) and Fairweather (1931) in Alaska, and the first aircraft-assisted climbs on Alaska's Mount McKinley (1930s).[64] Second, rock-climbing schools emerged, influenced by the development of technical climbing in Europe and modified for the demands of unique rock formations such as Yosemite's expansive granite walls in the California Sierra Nevada and the Devil's Tower in Wyoming. The Yosemite Valley became a centre for technical climbing following the Second World War, and the techniques pioneered there circled back to Europe.[65] During this era, climbing was an international arena of contested concepts, techniques, and practitioners.

The ACC, however, was not at this time in sync with international trends that veered toward technical climbing. Although it is frequently asserted that the club lagged behind international trends and stagnated in its development toward technical climbing, one could also say that while the club's manifestations of sport did not trend toward technical climbing they did change and were practiced in various ways concurrently. The culture of Canada's national alpine club was keen on classic alpine ascents, the ethics of first ascents, new route variations, and seeking out wild country, all still possible in Canada's far-reaching mountain ranges and remote lands. Adaptations associated with amateur guiding, winter sports, and backcountry huts emerged as the club's new sport and recreation agenda. The annual club camps reinscribed the dominant style and ethics of classic alpine ascents on mixed rock and snow. The *Canadian Alpine Journal* was a site where mountain sport and new ideas were discussed.

A trend toward amateur mountain guiding at the annual summer camps grew stronger in the ACC through the 1930s. Corporate cutbacks within the CPR and CNR reduced the number of professional mountain guides available for the club camps conducted in the national parks served by their lines. Swiss guides employed by the CPR, for example, had been cut to only three, all of whom were assigned to work, at the railway's expense, at the 1933 club camp in Paradise Valley. No mountain guides were retained by the CNR in 1934 due to a "measure of economy."[66] Alpine club executives worried that a shortage of "good guides" at camp might "cripple [their] climbing activities." To fill the gap, skilled climbers in the club were asked to volunteer service as amateur guides. Club executives called on experienced leaders to guide climbing parties during the 1934 camp, and, notably, Alex Dalgleish, Bill

Cleveland, Rex Gibson, Roger Neave, and Lawrence Grassi stepped up to assist.[67] Grassi was well known to refuse any payment from the club, in money or in kind, for guiding other climbers.[68]

These and other volunteers were committed to activating mountaineering by leading the ropes on the organized group ascents typical of ACC camps. In later reviewing the 1934 Chrome Lake Camp held in Jasper National Park, R.J. Cuthbertson from Saskatoon observed "contrary to the usual practice of the Club, guiding was done entirely by volunteer guides and on frequent occasions 95% of the membership were out of Camp."[69] Competent amateur guides willing to lead parties made possible a safe, active, climbing program that could instruct novice mountaineers; their work also reinforced alpine ascents with guided rope teams on peaks in the mountain parks as the dominant form and style of climbing at the national gatherings. They also played a direct role in encouraging the active memberships that were vital to the club's economic recovery during the worst of its revenue crisis—making a guided graduating climb was essential to qualifying new recruits as active members.

As ACC members gained their active memberships, they were able to read about international rock-climbing trends in the club's national mountaineering journal, even as classic alpine ascents remained the dominant form of sport in the club. "Modern Rock Climbing Equipment" in the 1932 *Canadian Alpine Journal* was written by American Robert L.H. Underhill, a Harvard philosophy professor in the Appalachian Mountain Club who was married to the famed Miriam O'Brien of the same club. Underhill experimented with new techniques in the Alps and American West, arguing that disparaging technical climbing as a "questionable mountaineering form" was outdated as climbers in Austrian Kaisergebirge and the Dolomites ensured "the piton has become a cornerstone of advanced technique, now looked upon as no more artificial than the ice-axe."[70] Hardware and aids—ring pitons, eye pitons, carabiners, snap-rings, piton hammers, and rock climbing shoes—were discussed with reference to practices in Europe and North America. Underhill's article challenged the assumptions asserted by an older British mountaineering ethic expressed by Stanley Mitchell to the club camp in 1937: "May this club never degenerate to the methods of what has been called 'The Hammer and Nail Co., Ltd.' Success won by skill, knowledge, and judgement is the only kind worth winning."[71] However, while dominant practices in ACC physical culture did not move toward technical climbing, some members did. Various club sections practiced

> ∧ Development of the piton (1), ring-piton (2), and eye-pitons (3) pioneered in Austria's Kaisergebirge and the Dolomites, shown in the 1932 Canadian Alpine Journal.

> Rock-climbing hardware illustrates carabiners or "snap-rings" (4), piton hammers (5), and piton catcher (6) in the 1932 Canadian Alpine Journal.

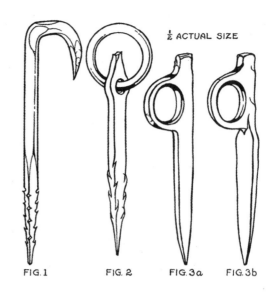

½ ACTUAL SIZE

FIG. 1   FIG. 2   FIG. 3a   FIG. 3b

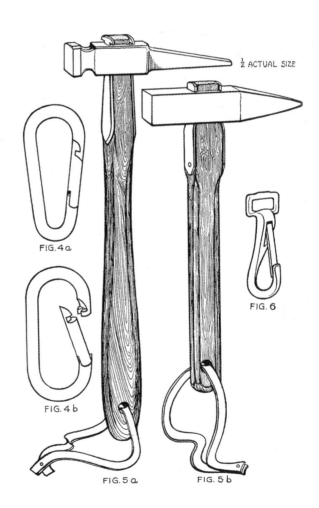

½ ACTUAL SIZE

FIG. 4a

FIG. 4b

FIG. 5a   FIG. 5b

FIG. 6

∧ Skiers tour across a lake during ACC ski camp in Jasper National Park, c. 1935. [EA-41-107]

rock climbing, often near home. In Manitoba, the steep walls of the Gunton dolomite quarries north of Winnipeg served as a training ground in the 1920s and 1930s for later climbs in the Rockies and Purcells.[72] On the West Coast, climbers such as Emmie Brooks were noted for their rock-climbing ability; she climbed in the Dolomites in 1949.[73]

The ACC also discussed ice climbing, the ascension of frozen water-falls, and skiing. In 1932 the *Canadian Alpine Journal* committed nineteen pages to debate on recent developments in equipment for winter sport. Another Underhill article presented a sophisticated under-standing of the relative design merits of crampons, crampon bindings, ice axes, ice-axe slings, ice pitons, boot nails, tent sacks, and the practical applications of this equipment in Europe and North America.[74] Skiing drew many ACC adherents beginning in the 1920s. The first ever ski-mountaineering guidebook, written by Sir Arnold Lund and published in 1920, signalled an emerging trend in the Alps.[75] During the same era, ACC members looked to the Canadian winter as a new frontier of recrea-tion and embarked on ski touring and ski mountaineering, particularly

∧ *"First Memorial Hut,*
Eremite Valley, ACC. Mount
Bennington and Para Glacier
—Jasper Park," 1939. ACC ski
camps promote winter sport
and backcountry huts in
national parks.
[WMCR, V14/AC1/P/01]

in the high mountains of Alberta and British Columbia.[76] Ski trips to the mountains and ski camps in backcountry areas were introduced as club activities in the 1920s. Sections in Vancouver, Edmonton, and Winnipeg took a strong interest in ski sports. H.J. Graves from Vancouver, for example, anticipated in 1930 that ski mountaineering would reshape the ACC sport roster as members opted to "alternate skis with hobnailed boots": "The sport of mountaineering may develop a new phase by the prompt introduction of winter expeditions and ascents by skis, thereby providing a field of activity throughout the whole cycle of the year."[77] Winter had previously closed the mountaineering season in Canada, but skiing opened the winter months and breathed fresh life into the ACC.

Manitobans in the ACC had an early affinity for skis and made winter trips to the Rockies and Selkirks as early as 1911, 1914, and 1922. Encouraged by trendsetter Alexander McCoubrey, who taught his friends how to ski on the banks of the Assiniboine River, the Winnipeg Section boasted a dedicated corps of skiers by the late 1920s. The section made repeated trips, riding the CPR from Winnipeg directly to Yoho National Park, to ski the Little Yoho Valley and Lake O'Hara on a quest for backcountry powder. McCoubrey and friends visited the Little Yoho Valley on many annual ski holidays, staying at Twin Falls Chalet before the Stanley Mitchell Hut was built.[78]

In British Columbia, the Coast Mountains offered slopes near Vancouver where the club skied Grouse Mountain, Mount Seymour, Hollyburn, and Strachan, and north into the Mount Garibaldi district. Skiing was particularly popular among young West Coast members at a time when the ACC was keen to renew its membership base.[79] Don and Phyllis Munday and friends in the Vancouver Section were quick to adopt skiing and make it part of their mountaineering way of life. In his account of the 1930 ACC ski ascent of Mount Baker, southeast of Vancouver, Don Munday observed that "ski-climbing in Canada" was an innovation that, "like most new things, is eyed askance by some climbers."[80] Vancouver members frequented nearby Mount Seymour— where there was snow on the upper slopes from November until mid-June—to learn and practice skiing. Don Munday argued that, although Mount Seymour and the local peaks were subalpine, "There was no reason to doubt that the skill developed here will be applied later in the ascent of truly alpine peaks."[81]

In Jasper National Park, the Edmonton Section had staked out its own ski terrain with a focus on the upper Tonquin Valley, supported by an alpine hut. Cyril Wates, Rex Gibson, Helen Burns, and H.E. Bulyea

were Edmonton club members committed to making repeated trips to climb and ski in the area encompassing Eremite Valley, the Ramparts, and Mount Geikie, set on making first ascents and finding new route variations, which were still possible in these back valleys of Jasper Park in the 1930s.[82] At the national level of club life, skiing was also gaining attention. Selby Walker noted that the ACC risked losing members to ski clubs if it did not adopt winter sports, reporting in 1934 that fifteen Calgary Section members had joined the Calgary Ski Club. He advised the club to open its Banff clubhouse to accommodate winter use by skiers and also to generate new seasonal revenues from facilities.[83] The Ski Mountaineering section in the *Canadian Alpine Journal* was started in 1930 under editor Alexander A. McCoubrey. It publicized trips undertaken for winter ascents as well as ski touring. Featured trips ranged from Monte Rosa in the Alps to Skoki Lodge in Banff and Mount Seymour. Russell Bennett's 1931 account of a ski mountaineering ascent on Snow Dome pointed to attractions at the Columbia Icefields, later explored from a national club ski camp there in 1947.[84] The ACC formed its national Ski Committee in 1931 under McCoubrey's direction, which set out to document skiing history in Canada, distribute information about skiing in the *CAJ*, create a skier's guidebook, map avalanche hazards, and do "pioneer work in the mountains in order to develop this side of mountaineering."[85]

Commenting on backcountry skiing, J.B. Harkin noted in 1933 "that the Alpine Club being the pioneer organisation supporting such recreation throughout the Parks will be in a position to offer suggestions."[86] Harkin was overlooking the many local ski enthusiasts and promoters, such as the Banff Ski Club, Calgary Ski Club, Mount Assiniboine Lodge, Skoki Lodge, and Sunshine. In 1934, following an accident-ridden season, Harkin requested the club's assistance "in the framing of regulations that would tend to prevent skiing accidents in the mountains." This consultation between the Parks Branch and the ACC built on the long-standing partnership between park policymakers and a key park user. Skiing added a new dimension to this old relationship, reinforcing the club's presumed status as an all-round pioneer in the field of mountain recreation. By 1930 events such as the Banff Winter Carnivals, skiing, and ski mountaineering were transforming Banff and Jasper national parks into attractive year-round tourist destinations.[87]

The rise of winter sports stimulated a push for shelters, and the club responded by constructing a network of alpine huts throughout the mountain parks during the late 1920s and into the 1940s as part of its agenda to keep ACC members in the backcountry throughout the year. ACC sections initiated huts in their favourite haunts for climbing, skiing, and ski mountaineering. The huts are a tangible legacy of the club's history that excite the imagination with thoughts of mountain adventure and rustic charm. They are also an extant cultural resource on public lands and a lasting legacy of antimodernism. Alpine huts were situated in the backcountry to serve as high take-off points for mountaineering ascents and as refuges against bad mountain weather or in case of accidents. Beyond these functional purposes, they continue to be social meeting places where mountaineers and guides gather to talk, drink, dry gear, cook, sleep, and swap stories.

Most of the ACC huts were located on national park lands, and so the club first had to obtain federal licenses for site occupation. Historically, the ACC stood out among other non-profit, recreational groups as a concessionaire occupying land in the national parks. Its status as a well-recognized authority on mountain recreation and an institution that opened up the mountains and offered excellent free publicity to the national parks helped it gain its licenses. Holding properties in turn reinforced the club's foothold within the national parks and made the renewal of future licenses and the approval of subsequent huts far more likely. The club and Parks collaborated on initiatives to provide recreational supports—such as the huts and trails to and near the huts—which drew travel into backcountry areas, reflecting their positive outlook in the 1930s on developing infrastructure and amenities in parks to promote public use and enjoyment. Fay (1927), Memorial (1930), and Elizabeth Parker (1931) huts were the first shelters initiated by the ACC in the mountain parks of the Rockies.

In addition to the chain of national ACC huts arising in the Rockies, a few section club huts were started for local use and enjoyment. Reports noted that local huts "contribute[d] to good fellowship and section unity." The Edmonton Section's succession of local huts provides a good example of the kind of "section unity" a hut could inspire in members. Edmonton's local club members built their first club hut in 1926 on Quesnell Heights and replaced it in 1932 with a secluded cabin in the Whitemud Creek ravine on the south side of the North Saskatchewan River just beyond the city. A stone fireplace was built by Dr. H.E. Bulyea. Members cut their own ski runs and trails and held "many happy parties around the leaping flames after the gathering shadows put an end to the stems and christies."[88] Sunday hikes in the local river valley, dinners, Christmas parties with children, singsongs, amateur theatre,

Early Alpine Huts in the Rockies

Fay, Memorial, and Elizabeth Parker

NEAR THE CROWN OF WATERFALLS streaming down to Tokumn Creek and overlooking Prospectors Valley perched the first alpine hut built by the club: Fay Hut. Here daylight ripples over rock headwalls chiselled from ancient seabeds, and the sound of glacier melt plummets into the night in Kootenay National Park. Situating a climber's hut on the west side of Mount Fay was an idea precipitated by club discussions at the Lake O'Hara Camp in 1925. Two years later, a party trailing a string of loaded pack ponies set out to construct the hut at a cost of $1,450 financed by donations from club members. Named after Professor Charles Fay, founder of the American Alpine Club and an early member of the ACC, the 1927 Fay Hut was built for climbers in the tradition of the Swiss alpine huts.[89] For climbers crossing over the spine of the Great Divide, the hut in Kootenay National Park, British Columbia, aided access from the Valley of Ten Peaks in Banff National Park, Alberta, via Wenkchemna Pass to Prospectors Valley and Opabin Pass to Lake O'Hara in Yoho National Park, British Columbia. Climbers could ascend from Fay Hut to Abbot Pass Hut, built by CPR Swiss guides, and cross back into Banff National Park above Lake Louise to make a circuit trip over high peaks and glaciers. Mountaineers continue to travel these routes.

A forest fire sweeping through Kootenay National Park burned the original Fay Hut to the ground in summer 2003, but Parks Canada granted approval for reconstruction on a nearby site. The ACC opened the new hut in 2005 as one of the club's centennial projects, but the hut was destroyed again (this time by a fire related to the hut's fireplace exhaust) in early 2009.

< Ice axes struck into the rustic logs of the original Fay Hut on visit by its namesake Professor Charles Fay, guide Edward Feuz (left), and the ACC's president Dr. Hickson (right), August 1930. Fay Hut was the first of a series of alpine huts in mountain parks that still draw climbers and revenue. [WMCR, V200/PA44/534]

Another early hut built by the club was Memorial Hut on Penstock Creek, located at the head of Astoria Valley in Jasper National Park. It was officially opened by members of the Edmonton Section on August 17, 1930. Designed by architect M.C. Wright, an Edmonton club member, and handcrafted in stone by Jack Hargreaves, a Jasper outfitter, Memorial Hut arose from the Edmonton Section's resolution to "devote its energies towards encouraging mountaineering in the Northern Rockies." With fewer than twenty members, the Edmonton Section managed to raise core funds and supplement construction through the national club from the Soldiers' Memorial Fund and the "Slark-Rutis" Memorial Fund. Memorial Hut jointly commemorated club members who had died in the First World War and climbers who had lost their lives in the Canadian mountains.[90] A map of the area published in the club's 1930 journal demarcated the route of the proposed trail from Cavell Lake, along the Astoria River, toward Chrome Lake and Amethyst Lakes, pushing for the vision of trail development. Access to the hut via Maccarib Pass took seven or eight hours in 1931, but by 1932 the club was pleased to report that a new trail to be built by Parks would render the hut "easily accessible in about four hours."[91]

Much of the early climbing in the Tonquin Valley involved Edmonton Section members. Rex Gibson bagged many first ascents and ski ascents there. One of his regular climbing partners was Cyril Wates, who made Memorial Hut a home base. Devotion to knowing the Tonquin Valley season after season "until every cliff and contour has become an actual part of one's being" indicates Wates's strong place attachment to one corner of Jasper National Park.[92] Wates married his second wife, Edmonton climber Helen Burns, a teacher who was a section chair and secretary, then died only two years later. As a result of his passion for the Tonquin, when the foundations of Memorial Hut were undermined by water run-off after seventeen years, a new log structure was

built in 1947 on the north shore of Outpost Lake and named the Wates-Memorial Hut. And a new log cabin was constructed on higher ground in 1961. It was rechristened the Wates-Gibson Memorial Hut. Insulated in 1979 for winter use, with a bequest from Helen (Burns) Wates, the third hut continues in year-round service.

The third shelter owned by the club in the Rockies was the Elizabeth Parker Hut, which opened in Yoho National Park in 1931, creating "an important link in the chain of cabins available to club members." When two log cabins were donated to the ACC from the remnants of the CPR bungalow camp in the meadow near Lake O'Hara—where the 1909 summer camp had been held—the Winnipeg Section led the project to create a club hut named after Parker, who was at that time seventy-five. Project costs amounting to $518 were funded by the Winnipeg Section with a loan from the national Club Hut Fund. A subcommittee of Winnipeg women furnished the necessary curtains, cutlery, and housewares. In exchange for an earlier two-acre lakeshore lease held by the club since 1912, a one-acre leasehold around the cabin was provided to the ACC by Parks in 1931 at the "nominal rental of ten dollars." The lease did not at first allow winter occupancy, but an amendment made way for the first ACC ski camp at the hut in 1937.[93] Climbs from Elizabeth Parker Hut radiated to peaks on Hungabee, Biddle, Odaray, Schaffer, Wiwaxy, Cathedral, Park, Ringrose, and Yukness.

By this time, the growing number of alpine huts in the mountain national parks was beginning to form a nodal system of facilities. Winnipeg member Edna Greer was "cheered by the sight of the cabin in the green meadows" and was not the only member to see the mountain backcountry as a colonized European-like landscape, domesticated by a rustic cabin and trails. As Greer wrote, the hut for her and many others was: "A haven of rest and...a base camp for climbing expeditions in the valley."[94]

∧ Section hut built for ACC weekend hikes, skiing, and parties on the outskirts of Edmonton. University of Alberta professors E.S. Keeping (far left), possibly Dr. Silver Dowding Keeping (top of ladder), and H.E. Bulyea (ladder), with Miss Helen Burns (right of Bulyea) and friends.
[EA-41-92]

and exchanging visits with Calgary Section members and the Edmonton Voyageur Canoe Club were also regular activities in the Edmonton Section in the 1930s and endured to the 1960s.[95]

The Seymour Hut near Vancouver was better known and had more vertical rise. Growing interest in skiing in 1930 led the Vancouver Section to propose a local hut on Mount Seymour. The section asked member Colonel W.W. Foster to obtain a 670-acre (271-hectare) leasehold from the Province of British Columbia and the Greater Vancouver Water District, where Seymour Hut was subsequently constructed in 1931. Club members carried lumber on their backs up the final 1,500 feet (457 metres) of elevation gain to the building site, even though "deep soft snow and much bad weather added to the toil and difficulties." Much like other volunteers in community organizations during the cash-strapped 1930s, local section members carried the full cost of the project, donated the materials, and volunteered the labour. The barn-style cabin could initially accommodate twenty overnight guests. "The summit views combine seascape and landscape, and...sometimes includ[e] Mt. Rainer, 180 miles away," noted Don Munday. Seymour Hut became a hub for local mountaineers, and the Vancouver Section welcomed other ACC members, even offering skiing and climbing outings for out-of-town guests.[96]

In the Rockies, the Ottawa Parks Department granted a lease to the Edmonton Section for the new Disaster Point Hut in Jasper National Park near Pocahontas in 1938. The idea for this hut arose after eighteen member climbers spent Labour Day weekend in 1937 rock climbing on the cliffs of Roche Miette. They "were greatly impressed with the beauty of this neglected area and its accessibility from Edmonton." To raise funds to build, the section staged a musical theatrical revue called *A Day at an Alpine Camp* at McDougall United Church, punctuated by movies of the annual summer camp in Jasper at Fryatt Creek and rock climbing in Banff at Bow Lake, thus promoting the club "with good publicity of the right kind." A pre-existing stone building under Roche Miette was upgraded for weekend section trips; other ACC members were accommodated based on available space.[97]

By 1935, however, the Depression put a hold on the building of national huts. It was not until 1939 that the club built the Stanley Mitchell Hut in the Little Yoho Valley, Yoho National Park, at a cost of $3,200 (of which $1,500 was donated by Montreal ACC member Miss Helen M. Trenholme). Alexander McCoubrey and his Winnipeg ski friends had already embarked on winter reconnaissance trips and site selection for the cabin, attracted by the snowfall and glacier terrain of the Little Yoho in the vicinity of Mounts Vice President and President, along with the Wapta Icefield. The hut was built in a spacious, if difficult to heat, one-and-a-half-storey log-cabin style with a sloped gable roof to support a tremendous weight of winter snow. The historic building continues in service year-round as an alpine hut for skiers and climbers.[98]

Until the Stanley Mitchell Hut was built, club managers steered the ACC toward generating revenue from camps, clubhouses, and huts during the recessive 1930s. Not surprisingly, camps and clubhouses brought in the bulk of revenue from facility operation, with backcountry huts generating modest revenues from overnight fees.[99] At a rate of 50 cents per night for members and 75 cents for nonmembers (accompanied by a member), the ACC managed to make a small profit on hut accommodations. For example, the Fay, Memorial, and Parker huts together produced a profit of $89.97 in 1934 and $63.33 in 1935.[100] Although similar in some respects to simple hostel shelters, such as the one operating in Bragg Creek, Alberta, at 25 cents a night,[101] alpine huts, especially high ones, were usually situated in less accessible areas and more costly to operate. And they were more socially exclusive.

Even as the Depression deepened, the club held onto its plan to form a network of shelters, particularly through mountain parks, akin to the system of huts in the Swiss Alps (where more people frequented alpine areas). Ironically, the club went to the mountains seeking a getaway from the city, yet, in seeking to develop a chain of huts to shelter and protect climbers, it implicitly repudiated wilderness through the colonization of space and mapping of an organized system engineered to make occupying the backcountry easier. Much as national parks and their partners aimed to offer services and infrastructure supports for travel, ACC climbers at the time may have seen themselves as simply being at home in the mountains while they enjoyed another cup of tea in the club's privileged domestic space amid the great outdoors. Despite its impecunious state and the sting of government funding cuts in the 1930s, the ACC was still a privileged sporting group.

While its sports activities diversified, the ACC retained a strong alpine focus. As early as 1928, when the Associated Mountaineering Clubs of North America branched out to become the Associated Outdoor Clubs of America, the ACC declined to continue its membership in the umbrella group. ACC Secretary Stanley Mitchell drew a distinction between omnibus outdoor "gangs" and his own alpine club.[102] The club was not keen to affiliate with a general outdoor association, preferring to retain its cachet as a specialized mountaineering club. Even while the ACC's roster of activities diversified into a year-round cycle of outdoor recreation, mountains remained its focus, as recreation in the mountains changed and access to those mountains became easier.

The club's first drive-up summer camp held at the Athabasca Glacier was a landmark change in 1938, coinciding with first ascents by women on peaks from Snow Dome to the Twins. The inauguration of the park road from Jasper to Banff allowed automobile access to peaks near the Columbia Icefields. The camp for 156 climbers and crew was situated near the foot of the glacier and "opened new climbing possibilities for members and friends and provided an innovation in that motor transport brought them and their baggage direct to Camp, instead of the old pack-train and its attendant hikers."[103] It was a first in the history of the club, reported a local Jasper newspaper also promoting the ease of travel

∧ A new road between Banff
and Jasper opened the way
to the Columbia Icefields
where the ACC held a "drive-
up" camp near Athabasca
Glacier in 1938. Auto tourism
expanded visitation after
the war. Edwin W. Mills
photograph. [WMCR, V14/
AC20P/1]

to this destination "reached by a quick and comfortable motor drive from Jasper station."[104] T.B. Moffat, past ACC president, asserted in *The Albertan* in 1939 that Alberta needed more tourists and the club played a role in economic development when it came to promoting mountain attractions.[105] Such news clippings reached the Ottawa Dominion Parks files dealing with ACC campsites. That 1938 mountaineering camp would be a precursor to major operations in the Columbia Icefields district during wartime and beyond.[106]

The ACC was not an unchanging citadel of tradition that rejected innovation through the interwar period. A classic style of mountaineering remained dominant within the ACC, but the club also demonstrated adaptability and debate through a difficult period of economic and organizational adjustment. If change did not occur overnight, it nonetheless affected the ACC, which began to conceive of and practice multifaceted mountain sports falling within its sphere of action. This transition ultimately led to a new set of priorities: sport and recreation—not conservation—solidified as the club's major preoccupation from the Depression into wartime.

Going to War for Canada

When Canada went to war, the ACC patriotically fell into step. The club mobilized on several fronts. While many members enlisted for military service, the club carried on with its associational life and played a direct role in alpine warfare training. In 1942 club President Eric Brooks observed that maintaining the club's "traditions and ideals" was an essential means of contributing to the national war effort on the home front: "Quite a number of our members are now on active service... Probably *our* greatest contribution, those of us who are left behind, is to make sure that the Club's activities and all they stand for are maintained. So that when the present conflict is over we may do our share in furthering the cause of international brotherhood which seems lacking in the world at large and yet is so evident around these campfires."[107] The flames kept burning, but the club's campfire circle grew smaller. Approximately eighty members dropped out of the club during wartime, leaving a membership of about 450 in November 1944.[108] Some of the enlisted members and those left behind formed a valuable pool of expertise when it came to mobilizing mountain troops for the Department of National Defence, and during wartime they found new ways to carry on the ACC's tradition as the national alpine club.

From 1942 to 1944 the ACC embarked on a major undertaking by instructing members of the Allied forces in mountain warfare. Alpine military training was launched to prepare for offensive tactical operations overseas: national parks in the Rockies simulated the terrain of the European Alps, Italian Alppenines, and Norwegian Kjølen. The ACC hosted troop-training exercises for the Canadian Army at its annual summer camps. Club members designed and instructed these training programs and were later commended for their proficiency by commanding officers and the Department of Defence.

In 1942 the ACC hosted seventeen Canadian Army officers at the annual summer camp in Banff National Park, held in Consolation Valley near Lake Louise, to learn mountaineering leadership skills for taking military units through "rough and semi-mountainous country." A two-week course with a six-day field test was designed "to give the officers practice in travel over all types of mountain terrain, rock, meadowland,

snow and glacier, to simulate as far as possible the sort of country which troops might be expected to encounter in actual operations of warfare." Military officials in Ottawa subsequently thanked the club "for the splendid cooperation and practical assistance rendered in respect to the training" and requested that the club provide a second training event for a large number of troops the following year, noting assessments from the officer trainees that the instruction appeared to have value to military operations and that furthermore "the best source of knowledge on the subject was undoubtedly contained in the membership of the Club." Following internal discussion, club President Eric Brooks and the executive responded by placing all personnel and equipment of the ACC at the service of the Canadian Forces. Brooks subsequently travelled to the US Army mountain training centre at Camp Hale, Colorado, and determined that the American training was very similar to the ACC's syllabus for military training.[109]

A camp the following summer was thus committed to the military. Known as the Canadian Army Mountaineering School, the camp hosted a series of training courses for several hundred men and officers in the Little Yoho Valley. A significant agenda of the 1943 training was to select a pool of soldiers with an aptitude for mountaineering who could become trainers. The school was based at the ACC Stanley Mitchell Hut, where twenty-two instructors from ACC sections in Canada and the United States stayed while introducing soldiers to basic climbing skills. Three US Army officers from Camp Hale and another observer from Washington participated. The exercises were also witnessed by General G.R. Pearkes of Pacific Command and Major General Ganong, GOC 8th Division; Pearkes asked the ACC for a three-week extension to train more troops, and the club obliged. Members of the press, National Film Board of Canada, and official photographers were also invited guests.[110]

The mainstay of the teaching staff at the Little Yoho military training camp were experienced amateur guides from the ACC, including Eric Brooks, John Brett, John Wheeler, Andrew Sibbald, and Don Munday. Troops were put through climbing instruction on Mounts Vice President and President, and surrounding areas. Munday later commented on rumours among the soldiers that their instructors were paid $10 a day for their services, a story that was "easier for them to believe than that of having given our services for free." The instructors had actually paid camp fees to the club to attend the training session. Because the Canadian Army had not been able to obtain climbing ropes on loan from the US Army, volunteers gave just as freely of their gear. As Munday

∧ *ACC men co-operated with the army during wartime. Instructors of the Canadian Army Mountaineering School at Stanley Mitchell Hut in 1943. Top row (left to right): Don Munday, John Brett, Andy Kramer, Henry Kingman, Harold Graves, Roger Neave, [Paul Blanc or Capt. John Jay], Ferris Neave, Russ Cuthbertson, Caufield Beatty, John Wheeler. Middle row: Hassler Whitney, unidentified, Brad Gillman, Ivor Richards,* J.S.T.G., *Fred LeCouteur, Major Jackman, Alan Lambert, Ludwig Randall, Henry Hall, Major Tweedy, Andrew Sibbald. Bottom row: three unidentified, Eric Brooks, Rex Gibson, Capt. Reg Nourse, unidentified. Canadian Army photograph.* [WMCR, V14/AC371P/1]

observed, "We used our own ropes and those belonging to the Club. Mine was worn out at the end, and I imagine most others were too."[111]

Munday's civilian assessment of the training school wryly critiqued efforts in which the ineptitude of the army fell far short of the standards of mountaineers. By the end of the second training period, when the number of instructors had dwindled to only half a dozen, Munday and young John Wheeler were "a bit scandalized" to be left the task of guiding ninety-six soldiers on Mount Vice President. It was an overwhelming task that compromised safety, even with the help of roughly six assistants from the "more skillful men" who had attended the first

∧ Troops and instructors with E.R. Gibson (standing right) on Mount Kerr, Yoho National Park, 1943. Canadian Army photograph. [LAC, E01106184]

>∧ Experienced mountaineers at ACC's Lake O'Hara Camp in 1943. Elizabeth Brett, Emmie Brooks, Dorothy Pilley Richards (back row), with Aletta Kramer (possibly), and Phyllis Munday (front row). Seasoned camper Mr. Chips (on stump) tangled with a porcupine. [BCA, I-66784]

> Abbot Pass Hut on the col between Mount Victoria and Mount Lefroy, 1943. Phyllis Munday photograph. [BCA, I-66786]

training period. The enormous party stretched out along a windy ridge, reached the summit, and began the descent. Below the bergschrund, the instructors were left with "an undisciplined mob plunging down" as it crossed crevassed terrain, blithely disregarding safety "in the fatuous self-delusion that if they reached camp not too long after the lunch hour the sergeant-cook might forget and give them an extra meal." Climbers began to break through the snow and fall into hidden crevasses, and none of the assistant leaders "had shown enough respect for the glacier" to rope up with a party. In this debacle, the soldiers' lack of respect for the authority of the guides and vague understanding of alpine hazards underscores, by contrast, how successful leaders at the ACC camps were in training and regulating men and women among the club's amateur climbers. Diminishing numbers of volunteer instructors for troop training put a pronounced strain on the amateur leaders, according to Munday, particularly considering that their own personal safety was also at stake.[112]

Mass ascents with large numbers of beginner climbers were recounted as amusing moments during the regular evening debriefing sessions held by the instructors at the Stanley Mitchell Hut. Stories were retold about a soldier who slid off a slope while carrying a stretcher below President Glacier, another who feared the instructor had the right to push him off a cliff if he refused to climb down, and yet more "duds" who

Women and Friends Camp at Lake O'Hara, 1943

THE SUMMER OF 1943 in Yoho National Park was not all given over to the military. Civilians in the ACC also conducted their own "Informal Camp" at Lake O'Hara. Thirty-five climbers and a dog named Mr. Chips camped in the meadows by Elizabeth Parker Hut. They carried on the summer mountaineering camp by modifying its usual format as most of the club's tents, gear, and male leaders were enlisted at the military camp. "What makes an Alpine Club Camp formal anyhow?" Dorothy Pilley Richards underscored in the CAJ, "Tweedy's book, bell and candle? Fixed meal hours, a Chinese cook and a vast enough fly to serve his offerings under? It was clear early enough that there would be none of these things this year."[113] Richards was a renowned English mountaineer, traveller, and climbing writer who had been an early advocate of "manless climbing"; she was in good company at Lake O'Hara Camp with a powerhouse of experienced climbing partners, particularly Phyllis Munday, Emmie Brooks, Elizabeth Brett, and Aletta Kramer. Phyllis Munday volunteered as a guide and safely led many climbing parties on peaks around O'Hara.

Some ACC leaders from the Canadian Army Mountaineering School in Yoho National Park came to pay a visit to the climbers camped at Lake O'Hara. Don Munday, Eric Brooks, John Brett, and Britain's Ivor Richards, came to see their wives and friends, and brought along Tom Waller of the Royal Canadian Air Force. Climbers mixed from both camps then teamed up on recreational ascents. Phyllis Munday and Tom Waller joined forces to lead the club climbers on an ascent of Mount Odarary. Phyllis Munday, Waller, and Aletta Kramer also formed a party to traverse Abbot Pass over the Great Divide while portering firewood on their backs to Abbot Pass Hut. At Lake O'Hara, women and older men like Herbert Sampson carried forth an alpine culture of ascents, knot lessons, singsongs, and happy recollections of earlier camps around the campfire— all in the midst of wartime.[114]

erred by throwing away their ice axes when they lost their footing on a slope rather than driving them into the snow to self-arrest. That these events were construed as comic narratives suggests insight into some of the risks involved in mountaineering, the tensions between troops and trainers and how they were managed. Soldiers did not necessarily see the alpine environment in the same way as mountaineers did, and a rough and rapid introduction to mountaineering may have seemed a contemptible assignment for some of them. Munday recalled that the climbing instructors never quite forgave one soldier who looked across his first panoramic view of the Rockies and Selkirks only to announce, "imagine asking a man to fight for a country like this…I'd give it all away to the Japs." Munday concluded that the real value of training the soldiers rested in the assurance that "among their number were a few, a goodly few, in whom had been aroused a love of the high places of the earth."[115]

Munday also remembered some comical scenes from the training. He wrote that, although Emerald Lake Chalet in Yoho was closed during the war, "the soldiers never quite realized that the park was not closed to tourists. As a result there were roadside incidents when men were not arrayed for civilian gaze." For example, the first contingent, carrying packs and rifles, hiked from Emerald Pass down to Emerald Lake one hot afternoon. It was spotted by tourists whose car rounded the bend where the road reveals the lakeshore, and "this day it revealed a hundred or more naked soldiers on the shore, and not all the occupants of the auto were males."[116] The Canadian Army Mountaineering School was caught in the tourist gaze as much as scenic landscapes were transformed in Yoho National Park.

Few places offered easy access to terrain and infrastructure to support mountain troop exercises in Canada as well as the national parks in the Rockies. Situated in prime climbing areas in the parks, alpine huts owned by the ACC were key facilities used by the military for high-mountain training. After military use, other buildings were obtained by the club, such as Saskatchewan Glacier Hut in Jasper National Park a mile below the tongue of the Saskatchewan Glacier, which was reconstructed by the Canadian Army Engineers from Calgary using materials left behind by mountain troops in the US Army 87th Infantry Brigade's 1942 camp for tracked vehicle tests and renovated for use by the ACC beginning in 1945. The club negotiated its lease through the Banff Park superintendent. The new hut made climbs on Mounts Andromeda, Athabasca, and Saskatchewan, and Castleguard Mountain feasible within a day by permitting closer access.[117] Obtaining buildings at a negligible cost may

Ordeal by Ice

Rex Gibson and "Secret" Winter Training in Jasper

IN 1943–44 E.R. (Rex) Gibson, a Canadian mountaineer and ACC leader, travelled to an army camp in Jasper National Park to teach skiing and high-mountain warfare to the Lovat Scouts, a British regiment from northern Scotland. Gibson teamed up with British Squadron Leader Frank Smythe, an English mountaineer well known for his attempts on Everest throughout the 1930s. Together they planned and implemented alpine field training for the British commandos. They chose Jasper as the site of operations over Vernon and Terrace in British Columbia, due to the appeal of high-mountain terrain at the Columbia Icefields, in the Tonquin Valley,

and in the Maligne Lake district.[118] The recently completed Banff–Jasper Road in the federal parks provided ease of access to a large mountaineering operation at the Athabasca Glacier.

Gibson (1892–1957) was an Englishman and a distinguished veteran of the First World War before immigrating to Alberta where he became a farmer and active leader in the Edmonton ACC Section and local Boy Scouts. The officer corps was typically filled by middle- and upper-class men, and amateur sportsmen like Gibson. He joined the Royal Canadian Artillery in 1941 and was promoted to the rank of major in 1944, after having served as a liaison officer between Canadian and British forces during the training of the Lovat Scouts. Careful and considerate with his students and willing to adjust his pace for less experienced climbers, Gibson was considered a good teacher.[119]

While training the scouts, Gibson was pleased to have eighty-five potential instructors who were Canadian soldiers trained at the ACC summer training schools in 1942 and 1943. About sixty-five made the selection cut to instruct the Lovat regiment after a rigorous three-week pilot course based at the Icefield Chalet beginning in mid-November 1943. The curriculum devised for the ACC training camp in Yoho was fully revised as the basis of the three-week Lovat Scout training school conducted in January 1944. The syllabus incorporated warfare tactics, along with instruction in mountaineering, backcountry skiing, crevasse rescue, ice climbing, medical evacuation, snowcraft, and winter survival. Ice climbing involved a hundred scouts on a fixed-rope route up frozen waterfalls in Maligne Canyon. Ski lessons at the Jasper Park Lodge led to higher camps and better snow at Chrome Lake in Tonquin Valley, Mount Edith Cavell Chalet, Maligne Lake Chalet, Watchtower, and Snowbowl. Winter mountaineering ascents by troops and instructors were completed on major peaks such as Andromeda, Athabasca, Columbia, Kitchener, Nigel, and Snow Dome. Members of the US Army and Air Corps, including expert mountaineers

Majors Walter A. Wood, Belmore Browne, and Innes Taylor, along with US Mountain Infantry men, also assisted the 1944 training program; after winter training in Colorado, the United States 10th Army Mountain Division deployed in Italy. The Lovat Scouts also went into battle in Italy beginning in July 1944 as Allied forces mounted major offensive operations.[120]

The National Film Board of Canada produced a documentary about the Lovat Scouts in the Rockies in 1945. *Ordeal by Ice* is part of the *Canada Carries On* series.[121] In propagandistic style, the film dramatizes the exercises as a triumph over nature and adversity, but it overlooks the introductory nature of the training program and the skill level of many newcomers to skiing and mountaineering, in contrast to the well-honed skills among specialized alpine troops in countries such as Finland, Italy, Austria, and Germany.[122] Scenes of mass manoeuvres with skiers descending the Athabasca Glacier and tracked vehicles invading the snowy Tonquin Valley, however, make military might in the mountain parks an impressive sight to an average observer. The film entirely obscures the fact that the same places were long-standing backcountry recreation areas for ACC members and other civilians. Local populations are also omitted, but in reality the Scottish troops met a warm welcome from residents of Jasper townsite whose winter season was busy with soldiers and commerce.[123]

have offered a small compensation to the club for its voluntary efforts collaborating with the army during troop training, which certainly had a higher dollar value than the annual $1,000 grant revoked by Bennett's Conservative government—and still not reinstated—a decade earlier.

Another result of the military training program for the club was recruitment among the men who had trained at the war camps. In assessing the ACC troop-training program, Eric Brooks commented that "another important outcome of the scheme which will bear fruit as time goes on is the fact that many of the boys whom we were privileged to train have developed a true love of the 'hills,' and some have already become valuable members of the Club."[124] The success of the military training programs, noted as "a bold experiment," was a point of pride to the club: "Besides teaching the Army, the members themselves learned a great deal. They have done a good job and proved themselves capable of giving instruction in the basic elements of mountaineering. At the same time the Alpine Club of Canada has justified its claim to be the leader in Canadian Mountaineering affairs and has shown that ability to advance which its founders foresaw."[125] By responding to the demands of the Canadian war effort through active leadership and volunteerism, the ACC reasserted its claim to status as the national mountaineering authority.

Much as harbours, hospitals, and universities were reassigned to military purposes, national parks served the nation during a time of war. In addition to testing military vehicles, housing prisoner-of-war camps, and generating hydroelectric power, the national parks were exploited for troop training in high-mountain warfare.[126] They effectively shifted into service to meet the needs of militarization, and the ACC actively participated in reconfiguring the Canadian national park idea to accommodate alpine warfare. Mountain parks were remade as nationalistic icons of Allied military power, much as masculinist mountaineering shifted in meaning from civilian leisure to armed combat. Ultimately, soldiers on skis fanning out across the Athabasca Glacier also prefigured the hordes of auto tourists that would be conveyed to the site by tracked Snocoaches, sightseeing tour buses, and private vehicles, not to mention the growing presence of the ACC and other mountaineers, in the years of peace and prosperity that followed the war. The ACC had made it through the Depression and the Second World War buoyed with pride, and it would soon identify a postwar park ideal based on a changed notion of Canadian alpinism that would result in a "hive of industry" in the national mountain parks emerging beyond the frontiers of Depression and war.

Limitless Playgrounds? 6

...the Alpine Club of Canada perhaps does more than any Club in the world to encourage the budding mountaineer and I ask all our members to further this, one of our major aims, "The encouragement of mountain craft and the opening of new regions as national playgrounds."

—E.O. WHEELER, 1954[1]

THE ALPINE CLUB OF CANADA lost two of its earliest supporters as the Second World War drew into its final months. Elizabeth Parker died at the age of eighty-eight on October 26, 1944. "The circle of the Canadian Alpine Club had lost a devoted friend...one of its most loyal supporters," noted her obituary in the *Canadian Alpine Journal*. Then, on March 20, 1945, Arthur Wheeler died suddenly at the age of eighty-five. He remained a grand figure even in death. Laid out in his Tyrolean cape, as he had requested, the green, white, and grey colours of the ACC were draped over the casket, wreathed by his climbing rope, ice axe, and Tyrolean hat. His remains were interred in the Banff cemetery where he had earlier obtained a plot, through negotiations with Parks officials, when planning his chosen resting place in Banff Park. "None who knew him can forget his genuine friendship or his broad vision and high objectives," stated his obituary in the club journal.[2] Former club presidents Patterson, Moffat, McCoubrey, Sibbald, and Wates also died during the war years, along with notables such as climber Bess MacCarthy, former secretary Stanley Mitchell, and mountain guides Edouard Feuz, Sr., and Christian Häsler, Jr.[3] These changes in the club membership came to pass as a new vision of national parks was taking shape.

At the time, mountain national parks stood out as protected spaces in Alberta and British Columbia amid an increasingly agricultural, industrial, and urban landscape. The Canadian West—the "last frontier" imagined by expansionists—was resettled by newcomers and broken by agriculture. Mountain ranges had been transected by railways, roads, and highways connected to metropolitan networks. New population settlement and growth from Manitoba west to British Columbia, between 1901 and 1941, rose from 598,200 to 3,239,700.[4] In 1945 Canada comprised more than 12 million people with a $10.5 billion gross national product; by 1951, more than 7.5 million people—62.9 per cent of the entire population—lived in urban areas.[5] The face of postwar Canada was predominantly urban with an industrialized core and regional economic hinterlands based on the exploitation of raw resources; notably, the 1947 discovery of major oil and gas reserves in Alberta triggered rapid development during "one of Canada's greatest resource booms."[6] Canada emerged from the 1940s with booming demographic growth and rising postwar affluence. All of these changes could not but affect parks, which were part of larger schemes of civil society and modern postwar development in Canada.

Canadians were encouraged to enjoy parks, recreation, and tourism as social benefits in the building of a better society and entitlements of citizenship according to postwar democratic liberalism.[7] And by enjoying the mountain parks, Canadians also constituted them. Through recreation, the public played a role in the social construction of postwar ideals of parks and tourism, shaped how they were realized, and influenced park planning. Escalating postwar park tourism mutually reinforced the successful transition to peacetime social and economic growth. The ACC was a constant presence in the mountain parks throughout this time, and, as the war came to a close, it looked ahead to planning the national parks, opening up new areas, and building access to wild places. The club's diverse approaches to mountain sport, to conservation and parks, and to recreational tourism at this time often pulled the club in different directions rather than straight along one path. A shifting interplay of stakeholders, politics, and mutable ideas shaped parks in Canada during this period. Relations between club members (and other park users), the state, corporations, and other interests would, in turn, shape the postwar mountain parks well into the 1970s. Recreation rose to the forefront of the club's agenda to open the "inner recesses" of the parks as "unlimited" tourist playgrounds throughout the 1950s and into the early 1960s. As popular access to Canada's national parks grew, postwar visitation skyrocketed. At the same time, ACC climbers travelled farther into the backcountry and northward to find "new" ground for the pursuit of wilderness mountain sport and solitude. In so doing, it reinscribed its vision of mountain parks as a climber's paradise.

Reconstruction
The ACC's Vision of Postwar Parks

Attention turned to Canada's postwar reconstruction in the national parks even before the end of the Second World War. The federal Advisory Committee on Reconstruction, appointed in 1943, set up a natural resources subcommittee that laid out several recommendations, including "the extension and improvement of National Parks facilities; study of methods for widening the economic basis for travel; [and] improvement of highways." Recommendations related to national parks showed up under tourism, illustrating how parks were directly linked to postwar growth.[8] In addition, the committee anticipated a rising need for parks at all levels of government.[9] Late in 1944, the ACC sent a formal submission related to policy development and planning to the Lands, Parks and Forests Branch of the Department of Mines and Resources. The main recommendation put forward in its proposal and published in the *Canadian Alpine Journal*, "Post-war Development of National Parks," was articulated as "the development and greater utilization of the National Parks of Canada by the general public." Within the document, the ACC claimed a special authority based on its long-standing mandates as a national club and its history of nearly forty annual summer mountain camps, facts highlighted to policymakers to enhance the club's status as a partner in public-park planning: "we feel especially qualified to submit the recommendations attached hereto."[10]

The club's proposal pointed out that it was "fully in accord" with the CPR's recent recommendations to the department—"Postwar Planning for Tourist Travel in Canada"—saying that "the time is ripe for the Canadian Government to do more to provide facilities for healthy outdoor recreation in its National Parks."[11] The link between tourism and outdoor recreation in parks was clearly drawn; in fact, opening the parks to mass tourism was the overarching theme of the proposal. The ACC reasoned that making parks more easily accessible stood to benefit not only climbers but also *"tourists in general*...Heretofore, many such areas have been accessible only to those able to afford expensive pack-pony trips, or to those physically fit to endure back-packing excursions of the most strenuous character...greater accessibility is necessary."[12]

"Accessibility" was the watchword of the postwar park ideal, and the club's historic role in opening up "new regions as national playgrounds" for the middle class resurfaced. Embracing mass tourism and its many recreationists sounded an inclusive chord, even as the club still held fast to its own particular agendas focused on alpine pursuits and access to terrain attractive to mountaineers.

According to the club's postwar vision, the function of parks was twofold. First, Canada stood to gain socially by deriving recreational benefits from its national parks. The argument that parks had value because they enhanced urbanites' health and productivity resonated with the philosophical underpinnings of late nineteenth-century social-reform movements that advocated nature pursuits, much as it paraphrased the turn-of-the-century philosophies of guiding lights A.O. Wheeler, Elizabeth Parker, and J.B. Harkin. But it went further by stating "unless they are made readily accessible and the public is encouraged to make use of them their value is lost."[13] The assumption that parks were without value unless the public used them, however, implied a more utilitarian ideal of material use than the previous high value placed on the intangible qualities of parks, such as the spirituality of nature and the inspirational power of beauty. In essence, mountain recreation was being reframed as a form of postwar recreational consumption, one that required a substantial infrastructure to support greater numbers of visitors.

The second part of the ACC's postwar vision was that parks could add prosperity to local and national economies. The club had participated in a regional tourist economy in the Rockies and Columbia Mountains for almost forty years and, by its presence, encouraged the growth of businesses such as railways, outfitters, hotels, and purveyors of various goods and supplies. It highlighted how developing parks stimulated economic benefits associated with the tourism industry: "whenever tourist travel is encouraged, services of various kinds will be required...and benefits will derive there from both to the individual and to the country at large."[14] In short, the ACC recognized the national parks as an economic asset, as did postwar public policy.

Five pages of recommendations in the ACC's 1944 submission requested specific "improvements" in Banff, Jasper, Yoho, Kootenay, and Glacier national parks, along with Mount Robson Provincial Park. Most of these recommendations pertained to the construction of highways, roads, bridges, trails, huts, and shelters—all with an aim of accessibility. The club was particularly interested in developing linked systems of roads, backcountry trails, huts, and shelters to allow more people into the "inner recesses" of the parks. The club also wanted to see upgraded systems of communications, maps, and trail signage. With respect to Jasper National Park, for example, the club summarized the value of "a whole scheme of trails" in the district of the Whirlpool Group and Athabasca Pass as it would connect to British Columbia at Boat Encampment on the Columbia River along the historic "Voyageur's Route": "Of inestimable scenic value."[15] Notably the club made pertinent the history of travel over Athabasca Pass during fur-trade explorations. This reference indicates an awareness of the park as a cultural landscape wherein such corridors signified the stories of earlier peoples in the mountains, underscoring the historical signification of the district to modern backcountry hikers and climbers in the parks. It also called for interjurisdictional management to improve trails across park and provincial boundaries. Not surprisingly, the ACC's suggestions for improvement were often in places where the club had staged past summer camps.

In one of its most striking proposals for Jasper relating to "opening new regions as national playgrounds," the club recommended construction of a new highway in Jasper to extend up the Astoria River drainage to Chrome Lake in the Tonquin Valley—an area that is today only reachable by trail beyond Mount Edith Cavell or over Maccarib Pass. Splendid terrain in the Tonquin Valley had already made it a highly attractive district to the ACC and various backcountry skiers, climbers, and hikers by 1944, along with military troops and all-terrain combat vehicles. The giant Mount Geikie was seen as the likely site of another ACC climbing hut, in addition to the existing Memorial Hut above Chrome Lake and below Outpost Lake, to enhance access to alluring mountaineering objectives in the western Ramparts. According to the club's proposed highway scheme, the wild Tonquin Valley in the Jasper backcountry was newly envisioned for intensive mass recreation as a drive-in destination through summer and winter. The proposal was never realized, but it offers a telling illustration of the ACC's wholehearted endorsement of development during the reconstruction era.

In 1944 the club also recommended that the area north of Horsethief Creek, from the Lake of the Hanging Glacier to the Bugaboo and Bobby Burns groups in British Columbia's Purcell Range be established as a new park or incorporated into Glacier National Park. This area had been marked by climbers as attractive to mountaineers as early as 1916— Conrad Kain guided the first climbing expedition to the Bugaboos that year and made a first ascent of Bugaboo Spire with Americans Albert and Beth MacCarthy. They were impressed by the granite spires and stupendous climbing terrain. In the case of the Bugaboos, the club felt the area had "little or no commercial value, but it contains some of the finest scenery and mountaineering problems in the Canadian Rockies."[16] The ACC could not have foreseen Hans Gmoser's venture in the Bugaboos, Canadian Mountain Holidays (CMH), launched in 1964 and now the world's largest commercial heli-skiing company.

The club's constitutional objective for "the preservation of the natural beauties of the mountain places and of the fauna and flora in their habitat" had receded from view in its new public agenda, much as its vocal conservation activism of the 1920s had faded forefront of its politics by the Depression.[17] The ACC wanted roads, trails, and facilities constructed to serve an expanding population of recreation seekers. Years of meager park budgets and delays through the Depression and war, along with the pent-up expectations and aspirations of the club, all added to its strong pressure for rapid postwar infrastructure development. Redolent with postwar optimism and unbounded expansionism, Alpine Club of Canada officials conceived of the mountains and parks in Alberta and British Columbia supporting limitless tourism, as it suggested in its proposals regarding Mount Robson Provincial Park. "The whole of this majestic region, containing the highest mountains in the Canadian Rockies, could be visited by *unlimited* numbers of tourists and travelers," proposed the club, and therein lay the main value of the postwar parks.[18] In the days of vigorous prosperity and optimism for better living through consumption that followed the war, the fragility of mountain environments was easily overlooked.

In this climate, the ACC's suggestions were well received by the Department of Mines and Resources. And, it would seem that the ACC continued to share many ideas "in line" with the Parks Branch—as it did when Harkin was commissioner, but now under a postwar-use philosophy. Ottawa director of the Parks Branch R.A. Gibson replied to the club's proposal, writing: "You will be glad to know that many of the ideas are in line with the suggestions which the Park Superintendents have made themselves."[19] The National Parks Bureau laid out a plan for its extensive "Post War Rehabilitation Programme" in preparation for the 1945 Dominion-Provincial Conference on Reconstruction. This five-year plan for capital investment and employment, amounting to $16.875 million, emphasized the role of the national parks in the Canadian economy, highlighting that "The possibilities...are almost unlimited."[20] In an attempt to thwart another recession after the war, Ottawa centralized power to weave a social safety net composed of health, education, and social benefits, while Minister of Reconstruction C.D. Howe's "super-push" approach to economic development sought to ensure a "high and stable level of employment and income."[21] Postwar Canada was ready to invest in rebuilding. Parks became one focal point of public spending, underpinned by policies that highlighted the social and economic values of tourism, recreation, and leisure in prosperous times. As recreation historians Wall and Wallis point out, "There was a surge in demand for camping and outdoor recreation had become an accepted government responsibility, due in part to the social utility associated with leisure and recreation as a necessary and enriching aspect of life."[22]

In March 1945, twenty-three national parks and national historic parks existed across Canada. Under the National Parks Act, the Lands, Parks and Forests Branch of the federal Department of Mines and Resources administered sixteen national parks—from Cape Breton Highlands, Nova Scotia, to Mount Revelstoke, British Columbia—and seven national historic parks. As the war effort peaked and the return of peace seemed more likely, total national park attendance grew by 42,041, from 415,351 tourists in 1943–44 to 457,392 in 1944–45—a total roughly the size of the 1941 population of New Brunswick. This shift marked the beginning of an accelerating trend toward increased postwar attendance in Canada's national parks.[23]

The provinces also spurred the development of parks after the war. Ontario, for example, had established eight parks between 1883 and 1944, but added forty-seven new parks between 1945 and 1960, most including campgrounds.[24] Alberta enacted parks legislation in 1930, but, between 1951 and 1960, it went from eight to thirty-four provincial parks with the goals of benefitting public recreation and conservation.[25]

It was no coincidence that the national parks were reorganized in 1950 as a branch of the Department of Resources and Development.[26] In Canada's overall reconstruction scheme, public parks were considered an important component of economic diversification, as well as egalitarian social development. Tourism was considered a limitless industry in an international marketplace and important to balance of trade; national parks were seen as a valuable asset to national and regional economic growth. J.G. Perdue of the National Parks Bureau made the link between parks, tourism, and resources clear to the Parks and Recreation Association of Canada in 1947: "The National Parks of Canada, besides providing for wildlife and preserving the natural beauty of the landscape, have become popular recreational areas for Canadians and are playing an important role in the tourist industry...About 20 percent of this year's million visitors were from other lands, particularly the United States."[27]

Economic prosperity and low energy costs through the 1950s and 1960s in North America boosted opportunities for leisure and travel. Postwar consumers were buying affordable commodities—automobiles, trailers, cottages, and televisions—befitting North American expectations for domestic life, family, and middle-class leisure. Suburban consumer desires and increasing family sizes in the 1950s fed growing markets for outdoor recreation vacations, car camping, and wildlife watching that Alexander Wilson identified with the postwar "culture of nature" popular in the white, urban, middle class in Canada and the United States.[28] More people living near major national parks, specifically Jasper and Banff, added to the number of regional visitors making local driving trips to the parks.[29]

Several factors worked to put more pressure on national parks after the Second World War. Geographer J.G. Nelson pointed to postwar immigration and rising birth rates that led to rapid population growth, while urbanization increased the size of cities and suburbs. The overall gross national product rose as Canadian industries expanded and diversified alongside advances like computerization and automation. In Canada and other Western countries, unions and other groups bargained for their share of increased prosperity and won higher wages, more holidays, longer vacations, and greater leisure time. Cars and airplanes improved transportation and mobility, particularly for middle- and upper-income earners. Nelson concluded that these factors "combined to put more and more pressure on recreational land and opportunities in Canada and the United States in the 1950s, 1960s and 1970s."[30] Without considering the cultural discourses of meanings and practices associated with nature and outdoor recreation, however, these factors alone do not fully explain why people went to recreate in parks after the war or how the idea of parks was constructed and understood. The ACC's participation in meaning-making in the outdoors helps us to understand how mountain parks became the mountain parks known in Canada. Most mountain park visitors were not climbers, yet imagining the mountain parks as the rejuvenating playground of mountaineers embraced the marvel, risk, and glamour associated with adventure in alpine sport and exploited it for tourism marketing. Notably absent in the new publicity materials were images depicting recent alpine warfare troop exercises on the Columbia Icefields, and other places; the parks were now politicized as innocent playtime venues for the middle class.

Castle or Eisenhower?

Postwar Toponyms and the ACC

AN INTERESTING EXCEPTION to the erasure of wartime images from Canada's parks arose in 1945 when Prime Minister Mackenzie King announced that Banff National Park's Castle Mountain would be renamed Mount Eisenhower, in honour of the man's contribution to the Second World War. The ACC objected strenuously, observing that "General Eisenhower is not a mountaineer" nor had he climbed the peak, and that James Hector of the Palliser Expedition had already named the peak in 1858.[31] Club President Eric Brooks officially wrote to the prime minister in 1946 to object, requesting that the ACC—as the "premier exploratory and mountaineering organization in the Dominion"—be granted representation on the Geographic Board of Canada or be consulted when toponym changes were being contemplated.[32] In this way, the ACC continued to position its authority with Ottawa on matters of mountain heritage. The American Alpine Club and the Government of Alberta also rebuked Ottawa for the proposed name change—Alberta immediately formed its own provincial geographic names board. Mountain enthusiasts were not convinced of the arbitrary and facile remaking of mountain landscapes as wholesale war memorials.

It wasn't until 1979 when the official geographic name reverted to Castle Mountain, with a tower named Eisenhower Peak as a compromise.

With federal and provincial government backing, public interest, and the support of the ACC, the gates to Canada's postwar mountain playgrounds were open. Millions of people swept into the national parks as visitation rose steadily from 1944 through the 1960s. A total of 457,392 people visited Canada's national parks and national historic parks from March 1944 to March 1945. The following year it grew to 602,409. By the close of 1969–70, attendance totalled 12,629,101 in the eighteen national parks (excluding national historic parks). Banff National Park typically took the largest share of tourism with, for example, 148,113 visitors in 1945–46; 980,069 in 1959–60; and 2,346,030 in 1969–70.[33]

What impact did postwar reconstruction and the changing visions of parks have? Significantly it was an impact measured in road and trail mileage. By the beginning of 1960, Canada's national parks were reported to offer 791.22 miles (1,273.35 kilometres) of motor roads, 117.54 miles (189.16 kilometres) of secondary roads, 599.14 miles (964.22 kilometres) of fire roads, and 2,446.02 miles (3,936.49 kilometres) of trail.[34] These figures quantified the extent of development largely realized as a cumulative outcome of Depression-era and wartime public works projects, and the postwar planning directions laid out by Parks in the mid-1940s.[35] The latter began with the vision of reconstruction and public works it generated and shared with the tourism industry and recreationists like the ACC, and ultimately materialized through public expenditures on capital investment according to the tenets of welfare state economics and through leisure consumption in Canada after the Second World War.

Opening Up the Mountains

As the club entered the postwar period, working on opening up new climbing terrain and encouraging guiding, it also articulated its vision of mountain recreation and conservation. This vision can be seen in the work conducted by the club's 1950–54 president, Brigadier Sir Edward Oliver Wheeler (1890–1962), Arthur's son. The younger Wheeler was also a mountain surveyor, an organizer, and a conservationist, but he was not a politically outspoken conservation activist like his father was.[36] As president, he focused on the economics of the club's camp operations, trying to open more remote regions for climbing, standardizing a planning process for advance campsite selection, and streamlining leasing procedures for club properties in national parks.[37]

The ACC promoted reconnaissance trips to delve into and publicize new climbing territories. The Hooker Icefield in southwest Jasper, the

French Military Group southwest of Kananaskis Lakes, the Freshfields Glacier in Banff, and the Bugaboos in the Purcells were all sought-after areas at the time. The club convened several of its annual camps after 1945 in these enticing destinations west and east of the Great Divide: Bugaboos in 1946 and 1959, Hooker Icefield (Whirlpool Valley) in 1953, the Freshfields in 1949 and 1969, Mummery (Blaeberry River) in 1958, and the French Military Group (Joffre Group) in 1964. Camps at Moat Lake on the Great Divide in the Tonquin district were held in 1957 and 1970, and at Fyratt Creek in 1960, promoting mountaineering and tourism in Jasper National Park closer to the spine of the Rockies.[38] These camps, farther from roads and railways, were expensive undertakings and often fell short of financial success, but they drew out the skilled mountaineers in the club, on whom beginners relied for amateur guides and rope leaders. The camps proved to be a financial balancing act: "The camps that pay off financially however, are those of previous experience, where the mountains and routes are known and where many newcomers will come," Oliver Wheeler stated. "Our difficulty is to find leaders, amateurs, who will generally insist on newer ground." The camps were still an occasion for mountaineering instruction.[39]

Wheeler attempted to convince the National Parks Branch that "the tourists bring the large money, but the Alpine Climber opens up the region for the tourist."[40] He considered himself unsuccessful in this respect. Efforts in 1952 and 1953 to renew the club's annual $1,000 federal grant failed. Rather than renew it, Deputy Minister H.A. Young advised park superintendents in Banff, Jasper, and Yoho in 1952 that "present policy was to provide facilities in the Parks for the different agencies and people interested, but...not...to give any financial assistance."[41] Still, Parks continued to assist the ACC by clearing out trails, repairing roads and bridges, and helping to maintain campsites, but Wheeler regretted that it refrained from "building roads to serve the mountaineer, who after all is also the pioneer, the forerunner of the tourist dollar."[42] In the end, with baby-boom demographics and prosperity fuelling the postwar market for commercial tourism, Parks viewed the club as just one of many recreational stakeholders, and the ACC found its days as "the pioneer" in the mountain playgrounds at an end.

Wheeler nevertheless persisted, planning summer camps in new locations in a competitive market for outfitters and escalating labour costs for packers, cooks, and hired help. The club's longtime outfitter, Ralph Rink, quit the club operations in 1943 after more than twenty years, and with the retirement and death of other "old hands," Wheeler had trouble

Beautiful Bugaboos

The Fortieth Anniversary ACC *Summer Camp*

"IT WAS DIFFICULT TO REALIZE," reflected Archibald MacIntosh, acting vice-president of Haverford College, Pennsylvania, "that there before us was so much country unexplored, so many mountains unnamed and unclimbed." His first ascent on Peak Three in the Quintet Group, south of Bugaboo Pass, ended with a 2,000-foot run glissading down a continuous sweep of snow. "The long snow climb of the morning was now an effortless rush. We came off the mountain with the celerity and smoothness of a dream."[43] On the walk back

∧ *Snowpatch Spire rises over the* ACC *Bugaboo Camp, 1946. Granite and glaciers primed a sense of adventure, yet the Bugaboos were near home to locals in the Columbia Valley. Edwin W. Mills photograph.* [WMCR, V14/AC20P/4]

to the ACC's fortieth-anniversary base camp at Bugaboo Creek with amateur leaders Elizabeth and John Brett from Montreal, Archie savoured "again a climb which was notable, not for its difficulty, but for the pleasure that we derived from it."[44]

Staged from July 14–28, 1946, this camp was "the largest club camp ever held, and altogether sixty-one tents, including three large marquees and the cook tent, were erected at the main campsite, while an additional ten were used at the outlying camps." Record attendance with "200 under canvas and 170 members or guests present at one time" marked the first club camp since the return of peacetime. The National Film Board of Canada even sent a camera crew to document this exciting event on film.

The Bugaboos provided a dazzling new location for the club, with attractive climbing problems. "Except for the Coast Range, where in the Waddington region in particular granite aiguilles abound, the Bugaboo and Bobbie Burns groups offer the finest rock climbing in Canada on sound granite," assessed Rex Gibson, "and it is to be hoped that many more mountaineers will be attracted to this veritable rock-climbers' Paradise."[45] Descriptions of the Bugaboos as "mountains unnamed and unclimbed," "country unexplored," and a "Paradise" for rock climbers rang a chord with the perennial adventure quest for imagined geographic frontiers and reinvention in the sport of mountaineering. The first ascent on Peak Three in the Quintet Group demonstrated the dominant form and underlying ethics of mountaineering typical of many climbers in the ACC and at the annual camps. The climb was a general mountaineering route, sloped with mixed snow and rock, and, as MacIntosh stated, notable more for its pleasurable enjoyment than its difficulty, yet it simultaneously embodied the ethics of the first ascent of a peak as the standard of significant achievement. "Celerity and smoothness" were all about the aesthetics of style and the embodied feeling of glissading on the descent. Rock climbing on steep faces and sheer vertical walls, with the use of technical aids such as bolts and pitons, was still an emergent form of the sport within the ACC in the 1940s. In 1946 the Bugaboos were an exciting frontier for rock climbers keen to test new routes and forms of ascent. As this climb suggests, classic first ascents were still possible, although the plum peaks in the main Bugaboo group had already been ascended.[46] Only two climbers present at the opening of camp—Albert MacCarthy and Polly Prescott—had ever climbed there

∧ Rex Gibson cuts steps in ice at Bugaboo Camp in 1946. Such photos were later used for a series of instructional slides. Edwin W. Mills photograph. [WMCR, V14/AC20P/11]

before, so "ropeleaders were pretty much 'on their own' and had all the thrill of working out routes afresh, or in some cases finding entirely new lines." In fact, J. Monroe Thorington's sketch map was their only guide to the district.[47]

The club intended to establish a new hut named in honour of Conrad Kain on the site of its 1946 Boulder Camp in the Bugaboos.[48] Ever seeking to claim an unclimbed paradise, amid the surge of postwar tourism, the club sought out and ventured to mountain playgrounds old and new—pushing out from its traditional terrain in the mountain parks to other ranges and destinations, exposing them to the public eye.

finding experienced help. Eric Brooks and Russ Cuthbertson stepped in to assist as club volunteers, managing and constructing the camps, and, starting in 1947, the club combined the efforts of its management committee, a camp manager, and the secretary-treasurer to supplement basic outfitting.[49] Throughout his term, Wheeler attempted to return to the old camp system run by one outfitter, but it was difficult to find a contractor who could juggle all the operations: "It has been impossible to obtain another 'Rink' who would contract for the whole camp organiz-ation."[50] Outfitting for the camps would prove difficult until 1954, when Bill Harrison took up a stalwart role as the club's outfitter and stayed on for the next three decades.[51] As Wheeler noted to the club in 1954, competition for outfitters was fierce at the time: "Not only are there more mountaineering and hiking clubs today who establish camps—at one time the Alpine Club of Canada was entirely alone in the field...for many years this was so—but also there are many, many more tourists seeking to hire ponies, guides, etc., and there are many more fishing and hunting parties than there used to be."[52]

Even though he realized that the increase in tourists was putting an "increasingly heavy drain" on parks, Wheeler acknowledged that club members—especially the experienced mountaineers—still wished to open up new areas for climbers and first ascents. With competition for resources in the parks came tension. Access to the backcountry was important, but demand for easy access was not unanimous within the club. Wheeler noted that some ACC members opposed more bridges, roads, and trails because these links would "put us more in sightseers' hands."[53] So, even though the club outwardly favoured infrastruc-ture developments to open the "inner recesses" of the parks, there was internal resistance from members who valued isolation in the backcountry.[54]

Opening up the mountains also implicated ongoing issues of how to deal with conservation management in the parks. Conservation initi-atives on the part of Oliver Wheeler during his presidency usually involved applied resource management in the education and conduct of the club's recreation activities more than concerted lobbying or galvan-izing outward political advocacy. For example, he strongly lectured the club on the importance of forest fire prevention, noting "it is for the old-timer to instruct the newcomer...about the danger of throwing a lighted cigarette or cigar butt into the bush." "Put it out—squeeze it in your fingers," he advised, adding that shaving mirrors should not be left against canvas tent flaps where they might lead to combustion, and that

< Ski parties, suppers, and Santa were popular with families. Ivan Hopkins (left), Frank Hollingworth (centre), and Don Campbell with daughter Barbara in the Edmonton Section's Whitemud Hut, c. 1955. [Barbara Campbell collection]

The proportion of men and women in the club in 1946 remained comparable to the interwar pattern, with males accounting for 58 per cent and females 42 per cent among 472 members. However, the distribution began changing in 1956, when among 871 members there were 550 men (63 per cent) and 321 women (37 per cent). There were also rising percentages of married women in the club after the war—31.8 percent in 1946 rising to 57.9 percent in 1967—and concurrent declines among single ones.[56] Near the height of the baby boom in Canada, women tended to marry earlier and begin families younger than their predecessors had; these changes likely impacted the proportion of women and men in the postwar ACC. As the prerogatives of conventional heterosexual femininity and domesticity characteristic of the 1950s were reasserted, there were setbacks for females in strenuous physical sports—like hockey and mountaineering—as well as in the paid workforce.[57] Social mountaineering at ACC camps was differentiated between climbs tacitly understood as more suitable for women and harder climbs typically assumed to be for men, which perpetuated unwritten yet entrenched gender sanctions and leadership within the club. By 1967 the falling number of women in the club was even more pronounced with only 32.4 per cent of women among a total of 1,268 members. These numbers were close to the pattern seen in 1907, and a drop of roughly 10 per cent compared to the number of women in the club in 1930, 1939, and 1946.[58]

In 1967 there were at least 157 married couples registered as individuals in the club. Household addresses and

Social Snapshot
Postwar Membership in the ACC

ACC MEMBERS—mostly middle-class urbanites—were well positioned to invest in leisure pursuits. After the war, club membership figures gradually surpassed previous levels: from 510 members in 1939 to 1,267 in 1967. As a result of increased membership, the club's income also rose: from about $3,500 in 1946 to $9,641 as men and women returned from the military and war-related duties to normal civilian life, renewing club memberships and leisure as part of that process.[55]

surnames indicate that 38.2 per cent of women in the
ACC had husbands who were also club members,
whereas 18.1 per cent of males were identified with wives
who were listed as members; thus a woman was more
likely to belong to the ACC with her spouse than was a
man.[59] Notably, some of these women had joined before
their husbands. Other relationships are less visible in
membership lists but included varied bonds and family
structures.

Regionally, almost half of the ACC was based in
British Columbia and Alberta during the postwar era.
The club's core group in these two provinces went from
41.9 per cent in 1939 to 47.2 in 1967. By 1967 there were
319 members in British Columbia and 279 in Alberta
among the 1,268 people registered in the club. The next
largest groups by region were United States with 334
members, Ontario with 137, and Quebec with 86. There
was also a small rise from nations other than Canada, the
United States, and the United Kingdom, suggesting a
slight lean toward more internationalization by 1967.[60]
The restructuring of ACC sections also reflected the
changing regional membership rolls. The British Section
disappeared after 1950, as did the Saskatoon Section in
1952–53. A New York Section returned in 1952, while
Chicago and Minneapolis consolidated a Midwest

Section by 1955. Montreal emerged in 1945, Ottawa in
1949, and Toronto revived in 1957. By 1957 ACC sections
operated in Victoria, Vancouver, Calgary, Edmonton,
Regina, Winnipeg, Toronto, Ottawa, Montreal, New
York, and the American Midwest.[61] By 1968 the Regina
Section had folded—but members from Saskatchewan
continued to enroll, even with the loss of this last section
in the province—and a new Kootenay Section operated
in Trail, British Columbia. American sections of the ACC
were regrouped as Eastern USA in New York, Midwest
USA in West Layfayette, Indiana, and Western USA in
Lake Oswego, Oregon.[62]

members should obey Parks' regulations about campfires. Parks authorities at this time insisted on strict practices and forest fire suppression policies.

Fire, of course, was not the only consideration. Cutting trees for tent poles had made a heavy cumulative impact on vegetation, as Wheeler pointed out, because it had been "grossly overdone in the past," leading authorities to restrict cutting permits:

> As with so many other "unlimited" resources, we are finding that this resource...too is being cut almost to extinction. Not necessarily by us; but by the cumulation of clubs of our sort, now taking to the mountains. There was a time when game was supposed to be inexhaustible; similarly fish; perhaps there was misjudgement there. The same applies to our trees, for tent and other poles, in the mountains. It seems to be for us to give what lead we can to younger organizations by curbing indiscriminate cutting of poles, brush and so on.[63]

He recommended using tents designed with fewer poles. Still the ACC was an older organization and its impact on popular sites for the large camps was cumulative, especially in repeat locations like Lake O'Hara meadows.

Wheeler duly put forward initiatives for controlling litter, disposing waste, and keeping streams clean,[64] and he also offered the club's assistance to parks officials in the collection of fish population data, based on creel survey cards, when fishing. Contact with Parks through the fish data questionnaires allowed Wheeler to cultivate good relations with Parks, which in turn smoothed work to simplify the licensing procedures necessary for building club huts in 1953.[65] The club's efforts on its own and in partnership with Parks show what "conservation" was understood to mean in the context of postwar park recreational use. Land-use conservation was in the doing.

Mountain sport and recreation were also in the doing. The club's participation in skiing, ice climbing, rock climbing, and mountaineering continued to move along the trajectories put in place during the war. Starting in 1945, the club hosted annual ski camps in Yoho, Jasper, Glacier, Banff, and Mount Robson.[66] The Banff–Jasper Road made for easier access to three ski camps at the Columbia Icefields by 1965. The club's increasing number of alpine huts allowed skiers to operate in popular summer climbing areas in the winter, and Parks was in favour of this kind of usage to promote backcountry skiing. The Little Yoho Valley

Ski Camp in April 1958 held by the ACC at the Stanley Mitchell Hut in Yoho National Park, for example, was strongly supported by the park superintendent who wrote to his Ottawa chief to endorse the good work of the club and request permission for a special food drop into the site by plane.[67] Ice climbing offered another winter sport, and the 1952 *Canadian Alpine Journal* reported on new ice-climbing routes being developed in the Rockies with the use of ice pitons.[68]

Just as they found favourite skiing places, regional ACC sections discovered local niches for rock climbing. In 1956, for example, several climbers canoed the Ottawa River from Deep River to search out rock-climbing routes on the cliffs. Precambrian cliffs afforded "most satisfactory climbing," and according to ACC member Pat Duffy, evoked the Valley of Ten Peaks in Banff National Park when "the crisp echoes from our yodels reminded us of Moraine Lake as we paddled home in a magnificent sunset."[69] Such references suggest the extent to which the landscape memory and vernacular of climbing was often inflected by the physical and social geographies of mountain parks in western Canada.

Even as some climbers were making new bids on rock and ice, Oliver Wheeler urged the club to move away from simply seeking first ascents on new mountain peaks toward another ethic of climbing based on finding new routes and redefining the sport based on grades of difficulty. Popular histories of climbing have broadly assumed the ACC lagged entirely behind the times on this score, but as early as 1954 Wheeler compared Canada to the Alps, calling out for leaders willing to change their climbing ethics:

> There is also a difference here in that many insist on new ground, first ascents and so on. How many first ascents are available in the Alps today? New (and increasingly difficult, improving the standard) routes, yes; but new mountains, no. Sooner or later, we must come to this also; meantime, bush-whacking is preferred by many and we, the Club, suffer in consequence from lack of good leaders—we rely almost entirely on the good will of our members for this chore (it is a chore) and many are unwilling to come to places they know by heart, though will come readily enough to "new" regions. This is also a major problem of management, for we never know how many leaders we may have at any given camp. An Alpine camp without any leaders would be as sorry a one as a camp without a campfire.[70]

Alpine Huts and Cultural Footprints

BY THE END OF the Second World War, the ACC occupied numerous properties subject to Crown licensing for alpine huts. In the 1950s, President Oliver Wheeler corresponded with James Smart, Ottawa director of national parks, wishing to simplify and organize the process by which club volunteers managed federal licenses of occupation.[71] Wheeler wanted the leases for club huts to be renegotiated at the same time and renewed on the same date.[72] Smart replied that "in years past, [the club] has been given strictly preferential treatment." Typical leasing fees of $10 or $15 had been reduced for the club to $1. Smart was willing to allow for longer term leases, "of 10 years instead of 5 years as in the past."[73] From new constructions (the Arthur Wheeler Hut in Glacier National Park, 1947), to buildings transferred from Parks to the club (Hermit Hut in Rogers Pass, 1946), to modern architectural designs—fibreglass igloos and prefabricated shelters—for newly built club huts (the Banff icefields huts, 1960s and 1970s),[74] the club slowly created a system of shelters for mountaineers.

The club was also interested in constructing bivouac huts above treeline in Jasper and Banff national parks,

especially from the Wapta to the Whirlpool. Peter Fuhrmann and Hans Gmoser, professional mountain guides originally from Austria and expert members in the ACC, took a keen interest in developing a hut-to-hut system in the national parks. However, it took some time for Parks Canada to share the club's interest in the venture. In 1961 ACC President Harry A.V. Green tried to persuade Walter Dinsdale, minister of the Department of Northern Affairs and Natural Resources, to have Parks build four or five rest huts for ski touring in the national parks for "those who still like to use their legs to enjoy the beauties and solace of our mountains."[75] However, Green's proposal was rejected: "a complete chain of glacier shelters is somewhat premature at this time," as Banff Superintendent D.B. Coombs expressed to the chief of the National Parks Service in Ottawa. Coombs was critical of high-altitude huts in part because of "unsatisfactory" experiences of vandalism at Abbot Pass, the only high-elevation bivy hut at the time. Jasper Superintendent J.H. Atkinson similarly rejected the proposal for ski-traverse huts; handwritten comments added to his letter noted that the ACC was one of few groups interested in wilderness travel.[76] Mountain guide Peter Fuhrmann recollected that Banff Superintendent Jim Strong had told him explicitly "No huts in the mountains."[77]

The push for high-level bivouac huts was delayed but not derailed. In 1965, after some informal (but influential) lobbying by a British countess and the Ottawa Capital Commission's chief planner (clients of Fuhrmann's), a prefabricated igloo was installed as the first Balfour Hut on the Wapta Icefields. Other clients of Fuhrmann's, Vicki and Lucio Mondolfo, donated the funding to buy the 1965 igloo shelter. The ACC was permitted to fly the shelter in by helicopter, and then Calgary Ski Club volunteers assembled it. Later, the Calgary Mountain Club (CMC) furnished it with benches and tables.[78]

The CMC initiated and built a few alpine huts in Banff, which were subsequently handed over to the Crown. However, the ACC continued to be the main hut builder in Canada's national parks. The property foothold secured by the ACC bivy huts in the mountain parks perpetuated the ACC's stakeholder status, despite the 1964 Parks policy to disallow private organizations to "lease land or construct permanent buildings" in national parks.[79] As senior national parks official Steve Kun noted in 1967: "There is no organization comparable to the Alpine Club that is building shelters in the Central or Atlantic Regional parks. The Alpine Club is the only organization that seems willing to go to the expense and trouble of building shelters which benefit the public and club members, even though these shelters become Crown property."[80]

The government asserted its 1964 policy against private holdings in 1972 when the ACC relinquished its Fay and Hermit huts to the Parks Branch, ostensibly to mitigate environmental damage associated with overuse. The Province of British Columbia also bumped the club out and assumed ownership of the Naiset Cabins (originally built for A.O. Wheeler's tours) in Mount Assiniboine

Provincial Park. Ten years of discussion with Parks Canada ensued, and the club was eventually allowed to control the operations of its huts in national parks. These shifts in policy reflect the expansion and contraction of government through the 1960s to the recessionary 1980s, as well as changing political ideologies in Ottawa. In their history of ACC huts, written during the Mulroney era, Herb and Pat Kariel observed that "both national and provincial parks have found it difficult to maintain the huts at a desirable standard, and so have turned back to the voluntary organizations for help."[81]

Of the ACC's twenty-four national backcountry huts, seventeen are in Banff, Jasper, Yoho, and Glacier national parks; five are in Bugaboo, Kokanee Glacier, and Elk Lakes provincial parks in British Columbia, and two others are in the Selkirk Mountains in the British Columbia interior.[82] The huts in national parks are now owned by the Crown and operated by the ACC as a continuing partner in park management.[83] Repairs and renovations conducted in the 1980s began to address the importance of environmental considerations related to water, waste removal, fuel use, and impact reduction— the ACC must comply with environmental standards required by Parks Canada Agency and other authorities.

As the huts age, some have been given more than just the usual repairs and renovations. In 1987 the Elizabeth Parker Hut, for example, was recognized as a federal heritage building, a tangible cultural resource with historical, architectural, and landscape associations with mountaineers in Canada's first national parks. Alpine huts are nodes on trails, climbing routes, and ski terrain that support ongoing recreational use and evoke a connection between past and present in the human history of mountain parks. They demand historical attention as social gathering points for mountain recreationists and as evidence of privileged space. These places tell stories of climbs and trips laden with diverse meanings, as well as the contested relations of power in the social construction of mountain parks in Canada. They reveal parks as a cultural way of seeing constructed in historical time and place.

His views challenged traditionalists in the club, who held strong affinities for first ascents, as well as skilled members who veered toward more technical climbing.

Continuing debates over the sport ethics of "hardware climbing" provoked contestations and a variety of reactions. Born in Czechoslovakia's Tatra Mountains, John L. Dudra (1926–58) was a leading ACC climber who put up challenging new mountaineering routes in the Coast Mountains, such as a first ascent on Mount Saugstad (1951) with Pete Schoening near Bella Coola and a second ascent of Monarch Mountain (1953), as well as ascents on Devil's Tower in Wyoming and Cathedral Spires in South Dakota (1952). Dudra served as the club's Vancouver Section chair of climbing and contended in the pages of the *Canadian Alpine Journal* that "unclimbed faces should be explored and vertical spires climbed... it is simply a matter of mountaineering evolution" that climbers would change their views on first ascents and pursue technical climbs as had happened in the Alps.[84] Dudra's outlook on technical climbing implicitly premised developments in terms of sport modernization based on a predictable and inevitable unilinear "evolution" of practices. He openly argued in favour of the use of climbing aids, in the pages of the *Canadian Alpine Journal:*

> *A man may look down on pitons, bolts and all other paraphernalia that the fanatics are supposed to carry, but never stop to ponder that he himself may be climbing in boots which have tricouni or vibram soles, or using an ice axe or crampons to help him move freely over ice...Where are we to draw the line? If we were to take away all aids we would be tackling a mountain with bare hands and feet regardless of circumstances or conditions.[85]*

Englishman F.S. Smythe's remark that he felt like a criminal for using a piton on Mount Colin in the Canadian Rockies—because "to knock pitons in all the way up a mountain in order merely to get to the top, is a profanation of that mountain and of the sport of mountaineering"—was indicative of the anti-piton sentiment still lingering among traditionalists in Canada in the 1950s.[86] After the Second World War, technical climbing finally expanded in Canada, but the ACC was not an institutional leader in the trend, especially as it tended toward classic mountaineering ascents at camp to train many beginners; even so, John Dudra, Elfrida Pigou, Fips Broda, and other individuals in the club were technical climbers. The mutability of mountain sport was not a unilinear evolution of inevitable progress, but an ongoing and contested process of change in the invention and re-invention of the sport as it was culturally adapted by climbers in various regions at different times for diverse objectives. And, as this contestation over sport ethics was taking place in Canada, a similar process was happening within the ACC in terms of its conservation ethics and its views on opening up new terrain. All of these changes were accompanied by a new focus on consumption, stoked by postwar affluence and advances in mountaineering gear and its availability in Canada.

Consumption, Terrain, and Conservation
Sustaining Sport

Changes in sport ethics and the ways in which the ACC "opened" the mountains for recreation—with first ascents, exploration of new terrain, and the gradual incursion of technical climbing—partnered with a focus on consumption—gear, huts, camps, roads—that challenged the ACC's vision of conservation and land-use practices in parks. Enhanced by wartime research and testing, climbing equipment and clothing was revamped and improved. New synthetic materials became available, such as nylon for ropes. Viking nylon climbing rope manufactured by the Dominion Wire Rope & Cable Company of Lachine, Quebec, was advertised in the 1953 *Canadian Alpine Journal*.[87] Popular gas stoves elicited the love of climbers like Paul Calcaterra, who wrote his own "Ode to a Mountain Stove" in the *CAJ* in 1957:

> *O hail the little mountain stove*
> *To thee we give our deepest love*
> *Because 'tis you that melts our snow*
> *And cooks our food at ten below.*
>
> *'Tis you that makes our Jello hot*
> *And burns the bottom from the pot*
> *'Tis you that makes the icicles tender*
> *And cooks the groats in all their splendour...*
>
> *But to a hungry mountaineer*
> *Your purr can bring unmeasured cheer*
> *Your flame can fill his tent with light*
> *And warm him on a wintry night*[88]

> Calgary's Alpine Equipment advertises in the Canadian Alpine Journal *1949 issue* before the advent of *REI* and Mountain Equipment Co-op.

> *The 1953 issue of the* Canadian Alpine Journal *advertises Canadian nylon climbing rope.*

NOW!

Your CLIMBING EQUIPMENT can be purchased in CANADA

| Famous Andenmatten Products Ice Axes Crampons Pitons, Etc. | Famous English Manilla Climbing Ropes Canadian Nylon Rope Swiss Avalanche Cord and Climbing Ropes | Hand Made Climbing Boots also A Good Low Priced Climbing Boot Tents, etc. |

BEST QUALITY — LOW PRICES — PROMPT SERVICE

Catalogue and Prices on Request

ALPINE EQUIPMENT
3530 - 15th St., S.W.   Calgary, Alta.

VIKING
Nylon
CLIMBING ROPES

Manufactured by

DOMINION WIRE ROPE & CABLE CO. LTD.
SYNTHETIC CORDAGE DIVISION

LACHINE, QUE.   CANADA

Primus and Svea gas stoves were familiar brand-name commodities and machines in Calcaterra's outdoor kitchen—emphasized as a masculine domain for cooking and companionship, much like the backyard barbecue in the 1950s.[89] At a time when the annual ACC summer camps still operated with a heavy outfit of gear and equipment that filled a railway freight car and was then packed by horses into camp,[90] light-weight backpacking stoves and drinking hot Jello at "ten below" also signified a lighter approach to mountaineering travel. Carrying compact stoves moved climbers a step away from dependence on woodcraft camping practices, as author James Morton Turner argued related to the emergence of the American wilderness backpacking movement in the 1970s, and closer to embracing the industrialized production and market-place of outdoor recreation commodities.[91] Backpacking mountaineers in the ACC may have diverted from the car-camping tourism typical of the 1950s, but they still shared commonplace gendered and sexual-ized understandings of a man's love for the purring machines of postwar consumerism.

All the gear could be purchased at a specialized camping and moun-taineering shop in Calgary called Alpine Equipment. In 1949 the shop offered ACC members a full range of products, from Andenmatten moun-taineering items to ice axes, crampons to English manila climbing ropes, pitons to Canadian nylon rope. "Now! Your climbing equipment can be purchased in Canada," the shop advertised in the club's journal.[92] In 1956 Monod's Sports Shop opened in Banff. Postwar Canadian shops and manufacturers were serving the domestic mountaineering market—an important factor in addition to mail order and purchasing from abroad, and another sign of the growing presence of climbing as a niche recrea-tional activity in Canada. Local climbing shops were not only convenient places to buy gear but also served as hubs for social networking between various outdoor enthusiasts and sport practitioners, from beginners to specialists. Likewise, they served a mobile economy radiating between the mountains and the city.

With better gear came the ability to explore more terrain. An old Everest explorer himself, Oliver Wheeler commented, "there can be little doubt that the development of light-weight and wind-proof clothes, sleeping bags and other equipment, has had much to do with the great ascents made in recent years, like Annapurna, Everest and others in the Himalayas, and some of the great peaks in the Andes, Alaska and Yukon."[93] Moreover, he clearly connected the material culture of the "luxurious" ACC camps and meals with its social culture and its sport and environmental ethics. He wondered if "pioneering camps" situated "25 miles off the beaten track" should not be lighter—"drastically cut the weight of tentage and other stores"—or if the club should considered cutting "such camps in number to about one-quarter of the total, in other years camping at well-known, near-by places easy to organize, easy to reach at minimum expense."[94] Heavy camps were expensive, and they also affected both climbing and land-use practices. However, Wheeler's pragmatic approach to the environment and management of camps, and his positive outlook on reinventing the sport, would soon be replaced by a throw-back vision of the mountains when Rex Gibson became ACC president in 1954.

Gibson, born in Essex in 1892, began as a banker in Paris and later immigrated to Alberta where he farmed at Winterburn, near Edmonton. He was active in the local ACC section, playing a central role in the club's alpine warfare training programs in the 1940s. With more than two hundred ascents in his own climbing career, many of them firsts, Gibson was keen on new terrain.[95] At the club's fiftieth anniversary in 1956, Gibson urged the club that "the opening up of new climbing areas to our members should be one of our prime aims." Gibson thus returned the club to the expansionist rhetoric and outlook of new frontiers for first ascents. "While the 'golden age' of exploration in the Rockies and the Selkirks is past, 'there remaineth yet very much land to be possessed' in the Coast ranges in British Columbia and in the great mountain groups in the Yukon Territory," he asserted, casting allusions to both Victorian exploration and the King James Bible. Gibson called on members to seek out climbing, expeditions, and new destinations for annual camps in these regions. "These unvisited ranges present a challenge to us as Canadians and if we do not take up the gage someone else will," he remarked in a nationalistic statement reminiscent of Elizabeth Parker's patriotic call leading to the formation of the club in 1906. He also reflected on "the institution of the annual summer camps" as an enduring driver for social cohesion within the club and as a vector pushing out the boundaries of access to recreation in mountain districts, such as north of Jasper where the Mount Sir Alexander Group was coveted as his next prize.[96] Gibson reiterated that there were still many first ascents to capture in Canada if the club but kept up the quest for unscaled summits. His sudden death on Mount Howson in 1957 led lawyer Harry A.V. Green to step in as the next club president.

However, while he was president, Gibson's style of rhetoric about frontiers for new first ascents and exploration persisted alongside the dynamic and shifting reinvention of the sport through technical climbing and other sport forms and styles making headway in Canada after the war. Oliver Wheeler and Rex Gibson differed on the matter of which directions the club ought to take, and this difference of outlook between the presidents shows the tensions and debates that were at work inside the club throughout the postwar era, calling into question interpretations that the ACC was archaically traditionalist, entirely and inevitably lagging behind the times in its thinking and practice of sport when compared to other climbers, clubs, and nations.[97] Mountaineering was not a simple march of unilinear technical advancement in sport and relentless territorial expansion represented as progress; it was a contested field wherein the relations of power circulated through outdoor pursuits as well as park-making. The two different perspectives connected to issues of exploration and "new" terrain, which were germane to land use and protection, as well as tourism access. These internal tensions also affected ongoing business with government and parks, as the annual summer camp of 1956 demonstrated.

That year, the ACC wanted to host the camp in the Bugaboos. These plans were "mooted," however, because, according to Oliver Wheeler, the Government of British Columbia had "no intention of catering to the mere mountaineer in that region, and the road at this moment is in very bad condition indeed."[98] Just as better roads improved for tourism were not a foregone outcome of postwar development and user demands from mountaineers, neither did local conditions and politics remain static and predictable. With changes in presidential visions of mountaineering as sport, the ACC's relationships with government also changed. Also in flux in the postwar period were the ACC's responses to development in the parks; its vision of conservation in the parks was put to the test in different ways. Club members wanted access, wanted to explore and open up new terrain, but their demands for that recreational terrain competed with the needs and demands of others among the public, government, and industry. How did the ACC's postwar response to development differ from its interwar and wartime response?

Hydro Power and Forestry Debates
The Ongoing Saga

The ongoing saga of hydro developments in Banff National Park demonstrates how the ACC was shifting its postwar attitudes about conservation and recreation. The 1930 park boundary changes had left the Alberta government free to negotiate with Calgary Power over the Spray Lakes water powers, but until 1950 the project waited on the drawing board. In the postwar era, it would be the Canadian National Parks Association (CNPA), created by the ACC in 1923, and its replacement in 1963, the National and Provincial Parks Association of Canada (NPPAC), that would take on the conservationist work that the ACC once championed. The ACC was itself focused mostly on recreation when the Spray Lakes project was forced through, but it recuperated a conservation advocate's position later in the postwar era when the second Sloan Commission on forestry was conducted in 1955. It would seem that just as technical climbing and first-ascent ethics persisted side by side in the ACC during this period, vocalized dissent and tacit consent also ran parallel in the club membership regarding conservation of resources in national parks.

In the late 1940s, Calgary Power again requested the alienation of more Banff National Park lands in the area of the Spray Lakes, which Selby Walker of the CNPA opposed. Minister of Mines and Resources J.A. MacKinnon responded to Walker: "I, as an Albertan, am deeply concerned regarding the maintenance of the attractions of our National Parks."[99] Meanwhile, federal Parks Director R.A. Gibson expressed to the acting deputy minister his department's exasperation with MacKinnon's failure to protect the principle of national park inviolability:

> *The Minister is fully aware and, I understand, has advised council that the officials concerned with National Parks administration are unfavourable to the proposed action as they consider it a violation of Section 4 of the National Parks Act. It is particularly unfortunate that a move of this kind should be made when there seems to be good ground for believing that the required power could be developed otherwise.*[100]

Pressure from Alberta Premier Ernest Manning and C.D. Howe, then federal Minister of Trade and Commerce, led to the excision of further Banff National Park lands preceding the construction of the Spray Lakes dam system in 1950. Manning and Howe both believed that the province was in need of more power, especially relative to the "new petroleum developments around Edmonton" and a nitrogen plant near Calgary. Howe emphasized that Alberta's "spectacular industrial expansion" should not be interfered with, advising that the Spray Lakes seemed to be the only option for power and that "this should be studied very carefully to determine whether something cannot be worked out that will still make the River scenically attractive. It would seem to me desirable to hold back the spring rush of water and maintain an even flow, even if this means a smaller flow than at present. In any event, it seems to me that the industrial growth of the province must be a first consideration."[101]

By this time, civic and business leaders in southern Alberta were staunch dam boosters, and the ACC had few comments on the issue. Manning's Social Credit government believed in a "minimum of interference" with business and, in practice, leaned hard toward natural resource exploitation, particularly in the growing energy sector. Ironically, the Spray Lakes were one of the last potential hydro sites within economic reach of major demand centres; after 1951, Calgary Power turned its sights to integrating coal-fired generating plants into electrical production, much as Selby Walker and the CNPA had urged ten years earlier.[102] Most of Alberta's electrical supply continues to derive from coal energy generation.

As far as the ACC was concerned, the Spray Valley had been lost in the 1930 Banff National Park boundary changes. By stepping out of hydro debates to focus on recreational sport and the national war effort in the 1940s, the club relinquished its stand on national park inviolability. The club overall was far more concerned with gaining recreational access to the mountain parks throughout the 1950s than with fighting open political battles against industry. Emblematic of this change was the expedited route the ACC travelled to its 1952 camp at Mount Assiniboine: "By using the Calgary Power Company road from Canmore to the Spray Canyon Dam, people were able to reach the main Camp in one day, from Banff or Canmore."[103]

Still, the ACC's stamp remained on the conservation advocacy conducted by the CNPA, which was active until 1950 when Selby Walker became ill and subsequently died in 1952. Walker had no successor. Without volunteer animation, the association also passed out of existence, as did Walker's extensive papers and correspondence records—kept at home in the style of many voluntary associations—which his widow threw out when moving out of their longtime family residence. The defunct CNPA was replaced in 1963 by a new organization, the NPPAC. It was, in turn, revitalized as the Canadian Parks and Wilderness Society (CPAWS) in 1986.[104] These specialized non-government agencies for park advocacy worked, much as the ACC did in the early 1920s, to lead the political struggles for conservation and wilderness in Canada.

Advocates of Nature Conservation

Aileen Harmon

EVEN THOUGH the ACC as a body was not engaging in conservation advocacy when the Spray Lakes hydro project finally found its feet, individual club members were. For example, Aileen Harmon's conservation advocacy work illustrates how the constituency of the ACC continued to incorporate nature advocates and overlapped with new specialized conservation organizations during the 1960s. Harmon was raised in Banff by her father Byron Harmon, the club's first official photographer. She became an early park naturalist who developed emerging park interpretation programs, interpretive literature, plant labels, and nature trails in the service of Banff National Park from 1938. She was also a long-standing member of the ACC, like her father, and an amateur photographer. She went to club camps, such as Steele Glacier Camp in 1967 and the Freshfields Camp in 1969. The club made her a life member.[105]

When the NPPAC formed, Harmon volunteered as a director of the Alberta chapter and was later a CPAWS founding member. She also sat on the first directorate of the Canadian Nature Federation, a national conservation and wildlife organization. The local Bow Valley Naturalists society was founded by Aileen Harmon and Bruce Gordan in the 1960s, and Harmon served as a board member for the Federation of Alberta Naturalists. These structures, committed to nature and park concerns at the local, regional, and national levels, benefitted from the work of conservationists such as Harmon, who knew the mountain districts and ecology of the parks first-hand due in large part to her professional work and active outdoor life engaged as a local naturalist and national park resident. Her many roles also indicate the laboured volunteer service committed to advocacy and nature education.

< *Park interpreter Aileen Harmon, hiking in the early 1950s. An ACC member from Banff, Harmon was an active Alberta conservationist. Lillian Gest photograph.*
[WMCR, V225/NS6/12/R182]

Although the ACC had remained silent about the Spray Lakes project, the Sloan Royal Commissions on forestry in British Columbia suggest how the club began to adjust its thinking about postwar growth and conservation by the mid-1950s and renew its collective public engagement in conservation debates west of the Great Divide. The first Sloan Commission, chaired by Chief Justice Gordon McGregor Sloan in 1945, articulated the origins of the province's "sustained yield" policy regulating timber harvesting; however, by 1955, the volume of timber cut in British Columbia had doubled, rapidly leading to alarm. Most of the postwar increase derived from new logging in the interior, cutting old-growth forests on the coast was on the rise, and reforestation was lacking. These concerns catalyzed the second Sloan Commission in 1955.[106]

ACC members frequenting lands in British Columbia for recreation witnessed the forests change, and some were publicly concerned. J. Fairley and a club committee composed of Dr. Bert Brink, Dr. Bill Mathews, Pat Duffy, Eric Brooks, Ernest E. Smith, and Fred H.H. Parkes prepared a written submission to the Sloan Commission on behalf of the ACC in March 1955. It stated that provincial parks and other public lands were not well protected in British Columbia for several reasons. Ambiguities in the forest management licenses that enabled logging could potentially jeopardize parks and other lands. Legal surveys for provincial parks, park reserves, and new potential parks were lagging behind the pace of lands alienated by private and corporate development. Significantly, the existence of provincial parks, park boundaries, and use classifications were subject to hasty ad hoc changes by Order in Council, rather than public legislative process, a situation the committee believed was "not in the best public interest." It recommended amendments to the Forestry Act to require public notification of such changes and input to decision-making processes; it also urged that amendments be passed into law to govern the specific boundaries, classifications, and restrictions on industrial activities respecting parks. The ACC urged the British Columbia government to protect provincial park lands from forestry harvesting, to reserve lands strategically for parks and recreational use, and to contemplate separating the administration of parks from the structure of the Forest Service in order to "eliminate the conflict of interest existing within the Forest Service between the Parks Division, which is concerned with the preservation of parks in perpetuity for public recreational use, and other divisions which aim, ultimately, at the commercial exploitation of our forests."[107]

In the brief, presented by Vancouver lawyer Fred Parkes, the club raised concerns about the need to prevent forestry encroachments for logging on provincial park lands, to safeguard from logging the unspoiled character of areas adjacent to parks, and "to preserve the inviolability of Park areas." Parkes argued further that remote alpine and subalpine districts in British Columbia's larger parks and glaciated and mountainous districts "often termed wilderness areas" should be left in a "natural state" forever.[108]

In a move that clearly shows how recreational development and conservation were working in tandem in the ACC's vision of parks at the time, the club's committee also recommended that British Columbia park policies be relaxed to allow the ACC and "organized mountaineering and outdoor groups" to fund and build backcountry cabins and shelters, following the model already at work in national parks. A permit system to allow clubs to pass through forested park areas during fire season closures en route to alpine districts for camps was also requested. The club requested that higher priority be given to developing walking trails in parks.[109] Notably, the ACC brief also recommended that active park advisory boards be established with broad representation to engage park users in dialogue and policy discussions with senior Parks officers, preferably superintendents, which reveals the postwar recreation tenor of democratic liberalism and citizenship.

The ACC's position about people in parks had changed. Only a decade earlier, the club's official line had proposed a discourse of limitless tourism and development in the mountain parks. Its approach to issues in 1955, however, suggests a repositioning alert to the pace of change and the role of parks "as our other wilderness areas decrease with the march of civilization. We are chiefly concerned with the preservation of such areas." People were still part of parks in the ACC's evolving vision, but the club now refocused on proposals for non-motorized recreation, swifter land protection, better governance, and safeguarding the "natural state" of alpine and wilderness areas.[110]

The concerns of provincial parks in British Columbia after the Second World War reiterated some of the problems the ACC and park advocates had encountered before with the administration of mountain national parks in the 1920s, such as executive governance by Order in Council rather than legislative process, and conflicts of interest implicit in the administration of parks within the same government ministries charged with industrial expansion for water power, irrigation, and forestry. When the club asked the Sloan Commission to consider the question "What safeguards exist or can be introduced to preserve the inviolability of Park areas?" it resurfaced a key principle argued by Arthur Wheeler during the 1920s era.[111] As stakeholders in outdoor recreation, ACC members were both pushing for access to public space and promoting their vision of parks as natural resources preserved for tourism. "We believe that Parks should be classified among natural resources. They are a potential source of income to the Province, an income which will increase as they are made more accessible to the public."[112] The crux of this argument went on in the brief to position the right to protect parks for perpetuity on a par with the right to protect timber, a rather risky strategy considering the weak state of provincial forest protection and Sloan's final recommendations, which have been linked to the transformation of forestry in the province to classic Fordism.[113] Was this the direction tourism would take in British Columbia's provincial parks? Nonetheless, by shifting forward in public debates over resources in British Columbia, the ACC promoted the public stake in the forests beyond cubic feet in timber to recreational values and other measures.

During the postwar era, the forces of development won the tired surrender of the ACC in the case of Spray Lakes in Alberta, but they also prompted renewed conservation advocacy to influence forest and park policy in British Columbia. By the early 1960s, growing demands on national parks as playgrounds were pushing the limits and would lead to new reckonings. The club's affiliation with parks, its interest in broadening playgrounds in wild mountain areas and redefining mountaineering sport ethics, and its seeming competing interest in preserving wild places would point the ACC northward in the 1960s as Canada celebrated its centennial, ultimately toward the formation of new mountain parks and new understandings of people in parks.

The Yukon Alpine Centennial Expedition
Making Memory and Parks in the North, 1967–1972

> *Whatever we remember, and the manner in which we remember, we get a different past, a different sense of place, and a different landscape every time.*
>
> —CHRISTOPHER TILLEY[114]

In the mid-1960s, as the tide of visitation to Canadian mountain national parks rose, postwar discourses of unlimited tourism were drawn into question even as the ACC reached farther for new terrain. The Yukon

Alpine Centennial Expedition (YACE) in 1967 produced a commemorative landscape of Canadian nationalism through sport and resulting narratives about the expedition, published in the club's own *Canadian Alpine Journal*, among other places, that illustrates the role of the ACC in shaping ideas of national parks in the 1960s. The club's involvement in YACE allowed members to know and remember a remarkable place through the cultural interactions of mountaineering and adventure tourism. Further, by the late 1960s, there was a growing push to establish new mountain parks in both northern and southern Canada. In this process, YACE exemplifies how cultural landscapes were produced as parks inscribed with multiple memories.

"Landscape histories are entangled, messy, contested and directly implicated in contemporary struggles for access and rights to use and enjoy the land," as Christopher Tilley has pointed out.[115] Kluane has long been part of the traditional territories of the Southern Tutchone peoples.[116] A Privy Council Order signed in December 1942 was the first step toward making Kluane into a park. Ottawa thereby reserved the southwest corner of the Yukon for consideration as a future national park, prompted by wildlife protection concerns brought on by the new Alcan Highway. In 1943 the Yukon Territorial government instituted a nearby game sanctuary. As a result, First Nations people who lived and hunted in the region were displaced from subsistence in their homelands in the restricted areas west of the highway. Authorities also noted a stretch of the highway that "offers something you can't get anywhere else...a view of the St. Elias Mountains containing the largest glaciers and mountain peaks in Canada."[117] It was these glaciers and peaks in Kluane that attracted the attention of mountaineers in 1967. The ongoing process of exploring mountain parks—and creating new ones—involves contested social relations and politicizing of spaces, listening to stories and silences. YACE is a microcosm of this process, an event that invoked the seemingly diverse forces of summit nationalism, conservation, and social activism.

When he recalls the Alpine Club of Canada's mountaineering camp, pitched in the midst of the vast terrain called Kluane National Park Reserve, David Fisher writes, "The sight of no less than six helicopters flying up the valley in the first two weeks made a control tower almost mandatory and the Camp looked like a heliport at times." In the midst of the spectacular St. Elias Mountains, the camp, tethered at the foot of the Steele Glacier, was buffeted by the rotor wash of Bell 47 helicopters, making their way from the Alaska Highway over the Donjek River

∧ *Guide Hans Gmoser,*
David Fisher, and Judy
LaMarsh (left to right) ramp
up the party for Canada's
1967 centennial in the
Yukon's St. Elias Mountains.
[WMCR. V46/42/44/R1C4]

Valley.[118] Over the noise the radio call out "bravo echo echo romeo" was still well understood by most climbers present as the summons for beer.[119] Judy LaMarsh, secretary of state for Canada's centennial celebrations, alighted with her entourage and Whitehorse reporters to visit the camp on July 20, where she joined a flight tour and lunch featuring the club's traditional turkey dinner laid on by the Harrisons. She was there to officiate the opening of this, one of many centennial events taking place across the nation.[120]

Large centennial initiatives in the North included a scientific expedition to the North Pole, a military search for Franklin's grave in the eastern Arctic, and a centennial barge on the Mackenzie River.[121] The Yukon Territory celebrated Canada's hundredth with parades, sports events, and other local cultural projects, as well as a new flag, a Yukon Pavilion at Expo '67, and YACE, a monumental mountaineering expedition.

Public commemorations are sites for producing social memory; as well, places can constitute memory-making.[122] As Helen Davies has argued, Canada's centennial celebrations were more than events directed by a state-driven script: the popular participation of ordinary citizens ensured events' successes.[123] YACE mobilized citizen sport involvement through mountaineering in the St. Elias Range to officially commemorate Canadian nationhood during the centennial, but the expedition also exposed what diverse sport and environmental ethics the ACC was championing at the time. While parts of the ACC were beginning to move toward challenging technical climbs, as noted previously, YACE captured the ACC's love of exploration and classic first ascents.

Mass ascents involving dozens to more than a hundred climbers are displays of embodied performance whereby many climbers ascend and descend peaks together. In contrast to mass ascents for military siege or religious pilgrimage, recreational ascents by mountain clubs assert sporting claims through the collective movements of many bodies mobilized in mountain landscapes. In the case of YACE, mass ascents were undertaken by numerous climbers making multiple ascents, thereby performing and inscribing an embodied narrative of cultural landscapes, which were in turn written about in the *Canadian Alpine Journal*.

Because YACE promoted mountaineering as a symbolic commemoration, ascents evoked narratives of summit nationalism that linked climbing to the making of nationhood and national memory. Just as the 1925 ACC's first ascent of Canada's highest peak, Mount Logan, was celebrated by Canadians as a triumph on "Canada's Everest,"[124] so YACE would open Canadians' eyes to mountaineering as a nationalistic achievement. Mountains have always been heavily invested with meanings and "it would be shortsighted to discount their significance and vitality as symbolic landscapes," Reuben Ellis observes.[125] Such landscapes—places where people and the land interact—are temporally and cross-culturally discursive places of social memory, and the St. Elias Range, where YACE found itself in 1967, had long been a place where people encountered the land; story-making—knowledge-making—resulted.

According to Julie Cruikshank, Aboriginal peoples and newcomers had direct encounters in the region that became shaped by their own stories. The social relations of local knowledge bound natural and cultural history together in a region that has often been marginalized from farther south.[126] Conceptually integrating the human and non-human is central to a philosophy of relational knowledge in which "humans and nature co-produce the world they share."[127] Jeffrey McCarthy suggests the stories of North American mountaineering writers depict experiences of nature presented in three primary narrative modes: national conquest, picturesque admiration, and the interconnection of human and non-human existence.[128] "Mountaineering is a conflicted site for symbolic configurations of human interaction with the environment,"[129] yet McCarthy contends that mountaineering literature has stories that can encourage readers to go beyond awareness of nation and ego, to think about historical encounters with the environment in terms of eco-consciousness.

YACE commemorated Canada's centennial in partnership with the state by writing a federalist-nationalist sport narrative of Canadian nationhood on the cultural landscapes of the Yukon's St. Elias Range. It reinscribed the ACC as a national institution and sport pioneer; it also fostered a reimagining of the Canadian North—in particular the Southern Tutchone homelands in this region—as a climber's paradise for mountaineering, conservation, and tourism. Kluane's park status was proclaimed subsequently by Parliament. At the same time, YACE and its outcomes cannot be oversimplified as acts of colonialism and nationalism on the march in climbing boots. Climbers and their writing articulated their own understandings of nature and culture in mountain landscapes in ways that challenge common assumptions.

The idea for YACE was officially articulated in June 1965, when ACC President Bob Hind and Eastern Vice-President David Fisher attended the Centennial Sports Governing Bodies Conference in Ottawa. Organized by the Athletic Division of Canada's Centennial Commission and the Department of National Health and Welfare's Amateur Sport Directorate, the meeting aimed at "accelerating and clarifying the plans being made for Centennial Year by Canada's sports governing bodies." Ottawa had a mandate to encourage, promote, and develop fitness and amateur sport in Canada based on the 1961 Fitness and Amateur Sport Act. Fisher later recounted, "We got our foot in the door of the Centennial Commission bank vault with a plan for an expanded 1967 camp in an area inaccessible without aircraft support, conceived in ten minutes on the back of an envelope."[130]

Really, though, as early as 1963, the club had looked ahead to planning projects for the centennial year. Member Fred Roots had proposed to hold a "semi-expeditionary" summer camp in the Yukon Icefield Ranges to mark Canada's centennial and to undertake a joint mountaineering ascent with the American Alpine Club to mark the centennial of the Alaska Purchase. Roots worked with the Department of Mines and Technical Surveys in Ottawa and consulted with Walter Woods, director of Icefield Ranges Research Project (IRRP) at Kluane Lake, to incubate early plans. Later, Bob Hind and David Fisher discussed convening the club's annual camp in the Yukon. At the Ottawa conference, a third set of actors surfaced from Whitehorse with their plan from the Yukon Territorial Government. Craig Hughes, legal advisor to the commissioner of the Yukon Territory, and Monty Alford, a mountain guide who was a Yukon hydrologist in the federal Water Resources Branch of Energy, Mines, and Resources, presented a plan they had conceived to make first ascents in the St. Elias Mountains: twelve peaks would be named after the respective Canadian provinces and territories, and two first ascents on the Yukon–Alaska border would confer the names "Good Neighbour Peak" and "Centennial Peak" to recognize both hundredth anniversaries. They hoped to "sell the idea" in Ottawa to obtain funding from the Centennial Commission.[131]

The Yukon group's plan was a compelling one that, according to Fisher's published account, captured the imagination of the conference delegates. "They certainly had the mountains; what they lacked was mountaineers," he recalled. "They came to me and asked for the support of the ACC and I readily agreed that we would co-operate in whatever way we could. In addition...we placed our own project before the Conference."[132] Combining these schemes resulted in YACE.

An extensive proposal, written by Fred Roots, was put forward by the ACC in January 1966 in concert with the Yukon government and key partners. YACE was described as "a many-sided mountaineering and exploration activity to take place in Canada's highest and most spectacular, and yet little known, mountain range."[133] The aims of the expedition were laid out as a metaphor for nationhood:

> *To commemorate the Centennial of Canadian Confederation in an epic and dramatic way, by means of a large-scale mountaineering tournament in which teams of the foremost mountain climbers in Canada, representing each Province and Territory, will challenge unclimbed summits in the country's highest and wildest mountain range. The parties of mountaineers, whose very lives depend on teamwork and whose linking rope signifies the greater power and strength to be found in concerted action than in individual effort, will be a symbol of the unity and freedom [that] characterizes the parts of Canada, each pushing into the unknown, challenging and overcoming obstacles as they are met.*[134]

Mountaineering was seldom conceived as a tournament sport, yet the expedition was further described as an exercise in "friendly rivalry." Size or wealth would not be privileged as "the smallest province or the poorest territory will stand on equal ground with its neighbours." Because co-operation between teams was critical, the expedition was seen to "set a most appropriate example for Canadian Confederation."

More foreigners than Canadians had seen the St. Elias region, according to the proposal, which overlooked the long presence of First Nations and their marginalization in 1966. YACE would be a means to visit Kluane: "Hundreds of Canadian climbers have dreamed of visiting these mountains, but only the few who have been able to take part in strenuous or lengthy expeditions have done so." The expedition would exemplify outdoor adventure and fitness, which were tied to the goals of the federal Fitness and Amateur Sport Directorate. A final objective was to create "a fitting permanent memorial on the maps of Canada, of the Centennial, of the Confederation of Canada, and of the friendship between Canada and the United States of America." To this end, it planned the geographic naming of "unnamed and unclimbed mountain peaks."[135]

Fisher became the ACC's lead on the YACE working committee, which put together an elaborate flow chart partnering the club with the Yukon Territorial Government, the Arctic Institute of North America (AINA), and a logistical advisor.[136] "One of the most exciting and ambitious Centennial projects, YACE will take place in a mountain range next in grandeur and dimensions only to the Himalayas and the Andes" forecast the club when it announced the centennial climbing teams early in 1967—an oblique reference to Mounts Everest and Aconcagua, the highest points in Asia and South America.[137] Touted in the Whitehorse daily news, it was "the biggest mountaineering expedition ever undertaken in the history of climbing."[138]

In the spirit of cost-shared co-operative federalism, provincial and federal governments supplied grants for YACE. To the frustration of ACC leaders, confirmations of final commitments and dollars, particularly by the federal Treasury Board, were slow to materialize until midway through preparations. The Centennial Commission, the Fitness and Amateur Sport Programme, Yukon Territorial Government, Northwest Territories, and the provinces of British Columbia, Alberta, Saskatchewan, Manitoba, Ontario, Quebec, and Newfoundland all supplied grants; funding was not forthcoming from the Maritime provinces, nor did they have local ACC club sections. The total grant budget amounted to $77,000 for all of the YACE projects, $60,000 of which was spent on aircraft, flight reconnaissance, and fuel costs.[139] "Due to the nature of the Centennial and other Government grants," club president Roger Neave stated, "it was only possible for a national Club such as ours to carry out this project."[140] In this case, status privileged access to public purse strings.

YACE involved three expeditionary phases. The first began in June 1967. The objective for the international ascent had refocused on Mount Vancouver, a massif with an unclimbed south summit close to or on the international border between the Yukon and Alaska. The ascent involved four Canadians and four Americans co-led by Canadian Monty Alford and American John "Vin" Hoeman. The joint team reached the unclimbed south summit on June 25 and called it "Good Neighbour Peak," then reported as 15,720 feet (4,791.5 metres). Canadian, US, and Canadian Centennial flags were planted at the summit, and although headaches, hard breathing, and snowstorms accompanied the fast descent, the team reached base camp successfully. On July 3, the team flew out to the staging camp at Kluane Lake. Vague international boundaries for the south summit on Mount Vancouver left it unclear whether the team had summitted in Canada or the United States.[141]

Co-leader Monty Alford[142] later reflected on the isolation and sense of the infinite he experienced climbing the St. Elias Mountains. In the 1968 *Canadian Alpine Journal,* he wrote:

> *The summit ridge was in excellent condition with firm snow. Blanketing the great glaciers which surround the Mt. Vancouver massif from view was a layer of cloud; an undercast at 10,000 feet. This gave the scene a particular enchantment. One felt so completely isolated. With other massifs made to look like islands as they penetrated the sun drenched canopy, the scene was breathtaking. Such a picture is not perhaps novel to the mountaineer but familiarity does in no way lessen the impact on the soul. One cannot help but feel extreme humility; so finite a form in such an infinite setting. The temperature was 9°F and the wind from the south at 5–10 knots.*[143]

Alford did not dwell on centennial commemoration, rather he described his summit moment as a philosophic musing on beauty and existence: he articulated his existential presence embodied through sensations and movement, feeling firm snow walking on the ridge and seeing the world as he climbed.[144] He measured temperature, wind speed, and time elapsed as a mountain guide attuned to physical conditions affecting embodiment. Later, he opted to write about it in a way that suggested an understanding of being in and of nature, in the sense that "mountaineering narratives...reveal a way of knowing predicated on unity with the environment instead of separation from it." "Mountain writing has utopian significance for contemporary conversations about wilderness," Jeffrey McCarthy postulates, "because it suggests the possibility of a lived relation with the natural world that is—fleetingly—a mode of oneness and not alienation."[145] Alford's account conveyed his sense of oneness lived through the climbing body.

The second phase of YACE took place to the northeast of Mount Vancouver in July. The "Centennial Range" peaks in the St. Elias Range were about 48 kilometres (30 miles) north of Mount Logan and 193 kilometres (120 miles) from the nearest road. To tackle them, fifty-two climbers were formed into thirteen teams to attempt thirteen first ascents throughout two weeks in mid-July. As per the YACE plan, one peak was to be named after each province and territory in Canada, along with a peak for the centennial. Snow, fog, and heavy cornices hampered conditions during many bids for these ascents.

"Some of Canada's climbing elite may have thought that YACE would be more a ceremony than an expedition," but, according to Ottawa Section chair and climber Stanley Rosenbaum, more than enough climbers applied to provide "highly competent" leaders and experienced teams. Reconnaissance climbs were needed to determine routes because maps for the area showed "contours only at 500-foot intervals."[146] Along with Swiss-born Jean-Robert (Hans) Weber from Gatineau, Quebec, and Canadian-born Klaus Boerger from Calgary, Rosenbaum was on the team that climbed Centennial Peak, led by expert mountaineer Waldemar Fips Broda from West Vancouver. It was not an easy ascent. While waiting out storms in the intimacy of a tent clinging to the mountainside, Broda divulged his harrowing Second World War experiences as a soldier in Austria's mountain troops. He encouraged the men to complete the ascent, and they pressed on to summit the highest peak in the range, newly named to honour Canada's Centennial. The team then flew out to the Kluane staging camp and toasted its success with champagne.[147]

Mount Quebec was ascended by a francophone team of three Montreal climbers led by Claude Lavallée from St. Bruno. They snowshoed through rotting snow across the glacier to approach the mountain. The CAJ published his account in French with English translation, emphasizing the involvement of French-Canadian climbers from

Quebec—notably the rival Club de Montagne Canadien. He expressed close identification with the peak after making the climb: "La première ascension du Mont Québec venait de se terminer après 28 heures d'efforts. C'est avec grand regret que je jetai un dernier regard vers le Mont Québec...J'avais l'impression d'y avoir laissé un peu de moi-même."[148] Leaving part of himself behind, he co-existed both with and as the mountain.

A team bound for Mount Manitoba was led by famed climber Paddy Sherman, an English-born Canadian journalist from Vancouver. Arriving to set up camp on the nearby central moraine, it was clear another helicopter had already been there. Contrary to notions of a pristine North, Sherman quipped, "old engine parts littering the moraine added a welcome touch." The team easily came near the summit on its first attempt and cached a flag pole for another attempt; on following attempts, it was forced back by rock fall, rotten snow and ice, and deteriorating conditions. "I felt that the safe retreat in good order was worth more than most summits," Sherman noted, "so we opened the summit brandy." He summarized, "Manitoba is not a difficult peak. In normal June weather, it would be a pleasant outing. But with bad snow, rotten rock and even worse weather, it just wasn't worth the gamble."[149] Bodily safety and enjoyment took priority over risks for nationalistic honour, and the team backed off.

Mount Saskatchewan was assigned to climbers who "had applied and been selected as an all women team to take part with the twelve men's teams." This rope comprised Helen Butling, ACC western vice-president from Nelson, British Columbia, Gertrude Smith from Vancouver, and Wendy Teichmann and Andrea Rankin from Montreal. Whether they climbed together with feminist intent went unstated, but an all-women's rope was an implicitly feminist way to climb.[150]

Seeing wildlife and Canada's highest peak from the air, then landing at the Divide operations camp on the icefields was an intersensory experience. Smith recounted: "The lower slopes of the mountains were fresh and green. Not far below us as we flew nearer the ridges, the Dall sheep and lambs skipped away from the noise of the aircraft. Each turn in the valley revealed scenery more and more beautiful and then breathtaking Mt. Logan spread its bulk across the horizon 30 miles away."[151] After enjoying a seventeen-hour sortie on Mount Saskatchewan, the women were surprised to see men from the Manitoba and Alberta teams out searching because the women were believed to be overdue and caught in an avalanche. "Although the last thing we wanted was for the other teams

> *Gertrude Smith (on lead) looks down to photograph Wendy Teichmann, Andrea Rankin, and Helen Butling on Mount Saskatchewan in pursuit of a first ascent in the Centennial Range. The peak has yet to be summitted.*

[Stan Rosenbaum collection]

to feel any extra responsibility towards us because we were women," wrote Butling about the search. "I think we all felt rather touched by their actions."[152] Notably, the Saskatchewan team framed the search in terms of social implications of gender, rather than mutuality among climbers.

Many daring collaborative attempts to climb Mount Saskatchewan's sharp ridge allowed the team to get to know the mountain well: "Several leads of the whole length of rope had to be made before a suitable belay stance could be found. The rock rose sharply and nowhere on that rotten mass of rock could a hand or foot hold be found that did not move and threaten to bring the whole thing down. On the southeast stretched the steep surface of the slope and on the northwest was the 1,500-foot drop-off. There seemed no alternative but to retrace our steps and find a way lower down to by-pass this unpleasant place."[153] On the final day, they turned back at 10,400 feet (3,170 metres) off route in deteriorating conditions. "To get back up entailed climbing up a steep snow slope sinking in up to the thighs which Gertrude very gamely tried to do but gave it up as too exhausting...We chose to strap on our crampons and using ice screws for protection go down the gully and cross the ridge lower down where we could see an opening."[154] Their friends again appeared looking for them, and all retreated back to the tiny tent, now packed with seven climbers, while the men cooked and "ordered" the women into sleeping bags to rest and tell their story after a thirty-hour attempt.

"Above 5000 feet the bare rocks appear to support little life. We saw a microscopic draba, a small blue butterfly and a wasp," Smith observed in the remote high alpine. "Often we had the sensation of having been transported back to the Ice Age." Her account, nonetheless, emphasized her position as one among other living organisms in a glaciated landscape peopled with climbers.[155] Teams relayed news about the weather, terrain, supplies, and each other while making visits. Ascents were eagerly awaited, and mountaineers were conscious of outcomes. Butling noted there was no party held on returning to Divide Camp because "with Manitoba and ourselves in the dog house and Centennial an unknown quantity no one felt like celebrating."[156] "Because the Expedition had placed us 'on stage,'" climber Andrea Rankin reflected thirty years later, "we felt more committed to success than we would have on an ordinary expedition."[157]

YACE mountaineering exploits also forged official social memory through commemorative ascents. The second phase of the expedition named peaks in honour of each province and territory, embodying and geographically inscribing a particular vision of federalist nationalism through the Centennial Range.[158] The Canadian Permanent Committee on Geographic Names (CPCGN) in Ottawa authorized these new toponyms to appear on official records and maps.[159] The Canadian Centennial Medal was bestowed on leading figures in YACE, such as Monty Alford and chief outfitter Bill Harrison. The silver medals, issued in 1967, were awarded by the Governor General to Canadians for service to the nation in all sectors of society, including sports.[160]

The third and final phase of YACE was the ACC general mountaineering camp (GMC—the new term for the annual summer camp), staged at the foot of the Steele Glacier during the last two weeks of

July and the first two weeks of August. It was not an easy sell to attract
and keep Canadian registrants due to "camp, travel, and equipment
costs," and organizers worked hard at marketing the camp, especially
to Americans.[161] Each two-week camp attracted about 115 people who

< ∧ The Centennial GMC
next to the surging Mount
Steele Glacier (centre)
in 1967. A fixed-wing Beaver
aircraft dropped new canvas
tents made in Edmonton;
mountaineers flew in
three-seater helicopters.
Supercharged piston engines
cranking auto rotations down
from 12,000 feet (3,657.6
metres) to land near camp
was "something that
everyone got used to" as
choppers whisked climbers
over an extraordinary
glacier surge.
[WMCR, V107/bx1-14]

< Bullock Helicopters fly
passengers and payload to
GMC at Mount Steele
Glacier in 1967. The new
mountain workhorses fuelled
at main camp for local flights.
Aviation fuel was cached
during late winter in 150
twelve-gallon drums, fifteen
feet (4.6 metres)above a
small lake near Steele
Glacier's snout; a sudden
glacier upsurge submerged
many and carried others
downstream. Recovery of
135 drums was improvised
with a raft christened the
Yukon Queen.
[WMCR, V46/42/44/R3C4]

staged near Burwash Landing on Kluane Lake. It was an unusual opportunity to visit a remote mountain district much farther afield than most
annual club summer camps. Lord Hunt and Lady Hunt of Llanfair
brought the YACE general camp a living link to the Everest first ascent;
Hunt had led the 1953 British expedition. Hunt offered his expertise
to lead climbing parties at the camp, as did well-known professional
mountain guides Hans Gmoser, Peter Fuhrmann, and Hans Schwarz.
Parties fanned out from the main camp, high camps, and heli-landing
points, seeking various climbing objectives. The surging Steele Glacier
was impassable, necessitating helicopter drops to reach many climbs.
Mounts Walsh, Wood, and Steele were key peaks climbed in the district,
also the only ones designated with official permanent geographic names.
A total of nineteen peaks were climbed from the main camp, of which
fourteen were recorded as first ascents.[162]

As the first ascents were gained, new names were subsequently
attached to various features overlooking the Steele Valley. Deceased ACC
presidents were honoured when twelve prominent peaks and associated
glaciers were named after them. With one exception, these peaks were
recorded as climbed and nine climbs were published as first ascents. By
ascending and naming peaks, the ACC left an imprint on the landscape
that emphasized a traditional institutional narrative of the club's "great
men"; left unstated was the history of women and men who provided
other volunteer, staff, and family supports to the club, particularly at the
local level, as well as that of co-founder and national secretary Elizabeth
Parker. After camp, the club applied to the CPCGN to approve the
submission of the new toponyms. Approval was officially granted after
the committee's deliberations and consultation with Yukon authorities,
who advised the committee that no Aboriginal names were known for
the proposed features.[162] However, since 1942, Indigenous geographies
had been obscured by the exclusion of First Nations' subsistence from
the region reserved for conservation.

Like clockwork, all campers and equipment were flown out by 5 PM on
August 14.[164] It appears that a major exception to the clean up was fifteen
barrels (180 gallons) of gasoline that presumably sank in the outflow
lake of Hazard Creek, dubbed "Drum Lake," or washed downstream.[165]
At the first club camp serviced by helicopters, there was little official

commentary to indicate an awareness of the environmental impacts of air traffic and noise, aside from it was "something that everyone got used to." However, Smith's references to how Dall sheep and lambs "skipped away" as her helicopter transport passed overhead suggest the effects of these disruptions.[166] Apart from abolishing campfires and firewood consumption usual at other ACC annual camps, the club's published accounts did not mention concerns related to environmental impacts, which suggests the club's institutional mentality and practices of the day with regard to "wilderness recreation" had yet to integrate emergent minimum-impact philosophies. Finally, near the campsite, a large 1967 Centennial logo was outlined in rocks and was still visible from a helicopter some thirty-five years later.[167]

The *Canadian Alpine Journal* issued in 1968 gave extensive coverage to YACE, complete with maps and illustrated accounts of the expedition logistics and ascents. David Fisher remarked to journal editor Phyllis Munday that the first-ascent accounts submitted for publication had required his close verification because, in many instances, heavy cornices overhanging peaks posed risks that complicated reaching the precise summit points due to changing natural conditions.[168] He made judgements about these practical considerations of summit claims by conferring with various climbers to verify and validate the first ascents before publication. Fisher's final business report about the expedition was also included in the same journal.

An illustrated book, *Expedition Yukon,* was published in 1971, edited by Marnie Fisher, married to David Fisher, with chapters written by YACE participants. It further commemorated events and fulfilled the goal for documentation set in the club's proposal to the Centennial Commission. The book details climbs and reports on the natural and cultural history of Kluane. It was sent to the sponsoring government agencies, just as flags and YACE medallions were distributed as commemorative artifacts.[169] The editor's introduction presented YACE as a monumental feat of firsts and a wellspring of climbing stories.[170] However, reviewed in 1972 by Dick Culbert, a leading-edge alpinist and member of the British Columbia Mountaineering Club, the book was written off as a "memento" for participants. He dismissed the style and substance of the expedition in a range that "had remained virgin through being overlooked by climbers, largely because its [sic] is overlooked by summits half again as high. The major climbs were eventful, and sizable chances were taken by several of the parties (in part because some of the members were out of their environment, if not clean over their heads)."

Here Mount Logan and higher peaks with tougher routes were the unstated prizes of the region, not the Centennial ascents. He judged the organization of the event as "the biggest challenge involved" in "a most massive and unusual undertaking."[171]

Faint praise for the ACC was characteristic of the emerging outlook among many skilled technical climbers; by this time certain clubs privileged different standards of climbing and new grades of difficulty. Climbers such as Culbert were apt to dismiss YACE as a centennial ceremony rather than serious climbing. Still, in 1997, an illustrated magazine edited by Marnie Fisher and R.W. Sandford, was published by the ACC for the thirtieth anniversary of YACE; it republished parts of the 1971 book and reinscribed the expeditions as "important events in the history of Canadian mountaineering," involving "the best of an entire generation of Canadian climbers."[172]

Reminiscences thirty years later stressed how the centennial climbs forged lasting personal memories for many of the individual climbers. "When your mind is truly focused, every second can seem like a hundred. And you are going to remember every one of those seconds for a long time," reflected Stan Rosenbaum. "Whatever else in their lives these people may have forgotten, the adventures of 1967 remained riveted in their minds, and still do today."[173] His historical essay and an extensive online photo archive placed the expedition within commemorations of the thirtieth anniversary of Expo '67 and Canada's centennial year.

Still, interpretations of YACE like those of Culbert persisted in recent historiography, often written by the generation of technical climbers contemporaneous with the early Calgary Mountain Club. In 2000 Chic Scott, a former CMC climber of that generation, offered ambiguous praise to the YACE ascents in his popular mountaineering history. He observed that "although the ACC has often been criticized for being out of touch with serious climbing, it has always been recognized for its organizational skills." He surmised that YACE was "the camp to end all camps."[174] Monty Alford contended in 2005: "Any history of mountaineering in North America must record YACE as a most imaginative event that was superbly planned and executed in the best tradition of alpinism," with praise for the organizers, climbers, and "those in federal and territorial offices who recognized the value of such an event as symbolic of the pioneering spirit, stamina and determination exhibited by the first explorers of this rugged part of northwest North America."[175] Divergent perspectives reflect divergent assumptions and subject positions. When faced with structuring the centennial climbs, the club could pursue innovative ascents by the best climbers, or broader participation by many climbers pursuing multiple objectives. In this respect, the style of YACE was a combination that aligned more with the participatory politics of centennial citizen commemorations across the country.

The YACE alpine ascents were not an innovation in the sport of alpine mountaineering nor did they reach for new technical feats, but as a mass performance they were a major national sporting event with strong nationalistic overtones of achievement in the North. By the end of YACE, the club had sent about three hundred people into the St. Elias Mountains in one summer season. Its mountaineers, mostly average amateur climbers on holidays with a number of elite climbers and professional mountain guides, had climbed thirty-three peaks in the Yukon, of which twenty-seven were first ascents.[176]

Just as the ACC had approached the 1925 first ascent of Mount Logan, in 1967 the club claimed that its quest would affirm Canadian nationhood through sport. This assertion came amid surging centennial-year nationalism, Canada's role as an international middle power under Lester Pearson, the co-operative federalism approach to federal–provincial relations and cost sharing, and growing national unity concerns spurred by rising Quebec nationalism. During this period, sport was understood as a bond for Canadian unity and pride even as it played on regional rivalries.[177] As well, the joint celebration of hundredth anniversaries on the Alaska–Yukon border emphasized friendly relations between Canada and its closest neighbour, all of this during an era of Cold-War American neo-imperialism and Canadian critiques of American branch-plant capitalism.

Naming twelve peaks after late ACC presidents on the south side of the Steele Glacier mirrored naming twelve peaks in the Centennial Range after provinces and territories. In this sense, the club's 1967 ascents—aligning the club with Canada itself—became a metaphor for federalist nationhood in a northern landscape long mythologized and co-opted by pan-Canadian ideologies. They also appear indicative of a representation of liberal pluralism in postwar Canadian citizenship that, by the late 1960s, was increasingly pressured to accommodate class, gender, language, ancestry, and regional tensions: in this case within a largely white mountaineering community formed around the ACC and YACE. First Nations were conspicuously absent from these representations of Canadian citizenship, which preceded the infamous 1969 federal White Paper. The ACC had laid nationalistic claims through mountaineering and willingly collaborated in nationalist agendas of the Canadian state. Its brief occupation of landmarks in the Yukon St. Elias Range, claimed as nationalistic symbols through multiple ascents and naming, simultaneously overlooked and overwrote Aboriginal claims and geographic names in the homelands of the Southern Tutchone peoples, as well as the long history of human migrations through the glaciated mountain and coastal regions subdivided by the colonial boundaries marked by the Yukon, British Columbia, and Alaska.[178] Adventure sports on traditional lands would serve to open what was considered rare and remote terrain to more tourism.

While YACE climbers were certainly not the only ones operating in the St. Elias Range that summer, the expedition was a magnet that drew more climbers north. YACE's pilots, outfitters, and guides were also recruited from the South, not locally, and the expedition served as a forerunner of greater helicopter tourism access to Kluane. Expeditioneers pursued travel and mountaineering objectives that they viewed as singular experiences in an undeveloped climbing area, an outlook influenced by a mythology of the northern wilderness frontier.[179] For example, Canadian climber Hugh Neave quoted Robert Service's "The Spell of the Yukon" to describe the YACE general camp, but such images erased a long human presence by imagining the North nameless, unpeopled, and untouched.[180]

YACE made future trips to the St. Elias Range more probable and enticing to mountaineers. The beauty and expanse of Kluane was undeniable to them, although the accounts discussed here rarely termed it wilderness. What they often described was termed "isolation," partly attributable to being on glaciated peaks at high altitude and at great distances from roads and settlements. Indirectly, isolation also implied the absence of local population, in this case because the national park reserve did not permit Indigenous peoples to subsist within its boundaries. Based on their cultural outlook, what climbers also saw was a tourism destination with a prime landscape for more mountaineering: once again, a climber's paradise. Roger Neave pointed out in his foreword to the 1968 CAJ, "To those who were not so fortunate as to be able to participate, they will perhaps give some idea of this fascinating country, and...inspire a desire to go and see it for themselves."[181] Overall, climbers expressed their own cultural ways of seeing landscape that also aligned with their ideas of southern mountain parks and nature conservation, which spurred the club on into lobbying for more mountain parks in the North.

Following YACE and the accumulated knowledge of the St. Elias Range, the ACC took an active role among proponents calling for the creation of new national parks in the North. In 1971 the ACC recommended that Kluane National Park Reserve be formally declared a national park. Club President David Fisher wrote to Jean Chrétien, then minister of Indian Affairs and Northern Development, to submit a proposal written by the club's conservation committee, chaired by Edmonton Section member Harry Habgood; Chrétien was also the ACC's honorary vice-president from 1969 to 1973.[182] Fisher emphasized their recommendation to expand the area of the park reserve in the vicinity of Quill Creek and Burwash Creek "to conserve it and to prevent the spread of development on the west side of the Alaska Highway." Fisher added he had "flown over this area in 1967 during our Centennial Expedition. I feel it is most important to include this region in the Park."[183] According to the club's proposal, crafted by Habgood, concessions to mining and prospecting were actively chipping away the Kluane park reserve lands and scarring a fragile northern habitat; it urged active support to advance the establishment of a national park before it was too late. The Carr Report forecast visitation to the Yukon would grow from a hundred thousand tourists in 1967 to triple or quadruple by 1985; tourism was proposed as an alternative economic generator "to help offset to some extent the vulnerability of the present extractive resource based economy." "With the added attraction of an outstanding National Park," the ACC reasoned that "tourism may well become a very important industry in the Yukon." Kluane was compared with Banff National Park's origins in the 1880s, when "Calgary was half the size Whitehorse is today." The ACC's proposal teamed economic and tourism arguments for an expanded Kluane National Park with rationales for protecting biophysical resources of wildlife and habitat, along with recognizing the St. Elias Mountains as "one of the largest non-polar glacier systems in the world."[184] Prohibitions against hunting and trapping in the existing Kluane Game Sanctuary were equated with protections granted in national parks. Although the proposal highlighted the need to understand Kluane's ecology and resources, it did not recognize the need to acknowledge the First Nations in the area, nor were First Nations mentioned in the club's proposal for a new national park in the Mackenzie Mountains in Nahanni.[185] However, Aboriginal peoples were recognized explicitly in the club's proposal for a national park on Baffin Island.

The Baffin Island proposal was strongly influenced by glaciologist Patrick D. Baird, a mountaineer and director of AINA in Montreal and a member of the ACC Ottawa Section.[186] A section on "Native Rights" emphasized the club "has no wish to force new modes of life upon the native people of northern Canada. Thus we strongly urge that every consideration be given to maintaining their rights if a park is created. Unless compelling reasons for other rules exist, the hunting and fishing regulations of the North West Territories should prevail."[187] Informed by Baird's extensive contact with Inuit during research in the eastern Arctic, this provision in the proposal preceded new directions that would emerge in northern parks in the 1990s, as collaborative management practices were instituted premised on Indigenous rights and land claims.

From 1969 to 1972, ACC leaders, along with other stakeholders, effectively lobbied Minister Jean Chrétien to support the creation of three mountain parks in northern Canada: Kluane in the Yukon Territory's St. Elias Range; Nahanni in the Northwest Territories' Mackenzie Mountains; and Auyuittuq in Baffin Island's Cumberland Range.[188] In fact, the minister had already been considering such directions. The Throne Speech in February 1972 announced formal commitments to designate the three national park reserves and next steps followed. Pending land claims, Kluane National Park Reserve (22,015 square kilometres) in 1972 was first, followed by the other two in 1976.[189] Kluane was then proclaimed a National Park Reserve in 1976 and, in 1993, renamed Kluane National Park and Reserve with the signing of the Champagne Aishihik First Nations Final Agreements.[190] Kluane was encompassed within a UNESCO World Heritage Site in 1979 that spans 9.8 million hectares of the Yukon, British Columbia, and Alaska.[191] Following the Yukon Indian Land Claim Settlement in 1995, Kluane National Park and Reserve gave rise to innovative co-operative land use and management agreements between First Nations and the Crown that significantly reshaped the conceptualization and management of national parks in northern Canada.[192]

After YACE, Kluane was imagined and occupied as a vast mountaineering playground. Outstanding land claims existed in the areas where YACE had operated, and the continued cultural imperialism of exploration and conquest in the conceptualization of parks in northern Canada initially overlooked the presence of Aboriginal homelands in the same territories that were redefined with new boundaries as territorial game sanctuaries, national parks, reserves, and World Heritage Sites. It is difficult to know if the expedition's first ascents were, in fact, "firsts," considering the more than eight thousand years of human history and travel—even at high altitude—in Kluane,[193] but clearly they were authorized and legitimated as such by hegemonic factors of sport and geography. How First Nations viewed YACE is unclear;[194] however,

Southern Parks, Too
Bugaboo Glacier Provincial Park

∧ *Bugaboo Spire and Vowell Glacier, 1966.* [BCA, I-21482]

NEW MOUNTAIN PARKS were not limited to federal lands in northern Canada. In the 1960s and 1970s, the provinces were also acting to create more mountain parks. On the British Columbia side of the Great Divide, the ACC had advocated the postwar designation of the Bugaboos as park land and recommended situating an alpine hut there as early as 1944. In 1969 the Province of British Columbia established Bugaboo Glacier Provincial Park (358 hectares) and granted the club a twenty-one-year lease to the location for the permanent new Conrad Kain Hut.[195] The new park protected the impressive granite spires and Bugaboo Alpine Recreation Area (24,624 hectares), including Conrad Glacier, Vowell Glacier, and Bugaboo Glacier, in response to growing public use and demand; they were later combined as Bugaboo Provincial Park (13,646 hectares) in 1996. The park's 1999 management plan highlighted rock climbing as "one of the most popular activities in the park and... a major impetus for preservation in the area"; it also concluded that the most popular climbs, such as Pigeon Spire, had reached social carrying capacity with line ups forming on the routes.[196] The popularity of Pigeon Spire was prefigured by the ACC annual camp as early as 1946: "Undoubtedly the most popular climb was Pigeon Spire.

Its firm rock always offered ample holds whenever its frequent exposure became particularly airy. On one day there was a traffic jam at the traverse to the final summit."[197] By 1999 the ACC was identified among the key stakeholders in the park planning consultation process, and the park management plan highlighted the club's role operating Conrad Kain Hut and holding one of four permits for commercial guiding in Bugaboo Provincial Park.[198]

Like Kluane, the Bugaboos represented the landscape aesthetics of sublime wilderness and peaks to ascend in awe-inspiring mountain ranges. Once considered new frontiers for a climber's paradise according to the ACC way of seeing and engaging in mountain landscapes, Kluane and the Bugaboos were ultimately reconstituted by the state as modern parks and protected areas that reinscribed the idea of mountain paradise. Unlike Kluane, the Bugaboos were a wilderness within closer reach of southern populations, and, by 1969, the area's role as a park was situated amid the growing economy for alpine recreation and tourism, such as heli-skiing with Canadian Mountain Holidays (CMH). In both cases, ACC members animated advocacy for mountain parks and recreation.

at least one local politician raised a dissenting perspective regarding the Centennial Range map: "We need no permanent reminders in this area that the Yukon Territory is a colony, certainly not from those who have consistently refused to allow the people of the Yukon...the same rights and freedoms as other Canadians resident in the Provinces," observed John Livesey, Yukon Councillor for Carmacks/Kluane Lake, a longtime northerner originally from England.[199] YACE and its state partners appropriated the St. Elias Range through sport to serve the goals of nationalistic commemoration and exploited the grandeur of northern wilderness by positing it as the essence of Canadian nationhood.

This interpretation may not be entirely satisfying, however, as the mass performance of first ascents ritualizing a national commemoration was constituted by individual mountaineers who made their own meanings and spoke with their own voices. Postcolonial narratives that homogenize the activities of colonizers as uncomplicated narratives of domination can overlook these complexities, ambiguities, and contradictions.[200] That YACE was given privileged access to areas of Kluane, in the Southern Tutchone homelands, on the basis of state funding schemes for an authorized centennial sport expedition is clear. Mountaineers were also part of an ongoing flux of human travel in the region, and they embodied a human presence on the land in a region with a long history as a peopled place.

Studying Athapaskan and Tlingit narratives about glaciers, Cruikshank argues that nature and culture in the St. Elias Range are deeply interconnected as one and the same through encounters and stories.[201] Exploring such interconnections with regard to YACE in the same mountain range underscores how postwar mountaineering narratives surfaced themes that went beyond commonly related stories of conquest or the Romantic sublime. An underlying narrative of mountaineering articulated a deeply interconnected way of knowing nature and culture as one through embodiment while climbing. Peak bagging and romanticism notwithstanding, published accounts of YACE mountaineers also expressed a sense of the St. Elias Range as a place where they were fleetingly in and of nature. Some mountaineers came to understand the region as a cultural landscape where they camped and climbed, a place that was potentially transformative as part of who they were, where they tied their stories to the land in an encounter as passing travellers in 1967. This outlook illustrates the potential Jeffrey McCarthy outlines for social transformation in Western relations with the environment.

YACE commemorated the culturally dominant idea of "Canada" in the 1967 climbs in Kluane.[202] Although individual climbers expressed varied understandings of YACE and thus of the centennial, the stories of YACE were always tied to a specific space, one from which local First Nations were barred from subsisting in 1967. Mountaineers with the expedition might appear in another story as passing non-Aboriginal travellers—such as the Klondikers or Alcan Highway builders—in a long local history of Indigenous occupation, but this was not the dominant understanding in texts produced by the climbers. YACE was a way to see mountaineering as the project of nationhood and to project the future of the Kluane St. Elias Mountains as a national park.

The ACC circled back to the St. Elias Mountains for the Yukon Alpine Centennial Camp (YACC) to commemorate the club's hundredth birthday in 2006. Today outdoor enthusiasts can see the Yukon by means of an elaborate commercial tourism industry, much as mountaineers relied on YACE and the ACC in 1967.[203] First Nations' rights are legally recognized and increasingly engaged through practices and procedures such as land and park co-management. In an era of climate change, species extinctions, rapid habitat depletion, intensifying resource extraction, and globalization, environmental protection and cultural survival in the Yukon are problematic but closely connected. "Aboriginal and non-Aboriginal alike are focusing on the land of the future, their land," highlighted Ken Coates, "shared and jointly occupied, developed and stewarded in a manner that is sustainable, achievable, and in the communities' collective self-interest."[204] YACE represents an event driven by multiple subjects and commemorated by dissonant memories, but those diverse elements work to transform cultural landscapes. The ambiguities and silences of commemoration can be the missing and lasting landmarks of a different sense of place and nation. Encounters with the land and the knowledge they produce in the midst of social and environmental flux may be a touchstone of cultural continuity. These encounters and stories also constitute and commemorate Canada.

Imbricated ideologies of liberal democratic citizenship, postwar economics, consumer culture, and welfare state intervention informed the directions of recreation, sport, and tourism that emerged while leading the mountain park idea, and the ACC, into a new era of environmental and ecological thinking. After the experience of YACE, environmental movements in the late 1960s and issues emerging in the Rocky Mountain national parks soon refocused public attention back to the ACC's old stomping grounds. Making mountain parks implicated place memories, land use, and sport tourism practices again, this time as changes were taking shape in the South. When the federal government proposed the first master plans for the "Four Mountain Parks," it set in motion a tidal wave of civic response from many Canadians, especially park users. The ACC emerged to rethink its ethics and social activism as it surged forward with them.

Belonging in Mountain Landscapes

The mountain parks are for all Canadians for all time and their value cannot be measured in terms of how many access roads, motels, souvenir shops and golf courses we've provided.

—BOB JORDAN[1]

WHEN THE ACC TRAVELLED TO the St. Elias Range for Canada's
centennial year and later lobbied for new national parks in the North, it
engaged a new environmental activism along with imagining Canada's
northern ranges as mountaineering playgrounds and protected areas. As
a result of Ottawa's proposals in 1968 to pave paradise in southern
national parks through the Rockies, this environmentalism—and
ongoing interest in recreation—produced vocal conservation advocacy
that led to re-examination. Specialized conservation organizations
emerged as the principal non-government advocates for parks and
wilderness, bolstered by the ACC as a recreational stakeholder.

By the late 1960s, the ACC had begun to realize how the postwar
tourism ideal had wrought unwanted side effects, such as vegetation
damage. Witnessing the cumulative effects of use in the mountain parks
through the 1950s and 1960s, especially in intensively visited areas
such as the Lake O'Hara meadows and Lake Louise, it was apparent that
strategies to better manage resource use and protection were needed.[2]
Moreover, as early as 1959 through the mid-1960s, the Parks Branch itself
came to realize that mushrooming visitation and its own race to keep
up with rising demands by providing public works and services were
having adverse effects on the environment.[3] In little more than a decade,

adherence to "limitless" postwar growth had produced a new generation of major management challenges that Parks grappled to reassess. As the postwar parks became host to a multiplying number of recreational stakeholders and intensified use, the role of the ACC diminished relative to the expanding population of recreationists. But its long-standing involvement in mountain parks and the North, and its commitment to recreation and protection in those places, continued to shape the national park idea.

Influenced by the new environmental movement, key ACC members rearticulated and renewed the club's commitment to conservation. The club intervened to challenge the direction of the federal government's master park plans declared for the Four Mountain Parks in 1968, and it reasserted the recreational importance of mountaineering, as well as minimum-impact ideologies and recreational use ethics. That many major valleys in these parks are unroaded today is a legacy of public conservation advocacy.

The Freedom of the Hills
Roads to Wilderness and Conservation in the Four Mountain Parks

Contentious federal government plans to build new scenic highways opening up more valleys to auto tourism in the mountain parks spurred public debate over the future of Banff, Jasper, Yoho, and Kootenay in the late 1960s. Sweeping new drive tours were on the drawing board for places such as the Pipestone-Cascade Valley, Howse Pass, Maligne River to Sunwapta River, and Fortress Lake, but the ACC and many other opponents to the proposals tended to see Ottawa planners driving the mountain parks from paradise to perdition on well-paved roads. Following the release of the provisional master plans for the contiguous Four Mountain Parks, approved early in 1968, Canada's National and Historic Parks Branch in the Department of Indian Affairs and Northern Development faced vocal opposition to the directions it had outlined to meet escalating tourism demands. Implementing a park zoning system with five land-use classifications, building new roads and mass campgrounds on valley floors, expanding service centres for automobile tourists, and encouraging more snowmobile recreation in designated areas were key proposals in the provisional plans released for discussion prior to public hearings. Formulated by the Parks Service Planning Division in Ottawa, the plans reflected an optimistic internal outlook on the strength of technocratic management and rational planning to design for and accommodate intensifying demands on the mountain

parks. However, "the view taken by an emerging environmental lobby argued for curbing growth and focussing on protecting wilderness areas," according to C.J. Taylor, and, ultimately, contestation through a newly launched public consultation process and lobbying prompted the national parks organization to reverse direction and shift its outlook.[4]

In the midst of this public policy debate, the ACC stepped forward to reinvigorate its advocacy role in the politics of national parks. It was concerned that the provisional master plans focused on automobile tourists, sightseers, and motorized recreation, while climbing, hiking, and ski touring in the mountain parks were scarcely mentioned as recreational activities. Moreover, it considered the preservation of wilderness to be seriously at stake. The ACC emerged from a re-examination of its own conservation ethics, prompted by social changes as well as its participation in YACE in 1967, and it galvanized against the vision of mountain parks proposed in the initial government plans and put forward its own countervision. Here it was influenced by contemporary trends in thinking about wilderness, ecology, and environmentalism in the late 1960s.

A new wave in the club's thinking about mountaineers and mountain parks began when six Edmonton Section members held a panel discussion to talk about conservation at a local section meeting. Soon afterward, in October 1969, the club's national board of management appointed them to form a new ACC Conservation Committee. The committee encouraged club members to engage the conservation objectives of the ACC and advised the national board of management on conservation concerns, reporting to Dave Wessel.[5] The chair of the new conservation committee and a leading thinker who articulated the club's changing philosophy of conservation and environmentalism during this era was Harry Habgood, who also worked on the proposal put forward in 1971 to proclaim Kluane National Park Reserve a national park.

The conservation committee sought to define a conservation policy for the club and spent two years preparing a submission to the Four Mountain Parks planning process and hearings. Habgood was this submission's chief architect. In its first policy statement, the committee judged the aims stated in the club's original mandate paradoxical. To reconcile the goals of mountain use and preservation, the committee stressed the importance of environmentally sensitive conduct to safeguard "mountain ecology" as it sought to define the club's conservation policy stance:

Henry Walter Habgood (1921–2008)

HENRY (HARRY) HABGOOD was an Alberta boy born in a Calgary family of English ancestry. In the mid-1950s, he moved from an appointment with the National Research Council in Ottawa to Edmonton, where he joined the Alberta Research Council and became vice-president of basic sciences. He held a PHD in chemistry from University of Michigan at Ann Arbor and a professional engineering degree from Queen's University, where he met Thelma Eskin (b. 1921) from Ottawa, the daughter of Russian Jewish immigrants. They married in 1946 at Ann Arbor. Thelma was an alkaloid chemist who held a master's degree from Queen's, a PHD from Ann Arbor, and a postdoctorate at University of Alberta; she became a researcher at the University of Alberta in the Department of Anthropology and Archaeology, studying palynology. Her diverse interests encompassed playing a Zuckermann harpsichord and hiking, and when she decided to join the ACC to pursue climbing in the mid-1960s her husband followed suit.

Harry attended two ACC summer camps and climbed on Baffin Island with fellow scientist Ted Whalley. Navigating off-trail without a guidebook

∧ *Thelma and Harry Habgood on their farm near Edson, Alberta. Habgood wrote the ACC's pivotal statements on the Four Mountain Parks master plans and national park advocacy for Kluane. [Helen Habgood private collection]*

appealed to him. Active in Jasper, Banff, and the Edmonton region, the Habgoods cross-country skied, backpacked, and scrambled. They carried three-month-old baby Helen in a sling on her first mountain camping trip near Jasper; Helen grew up to become an avid mountaineer. They loved plants, studied botany, and gardened on a weekend farm. The couple supported many outdoor groups but considered themselves "loners" more than "groupies." Both were scientists, deeply committed to nature and outdoor life. In 1974 they went trekking in Nepal, and a decade later moved to Nova Scotia where Thelma later took up life at a Buddhist monastery in Cape Breton. According to Thelma, Habgood was a modest man. A colleague said he was a "brilliant" intellectual and scientist who had little time for chitchat yet made time to hear university seminars with Margaret Atwood and other Canadian writers.[6] His acumen and zest for policy work brought strength to new environmental advocacy for parks and conservation.

The Alpine Club of Canada includes among its objectives the encouragement of mountaineering and also the preservation of the natural beauties of the mountain places and of the fauna and flora in their habitat. These objectives tend to be contradictory because, by his very presence, man alters the environment and most of his activities are damaging in some degree and to some aspects of the flora and fauna. A conservation policy for the Club, therefore, must be a set of guidelines whereby we can pursue mountaineering with minimum effect upon the mountain ecology. This policy is intended as a basis for our own activities and as a guide to the Club in its attitudes and policy statements concerning the actions of others including governments and corporations.[7]

The committee encouraged "Canadians to enjoy their mountain regions in ways that have minimum ecological effect on the Alpine wilderness" and advised its own club members to apply good conservation practices to set an example for other backcountry users. It laid out several internal management principles in 1969 to preserve protected areas and move toward minimum-impact practices:

1. *While we recognize that society may require the exploitation of natural resources such as timber and minerals in the mountain regions, we support efforts to set aside portions of these areas in which such exploitation is not allowed. In areas where development does take place, it must be regulated towards minimum impact on the surroundings.*

2. *National Parks are, in general, committed to the preservation of natural environments; hence we support the establishment of National Parks, especially in rocky and alpine regions.*

3. *The presence of a large number of people in a wilderness area can cause irreparable damage to the environment; hence we believe that the system of public roads in the mountains should leave major areas untouched as a discouragement to excessive visitation within these areas.*

4. *We believe that the maximum in human satisfaction combined with the minimum in ecological damage is achieved when the mountains are visited on foot, particularly on carefully made*

walking trails. We therefore support the development of a network of walking trails in mountain regions and feel that roads and horse trails should be limited to those required for reasonable access.

5. *We urge our members to exercise care and restraint both on the trail and in camp.*[8]

The ACC was awakened to ideas about ecology—the idea of minimum impact and "leaving no trace" was the latest philosophical concept to guide wilderness recreation—and it attempted to undo and prevent damage caused by increased human activity in the mountain parks.[9]

The ACC Conservation Committee began to publish regular reports in late 1969 to promote thinking about conservation and ethics in the club's national newsletter, *The Gazette,* issued twice yearly, and to discuss with club members issues of concern. "As Alpine Club members we have probably a deeper appreciation than the average citizen of the values of wild country and the wilderness experience," it advised in 1970, asserting its privileged cultural capital, "and of the fragility of the natural environments in the face of increasing population and development pressures." The committee recommended club members write directly to government and parks officials on issues such as counteracting demands for increased snowmobile use in national parks and wilderness areas, tighter regulation of outboard motors on alpine lakes (particularly Maligne Lake in Jasper, where oil discharges disintegrated slowly on the cold water), and clearing trees from reservoir sites before upstream flooding for power dams. They were also encouraged to suggest alpine areas "that the Club might recommend to governments for protection as National Parks, Provincial Parks, or wilderness areas" and to document them with pictures and maps. It wanted members to make recommendations for the establishment of well-constructed alpine trails to minimize damage and to watch for environmental abuses, such as poor waste disposal of garbage and serious erosion due to lumbering or mining operations. It also recommended that members join and support conservation groups, specifically the National and Provincial Parks Association of Canada (NPPAC), which aimed to expand federal and provincial parks to preserve natural and historic areas. NPPAC and ACC continued to share allied objectives, as well as certain members.[10]

A submission to the Four Mountain Parks planning hearings, co-ordinated and prepared in consultation with ACC section correspondents and the national board, was one of the conservation committee's major concerns. At the annual general meeting in August 1970, board member Dave Wessel applauded the club for becoming more actively involved in policy-making in this regard, and Reed Naylor stated he was pleased the club had formed the committee: "the new Board could fight our own Canadian battles and not have Canadians rely on such American Organizations as the Sierra Club...to do this for us." The committee was cautioned to proceed at the hearings without "being too emotional or in taking too strong a stance in banning snowmobiles from the Parks as we might lose the whole battle."[11] Following an internal club consultation and approval process, two briefs to Parks regarding conservation were published in *The Gazette* in May 1971: the first pertaining to the four mountain parks and the other recommending the formal establishment of Kluane as a national park in the Yukon.[12] The committee was ready for public hearings.

Several other initiatives were promoted by the conservation committee and the club. On the provincial front, the Edmonton and Calgary sections submitted briefs advising how to strengthen Bill 106 (1970) for the creation of wilderness areas in Alberta, and shortly after, the national conservation committee stepped forward to advocate protecting the full size of the provisional White Goat Wilderness Area when the province looked to reduce it in 1972.[13]

The conservation committee also promoted education. A list of films with conservation themes was circulated to interest club sections in discussion, and an illustrated pamphlet guide, called "Mountain Manners," was produced to promote better environmental practices on trips and climbs through applied conservation ethics to minimize impacts. "To enjoy and yet preserve is a real challenge. We believe that if we are careful when we visit the mountains we can have the enjoyment without causing significant damage. But as more and more people seek out the wild places," it cautioned, "we must all care a little more or soon there won't be much wilderness to enjoy." Instructions were proposed to take responsibility for garbage and fire hazards, and to minimize the use of horses and motorized vehicles such as snowmobiles. Backcountry users were advised to stay on trails, minimize campsite construction, dig latrines, store/hang food away from animals, use gas stoves as much as possible, and go easy on vegetation and trees. Campers were also encouraged to discuss conservation and clean up "messy campsites." "In short, do your best to leave no traces of your visit and to permit the next visitor to have the same thrill of unspoiled, quiet wilderness that you enjoyed." It concluded by quoting Aldo Leopold from *A Sand County Almanac*: "all conservation of wildness is self-defeating, for to cherish we must see and fondle, and when enough have seen and fondled, there is no wilderness left to cherish." *The Gazette* circulated the guide in 1972; 15,000 copies were provided for public distribution through the Regional Parks Office to national parks, such as Glacier.[14]

The conservation committee aimed, as it told ACC members, "to get something in each issue of the Gazette and in the Journal to keep you thinking about conservation matters and perhaps stimulating you to write something yourselves."[15] At about this time, the *Canadian Alpine Journal* also expressed renewed interest in conservation politics and recreation ethics. Environment and access were now related as twin concerns for climbers. "The serious problems of conservation, access, climbing regulations, etc., which have already become critical elsewhere," the new journal editor Andrew Gruff observed, "will soon begin to trouble us here, and will require an organized and informed approach if we are to cope with them."[16] Readers of the journal in 1971 found many articles pondering conservation and the future of the mountain national parks leading up to public hearings on the provisional master plans for the Four Mountain Parks.

James W. Thorsell, a University of British Columbia PHD student in conservation and recreation planning who joined the club in 1967, published an article in the *CAJ* titled "On Planning Canada's Mountain National Parks" in which he urged all mountaineers "to follow the results of the hearings with a critical eye, and to offer support to the Alpine Club's Conservation Committee in re-establishing an active voice in the development of the national parks."[17] He was technically attuned to the issues, having worked as a planner and researcher in Ottawa's Park Planning Division from 1966 to 1968, as well as conducting research in the mountain parks where he lived intermittently in Banff.[18] Thorsell was involved in work related to the Kluane Park Reserve in 1967, and he joined the first YACE general mountaineering camp as a climber.[19] He commended the Parks Branch public hearings as "a very positive way to encourage more public involvement in the planning process." Classifying four types of mountain park users—the group package tourist, the trailer-camping automobile sightseer, the wilderness traveller, and the abstaining "option user"—Thorsell critiqued the provisional master plans for catering to the motorized culture of "travelling armchair" visitors in the first two classes, while they overlooked the other two along with the big picture of ecological management and wilderness preservation in the western mountain parks. His assessment lamented the Parks Branch proposals to build 250 miles (402 kilometres) of new highway for thirteen more roads, turn Lake Louise into a townsite the size of Banff and Jasper, and zone more than a third of the total park area for uses other than wilderness. He also criticized plans to take up more wildlife habitat for campgrounds in montane valleys and to sponsor park snowmobile tours. "Inasmuch as areas of preserved wilderness are already in short supply, the prime function of most of the area of the western mountain parks *must* be the preservation of the Rocky Mountain landscape. This is primarily a wilderness landscape and should be presented to future generations as such." Based on his reading of the National Parks Act, Thorsell did not find use and preservation to be a contradictory tradeoff—provided that use caused no impairment and mass access was controlled. The overall question that emerged for him was: "In essence what do we want—national parks or regional playgrounds?"[20]

Thorsell aligned himself with the "wilderness traveller" in the parks, and he represented this group of user in tandem with a system of land zoning and the definition of wilderness. "He may be a mountaineer, backpacker, trail rider, ski tourer or canoer, but the common quest is active physical challenge and some sort of 'spiritual communion' with wild country...He demands little in the way of facilities but requires that large areas of undisturbed land be kept at a low use density." Perhaps influenced by the functionalist emphasis on land use and recreational activities in the paradigms of park planning, wilderness zoning in his description was in many ways defined by travelling bodies rather than roads or motor vehicles. "All remaining wilderness land in the parks should be left undisturbed with *physical ability* being the selective filter that will limit use," wrote Thorsell. He quoted controversial American ecologist Garrett Hardin, a professor at University of California Santa Barbara, to argue that the wilderness experience in many national parks was rightfully and "forever closed to people on crutches, to small children, to fat people, to people with heart conditions, and to old people in their usual state of physical disrepair."[21] This style of thinking constructed wilderness as a place occupied and territorialized by healthy, athletic, adult bodies—climbing, hiking, riding, skiing, and paddling— in a masculinist discourse of performance in a sporting landscape that excluded people by labelling bodies as fit versus unfit.[22] Thorsell's and Hardin's thinking also implicitly lacked acknowledgement of the long-standing Aboriginal and early settler presence on the land that predated the parks. At the time, Thorsell and others in the mountain sports community were constructing "wilderness" as essentially a hypermasculine place. This construction was represented by the newly vamped *Canadian Alpine Journal,* which now prominently featured glossy black-and-white photos of strong men on big wall climbs and mountaineering ascents in country like the Stikine.

In the same issue of the *CAJ,* a young geographer named John Marsh published his study of high-country recreational use in Glacier National Park, British Columbia, based on aspects of his doctoral research supervised by Dr. J.G. Nelson at the University of Calgary.[23] His analysis of climbing and ski touring commented on user statistics and long-standing regional traditions of mountaineering in the park. Climbers and ski tourers registered in 1967 were a small group of 890 recreationists, compared to 656,000 vehicles with more than 1.8 million passengers passing through the park. With consideration to "the expanding minority of park users," he concluded with his hope that the climbers and ski tourers in Glacier Park "will not be overlooked. They are certainly amongst the most legitimate of park users, and are in a position to cooperate with the Parks Branch in ensuring that the tradition of Glacier as an alpine recreation area of the highest quality is maintained, and its potential maximised."[24]

In 1971 Dan Phelps, a former University of British Columbia graduate student who had once played a role starting the conservation committee in his campus outdoor club, contributed the article "Conservation, Preservation—Same Thing."[25] It was an allegory satirizing a fictionalized political economy much like the mountain parks. It pointed at club members to pick up the slack by working together for the environment to save what they enjoyed in the mountains. In his story, he needled members to recognize themselves and their actions:

> *Once upon a time in a country on the continent of techno-quick-fix there were some mountains...many more people came to enjoy the view and to climb the mountains. Things were not quite the same for the peak baggers. The new people that came did not appreciate the same aspects of the mountains and had somewhat different values (when in the outdoors at least). The new people used more machines...Through all this, those who went to bag the peaks continued to do so. Some said that it was because they went there to escape from the situation they had helped create in the valleys and the lowlands; besides no one ever worried about how one square on the map affected another square on the map.*[26]

Phelps went on to enumerate a six-point plan for the club to aid "preservation/conservation" by encouraging more people to know and appreciate the mountains through publishing, engaging in active outdoor recreation, and working together with other outdoor groups to "present a much larger and more effective voice" to government. At the root of his arguments was the democratic assertion that mountain conservation stood a better chance if more people were involved and cared. The image of a mountain lake with a superimposed industrial mill spewing smoke skywards illustrated his story, hinting at how environmental concerns were caricatured, while his argument engaged principles of integrated land-use planning, ecological models, and coalition activism.

As these three articles illustrate, informed professionals, students, and researchers linked to the ACC were ready and willing to critique national parks and recreation policies. The ACC's and the public's re-examination of values and ideals related to national parks formed part of a larger wave of social, scientific, cultural, and generational change rolling through the late 1960s into the 1970s era of social movements and activism, not to mention new literatures—ecology, Beat poetry, and emerging Canadian Literature.[27] To the youth counterculture of hitchhikers, backpackers, and hippies travelling the major cross-Canada highway routes, national parks like Banff and Jasper were destination points.[28] The *Canadian Alpine Journal* acted as a platform for polemics among mountaineers just as the public hearings on national park planning approached.

Public hearings on the provisional master plans for the Four Mountain Parks were held in April 1971 in Vancouver, Edmonton, and Calgary,[29] and in Golden, British Columbia, in May.[30] This road show integrated extensive public consultation hearings into national park planning, aired multiple stakeholder perspectives, and diffused political dissent into a transformative decision-making process leading toward revised planning documents and management directions. The mountain parks hearings followed three other such Parks Branch hearings on the provisional plans for Kejimkujik, Fundy, and Cape Breton Highlands national parks in the Maritimes.[31] Stakeholders in the mountain park hearings involved many sectors including: regional chambers of commerce, gateway municipalities, local MLAs, provincial agencies, commercial business operators, and automobile associations. Natural resource and planning concerns were presented by university researchers, wildlife and fisheries biologists, vegetation and forestry specialists, and logging interests. Snowmobile clubs, ski clubs, commercial skiing, varsity outdoor clubs, climbing clubs, and the YMCA, among others, represented various sport and recreation interests. Conservation considerations were presented by local naturalist societies, various provincial federations of naturalists, and the NPPAC. Aboriginal speakers, high-school students, women's peace groups, farmers' institutes, various private individuals, and others brought diverse perspectives to the table. Among them all, the ACC argued for its vision of the future for the four mountain parks.

At the Edmonton hearings on the afternoon of April 22, Harry Habgood spoke on behalf of ACC President David Fisher and presented a written commentary endorsed by the club's national executive.[32] Habgood positioned the ACC as the national mountaineering club with a history of "sixty odd years" and organizational objectives for the enjoyment and preservation of mountain places that were "just the same as those of the National Parks Act." According to the club, roads, visitor centres, and tourist recreation facilities in the four mountain parks were already adequate. It preferred roads and service centres to develop regionally outside the parks and wanted "to establish and preserve the integrity of relatively large wilderness areas within the parks, perhaps to some extent even extending outside into provincial areas." Habgood voiced the club's considered opinion that "people should be encouraged to visit these blocks of wilderness, but to visit in ways that are in keeping with the wilderness character of the country and that cause minimum damage to the land and to its natural systems. And to us this means hiking, climbing, primitive back-pack camping, ski touring, snow-shoeing."[33] Building more roads to address surging demands and deal with overcrowding was a futile enterprise, according to the ACC. Habgood compared automobile traffic to existing Parks policy statements limiting aircraft in the parks, arguing the construction of proposed roads as thoroughfares would be to the detriment of "national park values." Working with provincial authorities to achieve "a comprehensive plan for the whole mountain area centered on the park" and offering federal subsidies for regional tourism development were recommended. He critiqued the classification system for land-use zoning in the parks and advised eliminating Class III zoning (Natural Environment Area) in favour of Class II (Wilderness Recreation Area) because Class III zones ambiguously "allowed some new roads and parkways" that might permit creeping development toward Class IV (General Outdoor Recreation Area).

Habgood highlighted "pedestrian travel" and "pack-in" camping as prime uses of parks. With regard to hiking, the club adopted some of the rubrics and language of recreational land-use planning: "A degree of rationing of land use could be accomplished by means of variations in the density and the difficulty of the trail network. In this way some of the more fragile alpine areas in the interior of the large wilderness zones, and in the Class I areas [Special Area, Wilderness], can be protected from excessive use in non-obtrusive fashion." Simple bridges—two or three well-anchored logs—were seen as a vital link to improve access up major stream valleys on existing trails. The club was not keen on horses using the same walking trails due to "drainage" concerns. The Great Divide Trail proposal for a north–south foot route through the Rockies was considered as "a good start on a system of cross-country touring trails." When designing campsites and shelters, planners were advised that "part of the pleasure of being in the wilderness is the feeling of freedom to go where you want and to stop where you want, and management policies should attempt to preserve that impression of freedom." With respect to more shelters and huts along certain heavily used trails, the club favoured enclosed huts because they were versatile enough for winter use. It also advocated more participatory decision-making in ongoing management through "the formation of advisory committees concerned with trails and huts."

Winter travel was part of the ACC's vision for the future of mountain parks, but recent attempts to allow recreational snowmobiling were seen as "unfortunate" and recreational snowmobiling was ruled out in the club's recommendations for all national parks. "We think that mechanized vehicles of this type are totally out of place in a wilderness," Habgood commented, "and should be used only where strictly necessary on park business." The club had, in fact, already made an earlier and separate submission to Parks specifically regarding snowmobile use. In contrast, the club again put forward its goals for a system of huts to "encourage extensive touring on skis and snowshoes and the further development of ski mountaineering." It also saw a need to extend the existing avalanche warning system. The club reasoned that facilitating backcountry use through more trails, shelters, huts, and primitive campsites would help to "defer" overcrowding problems, whereas proposals emphasizing roads and facilities in the master plans were seen to accelerate them.

Habgood concluded his presentation by emphasizing this picture of mountain parks: "we think the Department should take the initiative in encouraging people to enjoy the mountain national parks in ways that emphasize their distinctive natural features, and with all due respect, sir, we suggest that the activities of groups such as the Alpine Club of

Canada indicate the sorts of recreation that are distinctive to the mountains, are rewarding to participants, and cause minimum damage to the natural environment." The ACC and its outdoor practices were front and centre in this vision of recreation in mountain parks.[34]

After two days of hearings in Edmonton, the ACC was poised to comment again in the question and answer period. Valerie Stevens, an undergraduate student at the University of Alberta and chair of the Edmonton Section's conservation committee, asked why the Red Earth Creek Road had already been surveyed for a tentatively proposed road: "I've often wondered how many of you…have ever been into the back country of these parks, and really know why we, who have been there, fear what you are going to do by putting in these roads and dividing up the area so badly?"[35]

At the April 19–20 hearings in Calgary, the Calgary Section of the club had rallied its efforts to speak in defence of wilderness protection. Calgary Section Chair Erik Laerz spoke to the hearings on the evening of April 19 and pointed out that park plans would set policy parameters for later development in Village Lake Louise, even though Parks had designated it as a separate planning process. Particular concerns arose related to prospects for installing secondary sewage treatment, as Laerz identified: "This I find rather appalling, because this water will be leaving a national park. This is supposed to be a wilderness museum, a living wilderness museum, and secondary sewage essentially means that right below Lake Louise you are not able to drink that water safely, and this is rather frightening." He was critical of detrimental vegetation impacts due to snowmobile use off designated routes at Lake Louise: "…on one particular weekend we were skiing out of there with a group, and we had just followed about 12 to 14 snowmobilers, and I think you could count on one hand the number of avalanche slopes or alpine meadows that were not completely covered by snowmobile tracks on the way out, and there's quite a few of them. They seem to hit everywhere but…the road." He concluded that "preservation of the wilderness must be of paramount importance in formulating policy."[36]

On April 20, the Calgary Section spoke at the hearings again. Its local conservation committee submitted a written brief, endorsed unanimously by the section, which was summarized at the presentations by Bob Jordan. "The mountain parks are for all Canadians for all time and their value cannot be measured in terms of how many access roads, motels, souvenir shops and golf courses we've provided," Jordan began. "Rather their lasting value is in what might only be seen with a great deal of effort or perhaps never seen at all. The remote wilderness, we consider this to be the value of the National Parks and our comments on the master plans are based on this premise."[37] The Calgary Section objected "very strenuously" to proposed roads on the basis that they would carve through the "remaining three large wilderness areas in the parks, the Cascade-Pipestone, Red Deer Valleys, the area south and south-east of Maligne Lake and the north-west portion of Jasper National Park." It recommended that these areas in Banff and Jasper be reclassified as Zone I (Special Area, Wilderness) and left intact. Moreover, in Yoho all but two valleys were slated for road building, such as the extension of the Takakkaw Falls road to the foot of the Yoho Glacier. "Roads are the biggest single threat to wilderness and the parks," Jordan stated, presenting maps to indicate how proposed new transport corridors through mountain valleys would fragment wilderness areas and drastically subdivide the square mileage of the remaining pieces. The Calgary committee was dismayed that more consideration had not been given to ecological implications regarding habitat and wildlife in planning, specifically critiques arising from a 1969 report by the Canadian Wildlife Service (CWS), in which biologists pointed out that highly valued habitats, such as valley bottoms, were under great pressure in the mountain parks due to park development demands; there was "no evidence to suggest that the present roadless areas are more than adequate, and strong indications that in some parks they are inadequate."[38]

Jordan expressed that the proposed zoning lacked both "a sound and thorough scientific knowledge of the land involved" as well as "a feeling for the landscape." His presentation noted various inconsistencies in the proposed zoning system and how it applied on the ground as interpreted by the Calgary committee: "The Class I ["Special Area"] protection planned for the Athabasca Glacier mocks its purpose. For a price one can visit the Glacier via track vehicle. The terminal moraine is a parking lot and the south lateral moraine is now a road...Is a similar fate in store for the snout of the Yoho Glacier?...We strongly urge that...a new zoning plan aimed at protecting the parks, not at providing new corridors of visitor conveniences, be established. Until this has been done all undeveloped land should be given Class I or Class II protection.

"Even remoteness is no particular barrier to man's intrusion," Jordan illustrated with a photo of oil drums said to have been left as "a major oil company's legacy on the shores of Twin Tree Lake in north Jasper Park." Unmentioned was a similar legacy left by the ACC at the Mount Steele Glacier after YACE.

Cross-country skiing and ski touring in the mountain parks were popular among members of the Calgary Section, and they advocated the advancement of these activities through better trails, huts, and potential demonstration tours, along with trail maps and park information. "Approximately 850 people per month ski toured in Banff Park this winter," Jordan commented, and the sport was growing despite "a lack of marked trails and huts." High alpine refuges were promoted as invaluable emergency bivouacs for remote climbing, and the section made recommendations to enhance the shelter system for hiking, backpacking, climbing, and skiing. In the wake of controversial proposals through the 1960s to hold the Winter Olympics in Lake Louise, the Calgary ACC was pleased there were no references to the development of new downhill ski facilities in the mountain parks, and it recommended that the expansion of existing ski hills be subject to public input. It preferred downhill ski facilities to operate on provincial lands, noting that "the Alberta Government recreation policy has been getting a free ride from federally supported developments in the parks for decades, and we more than welcome recreation facilities outside the parks." Banning the recreational use of snowmobiles in the national parks was recommended as such use posed an "inevitable conflict with quieter types of winter recreation" and was difficult to oversee. Park interpretation was also endorsed by the Calgary Section, which wanted programs and material expanded beyond park boundaries to serve school groups and adults in large urban centres. Lastly, the Calgary Section noted it was concerned that prospects for condominium development at Lake Louise would breach park policies and requested that complete plans for "Village Lake Louise" be made available for public comment.

One young mountaineer in the ACC hit the road to follow the hearings across Alberta and British Columbia. He consumed a cumulative "eleven cups of federal government coffee" in three cities while listening to presentations, then spoke up on April 26 in Vancouver. Jim Thorsell made clear that he represented only himself and his personal views, speaking as a grad student who had logged "almost 2000 miles of back-country travel in the past ten years of living in and out of Banff Park"; he also identified his role as a British Columbia board member of the Provincial Parks Association.[39] He noted his comments were an abstract based on the article he had published that year in the *Canadian Alpine Journal* and on his observations of the hearings.

"Many people were somewhat bewildered as to how such development oriented plans could ever have been conceived in the first place.

Does the Department of Public Works really run the National Parks?" Thorsell questioned. "The difficulty here is that park planners are much further removed and less involved in the park than a dedicated inveterate park user." To contextualize the "puzzling" discrepancy between the provisional master plans and the reaction of the public at the hearings, Thorsell surmised that the plans were already obsolete when they were issued because they had been initiated four or five years "before the beginning of the environmental and social revolution we are currently undergoing." Looking ahead, he recommended that Parks "correct" its plans "in tune with this revolution": "what is called for are plans which would lead to a veritable greening of the National Parks."

Part of the difficulty clarifying fundamental planning goals for the master plans was confusion arising from the dedication clause of the National Parks Act, along with the lack of a "viable national outdoor recreation plan." Ecological management was the overriding concern Thorsell identified for the "greening" of the mountain parks, and he suggested "the ecological approach has changed the dimensions of all our planning and [I] would proceed to plan and zone the parks on an eco-system basis." Notably, one mechanism he proposed was the establishment of a Rocky Mountain regional planning commission to produce "a design theory for the Canadian Rockies as a whole, recognizing wilderness and industry alike as essential elements in an integrated land-use policy for the region." He reiterated: "All parks are not for all people. National Parks in the opinion of most people have the prime function of providing wilderness in the regional landscape." Backcountry travel, a hut system, and the proposed Great Divide Trail were recommended as appropriate, as was the exclusion of non-conforming bodies. He closed by underscoring the "spiritual values" underlying national parks as expressed by many speakers at public hearings, Aboriginal and youth voices particularly, and acknowledging the need to address the considerations of the underprivileged. As it turned out, mountaineer Jim Thorsell later emerged to become one of Canada's world leaders in conservation and planning, working for the World Conservation Union (IUCN) and advising UNESCO's World Heritage Committee.[40] His recognition of the merits of regional ecosystem planning and integrated land use on a vast scale was a significant idea in 1971, and analogous in some ways to the conceptual scope behind the Yellowstone to Yukon (Y2Y) scheme initiated some thirty years later.

Minister Jean Chrétien and his department moved to make changes after releasing the provisional master plans for the western mountain parks in 1968. In an atmosphere of growing political pressure, Ottawa planners—headed by English-born professional planner Ron Maslin, the co-ordinator of Parks master planning—grappled with input and changes. Most of the scenic road proposals were scrapped, Lake Louise village plans were curtailed, snowmobiling was prohibited as a non-conforming recreational use, and a new backcountry management approach was adopted.[41] According to C.J. Taylor, "a sea change in attitude" rippled incrementally through Canada's national parks administration and provoked an overall reassessment that moved closer toward ecological management. Assistant Deputy Minister Al Davidson noted in 1979 that the public hearings "had a profound impact on our planning emphasis and public participation leading to decision-making. Look back on some of the provisional master plans, at the emphasis on road building...and compare them with our present emphasis on programmes which will provide park experiences uniquely attuned to the environment."[42]

The government did not accept all the recommendations, but much of the public feedback hit the mark and the Parks Branch parlayed it into the revised set of master plans, which were implemented as working documents kept under a provisional title through the 1970s and 1980s.[43] These outcomes, along with the five volumes of critical public commentary from the hearings, suggest that a new watershed had been achieved for public participation in policy-making with the federal Parks Branch, one that shifted the balance of roles and expectations between citizens and the state and challenged centrist tendencies inside the branch.[44] Twenty years later, Parks Canada produced another generation of ecological shift in the next master plans, *In Trust for Tommorrow: A Management Framework for Four Mountain Parks* (1988), which treated the four parks as an ecological block and emphasized limiting development to existing corridors.[45] Leading up to 1988, the ACC again played an active stakeholder role in public park–planning consultations.[46]

The fact that many prime valleys and passes in Banff, Jasper, Kootenay, and Yoho parks are today unmarked by highways is a legacy of democratic social changes wrought by Canadian civil society in the late 1960s and early 1970s. Likewise, there was a lasting effect on national park governance and policy-making in Parks Canada, which came to institutionalize public consultation processes as part of successive ten-year planning cycles. The "greening" of national parks in the 1970s provides a counter narrative to paving the postwar parks after 1945, yet later decades were still fraught with the challenges and contradictions of land management and intensifying tourism growth. How the four mountain parks in the Rockies differed from some national parks in other regions, such as the Maritimes and southern Ontario, was indicated in the 1970s by the groundswell of emphasis on protecting vast zones of wilderness. The ACC's redefined vision of itself and national parks was emerging from public debates, and the dispositions of mountaineers featured prominently in it, as did discourses of wilderness premised on the social, spatial, and ecological concerns of mountain parks in the West.

The ACC's position as civic lobbyist was part of the club's redefined vision of itself and parks. Advocacy for conservation was strongly asserted through the national club, and the Edmonton and Calgary sections played leading roles as Alberta conservation stakeholders in Canadian park-policy formation. Following the hearings, Harry Habgood published an article in the 1972 *CAJ* to assess the outcomes: "Is the conservation effort worth while [sic]? Representations to officialdom do seem to produce some results. For example, according to a recent statement from the Parks Branch, the almost unanimous objections to new roads and visitor service centres in the four mountain parks have been heeded."[47] The promise of three new parks in northern Canada—Kluane, Nahanni, and Baffin Island—made in the 1972 Throne Speech was another outcome he observed in his article. He looked back on the club's shifting vision of national parks and how its emergent ethics now expressed "a stronger conservationist stance." Stirred into action by the master planning process, a consensus on principles had emerged from what he identified as broad-based and intense discussions within the club as to what was deemed appropriate for Banff, Jasper, Kootenay, and Yoho national parks:

> *Public opinion is changing, and Club policy is likewise shifting to give greater emphasis to preserving the park unimpaired for future generations while encouraging present use in ways that we think are most appropriate to the alpine wilderness, and are relatively undemanding on the environment...The Club submission on the provisional master plans was coordinated by the Conservation Committee so perhaps a conservationist point of view was to be expected. But there was a surprisingly broad and intense participation extending from the Board through the various committees, local sections, to individual members. The emphasis was on encouraging greater foot travel throughout the park by development of carefully sited trails, shelters, and huts. At the same time, while admitting*

*that members enjoyed the use of roads, the submission opposed
most of the suggested new roads as "any small gains in convenience of access that might result from additional roads would be
outweighed by the loss of wilderness values."*[48]

Henceforth, the club's vision of mountain parks highlighted the protection of "wilderness values" to safeguard the backcountry through zoning
and minimum-impact practices. It was a significant shift away from the
club's 1944 vision of postwar parks and the club's recommendation to
build a roadway through Jasper's Tonquin Valley, which Habgood noted
was "rather embarrassing to recall."[49] The club's 1971 emphasis on foot
travel, huts, shelters, and trails reaching into remote districts to serve
backcountry wilderness travellers, however, was not inconsistent with its
stakeholder outlook in 1944. Park wilderness was still defined as a place
for people but a regulated place to visit on foot in search of recreation for
the "well-governed" citizen.

The visions of national parks put forward by ACC mountaineers at
the hearings were not without certain ambiguities and contradictions.
Wildlife ecology was foremost in the planning discourse of habitat
protection and wilderness zoning adopted by the ACC from the CWS, but
this priority was closely combined with the intent for human recreational
use. The parks were increasingly seen by the ACC as interconnected
ecological systems supporting diverse life forms, along with a political economy of tourism and low-impact visitation in the backcountry.
Minimum impact necessitated conduct that veered away from the mass
gatherings, woodcraft camping, and campfire-burning practices still
common in the club in 1970, particularly at the annual general mountaineering camps. Shifting national park policy boded significant changes
for the ACC and its operations. As well, the masculinist discourse of a
wilderness territorialized by fit and able athletic bodies in a sporting
landscape—such as that championed by Thorsell—overlooked the history
of travellers of all ages, sizes, and abilities, along with families, who did
in fact go to the mountain park backcountry, some by direct means of
the ACC camps and huts, not to mention adaptive users who were yet to
stretch past previous limits by climbing with artificial limbs or riding
trail devices. This exclusive vision of humans in parks also overlooked
the contemporaneous ACC family camps premised on the inclusion
of children and camping for family leisure, as well as the history of
Indigenous families. The ACC vision of national parks as a wilderness
and recreation domain for backcountry adventures on foot was in many

ways an urban middle-class aspiration that contrasted with some of the concerns expressed by other stakeholders at the 1971 hearings.

But what about the flip side of wilderness backcountry, the frontcountry? How did respondents at the public hearings for the Four Mountain Parks discuss these areas of the parks and those who use them? The Edmonton YMCA drew attention to the needs of "families of limited means" and wanted to ensure that national parks had room for them, such as it had provided at its frontcountry camp on Lake Edith in Jasper Park since 1920, but which was newly jeopardized by changing national park leasehold policies coming into effect to phase it out.[50] At the hearings in Golden, British Columbia, Mrs. Minnie Wilder from Fairmont Hot Springs spoke out as a representative for the Windermere District Chamber of Commerce in favour of the park plans. "We hear an awful lot about people too lazy to use the trails. For your information there's babies come into the park, there's old age, there's people in wheel chairs, everyone cannot get out on the side roads, nor off on the trails." She went on to say that "most Canadian families start teaching their families the nature's way [sic] through the car window first...And we must take care of that whole family unit...not just the man who wishes to hike or the naturalist."[51] The boundaries and dividing lines between recreational uses and zoning classifications were seen in different ways and contested. "We use our machines to go to nature, not through it," stated Ron LaRoy for the Golden Snow Kings Snowmobile Club based in the blue-collar logging town near Yoho National Park. He made the case for snowmobilers touring the Amiskwi and Yoho valleys, arguing "the parks are ours, as much as they are the skiers,' or the hikers' or the campers.' If areas can be set aside for these groups, then why not for us?"[52]

On the other hand, the Northwest Mountaineering Club in Edmonton, associated with the Canadian Youth Hostel Association (CYHA), shared many of the same concerns expressed by the ACC with regard to wilderness and roads. It specifically supported the larger club's brief by making a statement in favour of encouraging hiking and climbing in the parks. It also stressed the experience of the CYHA and the ACC in running mountain huts.[53] Likewise, the views of naturalists' clubs and federations, both rural and urban, and those of the NPPAC held much in common with the ACC's vision of the mountain parks.[54] They also shared some of the same constituents as members. Aileen Harmon, for example, spoke to the hearings on April 20 in Calgary as a private citizen identifying herself as a "member of NPPAC and a Bow Valley naturalist." She was also a longtime ACC member. She emphasized how rising visitation and the attendant effects of "noise, many people and cars" would affect regional ecology, such as "prime caribou summer range" where the new Maligne–Poboktan road was proposed in Jasper. "The future of wilderness as part of our national heritage is at stake," she argued, and she proposed a definition of wilderness as "a place where plants, animals and the landscape can evolve without hindrance, where man is another animal passing by, where wilderness dictates its own terms if it is to survive at all." Harmon concluded by saying, "I know that some will classify this brief as the work of one of those who want to keep the wilderness for themselves. I assure you this is not the case. There are many of us who have enjoyed the best the parks have to offer and are able to evaluate these resources and their impact on the wilderness visitor. We know that in a rapidly changing world there will be vastly increased need for this experience."[55]

Contested social relations and the social reconstruction of what wild places meant were an ongoing process in the making of the mountain parks. The Four Mountain Parks planning exercise was a political process of contestation and control, sanctioned by the public and the state apparatus, whereby certain meanings were privileged and emerged as dominant. The influence of the ACC and similar stakeholders was embedded in the outcomes. "Wilderness values" emerging by 1971 were constructed as prime considerations for national park management to safeguard mountain ecosystems. This implied quiet, unroaded, unmotorized, and "natural" habitats occupied by non-consumptive human recreational uses; it sanctioned the outdoor practices of ACC mountaineers and like-minded people. Place is also a process, and part of what defined national parks as places was a behavioural regime constituting and constituted as cultural difference and relations of power. Park boundaries, zoning, regulation of trail networks, shelter systems, trip registration, and safety processes were rationalized design mechanisms running through space and time that rendered the mountain parks as places for the exercise and control of human activity on the part of the state, the "well-governed" citizen, and the "fit" bodies taking part in mountain recreation, sport, and tourism.[56] Ultimately, the ACC's input to the Four Mountain Parks provisional master plans and related political processes produced mountain national parks as a machine for the "freedom of the hills"—a romanticized dream of liberation, wilderness, and embodiment espoused and enacted by mountaineers.[57]

The realization among mountaineers that trail networks could regulate the frequency and density of visitation, for example, was embraced as a positive social control in wilderness management because it preserved the idea (illusion) of freedom while operating simultaneously as a constraint. Some self-reflecting mountaineers observed this duality, and the ACC brief expressed it at the 1971 public hearings. Similarly the new code of "Mountain Manners" promoted through the club's conservation committee produced a different economy of embodied resource-use behaviours for travel and camping in the mountains. They were presumed to be welcome self-disciplines to the well-governed citizen as a necessary part of stewardship to address the environmental concerns in the political economy portrayed in Dan Phelps's allegory of the mountain parks. One square on the map did indeed affect another, as the ACC was learning.

But the four mountain parks envisioned by the ACC were more than a disciplining mechanism of governance. They were home. Club members knew mountain park landscapes as places with faces, and they held strong affinities for them. Herein was the poetic potential for a largely urban-based constituency to conceive of wilderness as a home place.[58] Investing in place attachments to mountains produced landscapes with social and proprietary bonds. Humanist geographer Yi-Fu Tuan theorizes that garden landscapes "are a blending of nature and artifice" that reveal dominance and affection with neither taken to extreme; sociologist John Bale applies these ideas to "sportscapes."[59] In the case of mountaineering landscapes, the rationalized design and regulation of space by the state in the mountain parks occurred amid the production of geographic identities inspired by the affection of mountaineers, and others, in an historically mutable cultural landscape. Political contestations, such as the park-planning hearings, mobilized their topophilia for home. At the same time, sense of place was not unitary because mountains were also places subjectively layered with memories by different subjects and bodies.

Part of the sense of being "at home" in the mountains for many ACC members was produced through sensual geographies of the body in the outdoors. Embodied knowledge was generated through participating in mountain pursuits and returning to familiar places in the parks.[60] Mountaineers knew themselves as alive and part of nature through the body. Thinking and sensing came together as ways of knowing. No matter how the sense of self and the sense of nature were construed, there were epistemological and ethical ties between the two. Harry Habgood's swan song in 1974 after five years as chair of the club's conservation committee summed up knowing his personal outdoor ethic as "a striving for non-consumptive enjoyment of nature":

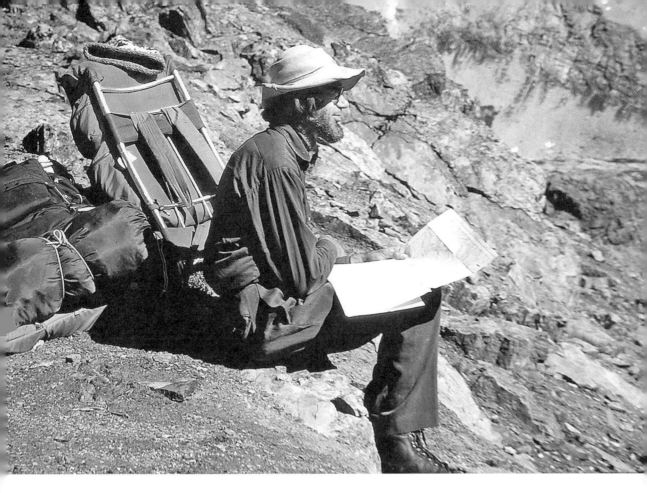

∧ Harry Habgood on
Noseeum Peak in Jasper
National Park in the early
1970s. [C.F. Richmond
photograph]

*This, of course, is only an ideal because, although the pleasure I
experience in the mountains is all in my head, I require some experience through my senses—seeing the wild streams and the ice-falls,
feeling the rock and the push of the wind, smelling the vegetation in
the hot sun, straining my muscles against gravity, and being aware
of the solitude—and in the course of this experiencing I consume a
bit of the naturalness, the wildness, and the solitude.*[61]

This intimate form of knowledge was often ingrained into place attachment in making meanings about mountains. An ecology of self and
world was thus known by mountaineers through their bodies, which were
in and of nature, and places grounded understandings of existence. "We
each build our own and create our own theatres of memory by reading
and experiencing sporting landscapes in very personal and often contradictory ways," writes Patricia Vertinisky, pointing out that "there is no
single 'sense of place'" shared by everyone.[62]

The dominant meanings of mountain national parks in western
Canada were under reconstruction through the late 1960s and the early

1970s. Embracing the scientized discourses of ecology and recreation management, along with the applied ethics of minimum impact, gave the ACC vision of mountain parks and its recreational philosophies a new lift. It conceded the excesses of postwar development had pushed the limits, and the club looked simultaneously to the ecological preservation of large tracts of land zoned as wilderness and visited on foot as the future of the mountain national parks. Rejecting the 1968 plans for the four mountain parks put forth by the Parks Branch, the club developed a heightened awareness of the environmental limits of recreation and tourism. In the newly articulated club vision, concepts of machine and home inhabited the idea of mountain parks and operated together despite apparent contradiction. Proposals for roads through wilderness led to re-examination and produced vocal conservation advocacy. No less vital to the club and national parks was the club's vision of parks as a peopled landscape incorporating concepts of wilderness and regulation that reflected the practices and newly emergent philosophies of the ACC in the early 1970s.

Mountaineering Landscapes
People and Place in National Parks

Clear weather led to an uninterrupted spree of climbing at the general mountaineering camp (GMC) when the ACC revisited the Freshfields district of Banff National Park in 1969, twenty years after its first camp there. Climbers who chased up nearby peaks—such as Bulyea, Forbes, Howse, Pilkington, and Walker—became "very fit and very tanned." Outfitters Bill and Isabel Harrison were praised for preparing the hearty meals in base camp as they had at the club's camps since 1954. The high camp situated in Niverville Meadows (7,200 feet; 2,195 metres) drew a full house of mountaineers spanning fifty years in age, described as "a very real meeting of the generations. Younger members were impressed by the mettle of their elders and the obvious joy they experienced just from being there."[63] Tangible traces of the spatial–temporal presence of mountaineers also surfaced at Freshfields Glacier:

> *The last Alpine Club camp held in the Freshfields was 1949. Of archaeological interest was an old boot heavily shod with muggers and clinkers carefully excavated and displayed...Phyl Munday's album of photographs from 1949 was of great interest especially as it recorded the position, at that time, of the tongue of the Freshfield Glacier. This tongue has retreated strikingly and*

now dips into a lake about a mile long. Our trail up to Niverville
high camp picked its way dustily over the moraines and around the
lake to reach the glacier further up the valley. The going was much
easier once the ice was reached and this had a dry and pleasantly
crunchy surface.[64]

Recovering the artifact of the climbing boot, recollecting the glacier from
Phyllis Munday's personal photos of camps gone by, and knowing glacial
recession as a longer walk across moraine fields to reach the ice surface,
enabled the club to read its own intergenerational memories inhabiting
landscape changes and the body.[65] Like the climbing boot, mountaineers
were imbedded in the historical geography of a cultured landscape in
Banff National Park.

    The club was also party to interactions within an administrative
framework of park management that had changed rules and expectations for camp operations related to conservation standards, and it was
expected to toe the line. Discussions with Parks authorities as early as

> British Columbia outfitter
Bill Harrison with dog
Chance at Mount Steele
GMC, 1967. Marjorie
Hind photograph.
[WMCR, V46/42-44/R4C2]

1968 heralded coming changes. "National Parks Policy, which is now under development, will have a great effect upon the type and extent of use allowed, especially in those areas being designated as perpetual wilderness," the club observed. Two thirds of ACC national summer camps (GMCs) in the preceding twenty-four years had been held in national parks and usually in wilderness areas. "With the imminent defining of those park areas which are to be maintained as wilderness areas...which are the usual sites for our camps—the type, size, and activities of these groups using these areas will be carefully scrutinized before permission for the camp is granted," club organizers noted. "It is possible that the General Mountaineering Camp as we know it today many not be permitted to use these wilderness areas in future."[66] Cutting firewood and trees for tent poles had emerged as vegetation concerns. Transport by horse and helicopter were still anticipated in national parks but costly. Campers in 1968 were reminded to keep things in tiptop shape to pass inspection by three senior Parks officials visiting the GMC, to maintain the club's reputation. At the Freshfields Camp in 1969, a similar inspection was conducted: "the official visit was anticipated by the Camp Manager as something of an examination. However all went well and the Superintendent, accompanied by Peter Fuhrmann in his official capacity with the Warden Service, expressed his approval of the camp operation."[67] Pressures on the institution of the annual GMC also mounted with efforts inside the club to reinvent its practices and image.

In the late 1960s, in an effort to appeal to members by diversifying its program offerings, the ACC initiated two other kinds of summer camps: an alpine mountaineering camp and a family summer camp. Competent mountaineers and "young tigers" were attracted to smaller more challenging alpine mountaineering camps first featuring the Adamants (1968), Mount Waddington (1969), Vowell Creek (1971), and Mount Clemenceau (1972).[68] Appealing to strong climbers was important to the retention and renewal of a rigorous athletic cohort. Distinct family camps started in 1969. The club reported "the first one was a big success and plans will certainly be made to repeat it." The following year two camps were held for adults and children at ACC alpine huts at Lake O'Hara and in the Little Yoho Valley in Yoho National Park.[69] Expanded through the 1970s to appeal to all ages and ability levels, these volunteer-led efforts also benefitted retention and recruitment by appealing to young families. The ACC also introduced ski mountaineering camps and local section camps and outings at this time.

"These are changing times and mountaineering is no exception to these changes," wrote President Roger Neave in 1968. Renewal was a problem facing the board of management as the club sought to update its image and operations. Survey questions and results that year were one indication. A question about the image of the club asked: "Do you feel that our Club is: 1) Satisfactory, 2) Friendly, 3) Conservative, 4) Exclusive, 5) Stuffy?" Most respondents identified it as "conservative, but friendly." The large majority of respondents were satisfied with the existing climbing programs—the GMC, alpine mountaineering camp, ski mountaineering camp, and section outings/camps. They also favoured existing membership requirements stipulating four graduating peaks and two years of climbing experience. Membership numbers totalled 1,243 members in 1968, but growth had stalled.[70] Outside the club, however, the image of the ACC was typically seen as stuffy and too traditional among younger climbers and immigrant climbers from areas such as Austria and California, where different styles and ethics prevailed in the sport. In the late 1960s and early 1970s, the Calgary Mountain Club positioned itself as a foil to the ACC, which it saw as a bastion of old-fashioned Anglo traditionalists more interested in wildflower slides than in a hard-drinking masculinist counterculture and pushing new routes up difficult faces in technical style.[71] The ACC's continued strong emphasis on beginner instruction, qualifying requirements for membership, classic alpine mountaineering, and organized camps were institutional aspects of its particular club identity that did not appeal to everyone, especially by the late 1960s.

With the implementation of the Four Mountain Parks plans, concurrent considerations arose about the viability of a GMC with more than a hundred mountaineers onsite. The scale and style of the GMC did not easily fit the new policy framework or the new outlook on ecology. In 1968 the GMC was still cutting tree poles for tents and burning volumes of firewood at Lake O'Hara, which leads to questions about how thoroughly the minimum-impact ethic had been adopted and applied. A move to multiple smaller GMC camps of approximately twenty-five people at a time did not begin until 1980. Declining enrolments at the GMC in the early 1980s led to financial losses that nearly ended the camp tradition, until it was renewed by dint of Louise Guy in Calgary and other dedicated volunteers working with Brad Harrison, a new contractor and son of Bill Harrison, in 1986–87.[72] Eventually, the GMC was reinvented with a smaller footprint, but it also moved out of the national parks most years because it did not easily fit the new policy framework arising out of the Four Mountain Parks planning directions and subsequent policies. Fewer restrictions outside national parks made it easier to serve the GMC with horses, helicopters, and firewood to accommodate many mountaineers. In this respect, the large-scale ACC institution and programs were slower to conform to the new ethics of conservation than its conservation committee, which had articulated a minimum-impact philosophy during the Four Mountain Parks planning process.

Changing Parks Canada management regimes, shifting conservation polemics, and diversifying the club's appeal to more people pushed the ACC to reassess the size and implementation of its large-scale annual camps on sites in the national parks. As the ACC was pressed to reassess the footprint of its camps, transformations in national park policy were partly the outcome of the club's own internal shift to embrace environmentalism and align with a new era of Parks policy. Nonetheless, the GMC remained a remarkable tradition unique in the world of mountaineering and carries on rejuvenated today.

The club's built infrastructure—huts, trails, routes, clubhouses, campsites—like its roving annual camps, also continues today, with some notable exceptions. The sites in the mountain parks frequented by the ACC are telling examples of the integration of people and place in cultural landscapes through the course of the last hundred years and more. As a component of cultural landscape, buildings figured in mountaineers knowing mountain parks in western Canada. Dwellings and campsites are nodes on trails and routes that support recreational use and function within an integrated park complex. There is a strong historical resonance in these places: mountaineers walk trails, ascend routes, and occupy huts in the mountain parks that were used by their predecessors generations ago. Several alpine huts in mountain national parks are cultural resources that have been designated as heritage buildings by the Federal Heritage Buildings Review Office (FHBRO) in Ottawa. They are now protected and presented as heritage resources by Parks authorities and operated as working huts by the ACC. Elizabeth Parker Hut in Yoho National Park and Abbot Pass Hut in Banff National Park are examples of two such successful advances, designated by FHBRO in 1987 and 1997 respectively, and furthermore the latter was also designated a National Historic Site in 1997.[73] On the other hand, the history of the demolished ACC Banff Clubhouse and Claremount House on Sulphur Mountain in Banff National Park is also instructive because of failures to recognize and protect cultural heritage landscapes. These hotspots put the problematic and peculiar issues of nature/culture into the urban backyard of Canada's first national park.

From the advent of its first club camp in Yoho and its clubhouse built near the Banff hotsprings, the ACC made its home in the mountain parks and was encouraged by the Dominion Parks to establish a presence. By the late 1960s, however, the future of the Banff Alpine Clubhouse on Sulphur Mountain was uncertain. The aging facility, built in 1909, required substantial renovation. At the same time, Parks Canada decided to eliminate private leaseholds that fell outside the Banff town boundaries, including the ACC clubhouse. Faced with this dilemma, in 1969 the club voted 675 in favour to seventy-eight opposed (with thirty-three ballots spoiled) to selling the clubhouse after considerable internal debate, and the lease was transferred back to the federal Crown.[74] "Surely the demise of the clubhouse in Banff symbolizes the end of an era,"

Les MacDonald stated in the *CAJ* in 1970. He equated the change with moving away from a tweed-clad mountaineering generation in the club toward a rejuvenating approach to attract younger climbers.[75]

But the loss of the clubhouse did not sit well with all club members. Past president Roger Neave had campaigned to retain the original clubhouse on Sulphur Mountain in recognition of its history and tradition.[76] At the annual general meeting held at the clubhouse in 1971, Yvonne Tremblay learned from club manager Pat Boswell that Parks intended to tear the building down, and so she "suggested that perhaps the Clubhouse building could be retained by the Government as an Historic Site."[77]

The club's executive initially hoped to relocate its headquarters to another location in the park. In 1970, after property in the Banff townsite was ruled out as "almost unattainable" and too costly, the club hoped to establish a "new Club Headquarters as a centre for Canadian mountaineering" in the coming village development proposed in park plans for Lake Louise.[78] By early 1971, however, this option, too, was ruled out. Costs for construction and operation were expected to be substantial, and the club anticipated "some difficulty" under the National Parks policies to obtain approval even though a developer would execute the lease.[79] The new clubhouse was eventually constructed but did not find a home within the boundaries of Canada's first national park. Built in an open-beam modernist style, it opened its doors in 1973 on a benchland overlooking the town of Canmore, Alberta, east of the national park boundaries.[80] The site on Crown land was approved by the Province of Alberta and local authorities.[81] In September 1974, Parks demolished the original clubhouse structure that had been the prominent symbol of Canada's national alpine club in Banff National Park for sixty-five years.[82] It was reduced to rubble as the direct result of a federal policy move to eliminate private leaseholds outside the Banff townsite boundaries, specifically leaseholds for the ACC clubhouse and the Rimrock Hotel on Mountain Avenue. Demolition erased one of the great landmarks of early Canadian alpinism in Banff National Park, along with its Edwardian architectural heritage. Had the building survived, today it would most likely be considered a national historic site and a prime architectural landmark.

Why did Parks Canada tear down the ACC's Banff clubhouse? The explanation given regarding townsite planning boundaries does not explain why the lease for the Rimrock Hotel, just up the road from the ACC clubhouse site, was never eliminated. Once a modest modernist slab structure, today's Rimrock is a prominent, eight-storey, luxury resort and conference centre. The inconsistent application of policy in these instances suggests that Parks Canada wanted to move the club off its leasehold property during a period of government spending and control, and that the ACC did not oppose Parks Canada loudly enough to avoid losing its lease. The club also did not secure a new one prior to relinquishing it. The hotel seems to have wielded more clout than the ACC, reflecting the shifting approach of federal management policy and the ongoing influential forces of entrepreneurial capitalist development in the park. It would seem that instead of viewing the demise of the clubhouse as part of the policy to eliminate leaseholds, we ought to ask critical questions about why the long-standing clubhouse was eliminated after more than sixty years whereas the hotel expanded.

The elimination of the ACC clubhouse deviated from the long record of overall co-operation between the club and the national park authorities and soured relations, especially with club members who did not support relinquishing the leasehold for the clubhouse. J.R. MacKenzie, a Calgary ACC member, expressed his concerns about the situation to Prime Minister Pierre Trudeau in 1969:

> *As perhaps you know, the Government of Canada is pressuring the Alpine Club of Canada to sell its lease at Banff. I would like to express an objection to this procedure in the strongest possible terms. Surely every encouragement should be given to outdoor activities in Canada, and particularly mountain activities, and the force of the government should be in the direction of making the Alpine Club of Canada a truly national club with broad membership, rather than helping to squeeze it out of existence. I really think that the Federal Government is so remote from the scene that the persons in positions of responsibility are incapable of even recognizing the problem, much less developing a rational solution.*[83]

MacKenzie believed Parks was jeopardizing the club and squeezing it out of the park. His last comment went directly to perennial concerns, commonly expressed by Banff leaseholders at this time, about the distance between decision makers in Parks Canada headquarters in Ottawa versus the local Banff area. As the minister responsible, Jean Chrétien replied to his letter with the rationale that "this sale was negotiated with the Club executive and I can assure you that there was no intention of 'squeezing' the Club out of existence. Indeed, it is our hope that this sale will allow the Club to redevelop in a more appropriate area in the town site." He elaborated further to assert "Our relations over the years with the Alpine

Club of Canada have been amicable. We have always appreciated the enthusiastic support of the membership for National Parks. I trust that this will continue to be the case in the years to come."[84]

The former site of the historic Banff Alpine Clubhouse, once marked by a bronze Parks Canada plaque, is now a grassy plateau forgotten among the trees within the Sulphur Mountain–Middle Springs Wildlife Corridor that prohibits public entry. One other building was closely tied to the club's history in the immediate area. Situated near the original site of the ACC clubhouse, Claremount House was constructed by 1923 as the summer residence of founding president Arthur Oliver Wheeler. The Craftsman-style bungalow, named after Wheeler's wife Clara, served as the base for Wheeler's Mount Assiniboine tour company and his home while director of the club. Claremount remained in the Wheeler family until 1953, and the site leasehold reverted to Parks Canada in 1991. After it was reviewed and designated as a recognized federal heritage building in 1993,[85] Banff National Park later left the house vacant and unheated, leading to the heritage home's slow demise even as Arthur Wheeler was commemorated as a significant person by the Historic Sites and Monuments Board of Canada with a plaque placed at the Columbia Icefields Visitor Centre in Jasper in 1998. Standing some fifty metres off busy Mountain Avenue, Wheeler's house remained boarded up and vacant within the boundaries of the wildlife corridor. By contrast, the construction of the new Middle Springs subdivisions bulldozed ahead with full approval through the forest nearby on the periphery of the townsite. From the mid-1990s, Parks Canada sidelined and effectively prevented active efforts to conserve Claremount House as a cultural resource, despite its architectural heritage, environment, and rich historical associations with Wheeler, the ACC, and Banff's past. The way Parks Canada chose to deal with this issue offers a cautionary tale of how acute conflicts arise when natural resources and cultural resources are pitted against each other by management decisions instead of being more effectively managed together as an integrated landscape whole. "Breaking the bond between people and place along arbitrary lines that separate cultural heritage from natural environment marks a decisive rift," commented anthropologist Julie Cruikshank. "How do management strategies shift with such designations, and with what consequences?"[86]

During a centennial speech to the ACC in 2006, mountaineer and surveyor Dr. John Oliver Wheeler, a retired glaciologist and past club president now in his eighties, drew attention to Claremount House near

∧ *Claremount House, designed by Arthur Wheeler, stands with boarded-up windows and a roof tarp, 1997. PearlAnn Reichwein photograph.*

Middle Springs. Growing up there as a boy during summers spent with his grandparents, John was touched by his family's commitment to mountains and mountaineering. The house provided a sense of place grounded in a cultural landscape, a place in the forests where he roamed, where he ate sandwiches filled with cress plucked from the yard, and where thermal waters trickled down Sulphur Mountain into a goldfish pond in the garden overlooking the Bow Valley—the same pond in which his white-bearded grandfather Arthur bathed. These are the "home places" Stan Rowe writes about, where humans are enveloped within the ecosystem and are part of it, and Bill Cronon's backyards where we live in the "middle ground."[87] Claremount House in Banff National Park stood as a cultural landscape representing the history of the ACC and of the Wheeler family's role engaging mountaineers in mountain parks until it was demolished on January 17, 2011, by order of Parks Canada Agency. Although Middle Springs refers to the thermal hot springs and karst outlet midway up Sulphur Mountain known during John Wheeler's boyhood, it is now more likely to evoke the name of the suburban subdivisions Middle Springs I and II, constructed in the 1990s as middle-class housing in the town of Banff, that press against the wildlife corridor on Sulphur Mountain.

The stories of these heritage buildings reveal a telling summary that encapsulates the changing visions of mountain national parks and the place of people in their cultural history, indeed the story of the ACC. The Alpine Club of Canada was encouraged early on to promote mountain recreation and Canadian heritage from its headquarters in the midst of Banff; subsequent land-use decisions, leading to demolition and resource neglect, have enacted an erasure of human presence from the same site, denying the human history of the area while upholding the legal mandate for ecological integrity in national parks emanating from the latest National Parks Act (1988). Where is the middle ground to reconcile the definition and governance of how we value nature and culture as resources for protection? Can natural resource and cultural resource protection be better integrated in places like Banff, taking a lesson from national parks in northern Canada where Aboriginal perspectives have informed integrated holistic approaches to land management, and from UNESCO World Heritage classifications that recognize cultural landscapes? Other alternatives may make possible a role for the integrated management of natural and cultural resources as a landscape whole.[88] Does one have to be at the expense of the other? These questions arise and demand answers in other contexts as land-use and management decisions in national parks attempt to cope with interests competing for park space, particularly considering relations between nature and culture that shape parks as landscapes. Can parks productively rethink how to manage cultural landscapes based on an integrated epistemology of place, particularly in cases that appear to set natural and cultural resource management in competition against each other for a few precious metres of space? This competition may actually be the product of how we frame our ways of thinking.

The demolition of the ACC Clubhouse and Claremount House constitute an erasure of local human presence and history in the urban backyard of Banff National Park. The loss of these sites may well be considered a serious social displacement due to the shifting priorities of regulatory and policy regimes. It is a view that can magnify over time, particularly when present use obscures the history we assign to a place. Whereas the success of the Sulphur Mountain–Middle Springs Wildlife Corridor has been measured in positive benefits to the protection of wildlife species, the loss of cultural heritage due to historically inconsistent public policies has yet to be accounted for in the positioning of public interests in contests of power. Good intentions, compromises, science, expediency, and the prevalence of capitalist development influence in the national parks have all figured in decision-making.

In 1991 Lake Louise International Hostel and Canadian Alpine Centre was opened jointly by the Alpine Club of Canada and the Alberta Hostelling Association. To some extent, it has filled the role once served by the Banff Alpine Clubhouse as a gathering point for alpine enthusiasts and travellers in Banff National Park. The ACC national office headquarters at the Canmore clubhouse stands outside park boundaries. While Parks Canada was willing to move the ACC out of its clubhouse in the 1970s, curtailed government spending through the 1990s returned partnerships with non-government groups to the forefront of national park initiatives. Increased government reliance on partnerships with private sector groups again cast the ACC as an active player regarding the operations and management of alpine huts in the national mountain parks. Huts act as reminders of the club's identity within park boundaries, just as the Banff clubhouse did, and they also generate substantial club revenues. Broader mountaineering communities and other travellers also opted to engage huts through affiliation with these places as part of the integrated nature/culture landscapes in mountain parks. Long-standing footholds of the human history of recreation and sport in the region, ACC huts are indicative of the club's privileged space, social status, and particular sense of place.

Mountaineers were part of the historical geography of a cultured landscape in Canada's mountain parks and protected areas. Remembering favourite campsites, revisiting the glacier ice, and witnessing local transformations through decades allowed the Alpine Club of Canada to read its own intergenerational memories inhabiting the landscape and the body. Along with fostering its own brand of outdoor pursuits and wilderness travel, the club contributed directly and indirectly to constructing an integrated landscape of park infrastructure and facilities. When its clubhouse and GMC moved out of the national parks, the ACC ended an era by symbolically leaving home. Technical planning and openings for meaningful democratic public consultation were characteristic of government into the 1970s era. As state planning strategies attempted to balance the objectives of use and preservation, the mountain parks paradoxically became increasingly managed wild places.

Epilogue

Reconnections in a Living World

What's going on just now? What's happening to us? What is this world, this period, this precise moment in which we are living?

—MICHEL FOUCAULT, "The Subject and Power"[1]

The past is now not a land to return to in the simple politics of memory but one of imaginary landscapes in imagined worlds.

—PATRICIA VERTINSKY, "Locating a 'Sense of Place'"[2]

<< Overleaf: Kiwa Glacier, British Columbia, 2006. PearlAnn Reichwein photograph.

∧ High Camp at Kiwa Glacier, Premier Range GMC, 2006. PearlAnn Reichwein photograph.

MY HAIR FLATTENS LIKE GRASS in the wind every time the heli-copter lands and roars off. Now it's my turn to fly to Kiwa Glacier in the Premier Range. We're about an hour from Jasper, near Valemount, British Columbia, west of Mount Robson and east of Wells Gray Provincial Park. As we fly up the forest drainage and turn into a hanging valley high in the Cariboo Mountains, a tiny camp appears below and grows larger as we approach a tented town. The annual summer moun-taineering camp is convening for the 101st time while the ACC commemorates its centennial year. It does not meet in a park. I hunch over to disembark as the helicopter rotor blades pass overhead, and then I walk into the storybook of my own historical imagination. The camp opens like the pages of an old photo album; black-and-white images spring to colour and life. A circus of geometric nylon tents in orange, silver, and white is laid out on the grassy meadow. Base camp is situated along a tumbling brook. Here is the canvas dining tent and cookhouse pulled taut with ropes, and over there the tea tent and another for drying. A woman in round glasses reminds me distinctly of Phyllis Munday, and two young brothers resemble Roger and Ferris Neave. I think of the heli-copter fuel, the specialized gear, and the sheer privilege complicit in carbon expenditures to achieve this moment.

Midweek, we fly through rain up to high camp, where a domed space station and smaller tents roost on a rock island in the midst of Kiwa Glacier. Climbing Mount Sir Wilfrid Laurier in this range with peaks named after prime ministers and crossing the snowfields roped with our guide takes us into an alpine world. Winds buffet the tents one night leaving ten centimetres of snow, which makes for a snowbound morning drinking coffee and talking in the dome expedition tent. I don't feel forty on the rock routes, but my knees do. More bad weather one evening holds us tent bound, this time drinking Scotch. We came so far to get away from the city, yet it followed us; there is nowhere to retreat from society, even on a rock island in a snowstorm, even if Mary Schäffer once went to seek out the "great un-lonely silence of the wilderness." A pair of ravens flies across the ice canyon of fissured blue-grey glacier. The pair keeps appearing when no one else is around. Black with horned beaks. What are they saying? They fly away across the canyon.

Tied to a rope with three other climbers, I get in step. Our synchronized swim across the snow plods on, step by step, in time with the guide ahead of us. Efficient walking can cover many more kilometres at a fast rate. Getting in sync. Getting it together. The rope team moves like dancers in a choreographed sequence: switch the rope from right to left, pirouette, keep it uphill, ready to catch a fall. It's a pedagogy of mountaineering. Wearing crampons means that a slip is unacceptable; I ponder this as the slope gradient increases up the shoulder of Sir Wilfrid Laurier, still remembering sliding past a man's face yesterday as we sailed on our backs through the snow in a minor avalanche called a sluff. Later, while downclimbing, facing the slope, I look between my feet to the climber below and remind myself not to step on her mittens. I visualize a crampon impaling her hand; that would not be good. Understatement is strong in mountaineering narratives, like other fictions of heroic adventure.

We carry on down, following an invisible ladder, step by step, until we regain the plateau of snow that spans the lower glacier. Our guide has moved ahead of the rope now, into the lead. "Drop coils and stretch out the rope in transition to glacier travel," he says. We sit down to eat lunch a long distance apart from each other, respectful of the glacier's crevasses. It is 11:30. My plastic CamelBak could bobsled downhill from here until it hits Kiwa Glacier lake far below. The water inside the pouch is so cold that it cools my internal tissues. And this is summer climbing in August. Of course, snow could arrive at any time, and perhaps it will in another hour. We march around a snowfield cirque, sweat dripping from my brow. Keep slogging, slogging, until we pass an orange safety flag in the snow and reach the rocks again. The rest of the group is relaxing with boots off, lounging on the rocks, drying gear, and watching our progress. The sun is strong off the glacier and heats the face. I need more sunscreen in this thin atmosphere. An endless show of cloud shadows and sunlight shifts across the snowfield and plays on the mountains as we look back to Laurier. It appears like a Byron Harmon silver print. One Calgary climber is fully absorbed, watching for any sign of the team on Mount Sir John Abbott; no one appears, and the suspense of this slow-action cinema is killing him. It's the best movie he's seen in years.

Life slows down after the climb. We hang out on the moraine. I let my RPM drop to nothing but glowing satisfaction after exertion. It's about 1:00 in the afternoon. No rush. Alpine starts at 4:30 in the morning give way to long afternoons. I lie on a flat rock, looking up to the drifting clouds and shadow play on the snow. Bare feet and drying socks. Now it's time to hang out and drink some coffee in the dome tent. I had skipped caffeine at breakfast to slow my heart down. The morning's dishes are washed up. Soup comes next. Inside the tent, orange light illuminates our skin until someone unzips a long oval door flap to open up a window onto the glacier. We can see out across the sheet of snow and ice seracs. The long wait for action on Mount Sir John Abbott finally breaks with the appearance of the cook and her other friends returning down the fractured glacier between Abbott and Mount R.B. Bennett. But the sky is changing. Thick grey clouds are developing on the horizon as a snowfall is coming toward the moraine, now. It feels like winter could arrive at any time. From the coffee tent, we watch the climbers' progress as the rope of four draws a black line down the slope and crosses the monumental icefield below the mountains. Time to get their soup on. "You could have dropped a bus down that crevasse," they tell us later, having crossed over a vital snow bridge still holding on the descent. Sentinels rise on the horizon as the last light passes into sundown. Red stripes wash over the peaks. An infinity of stars and galaxies lights the black night sky.

Here is the wonder and beauty of why I seek these faraway places.

When we stop talking, we can hear the brook running down the rocks into the valley. Mica dust sparkles everywhere, in the stream sediments, in our drinking water, all over our packs and clothes, in the cracks of our feet and hands, and no doubt inside our bodies as we ingest a daily dose of the mountain. You can see it gather as a deposit in the bottom of a Nalgene bottle. What are you drinking? Carcinogens in plastic or

DDT trapped in the glacier ice? Frozen memories of atmospheric pollutants. "There's much worse in the glacier," says our guide. "Have you seen *An Inconvenient Truth?*" someone asks. We drink the glacier; we climb the snow that makes meltwater. "How long will the glaciers last?" Melancholy infects our gaze as some of us foresee the glaciers shrinking away in our own lifetimes. A Jasper mountain guide mentions how he has seen the Athabasca Glacier shrink visibly in the last five years. I remember how my father drove directly to the foot of it when I was a child. We threw snowballs with my grandparents right where a parking lot now stretches out toward the ice. The glacier reached out even farther when Margaret Fleming rode past on a one-speed bicycle in 1945, after climbing at the ACC summer camp in Jasper. Phyl Munday observed that glacier and landscape change was a story told in the photos of the club's climbs and camps, and as early as 1930 she urged mountaineers to share the story:

> Our photographs are going to be in future, and have been in the past, our only record of our mountains. The glaciated areas change considerably, and if we do not keep records of our climbs and our Camps, other countries and individuals will feel that we are losing a splendid opportunity, because they naturally turn to the Alpine Club of Canada for records. If we do not keep these records, we are ourselves certainly losing...A great deal could be done throughout Canada by every Section trying at least once a year or once every two years to have a public exhibition in their town or city. A great deal of good work could be done for the Alpine Club of Canada, and the work that we are doing, because in this way we bring to the public our mountain scenery and our heritage.[3]

More recently, just such stories of memory in glaciated regions have documented phenomenal transformations in vanishing landscapes with Jeff Orlowski's film *Chasing Ice* screened at the White House on Earth Day and Paul Walde's oratorio "Requiem for a Glacier" staged on Jumbo Glacier in the Kootenay Mountains of British Columbia, both in 2013.[4]

Back at the Irish pub on Whyte Avenue, a few climbers gather together over beer after the club meeting in Edmonton. It's clear that routes on Mount Athabasca are changing due to glacial recession. It'll be a shooting gallery of rock fall. "You won't be able to climb that route in years to come," someone points out. Mountaineers are the intimate witnesses of disappearing glaciers and changing mountains. Privy to seeing, touching, feeling, hearing, and tasting the ice melt. The world is changing before our eyes.

"Climbing narratives that emphasize a state of connection with the natural world in all its threats and scars and beauty are narratives that point us all toward an understanding of place," contends philosopher Jeffrey McCarthy, "which is an understanding of our connection to the natural world that defines us and is defined by us." He also says that texts about climbing, about mountaineering "point readers toward a model of understanding human experience that transcends, if only briefly, the pressure to see the world from the confines of national-consciousness or ego-consciousness, and hints at the possibility of an eco-consciousness beyond."[5] Speaking our stories is meaningful. It can connect imagined and living worlds.

Mountaineers in the Cariboos hear the water sounding from summit to boulder field, to alpine stream, waterfall, brook, and wide river running with spawning salmon as the Fraser carves its way to the ocean. The widening breadth of water streams down from the mountains. What stands to be lost with the melting ice? "We don't miss the muddy river till the water has run clear," sings Alberta cowboy Sid Marty. "Where are the snows of yesteryear?"[6] Uneasy, we sense mountains stripped naked, rising shorelines, and shrinking polar caps. Dry fields. Parched cities.

Water is life.

What does it take to activate citizens and mobilize environmental concerns? Back in Rosebud, Alberta, later that summer, well water burns following recent coal-bed methane drilling and extraction.[7] Poor water quality jeopardizes health in many First Nations communities in Alberta and elsewhere in Canada, where good drinking water cannot be taken for granted.[8] Thousands of migratory birds drown in toxic tailings ponds at oil sands extraction sites near Fort McMurray.[9] Human cancer incidence concerns residents in the Peace-Athabasca Delta, farther down the Athabasca rivershed.[10] Whose job is it to protect the environment? The twentieth century would belong to Canada, said Sir Wilfrid Laurier, the late prime minister. Who will Canada's water belong to in the twenty-first century? I suck hard on the tube of my water pouch to stay hydrated on Mount Sir Wilfrid Laurier.

▲ Seeking the historical roots of early conservation movements in Canada and wanting to better understand the politics in the Rockies led me to study the Alpine Club of Canada. In Alberta, government leaders dismissed environmentalists as a fringe special interest group in the late

1980s. Minister of Environment Ralph Klein perpetuated this outlook then and as premier, while Alberta's lands and waters faced serious challenges in the midst of the changing fortunes in a boom–bust economy. The stakes are even higher today as southern Alberta's devastating floods from headwaters in the Rockies and plans for new dam projects illustrate. The 2013 floods can be considered a wake-up call to improve headwater protection.[11] And northern Alberta's industrial mega projects in the oil sands are debated as a global environmental concern. Writing off environmentalists may make it easy to achieve short-term political goals in a province like Alberta, which has a history of longstanding one-party governments. But look closely. A large number of Canadians, rural and urban, invest in conservation and the environment through parks, recreation, sport, and tourism, much as the ACC did throughout the twentieth century. They have a direct stake in the environment and heritage. They are citizens, and many of them vote or engage in various forms of democratic participation. They are stakeholders in the imaginative and political process of making parks and protected areas.

Political scientist C. Lloyd Brown-John says there is a changing balance between the state and the citizen with respect to national park management in Canada. "Contemporary public policy and administration—to say nothing of populist democracy—have witnessed massive alterations in the relationship between the citizen and the state. Public policymakers risk policies if they fail to fully appreciate the extent to which modern citizenship posits expectations about the relative roles of citizens and public officials in the process of governance."[12] Network processes involving stakeholders in national park management with the Parks Canada Agency have gained currency in collaborative public policy development. Roles for citizens in participatory governance underwrite a new management paradigm for protected areas. Governments cannot write off public stakeholders in parks and protected areas management and expect success. Nor can they diminish public funding and the public service without a fundamental loss and transformation in state–citizen relations. To go forward, public historian Lyle Dick observes that "in an increasingly complex political environment, addressing its mandate will require Parks Canada to build broadly based constituencies for the protection and presentation of national parks and other protected areas and to navigate between these different constituencies in ongoing dialogue and problem solving."[13]

Canada's national park idea has meant different things at different times. Ecological integrity, it is worth noting, is a historically contingent construct that was only recently inscribed as the dominant narrative in Canada's national park idea. It was legislated through milestones, such as the revised National Parks Act (1988), the Parks Canada Agency Act (1999), and the Canadian National Parks Act (2000). How it is conceptualized remains in flux. There are a variety of ways in which to see and talk about ecological integrity. The dominant perspective has been critiqued as a standard that presupposes nature–culture dualism and stems from Western assumptions that humans have no place in a "pristine" state of nature. As a result, this discourse can run against and impede new participatory governance for protected areas that involves communities in management. Another way of viewing and talking about the concept is based on how individuals create meaning and engage in collaborative learning that collectively produces ecological integrity. Overall, local participation and adaptive governance can give rise to diverse alternatives that mix several conceptual approaches. Such "new management" paradigms denote a dynamic understanding of socio-ecological management for integrity in concert with changing state–citizen relations.[14]

But how will ecological integrity fare in a Canada challenged by profound neo-liberal shifts in state–citizen relations that have left science undermined, environmental legislation and policy weakened, cultural institutions under duress, and the role of national parks (and often parks and protected areas in other jurisdictions) tilted hard toward increased profit-making?[15] Significant public sector cuts correlate with Ottawa's outlook that national parks are open for business and generating mass tourism is a priority. It now favours intensive tourism industry developments, such as the controversial "Glacier Skywalk," newly cantilevered into a ridge at the Columbia Icefields in Jasper, where paying visitors can also hop on a massive all-terrain vehicle to learn about mountains and climate change as it drives over the Athabasca Glacier; salvage tourism is about monetizing the chance to see ecosystems before they vanish, and that's definitely a limited-time offer. Yet praxis suggests rigorous and well-implemented knowledges are needed for best practices of integrated ecosystem management and heritage conservation. And in this process, well-informed governance, rule of law, free inquiry, and critique ought to come together in park and protected areas management as practices of democracy.

It is also consequential that learned human understanding of environmentally responsible behaviour and the intrinsic value of nature can be influenced through outdoor recreation. Take activities like mountaineering, camping, hiking, and walking. The understandings derived while engaged in nature-based leisure may be one of the foremost public-education purposes of national parks and protected areas in our own era. For example, declining visitation to US National Parks since 1987—following a steady fifty-year increase—prompted social scientists Oliver Pergams and Patricia Zaradic to investigate changing trends in nature-based recreation. Their recent conclusions point to a "fundamental shift away from people's interest in nature" evident in the United States and Japan. These findings suggest serious implications for conservation efforts because attempts to raise public awareness to address the current biodiversity crisis become less likely as people spend less extended time in natural areas. It is a problem both local and global in scope. Richard Louv raises an important question in *Last Child in the Woods* when he asks the vital question, "as the care of nature increasingly becomes an intellectual concept severed from the joyful experience of the outdoors, you have to wonder: Where will future environmentalists come from?"[16] Environmentalists come from people of all ages being outside to reconnect with the living world around them in all its wonder, beauty, and danger, and with their participation in the politics of social life rather than acquiescent withdrawal. Awareness of the environment grounded in place is critical to environmentalism. Cultures of mountaineering and nature pursuits of many kinds have potential to strengthen it. Early voices in the ACC took a leading role in Canada to provide a site for such pursuits and to fortify environmental resolve.

The city and the mountains can be reimagined as interconnected worlds, just as the ACC once posited. In 1971 mountaineer Dan Phelps wrote in the *Canadian Alpine Journal* that conservation relied on more people caring about the mountains by experiencing the outdoors. Likewise, the club's Calgary Section recommended extending Parks Canada's outreach programs to urban areas. These ideas touch on a key concern for today. For urbanites, nature outreach and free play can start with trees, parks, playgrounds, urban farmland, community gardens, ponds, kindergartens, animals, waterfronts, art, summer camps, and walking in the inner city and suburbs—concepts for the twenty-first century reconfigured from older ideas about nature and urban life drawn from thinkers like Frederick Frobel, Jane Addams, J.W. Woodsworth, Frederick Law Olmstead, Thomas Adams, Mary Hamilton, and Jane Jacobs, not to mention the Canadian Commission on Conservation of the early twentieth century. The example of the ACC speaks to the engagement of a largely urban population shaping a culture of nature in the mountain parks among middle-class Canadians and others, and to the significance of outdoor recreationists and NGO participation in governance in ways that bear historical relevance to current concerns. As Brown-John argues:

> As cities grow in population there is a reality that more and more urban Canadians have had little or no experience with national parks and, thus, it follows that the salience of and the mandate of Parks Canada is low in opinion and, with the exception of some very articulate interest groups (e.g. Canadian Parks and Wilderness Society; Sierra Club; the Nature Conservancy), those with a capacity to engage governments in a positive dialogue on national parks policy is limited. In some respects, for Parks Canada, promoting interest and support for national parks in growing urban communities is an immediate challenge.[17]

As NGOs continue to build capacity and dialogue, Parks Canada's Rouge National Urban Park in Toronto is also breaking new ground as the first urban national park in the country.[18]

Going beyond the urban middle-class orientations typical of the earlier social history of parks and the ACC to embrace diversity and diverse expectations among various urban and rural people is also important to participatory governance of national parks. Aboriginal perspectives—for so long excluded from white, middle-class, wilderness narratives—have fundamentally challenged assumptions about the meanings and management of national parks in Canada. We can also challenge standard discourses that shape thinking about mountain parks in spatial terms that subtly codify and politicize the so-called "frontcountry" as a hetero-familial commercial tourism strip and the "backcountry" as a masculine frontier in a wilderness devoid of human presence. These are exclusionary precepts based on class, gender, and ancestry that function through emparked nature and the social construction of the park idea.

Affordable access to mountain parks is another factor that merits closer inspection: some Canadians will never get to a national park. Rising user fees in national parks teamed with the closure of public campgrounds, group campsites, bridges, and basic public infrastructure in places like Yoho and Banff since the 1990s are trends that are unlikely to grow support for national parks. So, too, is declining social equity among Canadians since the waning of the postwar welfare state. Taking people out of mountain national parks may further sever the essential ties that lead them to care about the places they know and visit, that bind nature and culture as an integrated whole, and tell the story of parks as historical landscapes that include humans. To what extent do park management and design policies foster the highway windshield tour or commodified tourism "products" over accessible experiential interactions with nature? A subtle but creeping erasure of human history and presence in some mountain parks implies people never had a place there. There could be a finer reassessment of function and purpose that accounts for equitable and sustainable public recreation in tandem with the goals of ecological management. Some Albertans, certain climbers among them, now turn away from national parks in the Rockies toward provincial parks and lands on the eastern slopes where lower user fees are twinned with multiple-use management doctrines. Does this mean that regional markets are opting out of the national park idea and places that are seen as inaccessible to the average Canadian? Will such citizens care about Banff or Jasper or other national parks? And what about the effects of multiple-use provincial park policies on the eastern slopes and in other places? Linking exposure to pro-environmental recreation with the goals of ecological management may hold the promise of producing the next generation of park supporters and environmentalists. The natural and cultural worlds are interconnected. In practice, however, many difficulties can arise when implementing integration principles in highly politicized, high-stakes management situations, but great possibility can also reside in praxis.

"Protect the resource," the outfitter told us on day one in camp. "Whizz well away from the stream and use the outhouses located two hundred feet away from the watercourse." "Wash your hands properly," the camp doctor advises us succinctly. "Don't eat shit." Seems to make sense. It is the first time in a long time that many of us remember being able to drink directly from a clean mountain stream without fear of giardia or contamination. In the power play of global water supply, energy consumption, habitat loss, and extinctions, no one is a real winner.

What about mutual survival? One way to mobilize environmental concern is to recognize that people love the places that touch them and hold deeper meaning, the places they care about. Another way is to act on sharing mutual interdependence. It goes beyond parks and protected areas to larger ecosystem concepts. "The oilpatch made me angry the first time I went to work up there," an Alberta welder tells me. His grand-parents were homesteaders. "All living things are beautiful. The fact we have to build a four-way across a park to see it is ironic." Looking at the silent night sky as I stand in a field of sweet alfalfa and long grass, I see that he's right. I'm far from the mountains here, in eastern Alberta, about two hours west of the Saskatchewan border. These farms and ranches are fed by headwaters from the Columbia Icefields in Jasper. Bear scat filled with Saskatoon berry pulp is on the ground. Keening coyote wails break off into a series of yips. A marsh hawk is crashing into the aspen bush, diving after prey. Wild sounds in wild places. Wild and right at home. Just like the three tiny Eastern Phoebes nesting under the eaves of the farmhouse by the backdoor. We are all part of this living place.

When William Cronon launched "The Trouble with Wilderness; or, Getting Back to the Wrong Nature"—his now canonized social critique of urban American discourses of nature that construct wilderness as unpeopled—he concluded by urging readers to look for and after "wild-ness" and "nature" in their "own backyards," a worthwhile invocation even while his other arguments provoked substantial controversy in environmental history.[19] But whose backyards and where? For genera-tions, Canada's mountain parks were the "backyards" of ACC mountaineers, among many other climbers and recreationists, not to mention local residents. From this idea of the backyard came "play-ground" as a metaphor for parks in Canada throughout much of the twentieth century, as much as it was socially and spatially manifested in the club's physical pursuits in the parks. The club facilitated repeated park visits, seasonally, through individual lifetimes, and from one gener-ation to the next. If the mountain parks were the backyard of the ACC, it follows that some club members adopted some of these places as part of themselves and their own being, forging potentially profound relation-ships that touched both directions of knowing humans as in and of nature, thereby dissolving dualism and opening a way of knowing people and place as an integrated entity. As a result, there was an implicit reason for mountaineers to be aware of and responsible for their own power and privilege to know these areas. Moreover, the symbolic currency of Canada's many mountain parks—in the Rockies, Columbias, Cariboos, Bugaboos, Coast Range, St. Elias, Ragged Range, Laurentians, Cumberland Range, and east to the Torngats, to name but a few—extends beyond the scope of a specific region to national and international signification. It may render a big backyard, whose human constituents might care about an inte-grated way of knowing the mountain parks as places enriched with layered meanings and historical connotations, or, in the words of historian Simon Schama, to see their surroundings as "landscapes of memory."[20] Healing environmental ruptures begins with reconnections that move toward reuniting people and wild places. To this end, excavating the historic relationships of people and nature and explaining their importance is a key task in parks and protected areas, as well as in museums, archives, historic sites, galleries, schools, and universities.

What can we glean from history so we can understand the nexus of people and place that informs the pressing environmental concerns of our era? Is there transformative potential in understanding how key mountain park users know these places? "If the social world is not seen or understood as being of our own making, there is no way we can change it. And if we have no chance of changing it, it is quite conceivable that we are wasting our time in social science," observed sociologist G. Llewellyn Watson. "Not only should social science theory generate new knowledge, but such knowledge should be a means of transforming society."[21] This is also a role for arts and humanities scholarship. Mountaineers in the ACC past and present have forged understandings of mountain parks at crossroads of culture and nature, perhaps revealing a oneness of being in and of nature. What we imagine and create can determine what we see as the past and the future.

Canada's parks cannot be all things to all stakeholders. Common vision is hard to find. The fundamental questions concern what we want from parks and protected areas, and how we can reach a social contract long enough to sustain mutual goals and support the long-term needs of a living environment. Every generation must debate and renew this contract. The ACC periodically had to have debates, reach consensus, and set a model of environmental citizenship in its backyard. When civic responsibility to the public domain is abrogated, no one stands guard over the public trust of parks and protected areas, yet contending forces will always be present to challenge their purpose, which in part prompted J.B. Harkin's observation that "the battle for the establishment of National Parks is long since over but the battle to keep them inviolate is never won."[22] Arthur Wheeler observed as early as 1923 that "there will be assuredly, in the course of time, hundreds of other cases of varying types" to challenge the inviolability of the national parks.[23]

Do mountaineers matter to mountain parks? Participation in outdoor leisure can inculcate awareness and social commitment to values of biodiversity conservation, wilderness advocacy, and habitat protection. It can also awaken awareness of human history, cultural landscapes, and heritage protection—and how all these values interrelate. Another premise to foster in the interests of people and ecology is intergenerational political participation in civil society. If history can provide an analog for the present era, there may be something to be learned from the narratives of mountaineers and mountain parks to encourage a vision of the world that integrates people and place. Homecoming arises from the reconnection of people and place. The more backyards the better. Just as the ACC has encouraged and continues to encourage reinvention of the mountain parks—always in worlds both imagined and living—outdoor life and many kinds of learning can bring about nature-culture homecomings. Acknowledging the depth of connection between people and land in mountain parks helps dissolve boundaries between culture and nature, so that we might embrace and advocate the shared ground of cultural landscapes in Canada's parks and protected areas, and beyond. It is an outlook for mountaineers and the rest of us to contemplate, for ultimately, we all drink from watersheds in the same backyard.

▲ Kiwa Glacier demands honesty as my eye travels across the ice. Being here is also an imperative. The old alpine journal nests in my backpack. I have climbed the snow-covered mountain and the white paper tower. I will tell my story about this place. I will listen for other stories and silences. My arm slides through the strap, thoughts flowing like ink to paper, setting off on my way, like marginalia winding down the mountain to another home. A new page begins where we meet the road.

Appendix 1

Statistical Profiles of Alpine Club of Canada Membership

TABLE 1: Sex Distribution and Female Marital Status in the ACC, 1907–1967

Year	1907	1922	1930	1939	1946	1956	1967
Total Membership	201	599	652	510	472	871	1,268
Total Women	63	245	273	211	198	321	411
Total Men	137	354	379	297	274	550	857
% Female	31.3	40.9	41.9	41.4	42	36.9	32.4
% Male	68.2	59.1	58.1	58.2	58	63.14	67.6
Total Women Married	16	87	96	62	63	146	238
Total Women Single	47	158	177	148	135	175	173
% Women Married	25.4	35.5	35.2	29.4	31.8	45.5	57.9
% Women Single	74.6	64.5	64.8	70.1	68.2	54.5	42.1

Note: For analysis, marital status was determined by the honorific Miss or Mrs. in ACC membership lists. Women listed as Dr. or PHD, who were identified by female first names, were enumerated as single. Statistics derived from ACC list of members by year.

TABLE 2: Membership Distribution by Category in the ACC, 1907–1967

Year	1907	1922	1930	1939	1946	1956	1967
Active (Member)	93	549	341	336	300	644	903
Life Active	NA	NA	113	102	91	108	169
Graduating	90	NA	59	NA	22	61	NA
Subscribing	2	39	126	60	49	48	NA
Honorary	6	9	9	9	7	7	9
Associate	10	2	NA	NA	NA	NA	185
War	NA	NA	4	3	3	3	NA
Other	NA	NA	NA	NA	NA	NA	2
Total	201	599	652	510	472	871	1,268

Note: Statistics derived from ACC list of members by year.

TABLE 3: ACC Membership Distribution by Region in Figures, 1907–1967

Year	1907	1922	1930	1939	1946	1956	1967
BC	37	67	154	132	145	229	319
Alberta	79	149	101	79	79	193	279
Saskatchewan	3	35	17	13	12	11	18
Manitoba	30	52	29	17	12	13	14
Ontario	19	60	47	38	30	69	137
Quebec	2	10	10	6	29	50	86
Maritimes	1	2	4	1	0	1	4
Yukon	0	0	0	0	0	1	2
NWT	0	0	0	0	0	0	0
USA	16	124	197	182	129	263	334
UK	5	23	27	29	22	31	26
Other	3	6	7	7	3	9	49
Total	195	528	593	504	461	870	1,268

Note: Statistics derived from ACC list of members by year.

TABLE 4: ACC Membership Distribution by Region in Percentages, 1907–1967

Year	1907	1922	1930	1939	1946	1956	1967
BC	19.0	12.7	26.0	26.2	31.6	26.3	25.2
Alberta	40.5	28.2	17.0	15.7	17.1	22.2	22.0
Saskatchewan	01.5	06.6	02.9	02.6	02.6	01.3	01.4
Manitoba	15.4	09.8	04.9	03.4	02.6	01.5	01.1
Ontario	09.7	11.4	07.9	07.5	06.5	07.9	10.8
Quebec	01.0	01.9	01.7	01.2	06.3	05.7	06.8
Maritimes	00.5	00.4	00.7	00.2	0	00.1	00.3
Yukon	0	0	0	0	0	00.1	00.2
NWT	0	0	0	0	0	0	0
USA	08.2	23.5	33.2	36.1	28.0	30.2	26.3
UK	02.6	04.4	04.6	05.8	04.8	03.6	02.1
Other	01.5	01.1	01.2	01.4	00.7	01.0	03.8
Total	100	100	100	100	100	100	100

Note: Statistics derived from ACC list of members by year.

Appendix 2

Alpine Club of Canada National Executive, 1906–1974

Presidents

1906	A.O. Wheeler
1910	A.P. Coleman
1914	J.D. Patterson
1920	W.W. Foster
1924	J.W. Hickson
1926	F.C. Bell
1928	T.B. Moffat
1930	H.E. Sampson
1932	A.A. McCoubrey
1934	A.S. Sibbald
1938	C.G. Wates
1941	E.C. Brooks
1947	S.R. Vallance
1950	E.O. Wheeler
1954	E.R. Gibson
1957	H.A.V. Green
1958	J.F. Brett
1960	H.A.V. Green
1964	R.C. Hind
1966	R. Neave
1968	P.J. Dowling
1970	D.R. Fisher
1972	S.D. Rosenbaum

Director

1901–1926	A.O. Wheeler

Eastern Vice-Presidents

1906	A.P. Coleman
1908	J.D. Patterson
1912	F.C. Bell
1916	C.H. Mitchell
1920	C.B. Sissons
1922	G.M. Smith
1924	H.F. Lambart

1928	A.A. McCoubrey
1930	C.H. Mitchell
1932	W.J. Sykes
1934	J.B. Kay
1936	F. Neave
1938	W.J. Sykes
1941	J.F. Brett
1947	R. Neave
1950	J.F. Brett
1954	C.J. Woodsworth
1956	A. Bruce-Robertson
1958	R. Neave
1960	J.O. Wheeler
1962	R. Neave
1964	D.R. Fisher
1968	R.M. Thomson
1970	S.D. Rosenbaum
1972	M.A. Tyler
1974	W.T. Robinson

Central Vice-Presidents

1966	E. Hopkins
1968	E.M. Mills
1970	D.J. Forest
1974	J. Tewnion

Western Vice-Presidents

1906	J.C. Herdman
1908	M.P. Bridgland
1912	J.P. Forde
1916	W.W. Foster
1920	H.B. Mitchell
1922	T.B. Moffat
1926	C.G. Wates
1928	H.J. Graves
1930	A.W. Drinnan

1934	L.C. Wilson
1936	C.G. Wates
1938	E.C. Brooks
1941	S.R. Vallance
1947	W.A.D. Munday
1950	R.J. Cutherbertson
1954	R.C. Hind
1956	H.A.V. Green
1958	W.T. Read
1960	J.G. Kato
1962	W. Sparling
1964	S. Merler
1966	H. Butling
1968	W.P. Broda
1970	P. Sherman
1972	R.M. Paul
1974	D. Blair

American Vice-Presidents

1948	H.S. Kingman
1952	A.H. MacCarthy
1956	L. Gest
1958	P. Prescott
1960	S.B. Hendricks
1962	F.D. Chamberlin
1964	E.C. Porter

1966	H.S. Hall, Jr.
1968	D. Wessel
1972	L.L. McArthur

Secretary-Treasurers and Club Managers

1906	E. Parker
1908	S.H. Mitchell
1929	W.R. Tweedy
1944	E.C. Brooks (Acting)
1947	L.C. Wilson
1959	W.C. Ledingham
1969	P.A. Boswell
1974	E.S. Moorhouse

Canadian Alpine Journal Editors

1907	A.O. Wheeler
1928	J.W. Hickson
1930	A.A. McCoubrey
1942	M.D. Fleming
1953	P.B. Munday
1970	A. Gruft
1974	M. Irvine

Source: WMCR, ACC, List, 1976, 148-49.

Appendix 3

Alpine Club of Canada Camps

**General Mountaineering Camps,
1906–1974**

1906	Yoho Pass
1907	Paradise Valley
1908	Rogers Pass
1909	Lake O'Hara
1910	Consolation [Lakes] Valley
1911	Sherbrooke Lake
1912	Vermilion Pass
1913	Cathedral Mountain; Mount Robson
1914	Upper Yoho Valley
1915	Ptarmigan [Lake] Valley
1916	Bow Valley [Healy Creek]
1917	Cataract Valley
1918	Paradise Valley
1919	Yoho Pass
1920	Assiniboine
1921	Lake O'Hara
1922	Palliser Pass
1923	Larch Valley
1924	Mount Robson
1925	Lake O'Hara
1926	Tonquin Valley
1927	Upper [Little] Yoho Valley
1928	Lake of the Hanging Glacier
1929	Rogers Pass
1930	Maligne Lake
1931	Prospectors Valley
1932	Mount Sir Donald
1933	Paradise Valley
1934	Chrome Lake (Eremite Valley)
1935	Assiniboine [Lake Magog]
1936	Fryatt [Creek] Valley
1937	Upper Yoho Valley
1938	Columbia Icefields
1939	Goodsirs
1940	Glacier Lake
1941	Glacier, BC
1942	Consolation [Lakes] Valley
1943	Lake O'Hara
1944	Paradise Valley
1945	Chrome Lake (Eremite Valley)
1946	Bugaboo Creek
1947	Glacier, BC
1948	Peyto Lake
1949	Freshfields
1950	Maligne Lake
1951	Lake O'Hara
1952	Mount Assiniboine
1953	Hooker Icefield (Whirlpool Valley)
1954	Goodsirs
1955	Mount Robson
1956	Glacier, BC
1957	Moat Lake, Tonquin Valley
1958	Mummery, Blaeberry River
1959	Bugaboo Creek
1960	Fryatt Creek
1961	Goodsirs
1962	Maligne Lake
1963	Eremite Valley
1964	French Millitary Group
1965	Glacier Lake
1966	Mount Assiniboine
1967	YACE [Steele Glacier]
1968	Lake O'Hara
1969	Freshfields
1970	Moat Lake, Tonquin Valley
1971	Farnham Creek

1972	Fryatt Creek	1957	Maligne Lake
1973	Glacier Lake	1958	Little Yoho
1974	Mount Robson	1959	Assiniboine
		1960	Mount Robson

Alpine Climbing Camps, 1968–1974

		1961	Little Yoho
1968	Adamants	1962	Little Yoho
1969	Mount Waddington Area	1963	Eremite
1971	Vowell Creek	1964	Maligne Lake
1972	Clemenceau	1965	Columbia Icefields
1973	Ape Lake	1966	Little Yoho
1974	Battle Range	1967	Eremite
		1968	Glacier

Ski Camps, 1945–1974

		1969	Little Yoho
1945	Little Yoho	1970	Sphinx Glacier/Diamond Head
	(most previous camps held here)	1971	Little Yoho
1946	Little Yoho	1972	Glacier
1947	Columbia Icefields	1973	Eremite
1948	Glacier	1974	Little Yoho
1949	Eremite		Eremite
1950	Mount Robson		Adamants
1951	Little Yoho		
1952	Assiniboine		
1953	Mount Robson		

Sources: WMCR, ACC, List, 1976,
150-51; "General Mountaineering
Camp Locations," http://www.
alpineclubofcanada.ca/activities/
gmclocx.html; and CAJ.

1954	Skoki
1955	Glacier
1956	Columbia Icefields

Notes

Preface

1. Kootenay (established in 1920) comprises an area 1,406 km²; Waterton Lakes (established in 1895) 505 km²; Glacier (established in 1886) 1,349 km²; Mount Revelstoke (established in 1914) 260 km². See Finkelstein, *National Parks*, 19–21.

2. Isaac, "Relevance," 5.

3. Kidd, *Struggle*, 9–10.

4. For a sample, see: Bouchier, *Love of the Game*; Hall, *Girl and the Game*; Hargreaves, *Physical Culture*; Heine and Wamsley, "'Kickfest'"1996; Howell, *Sandlots*; Jasen, *Wild Things*; Kidd, *Struggle*; Loo, *Nature*; Metcalfe, *Canada Learns*; Morrow and Wamsley, *Sport*; Park, Mangan, and Vertinsky, *Gender*; Vertinsky, *Eternally*; Vertinsky and Bale, *Sites*; and Wall, *Nature of Nurture*.

5. McCarthy, "Place," 179.

6. Ibid.

7. Ibid., 190.

8. For discussion of the historical gaze turned toward borderlands, see Howell, "Borderlands," 251–70; and McManus, "Mapping," 71–87.

① **Imagining Canada's Mountain Parks**

1. Kidd, *Struggle*, 11.

2. Howell, *Blood*, 144–45.

3. Brown, "Doctrine," 46–62.

4. For examples of books in the expanding historiography of national parks in Canada, see Bella, *Profit*; Brower, *Lost Tracks*; Campbell, *Shaped*; Kopas, *Air*; MacEachern, *Natural*; MacLaren, *Culturing*; Sandlos, *Hunters*; and Waiser, *Prisoners*.

5. Julie Cruikshank's anthropology of glaciers in the St. Elias Range (*Glaciers*) and Reuben Ellis's analysis of neo-imperialism and mountaineering literature (*Vertical*) are two diverse examples of this.

6. Hart, *Selling*.

7. Jessup, "Tourist"; Hart, *Selling*; Leighton and Leighton, *Artists*, 28–32, 42, 65; and Zezulka-Mailloux, "Tracks," 302–39.

8. For how Romanticism transformed seeing nature and landscapes in touristic imagination, see Urry, *Tourist Gaze*, 20, 44; and Jasen, *Wild Things*, 8–9.

9. Kauffman and Putnam, *Guiding*.

10. Cited in Cavell, *Legacy*, 7.

11. Ibid. In 1914 Mary Vaux married Dr. Charles Doolittle Walcott (1850–1927), secretary of the Smithsonian Institute in Washington, DC, and the geologist and invertebrate paleontologist noted for his discovery of the Burgess Shale on Mount Wapta, British Columbia, see Cavell, *Legacy*, 13.

12. Berger, *Science;* Zeller, *Inventing;* Altmeyer, "Three Ideas," 21–36.

13. Campbell, *Shaped,* 199.

14. Ryden, *Mapping,* 76.

15. Donnelly, "Playing," 132.

16. Ramshaw, "Construction," 60.

17. McCarthy, "Place."

18. Ibid.

19. Various literature studies emphasize the symbolic currency and politics of mountains and mountaineering. Ellis, *Vertical,* 11. See also Slemon, "Climbing," 15–41.

20. Turner, "From Woodcraft," 462–84.

21. Louv, *Last Child.*

② Canada's Alpine Club

1. Parker, "Report (1908)," 323.

2. Fraser, *Wheeler,* 50–51.

3. Wheeler, "Origin and Founding," 85–87.

4. Wheeler, "Origin and Founding," 84; Green, *Among.*

5. Cavell, *Legacy,* 6.

6. Unless otherwise noted, biographical information on Wheeler draws on: Fraser, *Wheeler; Canadian Alpine Journal* (CAJ), "Arthur Oliver Wheeler," (1940), 205–12; CAJ, "Arthur Oliver Wheeler," (1944–45), 140–46.

7. Parker, "Clara," 252–53.

8. CAJ, "Brigadier," 160–63. Oliver Wheeler's photo-topographic survey and map of Everest is discussed in the saga of the early British expeditions organized by the Mount Everest Committee, a joint effort of the Alpine Club (London) and the Royal Geographical Society, see Howard-Bury, *Everest,* 319–37—for Major H.T. Morshead's comments, see p. 328; Bruce, *Assault;* Norton, *Fight.* For broader context, see Slemon, "Climbing," 15–35; Stewart, "Reaction," 21–39.

9. Parker, "Selkirk," 23.

10. Subsequently named the Canadian Institute of Surveying.

11. Wheeler, "Origin and Founding," 87.

12. Ibid., 88.

13. Parker, "A Joy," 20.

14. Parker, "Selkirk," 23.

15. Wheeler, "Origin and Founding," 88.

16. Ibid.

17. *Winnipeg Free Press,* "Mrs. Elizabeth," 11.

18. Henry J. Parker of Winnipeg was not visibly involved in mountaineering and remains a somewhat obscure figure who died in 1920. His occupation can be determined by cross-referencing the Parker family addresses with his name as listed in the *Winnipeg Directory,* 1892–1915. Some historians have erroneously identified Elizabeth Parker's husband as Herschel C. Parker, PHD, an American scientist at Columbia University and prominent mountaineer who was the first ACC life member; see LaForce, "Alpine," 5; and Selters, *Ways,* 61.

19. As her husband was incapacitated mentally, she made a living for herself by writing," stated Margaret Fleming about her older neighbour, Elizabeth Parker. Whyte

Museum of the Canadian Rockies (WMCR), Cyndi Smith Fonds, Cyndi Smith with Margaret Fleming.

20. *Winnipeg Free Press*, "Mrs. Elizabeth," 11.

21. Ibid.

22. Ibid.

23. Parker, "Memories," 56–57.

24. See WMCR, Cyndi Smith Fonds, Cyndi Smith with Margaret Fleming. According to Fleming, Jean Parker developed tuberculosis in her later teen years and Henry Parker suffered poor mental health.

25. Parker, "Backward," 21; Parker, "Holiday," 21; Parker, "A Joy," 20.

26. *Winnipeg Free Press*, "Mrs. Elizabeth," 11.

27. Parker, "A Joy," 21; for broader context to nature and reform, see Cook, *Regenerators;* and Berger, *Science*.

28. Parker, "Reviews: Rockies," 143; Parker, "Alpine Club," 8; Parker, "Matthew Arnold," 178–82.

29. Parker, "Report," 8.

30. Wheeler, "Memoriam," 125.

31. Parker, "Report," 7.

32. Draws on account in Parker, "Approach," 96–97.

33. Wheeler, "Origin and Founding," 89.

34. Ibid., 90.

35. Ibid., 91.

36. Ibid., 91–93. Clergyman and novelist Charles William Gordon served as a Presbyterian missionary in the Banff-Canmore area from 1890 to 1893, and is commemorated by the Canmore Ralph Connor Memorial Church, formerly Canmore Presbyterian Church.

37. Parker, "Report," 166.

38. Kelly, "Thrilling," 27.

39. Parker, "Report," 164.

40. Wheeler and Parker conflict on the total number of delegates who attended the 1906 Winnipeg conference. Parker reported 28 delegates. Although this figure may be correct, she does not list the delegates. For analysis, Wheeler's figure will be taken as the standard since he lists the delegates by name, notwithstanding that his list may have been subject to error. See Wheeler, "Origin and Founding," 91–93; Parker, "Report," 164.

41. Cited in Engel, *Mountaineering*, 120; for British alpinism, see Clark, *Men;* Keenleyside, *Peaks*.

42. *CAJ*, "Constitution," 178.

43. Ibid.

44. The ACC mission also reiterated common terms referring to national parks, such as "playground," "heritage," and "national asset." See Johnston and Marsh, "Club," 17.

45. *CAJ*, "Constitution," 178–81; WMCR, ACC, *List*, 1976.

46. WMCR, ACC, *Constitution and List,* 1958.

47. Wheeler, "Origin and Founding," 92.

48. *CAJ*, "Constitution," 178–81.

49. Ibid.

50. Ibid.

51. Ibid.

52. *CAJ*, "List," 182–83.

53. For influences in national culture formation in Anglo Canada, see Tippett, *Making*.

54. *CAJ*, "Constitution," 178–81.

55. *CAJ*, "List," 182–83.

56. Parker, "Report," 164; *CAJ*, "Report (1908)," 320; *CAJ*, "Report 1911 Camp," 146; *The Gazette*, "Schedules," 1934, 13–15, 18; ACC membership statistics based on Red Book membership lists published semi-annually by the club; see Appendix 1, Table 2.

57. Paid senior men accounted for 18,408 amateur athletes in the Amateur Atheletic Union of Canada (AAUC) in 1936. Kidd, *Struggle*, 90, 159.

58. The dominance of the male urban middle class of British ancestry in organized sport clubs and national amateur sport organizations in Canada through the turn of the twentieth century is well documented: Bouchier, *Love of the Game;* Howell, *Blood;* Kidd, *Struggle;* Metcalfe, *Canada Learns;* Morrow and Wamsley, *Sport*.

59. As LaForce noted from the 1907 and 1914–16 ACC membership lists, 50 per cent lived in Vancouver, Edmonton, Calgary, Regina, Winnipeg, Hamilton, Toronto, Ottawa, and Montreal, see LaForce, "Alpine," 6.

60. WMCR, Membership Applications.

61. On occupational status and social profile in The Alpine Club, see Hansen, "Albert," 310–11; LaForce, "Alpine," 2. For social characteristics of British mountaineers, also see Robbins, "Sport," 579–601.

62. LaForce, "Alpine," 6.

63. Ibid., 5–6, footnote 15.

64. See *CAJ*, "Report 1911 Camp," 144; Wheeler, "Origin and Founding," 94–95; for the original international honorary ACC members, see *CAJ*, "Report (1907)," 164; for affiliation with the London Alpine Club, see Wheeler, "Origin and Founding," 94–95; Wheeler, "Golden," 15.

65. LaForce, "Alpine," footnote 26, n.p. LaForce's early study emphasizes a decline of the western Canadian membership from 1906 to 1917: "In 1906, 75% of ACC members lived in Western Canada and 10% in Ontario and Quebec. By 1917, the West accounted for only 54%, and the two central provinces, for 16%. Americans now numbered 17% of the club, and Britons, 11%."

66. See Appendix 1, Tables 3 and 4.

67. The idea that women are connected more closely to the natural world than men has also been contended by more recent ecofeminist scholarship, and subsequently critiqued for excessive essentialism by feminist writers such as Janet Biehl. See Hessing et al., "*Elusive*," ix, xiii-xiv.

68. For how sport, games, and the outdoors figured in the construction of conventional masculinities in Canada, see: Kidd, *Struggle*, 26; Howell, *Sandlots*, 19, 28, 97–111; Bouchier, *Love of the Game*, 118–23; Mott, "Solution," 57–70; Barman, *Growing*, 71–77; Loo, "Moose," 296–319.

69. MacDonald, *Sons*, 117–57.

70. Cameron, "Tom," 185–208.

71. Parker, "Approach to Organization," 97.

72. Mummery, *Climbs*, 53, cited in Strasdin, "Easy," 72.

73. Clark, Men, 56, 76–77; Birkett and Peascod, *Women;* Kjeldsen, *Mountaineers*, 14–16.

74. Female physicality, medical history, and sport related to women and girls are discussed with reference to: Vertinsky, *Eternally*, 204–33; Mitchinson, *Nature*; Lenskyj, *Out*, 17, 39, 62; Hall, *Girl and the Game*, 27–33; Kidd, *Struggle*, 26–27; Prentice et al., *Canadian Women*, 145–47.

75. Jasen, *Wild Things*, 107–08, 114.

76. Hall, *Girl and the Game*, 31–37, 79.

77. Schäffer, "Breaking," 111–12, cited in Skidmore, *Wild*, 375–77.

78. Russell, *Blessings*, 210, 90–110, 215–19; Blunt, *Travel*.

79. Routledge, "Being," 31–58, see 58.

80. Parker, "Memories," 58.

81. Parker, "Reviews," 204.

82. *CAJ*, "Yoho," 170.

83. Wheeler and Parker, *Selkirk*, 178.

84. Strasdin, "Easy," 81, 74, and 78.

85. Crawford, "Mountain," 86.

86. Ibid., 85–91.

87. Ibid., 91.

88. Reichwein and Fox, "Margaret," 43.

89. See Appendix 1, Table 1; ACC Membership Database 1994.

90. See *CAJ* for section executives through the 1930s.

91. See *CAJ*, passim, for lists of executive members. For leaders in Edmonton, see Edmonton Section reports in issues of *The Gazette*, no. 45 (November 1949): 33–34; *The Gazette*, no. 46 (November 1950): 36–37; *The Gazette*, no. 47 (November 1951): 40–42; *The Gazette*, no. 48 (November 1952): 47–49; through *The Gazette*, no. 49 (November 1953): 34–37. Eric Hopkins took the chair in 1953 and made reference to female chairmen leading the section through the last five years: Harriett Inkster, Mrs. Doris Campbell, Sylvia Evans who served in the Royal Canadian Air Force, and Gladys Hartley.

92. Reichwein and Fox, "Margaret," 36–60.

93. See Appendix 1, Table 1.

94. Vaux to Walcott, 19 February 1912, cited in Skidmore, *Wild*, 208.

95. Parker, "Report," 166.

96. Cited in Leslie, *Western*, 52.

97. Cited in Smith, *Beaten*, 163.

98. Ibid., 194–95.

99. Routledge, "Being," 58.

100. *CAJ*, "Constitution," 178–81.

101. MacEachern, *Natural*, 166–69. Pretexts were devised by some hoteliers to turn away Jews and blacks, such as a lack of accommodation or avoiding embarrassment among guests who might object to their presence. MacEachern relates these cases were brought to the attention of the Ottawa Parks Branch staff and local superintendents but concludes the department did not respond decisively.

102. WMCR, Mitchell to Moffat, 3 September 1928; the men in favour of Mendelson's application were most likely L.S. Crosby and Byron Harmon of Banff.

103. WMCR, Moffat to Mitchell, 4 September 1928.

104. WMCR, Mitchell to Moffat, 26 September 1928.

51. Ibid.

52. *CAJ*, "List," 182–83.

53. For influences in national culture formation in Anglo Canada, see Tippett, *Making*.

54. *CAJ*, "Constitution," 178–81.

55. *CAJ*, "List," 182–83.

56. Parker, "Report," 164; *CAJ*, "Report (1908)," 320; *CAJ*, "Report 1911 Camp," 146; *The Gazette*, "Schedules," 1934, 13–15, 18; ACC membership statistics based on Red Book membership lists published semi-annually by the club; see Appendix 1, Table 2.

57. Paid senior men accounted for 18,408 amateur athletes in the Amateur Athletic Union of Canada (AAUC) in 1936. Kidd, *Struggle*, 90, 159.

58. The dominance of the male urban middle class of British ancestry in organized sport clubs and national amateur sport organizations in Canada through the turn of the twentieth century is well documented: Bouchier, *Love of the Game;* Howell, *Blood;* Kidd, *Struggle;* Metcalfe, *Canada Learns;* Morrow and Wamsley, *Sport.*

59. As LaForce noted from the 1907 and 1914–16 ACC membership lists, 50 per cent lived in Vancouver, Edmonton, Calgary, Regina, Winnipeg, Hamilton, Toronto, Ottawa, and Montreal, see LaForce, "Alpine," 6.

60. WMCR, Membership Applications.

61. On occupational status and social profile in The Alpine Club, see Hansen, "Albert," 310–11; LaForce, "Alpine," 2. For social characteristics of British mountaineers, also see Robbins, "Sport," 579–601.

62. LaForce, "Alpine," 6.

63. Ibid., 5–6, footnote 15.

64. See *CAJ*, "Report 1911 Camp," 144; Wheeler, "Origin and Founding," 94–95; for the original international honorary ACC members, see *CAJ*, "Report (1907)," 164; for affiliation with the London Alpine Club, see Wheeler, "Origin and Founding," 94–95; Wheeler, "Golden," 15.

65. LaForce, "Alpine," footnote 26, n.p. LaForce's early study emphasizes a decline of the western Canadian membership from 1906 to 1917: "In 1906, 75% of ACC members lived in Western Canada and 10% in Ontario and Quebec. By 1917, the West accounted for only 54%, and the two central provinces, for 16%. Americans now numbered 17% of the club, and Britons, 11%."

66. See Appendix 1, Tables 3 and 4.

67. The idea that women are connected more closely to the natural world than men has also been contended by more recent ecofeminist scholarship, and subsequently critiqued for excessive essentialism by feminist writers such as Janet Biehl. See Hessing et al., *"Elusive,"* ix, xiii-xiv.

68. For how sport, games, and the outdoors figured in the construction of conventional masculinities in Canada, see: Kidd, *Struggle*, 26; Howell, *Sandlots*, 19, 28, 97–111; Bouchier, *Love of the Game*, 118–23; Mott, "Solution," 57–70; Barman, *Growing*, 71–77; Loo, "Moose," 296–319.

69. MacDonald, *Sons*, 117–57.

70. Cameron, "Tom," 185–208.

71. Parker, "Approach to Organization," 97.

72. Mummery, *Climbs*, 53, cited in Strasdin, "Easy," 72.

73. Clark, Men, 56, 76–77; Birkett and Peascod, *Women;* Kjeldsen, *Mountaineers*, 14–16.

127. Ibid.; Foster, "Story," 51; for a report on the work of the field naturalist, see Laing, "Wild," 99–114.

128. Carpé, "Observations," 82.

129. For press clippings on the Mount Logan ascent collected in the Ottawa Parks administration files, see LAC, RG 84: "Will Mount Logan"; "The Assault"; "Mount Logan"; "Mt. Logan Conquered"; "Off to Attack." Also note news of the ACC annual summer camp held in Jasper's Tonquin Valley was collected in this file: "Hardy Mountaineers."

130. Discussion of the expedition is based on Foster, "Story," 7–58; MacCarthy, "Climb," 59–80 (MacCarthy cited from 80); also see Robinson and Reichwein, "Canada's Everest," 100–13. Regarding Lambart's injuries, see Carpé, "Adventure," 85–86.

131. Scott, *Pushing*, 96.

132. LAC, RG 84, "Highest of Canadian Rockies." The article erroneously situated Mount Logan in the Canadian Rockies.

133. *Toronto Daily Star*, "Mt. Logan Has Been Climbed for First time: Party of Six Canadians Reported Back From Successful Climb, Americans Drop Out, Bitter Cold and Blinding Blizzard Was Fought by the Hardy Alpinists," 1; *Calgary Daily Herald*, "Amateur Climbers Battle Storms and Extreme Cold to Scale Mount Logan: Canadian Leads Climbers to Logan Peak," 1. By contrast, American press coverage (*New York Times*) emphasized "Mount Logan Scaled by Six Climbers; American in the Lead," 1; for British coverage, see the *Times*, "Mt. Logan Climbed, Canadian Party's Exploit," 14.

134. Exploits of mountaineers were often elided as achievements for humanity based on modernistic assumptions of progress. Doug Brown points out that in the ACC, "They believed the accomplishments of a few elites could serve as legible symbols for all of humankind. In the case of mountaineering, reaching a new summit was heralded as an achievement for the human race." See Brown, "Fleshing-out," 362.

135. The CAJ (1925) issue devoted 126 of its 146 pages to articles reporting on the Mount Logan expedition, see 1–126; for the main expedition narratives, see Foster, "Story," 47–58, and MacCarthy, "Climb," 59–80.

136. Foster, "Story," 58.

137. LaForce, "Alpine," 26–27; LaForce cites Jones, *Climbing*, 86, regarding the psychological challenges that faced the 1925 Mount Logan expedition.

138. Jones, *Climbing*, 91.

139. Ibid., 86.

140. For a critique of the determinism implicit in seeing sport as an evolution on "the long march of modernization," see Gruneau, "Modernization," 9–32. Gruneau posits that sport be understood "as shifting social and cultural practices which help to constitute particular ways of life" and argues that sport "contributes to the ongoing production of social life itself" (19, 26).

141. Regarding innovations stemming from the 1925 expedition, see Selters, *Ways*, 73.

142. Selters placed the 1925 ascent of Mount Logan within the rise of major mountain clubs across North America and their role in first ascents on major summits. After 1925, he contended, most clubs receded from the leading edge of sport development, see Selter, *Ways*, 74–75. Moreover, in his discussion of the state of climbing since the late 1980s, Selter aligned the latest developments in mountaineering in North America as "a post-technical resurgence" whereby climbers "have reembraced mountaineering as climbing's most demanding and complex discipline, where any level of technical difficulty might be found but the technical challenge is compounded

by scale, environment, uncertainty and risk." He concluded that the "'grandfather' of the climbing game" has made a stronger comeback than ever (281). The "post-technical" interpretation of the sport moves toward recuperating classic mountaineering ascents, such as Mount Logan in 1925, in contrast to the interpretation put forward in the mid-1970s, seemingly predisposed toward technical climbing, as suggested by Jones.

143. WMCR, "Canadian Alpinists," 1–2; also see Robinson and Reichwein, "Canada's Everest" 115–16.

144. Scott contends the "glory days" of Canadian mountaineering, from 1886 to 1925, concluded as the "era of great first ascents in the Rocky Mountains and the Selkirks came to an end" with the climb of Mount Alberta. See Scott, *Pushing*, 105.

145. Mumm cited in Fraser, *Wheeler*, 146.

146. *CAJ*, "Arthur Oliver Wheeler," (1944-45), 146.

③ **Mountaineering Camp in the Tented Town**

1. Wheeler, "Golden," 19. Oliver Wheeler noted in his retrospective on the club's first fifty years that newly graduating members of the club were "welcomed in" in earlier days by this "nearly forgotten cry." The location of the club's first camp, Yoho National Park, was clearly imbedded in the words of the club's shout out, and also repeated the Cree word *Yoho*, meaning awe and wonder.

2. Yeigh, "Camp," 47, 51.

3. *CAJ*, "Mrs. A.L. Yeigh," 135; *CAJ*, "David Henry," 129; Hunter, "The Descendants." Annie and David Laird were children of Rev. Robert Laird, a clergyman, and his wife Barbara (Campbell); the Hon. David Laird, Sr., was their uncle and a father-in-law to David Laird, Jr., following his marriage to his cousin Fannie Louise Laird. The *CAJ* (1961) refers erroneously to David Laird, Sr., as Annie Laird's father. The Hon. David Laird, Sr., was a Liberal elected to Parliament in 1873 who held various appointments in the Canadian North West, as Minister of the Interior (1873–76), Lieutenant Governor of the Northwest Territories (1876–81), and Indian Commissioner (1898–1909). See Cameron, "Dominion," 45.

4. See the report of the chief mountaineer, M.P. Bridgland, "Report, Yoho," 171–73. Bridgland was noted to guide "with patience and good temper, and always with the utmost consideration for his party"; see Sissons and Wheeler, "Morrison P. Bridgland," 218–22. *CAJ*, "Graduating Members," 196. Also see MacLaren, Higgs, and Zezulka-Mailloux, *Mapper*, 71–76.

5. Parker, "Frank," 115–16; *CAJ*, "Mrs. A.L. Yeigh," 135; *Toronto Daily Star*, "Writer and Churchman," 5; Frank Yeigh, *Heart*; Strong-Boag and Gerson, *Paddling*, 102–103; Cameron, "Dominion," 38, 42, 45. Frank and Annie Yeigh maintained an interest in the ACC Toronto Section and received the *CAJ*. Annie Yeigh was a lifetime ACC member. Frank Yeigh donated books to the club library and published *Through the Heart of Canada* (1910) with stories about ACC camp. The Yeighs became active in social welfare movements, particularly as leading figures in child saving and international relief through the Canadian Save the Children Fund.

6. The term "invented tradition," as used in this text, follows Hobsbawm who means "responses to novel situations which take the form of reference to old situations, or which establish their own past by quasi-obligatory repetition." "Inventing traditions…is essentially a process of formalization and ritualization, characterized by

reference to the past, if only by imposing repetition," and relates to the development of collective social identities and/or nationalisms that he illustrates by discussing the adoption of certain sports, apparel, festivals, and spectacles as practiced by specific classes. See Hobsbawm, "Introduction," 1–4, 9; Hobsbawm, "Mass-Producing," 263–307; Williams, *Marxism*, 115–20. Also see Donnelly, "Invention," 235–43.

7. Geddes, "Call," 1. The editor of the songbook, Cyril Wates, had volunteered as the choirmaster of St. Paul's Church in Edmonton for several years and participated in music festivals. See *CAJ*, "Cyril," 277–81. Editor of the *Farm and Ranch Review*, Geddes perished in a climbing accident on Mount Lefroy in 1927. A cabin at the Banff Alpine Clubhouse was his memorial.

8. Wheeler, "The Alpine Club of Canada," 7–12.

9. Individuals attended ACC camps during the following periods: Coleman (c. 1913–1930s), Brooks (1929–62), Paget (1857–1927), Brigden (1934). Coleman, a painter as well as a geologist, attended "whenever possible," see *CAJ*, "Arthur Philemon," 131–32; Brooks attended eighteen camps in total, see *CAJ*, "Emmie," 1990, 99; for Brigden, see WMCR, McCoubrey to Tweedy, 27 June 1934.

10. Thomas Cook capitalized on the idea of taking large groups from the British middle classes on tour from Britain to the European continent during the mid-nineteenth century. The Swiss Alps and Chamonix glaciers were highlighted destinations. Cook & Son originated the tour business of today and filled an opening market for popular tourism. The early-eighteenth-century "Grand Tour" was by contrast aristocratic. Brendon, *Thomas*, 81; Schama, *Landscape*, 494, 502; Towner, "Grand," 5, 211–15.

11. Wheeler, "The Alpine Club of Canada," 7–12.

12. LAC, RG 84, A. Wheeler to Harkin, 19 October 1921.

13. Johnston, "Diffusion," 41–43.

14. Biographical information from: WMCR, M113, "James Bernard Harkin." Also see Taylor, *Negotiating*, 25–31.

15. Harkin, *History*, 7.

16. The ACC mandate referred to: "The encouragement of the mountain craft and the opening of new regions as a national playground." See *CAJ*, "Constitution," 178.

17. For list of secretary-treasurers and club managers, see WMCR, ACC, *List*, 1976, 149.

18. Unless otherwise noted, biographical information derived from *CAJ*, "Stanley," 101–06.

19. WMCR, Mitchell to Moffat, 16 September 1929. Parker, "Henry Bucknall," 87–89.

20. WMCR, Mitchell to Bell, 16 September 1926; WMCR, Mitchell to Bell, 3 November 1926.

21. WMCR, Mitchell to Bell, 26 October 1927.

22. WMCR, Mitchell to Bell, 12 January 1927.

23. WMCR, ACC, *List*, 1976, 148.

24. *CAJ*, "Stanley," 101–06.

25. WMCR, Mitchell to Bell, 30 December 1926.

26. *CAJ*, "Stanley," 101–06.

27. Ibid.

28. WMCR, Tweedy to Wates, 13 March 1940; WMCR, Tweedy to Wates, 21 March 1940.

29. *CAJ*, "Stanley," 101–06.

30. Regarding Miss Arneson, see WMCR, Sibbald to Tweedy, 11 June 1935; WMCR, Tweedy to Sibbald, 17 April 1936; WMCR, Tweedy to Sibbald, 21 May 1937. WMCR, Tweedy to Sibbald, 12 May 1935.

31. WMCR, Tweedy to Sampson, 18 April 1931.

32. WMCR, Tweedy to Sampson, 20 June 1932.

33. WMCR, Tweedy to Sampson, 2 January 1931.

34. These events are recalled by Wheeler in "Origin and Founding," 92–94.

35. Hart, *Diamond*, 75–81. Hart researched the history of regional guides and outfitters and discussed the ACC camps from this perspective, contending the ACC remained "an important factor in the financial security of the area's outfitters."

36. Loonsberry, "Wild," 139–52; Campbell, "Branding," 56–78; Bold, *Selling*, 1–69. MacDonald, *Sons*, 117–44.

37. Yeigh, "Camp," 56b.

38. Unless otherwise noted, biographical information derived from *CAJ*, "Wharton," 208–10.

39. WMCR, Tweedy to Sibbald, 26 May 1931; WMCR, Contract between Tweedy and ACC, 1 November 1932.

40. *CAJ*, "Wharton," 208–10.

41. WMCR, Tweedy to Wates, 7 March 1940.

42. WMCR, Tweedy to McCoubrey, 20 July 1933; WMCR, Tweedy to McCoubrey, 25 July 1933. Rink was the official ACC outfitter during the 1920s under Wheeler's Banff to Mount Assiniboine Walking and Riding Tours, see Hart, *Diamond*, 140–42.

43. WMCR, Wates to Tweedy, 25 September 1939.

44. Graves, "Little," 232.

45. WMCR, McCoubrey to Tweedy, 17 April 1933.

46. *CAJ*, "Wharton," 210.

47. Hart, *Diamond*, passim, 3. Hart described the region's guides and outfitters as "a group of rather unique individuals": "Instead of being drawn exclusively from backwoods environments...I found that many were from fine English, American and Canadian backgrounds; some were well-educated and most seemed to be of higher than average intelligence."

48. Murphy, "Homesteading."

49. For literature on the Swiss guides, see Kauffman and Putnam, *Guiding*; Kain, *Clouds*; West, "Swiss," 50–53; Griffiths and Wingenbach, *Mountain*; Longstaff, "Story," 189–97; *CAJ*, "Christian," 231–34.

50. Edward Feuz, Jr., cited in Kauffman and Putnam, *Guiding*, 113.

51. The Brewster family of Banff began its transport business in horse outfitting and later moved to automobile transportation and tours in the Rocky Mountain national parks. Brewster Transportation, currently operating regional bus tours in the mountain park corridor, is owned by Viad Corp.

52. Wheeler, "Report," 195.

53. WMCR, A.O. Wheeler to Parker, 6 May 1906.

54. WMCR, A.O. Wheeler to William Whyte, 31 March 1910.

55. WMCR, Mitchell to Moffat, 21 June 1929. Here Mitchell included relevant items of Wheeler's correspondence dated 1906–10 regarding the Brewsters.

56. Ibid.

57. Kauffman and Putnam, *Guiding*, 114.

58. WMCR, Osborne Scott to A.A. McCoubrey, 13 March 1934.

59. Kauffman and Putnam, *Guiding*, 114–15.

60. See *The Gazette*, "Annual Meeting, 1937," 7.

61. MacCarthy, "First," 18–26; Longstaff, "Story," 189–97; *New York Times* (Jones Library Special Collections), "Mrs. Stone."

62. *CAJ*, "Club Proceedings," (1944), 119. There were nineteen male and six women climbing leaders at the 1945 camp; four of the women had spouses among the male leaders: "Mesdames Brett, Finley, Hamilton, Kramer, Munday and Richards, and Messrs. Arbuckle, Blanc, Brett, Brink, Brooks, Cuthbertson, Gibson, Oilman, Hall, Hind, Innes, Kingman, Kramer, Marston, Munday, Parkes, Reid, Richards and Winram."

63. WMCR, McCoubrey to Tweedy, 30 January 1934. Mrs. MacArthur and Mrs. Phyl Munday led badge climbs. WMCR, Gibson et al. to Executive Board, n.d. 1940; WMCR, Wates to Tweedy, 14 November 1940. Miss Polly Prescott of Cleveland, Ohio, was rope leader on camp climbs from Mounts Athabasca, Hanbury, Vaux, Little Messines, Forbes, and Lyall; and the leader of "manless" ascents on Edith Cavell, Louis, Ptarmigan, and President, including new routes on Edith Cavell and "Waterfowl"—an unnamed peak west of Poboktan Creek. In 1940 she was awarded the ACC insignia of the Silver Rope. Regarding the phenomena of a woman leading climbs, see Underhill, "Manless," 3–12.

64. *CAJ*, "Club Proceedings," (1948), 242.

65. WMCR, Stanley Mitchell to H.E. Sampson, 26 February 1932.

66. See Yeigh, "Camp," 51.

67. *CAJ*, "Report 1910," 189.

68. Kauffman and Putnam, *Guiding*, 113.

69. WMCR, Stanley Mitchell to Fred Bell, 9 August 1927; WMCR, Mitchell to T.B. Moffat, 20 May 1929.

70. Tetarenko and Tetarenko, *Ken*, 92–93, 98.

71. LAC/NFTSA, 20th Century-Fox Film Corporation Collection, *Alpine Climbers*. The film most likely portrays July 1946 camp, judging by similar stills of a female cook taken by Jack Long. See LAC/NFTSA Alpine Club, Purcell Range.

72. For the Ontario youth camping experience, see Hodgins and Dodge, *Using*; and Wall, *Nature of Nurture*.

73. *CAJ*, "Clara," 252–53. Fraser, *Wheeler*, 64.

74. *CAJ*, "Edna," 130–31.

75. WMCR, Tweedy to Sibbald, 2 July 1936.

76. WMCR, Tweedy to Sibbald, 21 May 1937.

77. WMCR, Tweedy to Wates, 6 January 1939.

78. WMCR, Wates to Tweedy, 10 January 1939.

79. WMCR, Mitchell to Bell, 12 April 1928.

80. WMCR, McCoubrey to Tweedy, 20 July 1933.

81. WMCR, Tweedy to McCoubrey, 23 March 1934.

82. WMCR, Tweedy to McCoubrey, 10 April 1934.

83. WMCR, ACC Camp Costs Summary 1930-32; WMCR, Tweedy to McCoubrey, 30 August 1933.

84. Hind is also noted on the executive lists: WMCR, ACC, *List*, 1976, 148–49.

85. Cited in Andrews, "Passport," 25.

86. The ACC does not admit participants under the age of eighteen to annual General Mountaineering Camp currently due to safety and liability concerns.

87. Wates, *Songs*, 1.

88. Here I consider identity production in terms of the material artifacts historically found *in situ* at ACC camps and the production of the camp itself as a material artifact. Artifacts operate within particular social contexts. See Miller, *Material*, 109–30. Camps housed mountaineers, and, as temporary housing, they call attention "to examine the logic of the stuff itself, the form and underlying order of the built environment," see Miller, *Stuff*, 85. Taken out of situ, material artifacts associated with various sporting subcultures are also the stock and trade of collections exhibited and interpreted as symbols in many museum exhibits and sport halls of fame, see for example, Vamplew, "Gamble," 177–88; Gietschier, "International," 246–48.

89. Miller, *Material*, 122; also see Geismar and Horst, "Materializing," 6; Garner, "Living," 89.

90. Tetarenko and Tetarenko, *Ken*, 93–94.

91. Hart, *Diamond*, 80.

92. Yeigh, "Camp," 51.

93. For examples of camp stills see WMCR, Frank Freeborn Albums. For Byron Harmon image of sleeping campers, see Silversides, *Waiting*, 103. For other camp stills, see LAC/NFTSA, Alpine Club, Purcell Range, Item nos. 24587–690. For camp scenes circa 1940s, see LAC/NFTSA, 20th Century-Fox Film Corporation Collection, *Alpine Climbers*. For climbers going up tent pole, see WMCR, Lillian Gest Collection, *ACC Camp*. For 1946 campfire photos see Alpine Club, Purcell Range, Item no. 24587. For 1950 camp scenes, see LAC/NFTSA, National Film Board of Canada Collection, *Canada Carries On*.

94. WMCR, Sampson to Tweedy, 4 March 1931. Ten "English Alpine Club" ropes were ordered for the 1931 camp. Also see advertisement for ropes by Arthur Beale of London, England in the *CAJ* (1931): 211. WMCR, Tweedy to Sampson, 5 July 1932. Popular boot nails included the Tricouni and other "ordinary Hungarian" stock. WMCR, Sampson to Tweedy, 25 February 1931. Swiss paraphernalia included snow-glasses, badges, brooches, and rucksacks.

95. WMCR, Mitchell to Moffat, 11 February 1930.

96. WMCR, Tweedy to Sibbald, 18 March 1937.

97. WMCR, McCoubrey to Tweedy, 8 December 1933; WMCR, Tweedy to Wates, 8 March 1941.

98. WMCR, Tweedy to McCoubrey, 31 March 1934.

99. Fraser, *Wheeler*, 63.

100. See Ellis, *Vertical*; Slemon, "Climbing," 15–41.

101. Robinson and Reichwein, "Canada's Everest," 95–121.

102. LAC, RG 84, A. Wheeler to Harkin, 9 May 1916.

103. LAC, RG 84, Moffat to Stronach, 25 March 1922.

104. In the mid-nineteenth century, climbers in the Alps met the issue of exhausting their known ranges by seeking first ascents in other mountain ranges around the world, such as the Caucasus, Himalayas, Southern Alps, and the Rockies. The issue also drove mountaineering to innovate its form and goals as a sport, for example, adopting more difficult route variations to summits that had already been climbed, in keeping with the so-called "second generation" of climbers. See Donnelly, "Invention," 239.

105. LAC, RG 84, Wheeler to Smart, 20 October 1951. Sir Edward Oliver Wheeler served as ACC national president from 1950 to 1954. Fortress Lake, BC, is located in Hamber Provincial Park, 22 kilometres west of Sunwapta Falls in Jasper National Park.

106. LAC, RG 84, Wheeler to Hutchinson, 18 April 1953.

107. ACC camps were held in Paradise Valley in 1907, 1918, 1933, and 1944; WMCR, ACC, *List,* 1976, 150.

108. Crawshaw and Urry, "Tourism," 184; also see Jessup, *Antimodernism.* For reports mentioning that snowfall eight to ten inches deep on July 30 brought down two tents at camp, see *The Gazette,* "Larch Valley," 14.

109. A.O. Wheeler Diaries, 28 July 1923; I thank Jennifer Wheeler Crompton for access to papers in the Wheeler family collections. Osborne Scott was an ACC member and Winnipeg CNR man and J.B. Hutchings was an official of the national parks department.

110. Altitudes stated in Kruszyna and Putnam, *Rocky,* 232, 239, 240.

111. McDowall, *Quick,* 106–10. The Royal Bank encouraged its bankers to engage in whole-some middle-class sporting life. "Manly, outdoor pursuits"—such as boating, curling, golf, and hockey—were key sports according to McDowall. Mountaineering pushed the limits of the Royal Bank's responsible corporate image in some respects because of its inherent risk-taking nature. However, courage, determination, and team work in the face of calculated risk-taking were qualities viewed as common to both finance and mountaineering, qualities desirable in a strong image for a corporate bank and its leaders who were "paragons of amateur sport."

112. Cuthbertson, "Alpine," 4. I am grateful to Duncan McDowall for this reference.

113. For example, Edmonton climbers were intent on peak bagging first ascents in the Tonquin-Eremite region and on the interprovincial border the year prior to camp. Wates and Gibson, "Eremite," 63. Wates and Gibson graded the difficulty of the Ramparts and indicated the easiest routes had been taken, leading to their invitation: "Now that the last of the Ramparts has been conquered it may not be out of place to call attention to the unique character of this range from the climber's standpoint" (81).

114. Donnelly, "Invention," 238–41; Robinson, "Golden," 1–19; Williams, "Boundless," 70–87; Jones, *Climbing,* 69–98; LaForce, "Alpine," 25–27; Louie, "Gender," 123–24. Chic Scott maintains that Canada drifted from the mainstream of developments in mountaineering internationally from the 1920s to the 1950s, and, "while the world of mountaineering rapidly evolved, Canada was left behind in a time warp"; see Scott, *Pushing,* 107, 165, 371. For explanation of carabiners and pitons, see Cleare, *Guide,* 204. For historical overview of artificial climbing devices, see Hiebler, "Evolution," 320–23; Schneider, *Technology.*

115. Reichwein and Fox, *Diaries,* xviii–xix.

116. Ibid., 32.

117. WMCR, Jack Hargreaves to McCoubrey, 5 March 1934.

118. "The D'rector and the Secret'ry" quoted in Wilson, "The Camp," 226.

119. An unnamed female camper cited by Parker, CAJ (1910): 207.

120. See Kauffman and Putnam, *Guiding,* 113.

121. Huel, "Edward," 36–37. For further discussion of Edward Whymper's activities in the Canadian Rockies, see Parker, "Edward," 126–35; Huel, "Edward," 6–17; Huel, "CPR," 21–32. Whymper, *Scrambles.* Personal communication, Lawrence White to Author, 7 July 2005, regarding Whymper's ice axe at the clubhouse in Canmore, Alberta.

122. For references to campfire highlights, see Andrews, "Passport," 23. MacCarthy was a Lieutenant Commander in the US Navy who had ranched near Wilmer, BC, in the Windermere Valley and devoted his later years to his love for dogs through the SPCA

in the state of Maryland. The Mount Logan summit expedition is described in great detail in MacCarthy, "Climb," 59–80. *CAJ*, "Albert," 64–65. *CAJ*, "Fred," 66–67. Brigden was "not a mountain climber, but had a great love for mountains and sketched mountain and other Canadian scenery from Newfoundland to British Columbia...His pictures are hung in the National Gallery at Ottawa, the Art Gallery of Toronto and elsewhere."

123. Wheeler, "Report of 1910," 190.

124. For background on Canadian imperialism and nationalism see Berger, *Sense*.

125. Wheeler, "Report of 1910," 190.

126. MacDonald, *Sons*, 117–44; Anderson, *Chief*.

127. See Wall, "Totem," 542, 534; also see Deloria, *Playing*.

128. A photograph of the event belongs to the B. Silversides Collection and is identified with the caption "'Regina Alpinists Put on a Minstrel around the Campfire,' Jasper National Park." Silversides, *Waiting*, 107. For discussion of black minstrelsy at camps in the United States, see Paris, "Children's."

129. Binnema and Niemi, "Drawn Now," 724–50; Murphy, "Homesteading," 123–53.

130. Yeigh, "Camp," 54–55.

131. Ibid., 55.

132. Scott, *Pushing*, 157; *CAJ*, "Peyto," 138–39.

133. Andrews, "Passport," 23.

134. Parker, "Frank," 115. Cameron, "Dominion," 38.

135. For discussion of muscular Christianity, see Howell, *Blood*, 32–35, 49–50.; Kidd, *Struggle*, 14, 149; McKillop, *Matters*, 243–49.

136. Geddes, "Call."

137. Whyte, "Greetings," 1–2.

138. WMCR, Mitchell to Bell, 5 September 1927; WMCR, Mitchell to Bell, 28 September 1927; WMCR, Bell to Mitchell, 4 October 1927; Greene, *Who's*, 1522.

139. WMCR, J.A. Buckham to F.C. Bell, 19 September 1927. Buckham had obtained an appropriation for trail work a few years earlier and offered assistance to the ACC camp.

140. WMCR, Mitchell to Bell, 25 January 1928.

141. WMCR, Mitchell to Bell, 2 April 1928.

142. WMCR, Bell to Mitchell, 18 August 1928; WMCR, Mitchell to Bell, 31 August 1928.

143. The folk festivals began with a showcase of French-Canadian culture held at the Chateau Frontenac in 1926 and expanded to series of events that included the multicultural Great West Canadian Folksong, Folkdance and Handicraft Festivals at Regina's Hotel Saskatchewan and Calgary's Palliser Hotel, a Sea Music Festival at the Hotel Vancouver, and three "Highland Gatherings" held at the Banff Springs Hotel starting in 1927. A printed version of Gibbon's 1938 radio series *Canadian Mosaic*, sponsored by the CPR, merited a Governor General's award. Material on Dr. John Murray Gibbon is derived from files of the Canadian Pacific Railway Archives (CPRA) in Montreal. See CPRA, file B-07.15, "Memorial to Dr. John," 9; "New Book," 2; "John Murray Gibbon Ends," 10; "J. Murray Gibbon," 37; "A Profile," 5; "C.P.R.'s Gibbon," 5. Also see Henderson, "Still Time," 139–74; Hart, *Selling*, 105–09; Kines, "Chief."

144. See for example: *Canadian Pacific Railway Bulletin*, nos. 149 (1921), 173 (1923), 222 (1927), 224 (1927), 233 (1928), 258 (1930), 261 (1930).

145. WMCR, Mitchell to Bell, 9 August 1927.

146. WMCR, Mitchell to Moffat, 22 August 1928. Donald Station was situated on the CPR line immediately west of Golden, BC.

147. Ibid.

148. WMCR, Tweedy to Wates, 15 November 1938.

149. WMCR, Tweedy to Wates, 22 January 1940.

150. *CAJ*, "Alexander," 120–26; Fee, "Manitobans," 19–20; Reichwein and Fox, *Diaries*, 41–48; also see Reichwein and Fox, "Margaret," 35–60.

151. WMCR, McCoubrey to Management Committee, 31 May 1933; WMCR, McCoubrey to Management Committee, 5 June 1933.

152. WMCR, Sibbald to Tweedy, 17 August 1934.

153. Smith, *Jasper*. The Canadian Northern route through Jasper and the Mount Robson country was completed in 1915; it was consolidated under the Canadian National Railways flag in 1919 and absorbed the Grand Trunk Pacific Railway in 1923.

154. Smith, *Jasper*, 13. Thornton was a frequent visitor to the CNR's Jasper Park Lodge where he enjoyed horseback riding.

155. WMCR, Bell to Mitchell, 6 September 1927.

156. *CAJ*, "Where to Meet," 275.

157. WMCR, Sampson to Tweedy, 12 January 1932.

158. WMCR, Osborne Scott to McCoubrey, 13 March 1934.

159. WMCR, McCoubrey to Tweedy, 9 April 1934.

160. Department stores in Canada and elsewhere were actively involved in cultivating consumer tastes and education through entertaining techniques of exhibition and interpretation. Eaton's stores, for example, hosted exhibits from the National Gallery of Canada in the 1940s. The Hudson's Bay Company drew on its historic links to the frontier and adventure in various promotions and exhibitions. For discussion of retail education and exhibits, see Wall, "Fort," 10–14, 18–20.

161. *CAJ*, "World," 179.

162. *CAJ*, "Report Yoho," 177. *CAJ*, "Statement," 197–98.

163. MacLaren, Higgs, and Zezulka-Mailloux, *Mapper*, 72.

164. LAC, RG 84, Douglas to Harkin, 21 February 1912.

165. LAC, RG 84, Harkin to Rocky Mountains Park Superintendent, 25 May 1916.

166. For example, J.B. Harkin and J.B. Hutchings of Dominion Parks attended in 1923. A.O. Wheeler Diaries, 28 July 1923.

167. LAC, RG 84, Stronach to Smart, 13 April 1949, see note to Deputy Minister, 16 April 1949.

168. See for example, Department of the Interior, *Annual Report*, 1912, 8, 39–40; 1921, 24; 1928–29, 131.

169. LAC, RG 84, Harkin to A. Wheeler, 6 April 1922.

170. LAC, RG 84, Rogers to Mitchell, 31 October 1923; LAC, RG 84, Rogers to Wates, 28 November 1932.

171. LAC, RG 84, Homer Robinson letters 1946–48; *CAJ*, "Peyto," 138–39.

172. LAC, RG 84, O. Wheeler to James Smart, 19 March 1951; LAC, RG 84, Smart to Wheeler, 28 March 1951; LAC, RG 84, Smart to Superintendents, 28 March 1951; LAC, RG 84, J.R.B. Coleman to Smart, 4 May 1951.

173. LAC, RG 84, Harkin to A.O. Wheeler, 22 September 1933.

174. Strom, *Pioneers*; Yeo, "Making," 87–98; also see Scott, *Powder*.

④ **Advocacy for Canada's Hetch Hetchy**

1. LAC, RG 84, "Unique Views," 31 March 1922. James Outram quoted in *Calgary Herald*.

2. Great Plains Research Consultants (GPRC), *Banff*, 170–71.

3. Wheeler, "National Parks," 5.

4. Banff National Park Records (BNP), "Rocky Mountains of Canada," 1921.

5. BNP, Superintendent R.S. Stronach to J.B. Harkin, 21 February 1922.

6. LAC, RG 84, A.O. Wheeler to Roche, 9 February 1914.

7. LAC, RG 84, A.O. Wheeler to Roche, 9 February 1914; LAC, RG 84, J.B. Harkin to A.O. Wheeler, 10 March 1914.

8. Harkin, *History*, 14.

9. Ibid., 16.

10. For discussion of various groups marginalized in Canadian national parks as internees, prisoners, and work camp labourers, see Waiser, *Prisoners*. More historical research is needed to understand the lives of the working poor and disenfranchised social classes residing in the Canadian national parks, as well as Aboriginal populations excluded from living in the mountain parks.

11. LAC, RG 84, A.O. Wheeler to Roche, 9 February 1914; LAC, RG 84, J.B. Harkin to A.O. Wheeler, 10 March 1914.

12. BNP, "A Public Walking or Riding Tour." For other publicity, see BNP, "Special Route," 13 June 1921.

13. See LAC, RG84, Wheeler to Harkin, 26 March 1921. For the route map of these tours and the form of promotional material used by Wheeler, see LAC, RG 84, *Banff to Mt. Assiniboine*, (n.d., c. 1920–22). Also see CAJ, "Banff to Mt. Assiniboine," 274d.

14. CAJ, "Banff to Mt. Assiniboine," 274d.

15. Gray, *Bennett*, 24–27, 138–39.

16. LAC, RG 84, R.D. McCaul to James Lougheed, 25 November 1921. See also Winnipeg chair C.E. Fortin's letter, in which he wrote, "the wonders and beauties of our mountains should be opened up to all, be they either rich or in moderate circumstances," LAC, RG 84, C.E. Fortin to James Lougheed, 6 December 1921.

17. LAC, RG 84, Arthur Wheeler to the Members, 1 January 1922.

18. LAC, RG 84, vol. 102, file U36-1, parts 2 and 3, passim; LAC, RG 84, A.O. Wheeler to R.A. Gibson, 8 March 1922.

19. LAC, RG 84, Resolution, 11 February 1922.

20. LAC, RG 84, Cora J. Best to Minister of Interior, 17 January 1922.

21. LAC, RG 84, F.W. Waterman to Arthur Wheeler, 14 January 1922; LAC, RG 84, B.F. Seaver to Arthur Wheeler, 16 January 1922.

22. LAC, RG 84, Albert H. MacCarthy to Minister of Interior, 17 February 1922.

23. LAC, RG 84, A.O. Wheeler to W.W. Cory, 4 February 1922.

24. LAC, RG 84, J.B. Harkin to W.W. Cory, 14 February 1922.

25. LAC, RG 84, Harkin to A.O. Wheeler, 16 February 1922.

26. LAC, RG 84, J.B. Harkin to Marcus Morton, 27 January 1922. Descended from a distinguished Massachusetts legal family, Marcus Morton, Jr., served on Boston's Superior Court (1909–39). For ACC membership, see WMCR, ACC, *Constitution and List*, 1922; see also "Hon. James."

27. LAC, RG 84, Harkin to Stronach, 3 February 1922.

28. BNP, R.S. Stronach to J.B. Harkin, 21 February 1922.

29. LAC, RG 84, W.W. Cory to A.O. Wheeler, 8 March 1922.

30. LAC, RG 84, Harkin to W.W. Cory, 8 April 1925.

31. Potyandi, *Rivers,* 185–87, regarding 1919 Pincher Creek irrigation meeting; Denis and Challies, *Water,* 166–68, noted the Waterton Lakes Narrows as a potential power site; Ford and Whyte, *Hydrometric,* 193–217, for reports on the flow rates of the Waterton River, Belly River, and St. Mary River drainage basins, and diversions on the St. Mary River near Bab, Montana, and Kimball, Alberta; Getty, "History," 136–40, regarding the 1919 survey of Waterton Lake and the 1920 dam recommendation; hydrometric surveys in Alberta and Saskatchewan were conducted by the Canadian Irrigation Surveys from 1894 to 1909, from 1909 to 1911 by the Forestry and Irrigation Branch of the Department of the Interior, from 1911 to 1920 by the Irrigation Branch that was transferred with the Reclamation Service to the Dominion Water Power Branch in 1920, and reorganized as the Water Power and Hydrometric Bureau in 1924, see Department of the Interior, *Annual Report, 1921–22,* 61; Mitchner, "Development," 312, regarding the rise of the irrigation movement and the Lethbridge Southeast proposal.

32. The CPR took over the Alberta Railway and Irrigation Company in 1912, thus gaining entry into the Lethbridge-area irrigation market, see MacGregor, *History,* 202–03; also see Mitchner, "Development," 232–33; for a description of the Lethbridge Southeast project, see Department of the Interior, *Annual Report, 1923–24,* 90–91.

33. Harkin cited in Taylor, "Legislating," 130.

34. *Weekly Albertan,* "Farmers," 2; also see *Weekly Albertan,* "Industries," 4; *Weekly Albertan,* "Plan," 1.

35. *Lethbridge Herald,* "Thousands," 7; *Calgary Daily Herald,* "Influx," 1; *Calgary Daily Herald,* "Colonization," 1; *Calgary Daily Herald,* "Irrigation"; *Calgary Daily Herald,* "Legislation"; *Weekly Albertan,* "Interesting," 4.

36. *Lethbridge Herald,* "Finishing," 10; *Calgary Daily Herald,* "Problems," 7; *Calgary Daily Herald,* "Province," 1; *Weekly Albertan,* "Irrigation Mad," 20; *Weekly Albertan,* "Dominion," 2.

37. *Lethbridge Herald,* "Protest," 7.

38. Getty, "History," 145–46.

39. William Pearce was a former Department of the Interior senior surveyor who became an outspoken proponent of irrigation in his later career with the CPR, see Mitchner, "Development," chap. 2 passim, 374; Bella, *Profit,* 39–49. UFA locals were quick to react to the irrigation movement in southern Alberta, see Potyandi, *Rivers,* 185–86.

40. Getty, "History," 142, 145.

41. *Weekly Albertan,* "Irrigation Dam," 6.

42. LAC, RG 84, A.O. Wheeler to J.B. Harkin, 20 March 1922.

43. LAC, RG 84, J.B. Harkin to A.O. Wheeler, 6 April 1922.

44. Lothian, *History,* vol. III, 47.

45. LAC, RG 84, J.B. Harkin to A.O. Wheeler, 6 April 1922.

46. Getty, "History," 144.

47. LAC, RG 84, "Unique Views," 31 March 1922. For biographical background see *CAJ,* "James Outram," 127–28.

48. Cohen, *History,* 26–27, 50–51; Albright, *Birth,* 106–07: the National Parks Association was modelled after the American Civic Association and included distinguished national leaders and academics on its board.

49. Harkin to A.O. Weese, Ecological Society of America, 1 June 1922, cited in Getty, "History," 146–47, 149–50.

50. Wheeler, "Memorandum," 5. The memorandum, directed to the attention of all members of the ACC executive and all club section chairmen, reprinted passages of a letter received by Wheeler from J.B. Harkin on 6 April 1922.

51. *The Gazette,* "Annual Meeting, 1922," 17.

52. Ibid.

53. Lothian, *History,* vol. I, 46. *CAJ,* "Godsal," 90–93. For further background on Godsal's role in the creation of Waterton National Park and the current ecological state of the park, see Van Tighem, "Waterton," 26.

54. *The Gazette,* "Annual Meeting, 1922," 18.

55. Ibid.

56. Ibid.

57. Canada, *House of Commons Debates,* 1 June 1923, 3442.

58. Lothian, *History,* vol. III, 47; Getty, *Human Settlement,* 141–51; Potyandi, *Rivers,* 185–87.

59. University of Calgary Special Collections, Calgary Power Ltd., *Report,* 2–6; for background on Calgary's electrical supply and urban growth, see Foran, *Calgary,* 79; for Calgary population statistics, see Marsh, *Canadian Encyclopedia,* "Calgary."

60. Armstrong and Nelles, "Competition," 163–80; Oltmann, *Valley,* 37–50.

61. University of Calgary Special Collections, Calgary Power Ltd., *Report,* 2–6.

62. Armstrong and Nelles, *Monopoly's,* 303–09.

63. Andruschuk, *TransAlta,* 8; R.B. Bennett served on the Calgary Power board of directors (1909–19) and held shares in Calgary Power as well as the Canada Cement Company at Exshaw, see Gray, *Bennett,* 107–08, 136, 191; Aitken and Bennett were business partners who established successful mergers including the Canada Cement Company, the Calgary Light and Power Company, and the Alberta Pacific Grain Company, see Wilbur, *Administration,* 5.

64. For historical background on Calgary Power's hydropower developments on the Bow River and their significance to Alberta's economic growth, see University of Calgary Special Collections, Calgary Power Ltd., *Report,* and insert; University of Calgary Special Collections, Calgary Power Ltd., *Alberta.*

65. Department of the Interior, *Annual Report,* 1917–18 and 1918–19, 58–60.

66. University of Calgary Special Collections, Calgary Power Ltd., *Report,* 2–4.

67. Charles Stewart was a central Alberta farmer who began his political career as a Liberal member of the Alberta Legislature. He was the premier of Alberta from 1917 until defeated by Herbert Greenfield's United Farmers of Alberta in 1921. Then he entered King's federal cabinet as Minister of the Interior. See Betke, "Stewart, Charles."

68. GPRC, *Banff,* 170–77; Taylor, "Legislating," 129.

69. Canada, *House of Commons Debates,* 14 June 1923, 3940.

70. GPRC, *Banff,* 170–77. Taylor, "Legislating," 129.

71. GPRC, *Banff,* 173–74; LAC, RG 84, Banff Citizens Council to Park Commissioner Harkin, 12 September 1922; LAC, RG 84, "Will Not Permit," 29 January 1923; LAC, RG 84, "Banff Objects," 27 July 1922.

72. Cited in GPRC, *Banff,* 173–74.

73. LAC, RG 84, "Alpine Club at Annual," 29 March 1913.

74. *The Gazette,* "Notes," 20–21.

75. University of Alberta Archives (UAA), William Pearce Collection, Godsal to William Pearce, 19 May 1923; regarding the myth of nature's abundance, see Altmeyer, "Ideas," 27–31, 34.

76. UAA, William Pearce Collection, Godsal to T.O. West, 29 May 1923; UAA, William Pearce Collection, Pearce to Godsal, 14 May 1923; UAA, William Pearce Collection, Godsal to Pearce, 24 June 1923.

77. UAA, William Pearce Collection, A.O. Wheeler to W. Pearce, 18 May 1923. For background on Pearce's activities also see Bella, *Profit,* 13, 40, 51–56; Mitchner, "West, 1874–1904," 235–43; Mitchner, "Western Canada, 1882–1904."

78. UAA, William Pearce Collection, A.O. Wheeler to W. Pearce, 24 May 1923.

79. UAA, William Pearce Collection, Wheeler to *Calgary Daily Herald,* 8 June 1923.

80. Jones, *Muir,* 11, 94–99, 119–21, 182; Fox, *American,* 144. Groups that supported the creation of the society included the Boston Appalachian Mountain Club, the Seattle Mountaineers, the Portland Mazamas club, the American Civic Association, the American Scenic and Historic Preservation Society, and the General Federation of Women's Clubs. Albright, *Birth,* 106–07; Runte, *National,* 86–87, 102–03.

81. Wheeler, "National Parks," 4–5.

82. For club planning leading up to the meeting, see Markham-Starr, "Walker," 649–80.

83. *The Gazette,* "Annual Meeting, 1923," 17–18.

84. Ibid., 21–22.

85. Ibid.

86. The seven members in 1924 who also belonged to the ACC were: Dr. W.J.A. Hickson of Montreal, Hon. F.M. Black of Winnipeg, Mrs. W.C. McKillican of Brandon, Manitoba, Herbert E. Sampson of Regina, Mrs. J.W. Henshaw and Dr. Fred Bell of Vancouver, and Major F.V. Longstaff of Victoria. CNPA officers and executive members in 1924 are listed in *The Gazette,* "Canadian National Parks Association," 8, and were cross-referenced with WMCR, ACC, *Constitution and List,* 1921 and 1925. Prof. R.B. Thomson of Toronto and John Blue of Edmonton were the other two members of the CNPA executive committee in 1924; their names do not appear in the ACC list of members for 1921 or 1925; there was no extant 1923 list of members available for research, and it appears that one may not have been published that year. WMCR, Tweedy to Moffat, 27 May 1930.

87. WMCR, Tweedy to McCoubrey, 6 February 1934.

88. *The Gazette,* "Canadian National Parks Association," 6–11.

89. UAA, William Pearce Collection, W.J.S. Walker and T.B. Moffat, "National Parks and Power Sites."

90. *CAJ,* "Major," 128; *Calgary Herald,* "W.J.," 1–2; Canadian Hostelling Association, *Fifty,* 20, 31–39, 52, 60; MacEwan, *Colonel,* 159.

91. Markham-Starr, "Walker."

92. *CAJ,* "Major," 128.

93. UAA, William Pearce Collection, W.J.S. Walker and T.B. Moffat, "National Parks and Power Sites."

94. LAC, RG 84, A. Sibbald to Minister of the Interior, 14 August 1923; LAC, RG 84, Sibbald to Harkin, 9 August 1923; LAC, RG 84, W.J. Campbell to Minister, 29 August 1923; LAC, RG 84, Harold Parr to Minister, 30 August 1923; LAC, RG 84, A. McKay to Minister, n.d.; LAC, RG 84, D.J.M. McGeary to Minister, 10 October 1923; LAC, RG 84, E.J. MacKenzie to Minister, 8 November 1923; LAC, RG 84, Christina E. Henry to

Minister, 21 November 1923; LAC, RG 84, Rupert Reid to Minister, n.d. Among these CNPA correspondents, Campbell, Henry, and McGeary were registered ACC members from Saskatoon; Henry had joined in 1923 and McGeary in 1919. See WMCR, ACC, *Constitution and List,* 1921 and 1925.

95. LAC, RG 84, W.J. Campbell to Minister, 29 August 1923; WMCR, ACC, *Constitution and List,* 1925.

96. Bella and Markham, "Parks," 15–16; Bella, *Profit,* 54.

97. Canada, *House of Commons Debates,* 14 June 1923, 3940; *House of Commons Debates,* 1 June 1923, 3442.

98. Ibid., 3939–40.

99. Ibid.; Morton, *Progressive,* 161, 164, 171, 188.

100. *Weekly Albertan,* "King Offers," 1; *Weekly Albertan,* "Take the Resources," 1; *Weekly Albertan,* "Legislators Will," 1; *Weekly Albertan,* "Debate Tame," 1, 5; Mitchner, "Development," 104–06, 170.

101. LAC, RG 84, "Plans to Climb Mt. Logan," 5 February 1924.

102. Mitchner, "Development," 104–06.

103. Canada, *House of Commons Debates,* 10 April 1924, 1259–60.

104. Ibid., 1260.

105. Ibid., 1259.

106. LAC, RG 84, A.O. Wheeler to J.B. Harkin, 23 March 1925.

107. GPRC, *Banff,* 177–80.

108. Taylor, "Legislating," 131–32; GPRC, *Banff,* 182. New area added to Rocky Mountains Park included 268 square kilometres around Malloch Mountain and a 2,538-square-kilometre parcel of Jasper National Park. Surveyors R.W. Cautley and A.O. Wheeler were colleagues on the Interprovincial Boundary Commission through the 1920s.

109. *National Parks Act,* May 30, 1930, ch. 33, sec. 4.

110. GPRC, *Banff,* 183.

111. WMCR, Mitchell to Sampson, 18 October 1930. R.B. Bennett held investments in Calgary Power, CPR, and the Canada Cement Plant at Exshaw.

⑤ **Conservation, Sport Tactics, and War Measures**

1. *Saskatoon Star Phoenix,* "Industry," 13.

2. A.O. Wheeler Diaries, 17 January 1930, 1 and 18 February 1930, 7 March 1930, 31 May 1930, 1–2 June 1930, 27 July 1930 to 1 August 1930.

3. Taylor, "Legislating," 131–34; Lothian, *History,* vol. II, 10–17. The act also authorized the establishment of National Historic Parks by Order in Council.

4. Calgary Power became TransAlta Utilities in 1981. See Andruschuk, *TransAlta,* 44.

5. Hawkins, *Electrifying,* 208; *Calgary Daily Herald,* "Minnewanka," 13; GPRC, *Banff,* 183–84; Natural Resources Canada, "Power Development," 4.

6. *The Gazette,* "Resolution," 20–21.

7. Ibid.

8. In an early era of theorizing ecology, encouraging the use of fossil fuels to protect national parks was not uncommon even among conservationists as the implications were not fully apparent.

9. Wheeler, "Recent Proposal," 1.

10. *Saskatoon Star Phoenix,* "Industry," 13.

11. *Calgary Albertan,* "Ridiculous," 4.

12. Ibid.

13. *Calgary Albertan,* "Wide Objective," 3; *Calgary Albertan,* "Club Denies," 4.

14. *Crag and Canyon,* "Ridiculous," 4.

15. LAC, RG84, Revised Memorandum, Spray Lakes Hydro Electric Development, 14 January 1949; GPRC, *Banff,* 236–40.

16. The Department of the Interior observed rapid growth in water-power capacity through the late 1920s, see Natural Resources Canada, "Mid-Season"; Natural Resources Canada, "Power," 4; Natural Resources Canada, "Mid-Year," 1, 3; Natural Resources Canada, "Hydro-electric," 1, 3. For national power surpluses related to the Depression, see Regehr, *Beauharnois,* 169. For the Calgary Power situation and finances, see Hawkins, *Electrifying,* 169.

17. LAC, RG 84, Account of Cascade Power Development 1941; LAC, RG 84, Banff Electric Power-Lake Minnewanka; Taylor, "Legislating," 135; GPRC, *Banff,* 236–40.

18. Hawkins, *Electrifying,* 171.

19. *The Gazette,* "Honourary President's," 1943, 6–7; Ibid., 1940, 7.

20. LAC, RG 84, Walker to *Calgary Herald,* 5 September 1940; LAC, RG 84, Walker to *The Albertan,* 11 September 1940.

21. LAC, RG 22, W.J.S. Walker to J. Smart, 25 April 1941.

22. LAC, RG 84, "Banff Council Urges," 29 November 1940; LAC, RG 84, "Banff Power Proposal," 4 December 1940, 1; *Crag and Canyon,* "Advisory Council," 6 December 1940.

23. *The Gazette,* "Annual Meeting, 1931," 7; the federal grant in 1930 had been $1,000, see *The Gazette,* "Auditor's Report," 1931, 20.

24. LAC, RG 84, H.E. Sampson to T.G. Murphy, n.d.; WMCR, Sampson to Tweedy, 31 December 1931.

25. Canada, *Auditor Report 1928,* 222; Canada, *Auditor Report 1931-32,* 175. Grants to the Dominion Land Surveyors' Association remained steady at $125 per annum, while grants to the Canadian Forestry Association were reduced 50 per cent from $4,000 in 1928 to $2,000 in 1931. Other allocations were made to relieve needy settlers in Alberta and Saskatchewan, to schools and hospitals in the Northwest Territories, to wildlife conservation, to individuals, and to the Yukon local council.

26. WMCR, Mitchell to Sampson, 18 October 1930.

27. Hart, *Harkin,* 386–89.

28. *The Gazette,* "Annual Meeting, 1933," 7.

29. WMCR, Sampson to Tweedy, 3 October 1930. For issues with annual fees, see WMCR, Mitchell to Bell, 1 February 1928. For older club members passing away, for example five around 1929, see *CAJ,* "Proceedings and News," 1929, 129.

30. See Appendix 1, Table 1.

31. WMCR, Sampson to Tweedy, 26 August 1930. Sampson noted: "Any method you adopt for the saving of expense will be satisfactory to the Treasurer and myself. We are anxious to keep expense down as much as possible." WMCR, ACC Camp Costs Summary 1930-1932; WMCR, McCoubrey to Tweedy, 5 May 1933; WMCR, Tweedy to McCoubrey, 26 May 1933; WMCR, Sibbald to Tweedy, 17 August 1934.

32. *The Gazette,* "Report of Auditor," 1936, 16–17; camp budget figures totalled Mount Sir Donald/Glacier Camp (1932) $3,330.17 income to $2,417.82 expenditure, Paradise Valley (1933) $2,679.64 income to $2,531.63 expenditure, Chrome Lake (1934) $3,250.21

income to $2,859.01 expenditure, Mount Assiniboine (1935) $7,101.28 income to $6,030.03 expenditure.

33. WMCR, McCoubrey to Tweedy, 5 May 1933.

34. For number of ACC campers at 1935 Lake Magog Camp, see *CAJ*, "Proceedings and News," 1934 and 1935, 118-20.

35. Tetarenko and Tetarenko, *Ken*, 94.

36. *The Gazette*, "Annual Meeting, 1933," 8.

37. Ibid. The cost of the 1925 Mount Logan expedition totalled $12,793.48, which was financed by contributions from club members and corporate donors, see *CAJ*, "Annual Meeting 1926," 248; *The Gazette*, "Contributions," 24.

38. WMCR, Mitchell to Moffat, 8 December 1928. For notes related to subscribing members by region, see WMCR, ACC Candidates for Election, n.d.

39. WMCR, Mitchell to Moffat, 16 September 1929; WMCR, Mitchell to Moffat, 10 October 1929; WMCR, Mitchell to Moffat, 4 December 1929; WMCR, Mitchell to Moffat, 27 December 1929. Mitchell's increasing frustration with the lack of leadership in the Toronto Section is evident in his letters to the ACC national president.

40. WMCR, Mitchell to Moffat, 4 December 1929; WMCR, Mitchell to Moffat, 21 January 1930. Reichwein and Fox, "Margaret," 38.

41. WMCR, Mitchell to Moffat, 10 October 1929. United States residents comprised 33.2 per cent of the total ACC membership in 1930 and 36.1 per cent in 1939. See Appendix 1, Tables 3 and 4.

42. See Appendix 1, Tables 3 and 4. For the situation of key national sport organizations across Canada, see Kidd, *Struggle*, passim.

43. *The Gazette*, "Annual Meeting, 1933," 26.

44. Ibid., 25-26.

45. WMCR, McCoubrey to Tweedy, 1 December 1933, regarding Lambart. WMCR, *Constitution and List*, 1933, 7, regarding rate of annual fees. WMCR, Tweedy to Sibbald, 28 December 1934, regarding Calgary Section executives.

46. WMCR, List of Members in Arrears, 1 October 1933. The bulk of membership was Canadian, centred in Calgary, Vancouver Island, and Vancouver. Auditor's figures from *The Gazette*, "Schedules and Report," 1934, 20-23.

47. *The Gazette*, "Schedules and Report," 1935, 13-15, 18.

48. *The Gazette*, "Annual Meeting, 1935," 18.

49. Ibid.

50. *The Gazette*, "Annual Meeting, 1936," 5-6.

51. Ibid., 5-7.

52. *CAJ*, "Andrew," 274-77.

53. *The Gazette*, "Annual Meeting, 1936," 5-7.

54. *The Gazette*, "Annual Meeting, 1937," 12. Regarding age requirements for membership in the ACC, see WMCR, ACC, *Constitution and List*, 1907 through 1958.

55. LAC, RG 84, R.J. Cuthbertson to J.B. Harkin, 28 March 1935; LAC, RG 84, Cuthbertson to Parks Branch, 7 September 1934. For further discussion of grant renewal, see LAC, RG 84, Harkin to Cuthbertson, 19 September 1934; LAC, RG 84, Cuthbertson to Murphy, 16 August 1934; LAC, RG 84, Harkin to Gibson, 29 August 1934; LAC, RG 84, Assistant Deputy Minister to Harkin, 31 August 1934; LAC, RG 84, Harkin to Cuthbertson, 15 July 1935.

56. *The Gazette,* "Report of Auditor," 1938, 19–21; *The Gazette,* "Report of Auditor," 1939, 15–17; *The Gazette,* "Annual Meeting, 1938," 12.

57. Wheeler's comments cited in *The Gazette,* "Annual Meeting, 1934," 8.

58. *The Gazette,* "Annual Meeting, 1938," 19.

59. Wright, "Urban," 449.

60. Department of the Interior, *Annual Report,* 1931, 99; Department of the Interior, *Annual Report,* 1932, 8; Wall, "Recreational," plate 36, n.p. Visitation to Point Pelee and Riding Mountain national parks, in close proximity to the large urban centres of Toronto and Winnipeg respectively, suffered less fluctuation.

61. The national parks Engineering Service in Ottawa and Banff directed these highway projects, see Lothian, *History,* vol. II, 18; for unemployment relief works and labourers in the construction of the Banff–Jasper Road, see Waiser, *Prisoners,* 81–91.

62. Clark, *Men,* 144–48, 150, 155–56, 214; Keenleyside, *Peaks,* 64, 74; Unsworth, *Heights,* 286–87; Irving, "Trends," 53–63; Donnelly, "Invention," 235–43; Donnelly, "Paradox," 189–99.

63. Hansen, "Vertical," 48–71; Höbusch, "Germany's," 137–68; Bayers, *Imperial;* Slemon, "Climbing," 15–41.

64. Wiessner, "Waddington," 18–24.

65. Clark, *Men,* 157–61; Keenlyside, *Peaks,* 144; Kelsey, *Climbers,* 506–15.

66. For the CPR's guides and $200 corporate donation to camp in 1933, see WMCR, McCoubrey to Management Committee, 31 May 1933; WMCR, McCoubrey to Management Committee, 5 June 1933; the CNR provided a $200 credit toward freight costs to ship club cargo from Calgary to Jasper for Chrome Lake Camp in 1934, see WMCR, Osborne Scott to A.A. McCoubrey, 13 March 1934.

67. As early as 1930, the ACC requested Lawrence Grassi to attend camp as a mountaineering guide, see WMCR, Mitchell to Grassi, n.d., c. April 1930; WMCR, Mt. Little Climb, 30 July 1930; regarding the 1934 amateur guides, see WMCR, McCoubrey to Tweedy, 7 June 1934.

68. WMCR, McCoubrey to Tweedy, 27 June 1934.

69. Cuthbertson, "Alpine," 4.

70. Underhill, "Modern Rock," 165.

71. See the address of the honorary secretary, *The Gazette,* "Annual Meeting, 1937," 9.

72. Fee, "Manitobans," 19–20.

73. *CAJ,* "Emmie," 1990, 92.

74. Underhill, "Modern Ice," 116–32.

75. Unsworth, *Encyclopedia,* 211, 148.

76. For background on skiing in Canada, see: McCoubrey, "Contribution," 116–19; Graves, "Ski," 5–7; regarding the Scandinavian roots of Manitoba skiing, see Lund, "History," 214–20; Lund, "Skiing," 48–53; for a US example of female skiing, see Allen, "Sierra," 347–53; an ACC ski camp is described in *Weekend Picture Magazine,* "High," 1–5; with regard to the development of skiing in the American Rockies, see Coleman, *Style.*

77. Graves, "Ski," 7.

78. Fee, "Manitobans," 19–20; Neave, "Spring," 122–27; McCoubrey, "Skis," 164–66; Reichwein and Fox, "Margaret," 35.

79. WMCR, Mitchell to Moffat, 29 April 1930.

80. Munday, "Baker," 7–10.

81. Munday, "Seymour," 117–19; for a survey of developments, see Baldwin, "Mountaineering," 24–25.

82. Gibson, "Resplendent," 111–13;

83. *The Gazette,* "Annual Meeting, 1934," 14.

84. d'Egville, "Ski-mountaineering," 96–99; O'Brien, "Monte Rosa," 100–06; Bennett, "Snow Dome," 107–10; Kingman, "Skoki," 114–16; Munday, "Seymour," 117–19; CAJ, "Ski Camps," 151.

85. CAJ, "Interim," 240.

86. LAC, RG 84, Harkin to A.O. Wheeler, 22 September 1933.

87. Department of the Interior, *Annual Report,* 1929–30, 107–09; Yeo, "Making," 87–98; Strom, *Pioneers;* also see Scott, *Powder;* and Mittelstadt, *Calgary.*

88. *The Gazette,* "Notes from Sections," June 1938, 12. Bob Hind and Rex Gibson were noted to teach skiing to club members and associates.

89. Kariel and Kariel, *Alpine,* 9, 24–27; *The Gazette,* "Hut Fund," 1926, 13–14; CAJ, "Annual Meeting, 1926," 247.

90. Wates, "Memorial Cabin," 124–29, 124 cited. Haberl, *Alpine,* 121. Slark and Rutishauser, the first climbers to ascend Redoubt Peak in the Ramparts, met with accidental death on their descent in 1927.

91. Wates, "Memorial Cabin," 127, 129; also see foldout map "Alpine Club of Canada Sketch Map of Region Surrounding Memorial Cabin." Wates and Gibson, "Memorial Cabin in 1931," 5–29, 8 cited.

92. Wates and Gibson, "Memorial Cabin in 1931," 5.

93. Greer, "Elizabeth," 159–61, 159–60 cited; LAC, RG 84, Lake O'Hara-Elizabeth Parker Hut 1908–54, passim; LAC, RG 84, Lake O'Hara-Elizabeth Parker Hut, 1928–56, passim; Kariel and Kariel, *Alpine,* 17–23.

94. Greer, "Elizabeth," 159–61, with photos; LAC, RG 84, Lake O'Hara-Elizabeth Parker Hut 1908–54, passim; LAC, RG 84, Lake O'Hara-Elizabeth Parker Hut, 1928–56, passim.

95. *The Gazette,* "Edmonton," May 1937, 7–8; *The Gazette,* "Edmonton," November 1964, 28.

96. Munday, "Seymour," 118.

97. *The Gazette,* "Notes from Sections," June 1938, 11–15. The revue featured scenes titled "Early Morning at Camp," "The Summit," and "The Evening Campfire," with music derived from the club songbook. The evening also included home movies of club camp at Fryatt Creek and rock climbing at Bow Lake, along with slide talks about climbing: an intriguing representation of club culture.

98. *The Gazette,* "Annual Meeting, 1935," 20; LAC, RG 84, Upper Little Yoho Valley-Stanley Mitchell Hut, 1937–58, passim; *The Gazette,* "Stanley Mitchell Hut Fund," June 1938, 13; *The Gazette,* "Stanley Mitchell Hut," 8, illustration of hut design on facing page; *The Gazette,* "Stanley Mitchell Hut Fund," November 1938, 26; *The Gazette,* "Business Arising," 1939, 5; Kariel and Kariel, *Alpine,* 28–34.

99. *The Gazette,* "Schedules and Report," 1934, 20–23.

100. *The Gazette,* "Hut Committee Report," 1935, 20; *The Gazette,* "Hut Committee," 1936, 12.

101. *The Gazette,* "Hut Committee," 1936, 13; hostel accommodation in Bragg Creek, Alberta, cost 25 cents a night in 1933, see Canadian Hostelling Association, *Fifty,* 1–25.

102. WMCR, Mitchell to Bell, 2 March 1928. The Associated Mountaineering Clubs of North America was an umbrella body formed in 1916 by Leroy Jeffers of the New York Public Library. The ACC joined in 1917, and in 1919 Toronto ACC member Frank

Yeigh encouraged J.B. Harkin to have the Dominion Parks Branch join, which it did from 1921 to 1931. During the 1920s, the organization rang out as a pro-park advocacy group, for example, opposing hydro developments in Yellowstone National Park. See LAC, RG 84, vol. 170, file U125-5, part 1, passim.

103. *CAJ*, "Icefields Camp," 145–47. Female first ascents during camp were recorded on eight peaks, including Athabasca, Columbia, Snow Dome, North Twin, and South Twin.

104. LAC, RG84, "Columbia Icefield," 31 March 1938, n.p.

105. LAC, RG 84, "Alberta Needs More," 5 May 1939, n.p.

106. *CAJ*, "Ski Camps," 151.

107. *The Gazette*, "E.C. Brooks," 14.

108. Among the 450, the club carried 70 enlisted members without payment of dues. By 1944-45, 18 women and 76 men from the ACC were serving in the Allied forces, many among the officer corps. *The Gazette*, "Letter from President," 1944, 3; *CAJ*, "Members on War," 175–76.

109. For references to 1942 training, see Graves, "Little," 230–46; for winter training at Camp Hale, see Coleman, *Style*, 100–04.

110. Graves, "Little," 232–38; Taylor, *Highland*, 16–17.

111. For references to Munday's version of events at the 1943 training school, see Munday, "Troops," 83–90.

112. Ibid., 88–89.

113. Pilley Richards, "Proceedings Lake O'Hara," 118. Also see Pilley, *Climbing*.

114. Pilley Richards, "Proceedings Lake O'Hara," 118–21.

115. Munday, "Troops," 83–90.

116. Ibid., 90.

117. Gibson, "Saskatchewan Glacier," 202–03; Kariel and Kariel, *Alpine*, 28–34, 92–93; Taylor, *Highland*, 76; the US Army 87th Infantry Brigade later became part of the 10th Mountain Division, see Coleman, *Style*, 97–107.

118. Gibson, "Training," 177–91; *The Gazette*, "1943 Summer," 2; *The Gazette*, "Letter from President," 1944, 4; Taylor, *Highland*, 58–59.

119. Biographical information about Rex Gibson is drawn from the following sources unless otherwise noted: Hind, "Gibson," 111–14; Taylor, *Highland*, 56–59.

120. The Amercian Alpine Club and various skiing and outdoor groups encouraged the US military to begin training mountain troops; see Gibson, "Training," 177–91; Taylor, *Highland*, 57, 66–68, 73, 105.

121. Daly, *Ordeal*. The feature on troop training was ten minutes long and portrayed winter as a hostile and challenging environment.

122. Preliminary ski instruction in Jasper for five hundred Lovat Scouts required forty instructors. Experienced with climbs in the Himalayas, Frank Smythe expected British and Canadian troops to meet high standards. He was critical of the calibre of skiing and mountaineering among the Canadian instructors, see Taylor, *Highland*, 67, 71–72. Rex Gibson noted there were more competent skiers than mountaineers available in Canada: "The problem really resolved itself into one of 'teaching mountaineers how to ski and skiers how to climb mountains," see Gibson, "Training," 18.

123. The St. Andrew's Society in Jasper hosted three hundred soldiers at a Robert Burns Supper, January 25, 1944. It was noted by one Scottish soldier as "an example of the

great and generous welcome we have received everywhere from Canadians." See Melville, *Lovat*, 87.

124. *The Gazette*, "Letter from President," 1944, 4.

125. Graves, "Little," 245–46.

126. Regarding prisoner-of-war camps in national parks, see Waiser, *Prisoners*, 175–226.

⑥ **Limitless Playgrounds?**

1. Wheeler, "Foreword," 6.

2. CAJ, "Elizabeth Parker," 122–27; Ibid., "Arthur Oliver Wheeler," 140–46; Fraser, *Wheeler*, 156.

3. Wheeler, "Golden," 17.

4. Lower, *Western*, 316.

5. The total population of Canada was 12.07 million in 1945, and the urban population was 7,511,539 in 1951. For census data, see Finlay and Sprague, *Structure*, 481–84; Lower, *Western*, 317.

6. Richards and Pratt, *Prairie*, 44.

7. These implications of postwar recreation and tourism are discussed further in Tillotsen, *Public*, 3–43; Wilson, *Culture*; Reichwein, "Holiday," 49–73.

8. Thorpe, "Historical Perspective," 9–10.

9. LAC, RG 84, T.A. Crerar to Mr. Whitaker, 28 July 1944. Minister Crerar wrote to Whitaker, head of the Ontario Parks Association.

10. CAJ, "Post-war," 168–69.

11. Ibid.

12. Ibid., 169 (italics in original source).

13. Ibid.

14. Ibid.

15. Ibid., 170.

16. CAJ, "Post-war," 173.

17. The key objectives with respect to park use were "The promotion of scientific study and exploration of Canadian alpine and glacial regions" and "The encouragement of the mountain craft and the opening of new regions as a national playground"; see CAJ, "Constitution," 178.

18. CAJ, "Post-war," 169; emphasis added.

19. Gibson, "Department," 174.

20. LAC, RG 22, "Post War Rehabilitation," 21 July 1945.

21. Francis and Smith, *Destinies*, 298–308; Bothwell and Kilbourn, *C.D. Howe*, 180–96; Morton, *1945*, 3, 14–18.

22. Wall and Wallis, "Camping," 349.

23. The national parks were Banff, Cape Breton Highlands, Elk Island, Georgian Bay Islands, Glacier, Jasper, Kootenay, Mount Revelstoke, Nemiskam, Point Pelee, Prince Albert, Prince Edward Island, Riding Mountain, St. Lawrence Islands, Waterton Lakes, and Yoho; for reference to park attendance, see Government of Canada Annual Reports (GCAR), "Report of the Department of Mines and Resources, March 31, 1946," 81, 84; national park attendance figures published in annual reports were subject to methodological discrepancies varying between parks and years but are taken as reported values for the purpose of this analysis. The 1941 population of New Brunswick was 457,401; see Finlay and Sprague, *Structure*, 481.

24. Wall and Wallis, "Camping," 341–53; Killan, *Protected*, 74, 121.

25. Swinnerton, "Alberta Park," 112–13.

26. Lothian, *History*, vol. II, 19.

27. LAC, RG 84, J.G. Perdue to the Parks, 11 September 1947.

28. Wilson, *Culture*, 21, 27, 31, 43; Owram, *Born*, 84–110; MacEachern, *Natural*, 161.

29. Taylor, "Changing," 216–7.

30. Nelson, "Canada's," 41–6; Taylor, "Changing," 199–23.

31. *CAJ*, "Eisenhower," 305–06.

32. Ibid.

33. GCAR, "Report of the Department of Mines and Resources, March 31, 1945," 84; GCAR, "Report of the Department of Mines and Resources, March 31, 1946," 100; GCAR, "Department of Resources and Development," 36; GCAR, "Department of Northern Affairs and National Resources," 100; GCAR, "Department of Indian Affairs and Northern Development, 1969–70," 4.

34. Banff and Jasper were the leaders in this development: 216.5 miles of motor road and 704.75 miles of trail existed in Banff; 146.5 and 620.55, respectively, in Jasper. GCAR, "Department of Northern Affairs and National Resources," 100.

35. The labour history of public works development in western Canadian national parks and the nature of a changing workforce of "alien" internees, relief workers, transients, conscientious objectors, prisoners of war, and others is discussed in Waiser, *Prisoners*; Wright, "Urban," 440–52; and MacEachern, *Natural*, 43–44, 65, 76. Wright describes the Depression and Second World War eras as "a virtual no-growth condition in park development for a period of almost thirty years" that led to a later massive resurgence of public investment in new and existing parklands and facilities from 1945 to the late 1960s; Waiser and MacEachern, respectively, contend the extent of public works in Canadian national parks through the Depression era was substantial due to government relief programs. Moreover, as MacEachern describes, the first Maritime national parks, Cape Breton Highlands and Prince Edward Island, were created as new additions to the system circa 1936 and benefitted local economies through trail- and road-building construction projects. In Cape Breton Highlands, park construction of the early Cabot Trail advanced from 1937 to 1939 with more than a hundred local labourers (65). Projects such as the Banff–Jasper Road, Banff Administration Building, and Cascade Gardens, as well as other public works were enduring facilities constructed in the western mountain parks by relief labourers funded through the interwar period.

36. Author's Interview with John Wheeler, 11 August 1993. Sir Edward Oliver Wheeler was Dr. John Wheeler's father. For biographical background, see *CAJ*, "Brigadier," 160–63.

37. LAC, RG 84, E.O. Wheeler to J. Smart, 11 February 1953; LAC, RG 84, J. Smart to Wheeler, 18 February 1953; LAC, RG 84, Wheeler to Smart, 27 February 1953; LAC, RG 84, Oliver Wheeler to J. Smart, 19 March 1951; LAC, RG 84, J. Smart to Wheeler, 28 March 1951; LAC, RG 84, Smart to Superintendents, 28 March 1951; LAC, RG 84, J.R.B. Coleman to Smart, 4 May 1951; LAC, RG 84, J. Smart to Superintendent Steeves, 28 December 1951; LAC, RG 84, Wheeler to Steeves, 31 January 1953; Wheeler, "Foreword," 1–6.

38. *CAJ*, "General," 150.

39. Wheeler, "Golden," 19.

40. LAC, RG 84, E.O. Wheeler to J.A. Hutchinson, 18 April 1953.

41. LAC, RG 84, H.A. Young to Superintendents, 26 May 1952. The letter followed Young's meeting with Col. William Foster who requested renewal of the $1,000 federal grant to the ACC. Also see LAC, RG 84, L.C. Wilson to Robert Winters, 17 February 1953.

42. Wheeler, "Foreword," 4.

43. MacIntosh, "First Ascent," 153.

44. Ibid.

45. Gibson, "Climbs," 160.

46. For example, first ascents on these peaks had been recorded on Bugaboo Spire by Albert and Beth MacCarthy with Conrad Kain in 1916, Pigeon Spire by Paul Kaufmann and Eaton Cromwell in 1930, and Snowpatch Spire by J. Arnold and R. Bedayn in 1940.

47. Gibson, "Climbs," 154, 158, 160.

48. Gibson, "Climbs," 154, 158, 160. Polly Prescott was a longtime member of the ACC and received the Silver Rope award (see Chapter 3). For the account of her 1938 climbs with Sterling Hendricks, Lawrence Coveney, and Marguerite Schnellbacher in the Bugaboos, see Olton, "Bugaboos," 292–98.

49. Wheeler, "Golden," 21–22; Wheeler, "Foreword," 1.

50. Wheeler, "Golden," 22.

51. William Orton Harrison (1904–93) helped to outfit ACC camps in 1946 and 1947. Beginning in 1954, "Bill" Harrison and his family were involved as outfitters for general mountaineering camps. Brad Harrison, his son, took up more duties in the 1980s and inherited his father's role. He continues to outfit the current annual general mountaineering camps. Shokoples, "Harrisons," 61–62. Also see Robinson, *Family*.

52. Wheeler, "Foreword," 1.

53. Ibid., 2.

54. The British Columbia Mountain Club was similarly pulled in two directions with regard to building postwar roads and facilities. See Dummitt, "Risk," 12.

55. See Appendix 1, Table 1; *The Gazette*, "Statement," 27.

56. See Appendix 1, Table 1.

57. Owram, *Born*, 4–5; Hall, *Girl and the Game*, 110–23; Prentice et al., *Canadian Women*, 311, 330.

58. See Appendix 1, Tables 3 and 4.

59. This conclusion was based on the 1967 ACC Red Book list of members. Analysis categorized a man and a woman who listed the same surname and the same mailing address to be a married couple living in the same household when the female was listed by the prefix "Mrs." See Appendix 1, Table 1.

60. *The Gazette*, "A Letter," 1942, 14; see Appendix 1, Tables 1, 3, and 4.

61. CAJ, "Local Section," vii; for lists of sections, see opening pages of CAJ 1944 and 1945 to 1957.

62. CAJ, "Local Sections," v.

63. Wheeler, "Foreword," 4–5.

64. Wheeler, "Golden," 17.

65. LAC, RG 84, Wheeler to Smart, 11 February 1953. Wheeler noted that the club was co-operating on issues of the Park Fishing Creel Census, litter and fire control, and minimizing pole cutting for tents when he wrote to the director of national parks to discuss simplifying site licensing procedures for ACC huts in the national parks. LAC,

RG 84, J. Smart to Oliver Wheeler, 18 February 1953. With regard to the creel census cards, Smart commented to Wheeler, "The efforts you are putting forth to make more widely known this phase of our conservation work is greatly appreciated," and commended the ACC's good work in conservation. LAC, RG 84, O. Wheeler to J. Smart, 17 March 1952, outlined that the ACC planned to participate in a creel census during its 1952 camp at Mount Assiniboine Provincial Park and sought input on fish stocking in the national parks for an article in the newly reintroduced scientific section of the *Canadian Alpine Journal*. Smart replied, "This section in the former issues has been a source of valuable information to many persons outside of the actual members of the club." See LAC, RG 84, O. Smart to Wheeler, 25 March 1952.

66. *CAJ*, "Ski," 151.

67. LAC, RG 84, C.E. Doak to Chief of National Parks Branch, 2 April 1958.

68. Wilts, "Unusual," 160.

69. Duffy, "Climbing," 81–84; Moraine Lake lies in the Valley of Ten Peaks, near Lake Louise, Alberta, in Banff National Park.

70. Wheeler, "Foreword," 2–3.

71. LAC, RG 84, E.O. Wheeler to J. Smart, 11 February 1953. Wheeler noted that the club was co-operating on issues of the Park Fishing Creel Census, litter and fire control, and minimizing pole cutting for tents.

72. LAC, RG 84, E.O. Wheeler to J. Smart, 27 February 1953.

73. LAC, RG 84, J. Smart to Oliver Wheeler, 18 February 1953.

74. Kariel and Kariel, *Alpine*, 72–77, 124–28, 171.

75. LAC, RG 84, H. Green to W. Dinsdale, 10 July 1961.

76. LAC, RG 84, J.H. Atkinson to Chief of National Parks Service, 7 February 1962; LAC, RG 84, D.B. Coombs to Chief, 1 March 1962.

77. Kariel and Kariel, *Alpine*, 46–47.

78. Ibid., 172.

79. Ibid.

80. LAC, RG 84, S.F. Kun to A.J. Reeve, 10 August 1967.

81. Kariel and Kariel, *Alpine*, 171–74.

82. ACC, "Backcountry." The 24 national ACC huts currently include 17 huts in national parks. The 24 current backcountry national huts encompass: 6 in Banff National Park comprised of Abbot Pass Hut, Bow Hut, Castle Mountain Hut, Peter and Catharine Whyte (Peyto) Hut, R.J. Ritchie (Balfour) Hut, Neil Colgan Hut; 4 in Jasper National Park comprised of Mount Colin Centennial Hut, Wates-Gibson Hut, Lloyd MacKay (Mt. Alberta) Hut, Sydney Vallance (Fryatt) Hut; 3 in Yoho National Park comprised of Elizabeth Parker Hut, Stanley Mitchell Hut, and Scott Duncan Hut; 4 in Glacier National Park comprised of A.O. Wheeler Hut, Asulkan Cabin, Glacier Circle Cabin, and Sapphire Col Hut; 1 in Bugaboo Provincial Park, BC, comprised of Conrad Kain Hut; 3 in Kokanee Glacier Provincial Park, BC, comprised of Kokanee Glacier Cabin, Silver Spray Cabin, and Woodbury Cabin; 1 in Elk Lakes Provincial Park, BC, comprised of Elk Lakes Cabin; and 2 in the Selkirk Range, BC, comprising Bill Putnam (Fairy Meadow) Hut, Ben Ferris (Great Cairn) Hut. Additional ACC properties include various section huts and cabins in British Columbia, Ontario, Quebec, and New York state, as well as frontcountry national clubhouses, and cabins in Alberta. The Canadian Alpine Centre and Hostel is located in Lake Louise, AB, in Banff

National Park. In 2009 the newly rebuilt Fay Hut in Kootenay National Park burned down.

83. Haberl, *Alpine*.

84. Dudra, "Defence," 150–51. Dudra was a strong ice and rock climber who belonged to the ACC and AAC before his untimely death in a plane accident. For biography, see *CAJ*, "Dudra," 92; also Scott, *Pushing*, 226.

85. Dudra, "Defence," 150–51.

86. For Smythe's remarks, see Lewis, "Climbs," 153–54.

87. *CAJ*, "Viking," advertising end pages, n.p.; Mears, "Rope," 129–45.

88. Calcaterra, "Ode," 81.

89. Dummit, "Finding," 209–23.

90. Wheeler, "Foreword," 2.

91. Turner, "From Woodcraft," 474–75, 479.

92. *CAJ*, "Alpine Equipment," advertising end pages. Alpine Equipment was located at 3530 15 Street SW, Calgary, in 1949, and advertised regularly in the *CAJ* for many years.

93. Wheeler, "Golden," 17.

94. Wheeler, "Foreword," 2.

95. Hind, "Gibson," 111–13.

96. Gibson, "Jubliee," 1.

97. For influential examples of historiographic interpretations of the sport modernization thesis and its underlying teleological assumptions, see Jones, *Climbing*, 89–99, 319; and Scott, *Pushing*, 165–67, 313. Scott further characterizes the 1950s era as Canada's coming of age, portraying developments in technical climbing within the sport of mountaineering as part of a nationalist narrative of Canadian history.

98. Wheeler, "Foreword," 4.

99. LAC, RG 84, Selby Walker to R.A. Gibson, 15 November 1948; LAC, RG 84, J.A. MacKinnon to Walker, 22 November 1948.

100. LAC, RG 84, R.A. Gibson to Acting Deputy Minister, 2 November 1948.

101. LAC, RG 84, Ernest Manning to James A. MacKinnon, 21 May 1948; quoted from LAC, RG 84, C.D. Howe to MacKinnon, 15 June 1948; LAC, RG 84, Manning to W.L.M. King, 23 June 1948; LAC, RG 84, Manning to James A. MacKinnon, 18 June 1948; LAC, RG 84, MacKinnon to Howe, 25 May 1948; LAC, RG 84, Manning to MacKinnon, 19 October 1948; MacKinnon to Manning, 30 October 1948; LAC, RG 84, R.A. Gibson to J. Smart, 26 October 1948; LAC, RG 84, Spray Lakes Power Development Water Diversion 1948–1955; LAC, RG 84, Spray Lakes Power Development 1946–1949; GPRC, *Banff*, 183–84; Andruschuk, *TransAlta*, 35–36.

102. For background on the Social Credit government in Alberta during this period, see Finkel, *Social*, 99–140, 166; Andruschuk, *TransAlta*, 38.

103. *CAJ*, "Assiniboine Camp," 173.

104. Bella, *Profit*, 112–13, 155; Taylor, "Canadian National," 1–11. The new name, CPAWS, also bore some resemblance to the Wilderness Society founded in the United States in 1935 by leaders such as Aldo Leopold, Arthur Carhardt, Bob Marshall, and Olaf and Margaret Murrie. See Waterman, *Nameless*, 3–4, 62, 114, 175; Craighead and Kreps, *Dreams*, 68, 71, 79.

105. Biographical information about Aileen Harmon is from Harmon Photography, "Aileen." I am grateful to Carole Harmon.

106. Hayter, *Flexible*, 48–49; Pedersen, "Allowable," 5–7; Sloan, *Report*; British Columbia Royal Commission on Forest Resources, *Report*. In total, 219 witnesses presented before the commission at meetings held throughout the province in 1955, see list in Appendix C of the second commission report.

107. Parkes, "Brief," 126. The brief noted that annual club camps had been conducted in BC provincial parks at Mount Robson and Mount Assiniboine, members used Garibaldi Park and Manning Park, and members were early users in Mount Seymour Park.

108. Ibid., 125–28; *CAJ*, "Fred," 164–65.

109. Parkes, "Brief," 128.

110. Ibid., 125–28.

111. Ibid., 125.

112. Ibid., 125–26.

113. See Hayter, *Flexible*, 48–49.

114. Tilley, "Identity," 29.

115. Ibid., 26.

116. Kluane First Nation is headquartered at Burwash Landing, and the Champagne and Aishihik First Nation is in Haines Junction, see Council of Yukon First Nations, "Champagne"; Council of Yukon First Nations, "Kluane."

117. Overhunting and conservation concerns arose with the influx of military and construction workers on the Alcan Highway project during the Second World War. As the liaison officer between the Dominion departments and the United States Army officers building the Alaska Highway, Charles LeCapelain advised Ottawa's R.A. Gibson to establish a protected area. LeCapelain was a highway engineer familiar with mountain parks and wildlife conservation in southern Canada from his earlier work as superintendent of Waterton Lakes National Park in Alberta. His letter to Gibson is cited in McCandless, *Yukon*, 79; Cruikshank, *Glaciers*, 251–53.

118. Fisher, "Report," 253–54.

119. Ibid., 254; Neave, "Second Steele," 115.

120. *Yukon Daily News*, "Alpine Dinner," 1; Fisher, "Report," 253.

121. Arctic Institute of North America (AINA), "Northern Highlights," 223–26.

122. Schama, *Landscape*; Cruikshank, *Glaciers*; Ellis, *Vertical*; Fentress and Wickham, *Social*; Opp and Walsh, *Placing Memory*.

123. Davies, "Politics"; regarding the 1967 Voyageur Canoe pageant enacting an exclusionary narrative of Canadian nation-building perpetuated through sport and myths of the canoe, see Dean, "Centennial"; Reichwein, "Expedition."

124. Robinson and Reichwein, "Canada's Everest," 95–121.

125. For the symbolic currency and politics of mountaineering, see Ellis, *Vertical*, 11; Slemon, "Climbing," 15–41.

126. Cruikshank, *Glaciers*, 243, 12.

127. Tim Ingold cited in Ibid., 243.

128. McCarthy, "Place," 184–86.

129. Ibid., 179.

130. Fisher, "Yukon Alpine," 1.

131. Alford, *Raven*, 102–07. Hughes advised, "We would want peaks lying east to west, so that they could be named in the same geographical orientation as the provinces; that way there would be no squabbling over peak dominance" (102).

132. Fisher, "Yukon Alpine," 1–2.

133. WMCR, David Fisher Papers, Yukon Territorial Government and the Alpine Club of Canada, et al., "Yukon."

134. Ibid., 1.

135. Ibid., 2–3.

136. Fisher, "Yukon Alpine," 12–13.

137. *CAJ*, "Yukon Alpine," 1.

138. *Yukon Daily News*, "Climbers," 1.

139. Fisher, "Report," 252–53.

140. Neave, "Yukon," xii.

141. *Yukon Daily News*, "Climbers," 1. Boundaries on Mount Vancouver remain unresolved.

142. Hancock House Publishers, "Monty."

143. Alford, "South," 37.

144. On these climbs, walking on snow was integral to alpine mountaineering. For embodiment as kinesthetic and intersensory consciousness, see Merleau-Ponty, *Phenomenology*; Lewis, "Climbing Body," 58–80.

145. McCarthy, "Place," 190.

146. Rosenbaum, "Photographic"; Interview, Stan Rosenbaum with Author, Ottawa, 28 May 2009.

147. Broda, "Centennial," 42–49. For Broda's leadership, see Rosenbaum Interview.

148. Lavallée, "Mont Québec," 84.

149. Sherman, "Mount Manitoba," 55–58; Fisher, "Summary Centennial," 100.

150. Butling, "Mt. Saskatchewan," 10, 16. For non-activists as participants in the women's movement, see Rak, "Social Climbing," 109–46, 131.

151. Smith, "Mount Saskatchewan," 87–88.

152. Butling, "Mt. Saskatchewan," 16.

153. Smith, "Mount Saskatchewan," 91.

154. Butling, "Mt. Saskatchewan," 22.

155. Smith, "Mount Saskatchewan," 87–88.

156. Butling, "Mt. Saskatchewan," 25.

157. Rankin, "Climbs," 26.

158. Various attempts were made to inscribe nationalizing place names in the St. Elias Range. Mount Logan was named after Sir William Logan, Geological Survey of Canada founder; renaming it Mount Trudeau was proposed in 2000 but quashed.

159. Official approval from the CPCGN was sought by the ACC to authorize permanent names for peaks and glaciers in the Centennial Range, for example Mount Alberta. For details, see Fisher, "Summary Centennial," 97–103.

160. Yonatan Yew, Rideau Hall, Ottawa, to Author, 4 May 2009. Medals were awarded to select YACE leaders, but David Fisher was not listed as a recipient. Hancock House Publishers, "Monty"; Robinson, *Family*, 13.

161. WMCR, David Fisher Papers, Eric Brooks to Dave Fisher, 6 May 1967.

162. For camp information, see Fisher, "Report," 252–55; Fisher, "Summary Climbs," 131. Kluane Lake—Lùù'ààn Man in Southern Tutchone and Lùùxhààníí in Tlingit—is the largest Yukon lake.

163. Geographic names were also suggested for features to the north side of the Steele Glacier. Fisher, "Summary Climbs." The fold-out photo taken by Walter Wood provides a panorama (132–33). Mount Coleman (Peak 7A) was not climbed. Dunnell,

"First," 104–12. WMCR, David Fisher Papers, G.F. Delaney to D.R. Fisher, 1 December 1970.

164. Fisher, "Report," 254.

165. Fisher, "Yukon Alpine," 29.

166. Fisher, "Report," 254; Smith, "Mount Saskatchewan," 87–88.

167. David Neufeld to Author, May 20, 2008.

168. WMCR, David Fisher Papers, David Fisher to Phyllis Munday, 13 February 1968. For details related to cornices and judging first ascents, also see Fisher, "Summary Centennial," 99.

169. WMCR, David Fisher Papers, P.B. Howard to D. Fisher, 4 August 1971; D. Fisher to J.R. Chalker, 2 July 1971; J. Smith to D.R. Fisher, 4 August 1971; Jean Alarie to D. Fisher, 9 August 1971; L.J. Wallace to D. Fisher, 10 August 1971; S.M. Hodgson to Fisher, 14 September 1971. David Fisher also sent YACE medallions and flags to museums, see Hodgson to Fisher, 2 December 1968; also see David Ross to D.R. Fisher, 3 December 1968. Royal Alberta Museum holds a YACE medallion.

170. Fisher, *Expedition Yukon*, 9.

171. Culbert, "Book Reviews," 58.

172. Fisher and Sandford, *Expedition Yukon*, 3.

173. Rosenbaum, "Photographic."

174. Scott, *Pushing*, 313.

175. Alford, *Raven*, 115, 113.

176. Fisher, "Report," 254.

177. Macintosh, *Sport*, 37, 53, 173, 186. The 1969 Task Force on Sport linked sport to federalist nationalism.

178. Cruikshank, *Glaciers*, 251–54.

179. Grant, "Arctic," 27–42.

180. Neave, "Second Steele," 120.

181. Neave, "Foreword," xii.

182. Until 1989 the ACC commonly appointed federal and provincial ministers responsible for parks as its honorary vice-presidents. Such well-known politicians as federal MPs Jean-Luc Pepin, Judd Buchanan, Warren Allmand, Hugh Faulkner, John Roberts, Tom McMillan, Lucien Bouchard, and Alberta MLAs Allen Adair and Peter Trynchy held the role. Through such appointments the club fostered ties with the federal and provincial governments responsible for key mountain parks.

183. WMCR, David Fisher Papers, David Fisher to Jean Chrétien, 2 March 1971.

184. WMCR, David Fisher Papers, "A National Park in the Yukon."

185. WMCR, David Fisher Papers, "Ragged Range."

186. MacAdam, "Pat," 35; AINA, "Exploring."

187. WMCR, David Fisher Papers, "A National Park in the Cumberland Peninsula."

188. WMCR, David Fisher Papers, "A National Park in the Yukon"; WMCR, David Fisher Papers, "Ragged Range"; WMCR, David Fisher Papers, "A National Park in the Cumberland Peninsula."

189. LAC, RG 22, Fred E. Vermeulen to Jean Chrétien, 25 March 1970; LAC, RG 22, Chrétien to Vermeulen, 8 May 1970; Parks Canada, "Kluane."

190. Cruikshank, *Glaciers*, 251–52.

191. For Kluane/Wrangell–St. Elias, Glacier Bay, Tatshenshini-Alsek World Heritage Site, see United Nations Educational, Scientific, and Cultural Organization (UNESCO), "World Heritage."

192. Two First Nations play a significant role in land management in Kluane National Park and Reserve, see Parks Canada, "Kluane." With regard to First Nations and collaborative park education initiatives, see Parks Canada, "Time." The example of collaborative management in Tatshenshini-Alsek Park and World Heritage Site is discussed in Canadian Parks Council, *Aboriginal*, 91–94. For concerns pertaining to UNESCO World Heritage designations affecting local First Nations in the St. Elias region, see Cruikshank, *Glaciers*, 251–52.

193. Archaeological and biological studies indicate at least eight thousand years of human history. Human remains almost six hundred years old were recovered from a glacier, see Cruikshank, *Glaciers*, 245–47, 250–59.

194. For pluralistic constructs of Aboriginal cultural landscapes and commemoration in northern Canada, see Prosper, "Wherein," 117–24.

195. The ACC sought to build a permanent hut as early as 1968 to replace a pre-existing temporary shelter. Hut Committee Report cited from *CAJ*, "ACC," 111; with regard to the new lease see *The Gazette*, "Conrad Kain Hut," 2; *The Gazette*, "Alpine Club Huts," 2; with regard to permission to build a hut not yet granted, see *The Gazette*, "Club and Other Huts," 5.

196. BC Parks Kootenay District, *Management*, 6, 26, 29, 31.

197. Fuller, "Fortieth," 150–51.

198. The Bugaboos are noted to be culturally significant as "the historic birthplace of the provincial heli-ski industry" and "home to the largest heli-ski company in the world." See BC Parks Kootenay District, *Management*, 6, 26, 29, 31. The park is closely identified with a regional tourism economy, which was built on the scenic and sporting attractions of mountain terrain long extolled as parkworthy by the ACC and its members, as well as its journal, along with private operators such as Canadian Mountain Holidays.

199. Yukon Archives, John O. Livesey to H.J. Taylor, 24 May 1968.

200. Cruikshank, *Glaciers*, 181.

201. Ibid., 3–20, 243–45.

202. For dissonance in centennial commemorations, see Rutherdale and Miller, "Our Country." For an Aboriginal perspective, see Tallentire, "Shining moment," 19–20. Yukon Centennial celebrations featured local parades and river regattas involving Aboriginal, newcomer, and tourist populations; for example, YACE climber Maurice Haycock filmed the parade in Dawson, see LAC, Maurice Hall Haycock Fonds, "Yukon 1967."

203. With regard to how "Green is the new Gold" in Yukon tourism, see de la Barre, "Place," xxii. She argues, "...it is the Yukon's vast space and virtually untouched wilderness—often referred to as 'pristine'—combined with its growing infrastructure that is increasingly at the heart of its present appeal. Under the maxim that 'Green is the new Gold,' modern adventurers are making their way north in pursuit of a new kind of rush."

204. Coates, *Land*, 315.

⑦ **Belonging in Mountain Landscapes**

1. From Canada, *Transcript of Proceedings*, vol. II, 45–49.

2. Backcountry use and cumulative impacts in the mountain national parks were the subjects of various studies, for example, see Trottier and Scotter, *Survey.*

3. MacEachern, *Natural,* 222–23. MacEachern contended that the Parks Branch saw its own actions contributing to "manmade change" and that this realization, along with other factors, contributed to an ideological shift away from interventionism; however, a disjuncture between ideology and action was evident as continuing demands to accommodate visitors mitigated against entirely adopting a new philosophy and park development continued in the 1960s. I situate the early provisional Four Mountain Parks master plans at this disjuncture.

4. For further context on debates over these provisional master plans and an insightful analysis of the critiques that emanated from a key conference hosted at the University of Calgary in 1968, see Taylor, "Canadian National," 2, 8. For an indication of critiques arising in the academic papers presented at the 1968 conference, see Nelson with Scace, *Canadian;* also see Nelson with Scace, *Perspective.*

5. *The Gazette,* "Conservation," 1970, 11–12. Habgood was a member of the initial panel discussion in Edmonton. Members of the national conservation committee, as reported by Harry Habgood to the annual general meeting on August 9, 1970, included Sylvia Evans, Phil Fransen, Neil Graham, Bob James, John Root, and Fred Vermeulen. Additional members were Brian and Val Stephens, and Rolf Kellerhaus in the Edmonton Section. Corresponding members in other sections were Walter Robinson and John Osborn in Toronto, Don McDiarmid in Ottawa, Norm Purssell in Vancouver, and Jim and Linda Jones in Calgary.

6. Harry Habgood died at the age of eighty-five on September 7, 2008. See Gampo Abbey, "Death."; Habgood, "Dielectric." Thelma (Eskin) Habgood was born in Ottawa and later in life became a Buddhist nun, see Gampo Abbey, "Fortunate," 3; for Thelma Habgood's palynology work, see Hickman, Schweger, and Habgood, "Lake Wabamun," 1438–65. E-mail Interview, Migme Chödran with Author, March 11–16, 2010; Personal Communication, C.F. Richmond to Author, March 16, 2010. I appreciate the insights of Ani Migme Chödran, Helen Habgood, and former colleague C.F. Richmond.

7. *The Gazette,* "Conservation Committee," 1969, 3–4.

8. Ibid.

9. For discussion of minimum-impact ideologies and outdoor recreation, see Turner, "From Woodcraft," 462–84.

10. NPPAC sponsored the Canadian National Parks Today and Tomorrow conference at the University of Calgary in October 1968 to mobilize critiques of Parks and directions in the proposed master plans. See Nelson with Scace, *Canadian;* the conference also led to the well-known book Nelson with Scace, *Perspective.* Notably, Nelson's graduate students Robert Scace and John S. Marsh wrote papers in the volume, as did biologist Dr. Ian McTaggart-Cowan from University of British Columbia. Many leading academics in national park research contributed briefs and presented at the Four Mountain Parks hearings.

11. *The Gazette,* "Conservation," 1970, 11–12. Snowmobilers had been reported near the club's huts and in remote areas in the mountain national parks.

12. *The Gazette,* "Conservation," 1971, 4.

13.   *The Gazette*, "Conservation Committee," 1970, 6; also see *The Gazette*, "Conservation," 1972, 16.

14.   For detailed advice to campers see draft copy in WMCR, M200, "Mountain Manners." Also see *The Gazette*, "Conservation," 1971, 14–15; for reference to the enclosure of the pamphlet, see *The Gazette*, "Mountain Manners," 6; for reference to the wider distribution of the pamphlet, see *The Gazette*, "Conservation," 1972, 16.

15.   Ibid.

16.   Gruff, "Editorial," 45.

17.   Thorsell, "Planning," 18–19. Subsequent references to the Thorsell article draw on these pages. Thorsell joined the club as an associate member in 1967 and listed his mailing address in care of the Planning Division in the National Parks Branch in Ottawa, see WMCR, *List,* 1967, 34.

18.   Lumley, "Thorsell," 1285; for an example of his early research studies, see Thorsell, *Analysis.*

19.   WMCR, "YACE List," 25 May 1967, 3.

20.   Thorsell, "Planning," 18–19.

21.   Thorsell quoted Hardin, "We Must Earn," n.p.; see Thorsell, "Planning," 18–19.

22.   The discursive production, discipline, and surveillance of fit and unfit bodies has been analyzed in Foucauldian sport sociology studies, see Pronger, *Body;* Smith-Maguire, "Foucault," 293–314; Markula and Pringle, *Foucault,* 51–71.

23.   John Marsh completed his PHD at the University of Calgary in 1971. His dissertation was titled "Man, Landscape and Recreation in Glacier National Park, British Columbia, 1890 to Present." He was appointed a professor of geography at Trent University from 1972 to 2002, contributed to the Frost Centre for Canadian Studies, and organized many conferences about parks, protected areas, and conservation, including the first Rails to Greenways Conference in 1993. He is actively involved in the conservation work of CPAWS (formerly the National and Provincial Parks Association of Canada). Trent University Archives, Professor John Marsh Fonds.

24.   Marsh, "Glacier," 40; for further background, see Marsh, "A History," 66–67.

25.   Phelps, "Conservation," 58–59. Subsequent references to the Phelps article draw on these pages.

26.   Ibid.

27.   In addition to the scientific literature of ecology, travel fiction and nature poetry was also influential, see for example Synder, *No Nature;* Kerouac, *Dharma;* Campbell, *Beat Generation;* mountain life and nature in the Canadian Rockies figured specifically in works by Marty, *Headwaters.*

28.   For a park warden's perspective on the youth generation transient in Jasper National Park in the 1960s, see Schintz, *High Walls,* 158–66.

29.   Canada, *Transcript of Proceedings,* vols I–V. Hearings were held in Calgary on April 19–20, Edmonton on April 22–23, and Vancouver on April 26.

30.   Canada, *Preliminary Report.*

31.   For further discussion of public hearings related to provisional master park plans for national parks in the Maritimes, see MacEachern, *Natural,* 234–39.

32.   Canada, *Transcript of Proceedings,* vol. III, 97–101. Subsequent references to Habgood's presentation draw from these pages.

33.   Ibid., 98.

34.   Ibid.

35. Ibid., vol. IV, 107.

36. Ibid., vol. I, 127.

37. Subsequent references to Bob Jordan's presentation are drawn from Canada, *Transcript of Proceedings,* vol. II, 45–49.

38. Canadian Wildlife Service (cws), *Some Ecological,* 1, 4, 5, 10, 14. The cws specifically opposed the classification for Class III Natural Environment Area, as did the acc, as it was seen to jeopardize Class II lands with the risk of creeping development, see p. 2. cws also opposed more commercial ski hills in the national parks. On the other hand, walking was prioritized based on the following rationale: "The resources of national parks should be used but not consumed. Nonconsumptive use if regulated is perfectly compatible with nature preservation. The best example of nonconsumptive use is hiking. Walking through wildlands unaltered by man's action can be equally refreshing to body and spirit yet leave the landscape unimpaired. To facilitate foot travel a well planned network of trails should be established in zones named 'Wilderness Recreation Area.' The construction of trails involves minor alterations of the landscape. However, if well planned and executed the damage is minimal. Along the network of trails, cabins spaced at intervals of one day's walking, should be constructed" (5).

39. Canada, *Transcript of Proceedings,* vol. V, 54–60. Subsequent references to Jim Thorsell's presentation draw from these pages.

40. At the Calgary hearings, Adolph Hungrywolf of Golden, BC, raised concerns from an Aboriginal perspective, stating: "You are proposing changes here today in the Rocky Mountain national parks. These parklands are among the last of the old time natural, sacred places. Your proposed changes would set in motion the possible destruction of the spiritual peace found in these remote places. My children's children may never forgive you for this." See Canada, *Transcript of Proceedings,* vol. I, 96. Lumley, "Thorsell," 1285. Thorsell obtained his phd from the University of British Columbia in 1971 and went on to a distinguished international career in conservation and planning. The Great Divide Trail was one of the early initiatives he promoted in western Canada. He was a private environmental consultant (1971–76), an assistant professor at the University of Alberta (1977–79), and become a senior advisor of the iucn (World Conservation Union) to unesco's World Heritage Committee in 1984. In 2006 he was the recipient of the University of Alberta Alumni Association's Distinguished Alumni Award, see University of Alberta, "People, James Thorsell." In 2009 the University of Alberta awarded him an honorary doctorate of laws.

41. For an example of the emerging approach to backcountry management, see Sheppard, Woledge, Hermanrude, Wood, and Vroom, *Backcountry.*

42. Taylor, "Canadian National," 8–9. Davidson is quoted by Taylor from publications of the 1979 Canadian National Parks for Tomorrow conference.

43. I appreciate the comments of librarian Katharine Kinnear, Parks Canada Agency, Calgary, who assisted with information related to the series of documents produced as provisional master plans for the four mountain parks. The plans that were revised following the 1971 public hearings became working documents under "provisional" titles until replaced by Canada, *In Trust.*

44. While centrism was certainly not demobilized, the provisional master plan hearings nonetheless marked a beginning in the transformation to participatory governance that led to later management changes, see Brown-John, "Policy"; Kopas, *Air,* 93.

45. See Taylor, "Canadian National," 8–9.

46. ACC, "Brief to the Four."

47. Habgood, "Preservation," 67–68. Subsequent references to Habgood's article draw on these pages.

48. Ibid.

49. Ibid.

50. Canada, *Transcript of Proceedings*, vol. III, 94–97. Mr. A.E. Nightingale presented the brief for the Edmonton YMCA. He further commented: "There are many people…who lack the facilities for camping, or for reasons of health, physique, or inclination, will not wish to camp out. These people should not be ignored in developing policy for national parks. They should not be greeted with a no-admittance sign at the gates, because if they are so greeted, they are put in the position, perhaps, of helping finance facilities which they themselves cannot afford." The YMCA also advocated for wilderness protection and conservation, partly through education, suggesting that nature study centres would contribute to producing "a better informed public which will result in more citizen self-control of pollution within our parks and country" (96).

51. Canada, *Preliminary Report*, 20–23.

52. Ibid., 13–15. Ron LaRoy emphasized that his club did not want the whole of the parks opened to snowmobiling, rather it hoped for "a couple of good areas." It is worth noting that in 1971 the two areas he identified in Yoho National Park were described as "developed areas" in his brief: Takakkaw Falls was described as a campground and Amiskwi Valley was a known logging area.

53. Canada, *Transcript of Proceedings*, vol. IV, 72–74. Edward Frost spoke on behalf of the eighty-five members of the Northwest Mountaineering Club, founded in 1964 under the auspices of the Northwest Region of the Canadian Youth Hostel Association in Edmonton. The club was oriented to novice mountaineers, male and female, with an emphasis on basic instruction in mountaineering and rescue. The club was affiliated with Northwest Cross-Country Ski Club and the Northwest Voyageurs Canoe Club under the umbrella of the Canadian Youth Hostel Association, and much of its membership shared an interest in these winter and summer activities.

54. For example, John W. Rettenmayer spoke on behalf of the Edmonton chapter of the NPPAC, Canada, *Transcript of Proceedings*, vol. III, 48–50.

55. Ibid., vol. II, 24–29. In the transcripts, she was identified as "Eileen Harmon" of Banff, AB.

56. Segmentation, territorialization, and surveillance worked to discipline park space and its users through rationalized design and controls. Bale theorized the ordering of land for sportscapes with reference to Foucauldian theory and the panopticon, see Bale, *Landscapes*, 67–84. Internalizing embodied regimes and regulating the self are central to how Foucault conceptualized panopticism/discipline and bio-power/governmentality. Self-surveillance was also instrumental in affecting discipline and generating disciplinary power as an integrated network of relations, see Foucault, *Discipline*, 176–77, 201–03. For discussion and reflections on these concepts in studies of sport and physical activity, see Cole, Giardina, and Andrews, "Michel," 207–23; Smith-Maguire, "Foucault," 293–314.

57. The French architect Le Corbusier discussed landscapes as machines for sport, see Bale, "Human," 180. Manning, *Mountaineering*, was published as the second edition of this famous book, first published in 1960 by the Mountaineers of Seattle, Washington,

and employed as a textbook of mountaineering and climbing in the United States and Canada. Its seventh edition was published in 2003. I have taken the book and its subtitle as synonymous with ideological pursuits of mountaineering in North America.

58. Similarly, Bale discussed how sporting landscapes, such as stadia, can generate topophilia and a sense of place associated as home by those who frequent there or know it. Topophilia for home can exist in sporting landscapes in apparent contradiction and tension with topophobia for landscapes that constrain, see Bale, *Landscapes*, 120–21, 131–34, 146. For reflections on ecologies of home, see Rowe, *Home;* Vertinsky and Bale, *Sites,* 1–7; Tuan, *Space;* Tuan, *Topophilia.*

59. Tuan, *Dominance,* 21–23; see Bale, "Space," 167; Bale, *Landscapes,* 43–47.

60. Bale, *Landscapes,* 132–33, 144. Humans in motion experience places through their senses and feelings of vitality during physical activities such as running, skiing, walking, or orienteering. For Bale, sporting landscapes include built structures like playing fields, as well as nature-based places like forests. He writes that forests and hills have signified home and generated intense topophilia, which is extended here to mountains.

61. Habgood, "Swan," 5.

62. See Vertinsky, "Locating," 24.

63. White, "Freshfields,"76.

64. Ibid.

65. Embodiment, landscape, and memory are interrelated, as Christopher Tilley noted, "places and landscapes anchor memories because we do not remember in a disembodied placeless manner." For further discussion, see Tilley, "Identity," 22, 25.

66. *CAJ,* "Annual General Meeting, 1968," 107–08.

67. White, "Freshfields," 76. Peter Fuhrmann was a professional mountain guide and alpine specialist in safety and rescue with the Warden Service; he was also well known to the ACC and later became a club president. He was a postwar immigrant from Germany.

68. *CAJ,* "Alpine Climbing," 151. Other alpine mountaineering camps were held at Ape Lake (1973), the Battle Range (1974), the Mount Alberta area (1975), and the Premier Range (1976).

69. See camp reports in *The Gazette* (February 1969 to May 1980) regarding family camps.

70. *The Gazette,* "Roger Neave to Members," 10 May 1968; *The Gazette,* "Questionnaire Results," 2.

71. The CMC is described in Scott, *Pushing,* 186.

72. Robinson, *Family,* 14, 16. Louise Guy chaired the ACC Camp Committee beginning in 1986 and was instrumental in writing letters to past GMC participants to renew registrations for the camp held successfully at Farnham Creek in 1987. Brad Harrison, son of Bill Harrison, became the new contractor for the GMC during the same year and continues his family's tradition of outfitting the ACC summer camps.

73. Personal Communication, A.L. Sandy Aumonier to Author, 30 June 2008. I thank Sandy Aumonier, Community Planner and Cultural Resources Planner for Parks Canada Agency, Western and Northern Service Centre in Calgary, Alberta, for providing information as to the dates of these designations.

74. *The Gazette,* "Clubhouse Ballot," 1. The results of the ballot on selling the clubhouse was certified by the club president on December 23, 1969. There were 756 total ballots cast.

75. MacDonald, "Oh, Canada," 2–3.

76. Personal Communication, Gil Parker to Author, Lake Louise, Alberta, 23 October 1993. Gil Parker kindly shared his recollection of Neave's work to retain the original Banff clubhouse. Neave's club obituary underscored a retrospective assessment of the outcomes, see Hutchinson, "Roger," 117–18: "He led a spirited campaign to keep the old clubhouse on Sulphur Mountain, in Banff, and vigorously opposed the move to Canmore: many consider his position the correct one in retrospect."

77. *The Gazette,* "Clubhouse," 1971, 14. The ACC phased out summer use at the clubhouse gradually, running well for a few years with a modified management approach geared to a more casual style. This approach, with a self-serve kitchen, accommodated members young and old, along with nonmembers, with much satisfaction until the clubhouse site was shut down. *The Gazette,* "1970 Clubhouse," 2. Interview, Stan Rosenbaum with Author, Ottawa, 28 May 2009.

78. *The Gazette,* "Clubhouse," 1970, 2. The ACC Board of Management noted there were more potential benefits to negotiating for a site at Lake Louise: "No property acquisition would be required at Village Lake Louise and we would be dealing with the developer on a long lease rather than with the Government. Furthermore, Lake Louise is nearer the centre of climbing activities."

79. *The Gazette,* "President's Message," 1971, 1.

80. Rosenbaum, "President's Message," 1973, 1; Boswell, "Clubhouse," 3.

81. *The Gazette,* "President's Message," 1971, 1; *The Gazette,* "Clubhouse," 1971, 2.

82. Edmonton Federal Records Center, RG 84, Realty file on Alpine Club of Canada Banff Clubhouse property, passim; LAC, RG 84, Realty file on Alpine Club of Canada Banff Clubhouse property, passim; Cowell, "Old Lady."

83. LAC, RG 22, J.R. MacKenzie to Pierre Elliott Trudeau, 11 December 1969.

84. LAC, RG 22, Jean Chrétien to J.R. MacKenzie, 19 February 1970. This letter was copied to the regional director of Western Region.

85. Personal Communication, A.L. Sandy Aumonier to Author, 30 June 2008.

86. Cruikshank, *Glaciers,* 251.

87. Rowe, *Home.* Cronon, "Trouble," 7–28. Among the "wild places much closer to home" that Cronon remarked on celebrating because "they remind us of the wildness in our own backyards, of the nature that is all around us if only we have eyes to see it" was a group of ponds, near his house, where warm water from a limestone spring kept the pools open through the winter and attracted waterfowl, see pp. 21–22.

88. Innovative collaborative resource management and land use with Aboriginal peoples in Canada's northern national parks and Gwaii Haanas demonstrate holistic alternatives that value the integrated whole of natural and cultural concerns that are epistemologically united within Indigenous worldviews, not divided. See Peepre and Dearden, "The Role," 323–52; Berg, Fenge, and Dearden, "Aboriginal Peoples," 225–55. UNESCO merged its assessment criteria for the selection of World Heritage Sites to integrate natural and cultural heritage under one matrix in 2005; see United Nations Educational, Scientific, and Cultural Organization, Intergovernmental Committee for the Protection of the World Natural and Cultural Heritage, *Operational,* 20–21, refer to paragraph 77 and marginalia related to criteria changes. The IUCN Category

5 classification for cultural landscapes offers another alternative model, see Dearden and Rollins, "Still A-Changin,'" 12.

Epilogue

1. Kant's query "Was heisst Aufklärung?" prompted this interpretation. Foucault, "Subject," 785; also see Cole, Giardina, and Andrews, "Michel," 207–22.
2. Vertinsky, "Locating," 24. She draws on the directions of Appadurai, *Modernity*.
3. Phyllis Munday made these comments as the ACC honorary photographic secretary, see *The Gazette*, "Annual Meeting, 1930," 12. She further urged members to donate photos to the club collections and to compete in club photo competitions.
4. "Chasing Ice"; Metcalfe, "Orchestra."
5. McCarthy, "Place," 190–91.
6. Marty, "Snows."
7. Klaszus, "Trouble," 28–33.
8. Smith, Guest, Svrcek, and Farahbakhsh, "Public Health," S1–S17; Struck, "Evacuates," A22.
9. R. v. Syncrude Canada Ltd.; CBC News, "Syncrude." EcoJustice.ca, "Environmentalists."
10. Weber, "Proposed."
11. Van Tighem, "Safeguarding," 28–35; Heuer, "Wake-up," 18.
12. Brown-John, "Policy," 18.
13. Dick, "Epilogue," 381–82.
14. For analysis of four ecological integrity discourses, see Clark, Fluker, and Risby, "Deconstructing," 154–64.
15. Schindler, "Climate," 19. For far-reaching impacts on Parks Canada, Library and Archives Canada, and Museum of Civilization, see "Canada's Past Matters." Gerson, "Mountain."
16. Louv, *Last Child*, 146–47.
17. Brown-John, "Policy," 13.
18. Parks Canada, "Rouge."
19. Cronon, "Trouble," 21–22.
20. Schama, *Landscape*, passim.
21. Watson, *Social*, 97. Notwithstanding the main point of his contention about the role of social science in catalyzing social transformation, Watson nonetheless dichotomized nature and culture in his related assertion that "men and women are more than mere objects existing in the natural world. They are the creators of the liveable world—the cultural world." His discussion deals further with a fundamental alienation of man and nature characteristic of Karl Marx's writings. I contend the seam between these worlds is permeable and subject/object identities are changeable and contingent.
22. Harkin, *History*, 14.
23. UAA, William Pearce Collection, A.O. Wheeler to W. Pearce, 18 May 1923.

References

Archival Sources

▲ Banff National Park (BNP) Records

BNP, RG 84, FILE 6.2/5-L3.1/A-11, VOL. 1, BOX 80:

Advertisement "Rocky Mountains of Canada: A Public Walking or Riding Tour for 1920 Under the Patronage of the Alpine Club of Canada."

Advertisement "Rocky Mountains of Canada: Banff to Mount Assiniboine," 1921.

"Special Route Prepared for Tourists Wishing to Visit Mt. Assiniboine," *Calgary Herald*, 13 June 1921.

Superintendent R.S. Stronach to J.B. Harkin, 21 February 1922.

▲ Canadian Pacific Railway (CPR) Archives

FILE B-07.15, JOHN MURRAY GIBBON:

"A Profile of John Murray Gibbon." *CP Rail News*, 25 July 1984.

"C.P.R.'s Gibbon Celebrated 'Mosaic.'" *CP Rail News*, December 1988/January 1989.

"J. Murray Gibbon." *Spanner*, August/September 1952.

"John Murray Gibbon Ends Notable Company Career." *Canadian Pacific Staff Bulletin*, July 1945.

"Memorial to Dr. John Murray Gibbon." *Spanner*, September/October, 1955.

"New Book on Canadian Pacific History Comes from Pen of J. Murray Gibbon." *Canadian Pacific Staff Bulletin*, 1 October 1935.

▲ Edmonton Federal Records Center

RG 84, ACC. S876-S881, BOX 16, FILE 62/5-L2.1/V BLOCK 20, VOL. I:

Realty file on Alpine Club of Canada Banff Clubhouse property.

▲ Jones Library Special Collections

"Frederick L. Stone Family Papers, 1891–1991, Finding Aid." http://www.joneslibrary.org/specialcollections/collections/stone/. Accessed 8 January 2010.

"Mrs. Stone Resting in Mountain Camp." *New York Times*, 30 July 1921.

▲ Library and Archives Canada (LAC)

Department of Indian and Northern Affairs, LAC, RG 22:

A-1-A, FILE 300-66, PART 2, VOL. 977:

J.R. MacKenzie to Pierre Elliott Trudeau, 11 December 1969.

Jean Chrétien to J.R. MacKenzie, 19 February 1970.

Fred E. Vermeulen to Jean Chrétien, 25 March 1970.

Chrétien to Vermeulen, 8 May 1970.

A.2, VOL. 78, FILE 490:

"Post War Rehabilitation Programme—National Parks Bureau," revised 21 July 1945.

A.2, VOL. 238, FILE 33-4-4, PART 3:

W.J.S. Walker to J. Smart, 25 April 1941.

National Parks, LAC, RG 84, Series A.2.a.:

ACC. S876-S881 BOX 16, FILE 62/5-L2.1/V BLOCK 20, VOL. II:

Realty file on Alpine Club of Canada Banff Clubhouse property, Villa Block 20.

VOL. 1, FILE R62, PART 2:

A. Wheeler to Harkin, 9 May 1916.

Harkin to Rocky Mountains Park Superintendent, 25 May 1916.

VOL. 102, FILE U36-1, PART 2:

A. Wheeler to Harkin, 19 October 1921.

Arthur Wheeler to the Members of the Alpine Club of Canada, 1 January 1922.

A.O. Wheeler to R.A. Gibson, 8 March 1922, enclosure.

C.E. Fortin to James Lougheed, 6 December 1921.

Harkin to A. Wheeler, 6 April 1922.

Moffat to Stronach, 25 March 1922.

R.D. McCaul to James Lougheed, 25 November 1921.

Rogers to Mitchell, 31 October 1923.

Wheeler to Harkin, 26 March 1921.

VOL. 102, FILE U36-1, PART 3:

"Alpine Club at Annual Dinner," *Daily Colonist*, 29 March 1913.

"Alpine Club of Canada Plans to Climb Mt. Logan," *Calgary Herald*, 5 February 1924.

A.O. Wheeler to J.B. Harkin, 20 March 1922.

A.O. Wheeler to W.W. Cory, 4 February 1922.

Albert H. MacCarthy to Minister of Interior, 17 February 1922.

B.F. Seaver to Arthur Wheeler, 16 January 1922.

Banff to Mt. Assiniboine: A Public Walking and Riding Tour Amidst Magnificent Mountain Scenery (c. 1920–22).

Cora J. Best to Minister of Interior, 17 January 1922.

F.W. Waterman to Arthur Wheeler, 14 January 1922.

Harkin to A.O. Wheeler, 16 February 1922.

Harkin to Stronach, 3 February 1922.

J.B. Harkin to A.O. Wheeler, 6 April 1922.

J.B. Harkin to Marcus Morton, 27 January 1922.

J.B. Harkin to W.W. Cory, 14 February 1922.

Resolution, 11 February 1922.

"Unique Views of Mountains are Exhibited," *Calgary Herald*, 31 March 1922.

W.W. Cory to A.O. Wheeler, 8 March 1922.

VOL. 102, FILE U36-1, PART 4:

A.O. Wheeler to J.B. Harkin, 23 March 1925.

"The Assault on 'The Canadian Everest' Mount Logan," *Edmonton Journal*, 4 March 1925.

"Hardy Mountaineers at Alpine Club Camp Had Thrilling Times," *Edmonton Journal*, 28 August 1926.

Harkin to W.W. Cory, 8 April 1925.

"Highest of Canadian Rockies Is Conquered by Expedition of Amateur Alpine Climbers,"
       The Globe, 15 July 1925.

"Mount Logan: The attack begins on Canada's mighty peak," *Edmonton Journal*, 30 May
       1925.

"Mt. Logan Conquered! An epic of Canadian heroism, victory over fearful odds," *Calgary
       Daily Herald*, 22 August 1925.

"Off to Attack King of Canadian Peaks," *New York Times Magazine*, 3 May 1925.

"Will Mount Logan Be Conquered?" *Montreal Daily Star*, 7 February 1925.

VOL. 102, FILE U36-1, PART 5:

"Alberta Needs More Tourists: Mountain Attractions," *The Albertan*, 5 May 1939.

"Columbia Icefield Site of Alpine Club Camp," *Edson-Jasper Signal*, 31 March 1938.

Harkin to A.O. Wheeler, 22 September 1933.

Rogers to Wates, 28 November 1932.

VOL. 107, FILE U125, PART 1:

A. McKay to Minister, n.d.

A. Sibbald to Minister of the Interior, 14 August 1923.

Christina E. Henry to Minister, 21 November 1923.

D.J.M. McGeary to Minister, 10 October 1923.

E.J. MacKenzie to Minister, 8 November 1923.

Harold Parr to Minister, 30 August 1923.

Rupert Reid to Minister, n.d.

Sibbald to Harkin, 9 August 1923.

W.J. Campbell to Minister, 29 August 1923.

VOL. 170, FILE U125-5, PART 1, PASSIM.

VOL. 171, FILE U125-17, PART 1:

J.G. Perdue to the Parks and Recreation Association Annual Convention at Fort William,
       11 September 1947.

VOL. 189, FILE U36-1, PART 1:

Homer Robinson Letters, 1946–48

J.R.B. Coleman to Smart, 4 May 1951.

O. Wheeler to James Smart, 19 March 1951.

Smart to Wheeler, 28 March 1951.

Smart to Superintendents, 28 March 1951.

Stronach to Smart, 13 April 1949, see note to Deputy Minister, 16 April 1949.

VOL. 189, FILE U50-1-1:

Assistant Deputy Minister to Harkin, 31 August 1934.

Cuthbertson to Murphy, 16 August 1934.

Cuthbertson to Parks Branch, 7 September 1934.

H.A. Young to Superintendents of Banff, Jasper, and Yoho, 26 May 1952.

Harkin to Cuthbertson, 15 July 1935.

Harkin to Cuthbertson, 19 September 1934.

Harkin to Gibson, 29 August 1934.

H.E. Sampson to T.G. Murphy, n.d.

L.C. Wilson to Robert Winters, 17 February 1953.

R.J. Cuthbertson to J.B. Harkin, 28 March 1935.

VOL. 238, FILE 33-4-4, PART 3:
Banff Electric Power-Lake Minnewanka Power Project Calgary Power 1941–48.

VOL. 491, FILE R39-5-2:
Banff Citizens Council to Park Commissioner Harkin, telegram, 12 September 1922.
"Banff Objects to Lake Minnewanka's Level Being Raised," *Calgary Daily Herald*, 27 July
    1922.
"Will Not Permit Minnewanka Levels Changed," *Morning Albertan*, 29 January 1923.

VOL. 505, FILE B39-8, PART 1:
Spray Lakes Power Development 1946–1949.

VOL. 539, FILE B39-5A:
Account of Cascade Power Development 1941.

VOL. 539, FILE B39-8, PART 1:
Spray Lakes Power Development Water Diversion 1948–1955.

VOL. 539, FILE B39-8, PART 9:
C.D. Howe to MacKinnon, 15 June 1948.
Ernest Manning to James A. MacKinnon, 21 May 1948.
J.A. MacKinnon to Walker, 22 November 1948.
MacKinnon to Howe, 25 May 1948.
Manning to James A. MacKinnon, 18 June 1948.
Manning to W.L.M. King, 23 June 1948.
Manning to MacKinnon, 19 October 1948.
MacKinnon to Manning, 30 October 1948.
R.A. Gibson to J. Smart, 26 October 1948.
R.A. Gibson to Acting Deputy Minister, 2 November 1948.
Revised Memorandum, Spray Lakes Hydro Electric Development and the Calgary Power
    Limited, Ottawa, 14 January 1949.
Selby Walker to R.A. Gibson, 15 November 1948.

VOL. 931, FILE B39-5NC:
"Banff Council Urges Power Plant Support," *Calgary Herald*, 29 November 1940.
"Banff Power Proposal Backed by Trade Board," *Calgary Herald*, 4 December 1940.
Walker to *The Albertan*, 11 September 1940.
Walker to *Calgary Herald*, 5 September 1940.

VOL. 2019, FILE U36-1, PART 6:
O. Smart to Wheeler, 25 March 1952.
O. Wheeler to Smart, 20 October 1951.
O. Wheeler to J. Smart, 17 March 1952.

VOL. 2019, FILE U36-1, PART 7:
D.B. Coombs to Chief, 1 March 1962.
H. Green to W. Dinsdale, 10 July 1961.
J.H. Atkinson to Chief of National Parks Service, 7 February 1962.

VOL. 2019, FILE U36-1, PART 8:
S.F. Kun, Assistant Chief of National Park Operations to A.J. Reeve, National Parks
    Assistant Director, 10 August 1967.

VOL. 2243, FILE Y16-3, PART 1:

A.O. Wheeler to Roche, 9 February 1914.

Crerar to Mr. Whitaker, 28 July 1944.

Douglas to Harkin, 21 February 1912.

E.O. Wheeler to J.A. Hutchinson, 30 April 1953.

J.B. Harkin to A.O. Wheeler, 10 March 1914.

O. Wheeler to Hutchinson, 18 April 1953.

Lake O'Hara–Elizabeth Parker Hut 1908–54, passim.

VOL. 2248, FILE Y16-26:

Lake O'Hara–Elizabeth Parker Hut, 1928–56.

VOL. 2249, FILE Y16-40, PART 1:

C.E. Doak to Chief of National Parks Branch, 2 April 1958.

E.O. Wheeler to Smart, 11 February 1953.

E.O. Wheeler to J. Smart, 27 February 1953.

J. Smart to Superintendent Steeves, 28 December 1951.

J. Smart to Oliver Wheeler, 18 February 1953.

Upper Little Yoho Valley–Stanley Mitchell Hut, 1937–58.

Wheeler to Steeves, 31 January 1953.

LAC, Maurice Hall Haycock Fonds

accn. 1993-0193, ISN#213897, "Yukon 1967."

LAC/NFTSA, 20th Century-Fox Film Corporation Collection

Alpine Climbers in Canada, (Fox, n.d.), 35mm sil b&w ans print, acc. no. 1981-0152,
    no. 8203-0265.

**LAC/NFTSA, National Photography Collection, National Film Board of Canada
Collection**

Canada Carries On, (NFB, 1950), 16 mm sd col. print, 11 mins, acc. no. 1977-0207,
    no. 7709-1326.

Alpine Club, Purcell Range, BC, July 1946. Photos by Jack Low. Item nos. 24687, 24609.

Alpine Club, Purcell Range, BC, July 1946. Photos by Jack Low. Item nos. 24587–690.

▲ Trent University Archives

Professor John Marsh Fonds, 1971–1999. http://www.trentu.ca/admin/library/
    archives/03-002.htm. Accessed 16 November 2010.

▲ University of Alberta Archives

William Pearce Collection, accn. 74-169-421

A.O. Wheeler to W. Pearce, 18 May 1923.

A.O. Wheeler to W. Pearce, 24 May 1923.

F.W. Godsal to William Pearce, 19 May 1923.

Godsal to Pearce, 24 June 1923.

Godsal to T.O. West, Calgary ACC Chair, 29 May 1923.

Pearce to Godsal, 14 May 1923.

Wheeler to *Calgary Daily Herald*, 8 June 1923.

W.J.S. Walker and T.B. Moffat, "National Parks and Power Sites," news clipping.

▲ University of Calgary Special Collections

Calgary Power Ltd. *Report*. March 1930.

Calgary Power Ltd. *Alberta: Province of Opportunity*. Calgary: Calgary Power, 1958.

▲ Whyte Museum of the Canadian Rockies (WMCR) Archives

M113, ACCESSION 1947, FOLDER 6:

W.F. Lothian, "James Bernard Harkin: A Brief Biographical Sketch," Ottawa, 31 October
1972.

Alpine Club of Canada Collection, M200/s6/v14

ACCN. 6375, BOX 2:
"Mountain Manners."

ACCN. 6375, BOX 3:
"YACE List of Participants in First and Second Camps," 25 May 1967.
AC *List of Members*, 1976.
AC *Alpine Club of Canada Constitution and List of Members*, 1921; 1925; 1933; 1967; 1976;
1907–58.

AC O 54:
"Canadian Alpinists' Brilliant Conquest of Mount Logan: Expedition Added Greatly to the
Store of Geographical and Meteorological Knowledge." *Natural Resources Canada* 4,
no. 9 (September 1925).

AC O 61:
Wheeler to Cory, n.d.

AC O 64:
Craig to Cory, 20 December 1924.

AC 00M/001:
Mitchell to Bell, 16 September 1926.
Mitchell to Bell, 3 November 1926.
Mitchell to Bell, 30 December 1926.
Mitchell to Bell, 12 January 1927.
Mitchell to Bell, 26 October 1927.

AC 00M/002:
Bell to Mitchell, 6 September 1927.
Bell to Mitchell, 4 October 1927.
Bell to Mitchell, 18 August 1928.
J.A. Buckham to F.C. Bell, 19 September 1927.
Mitchell to Bell, 5 September 1927.
Mitchell to Bell, 28 September 1927.
Mitchell to Bell, 25 January 1928.
Mitchell to Bell, 31 August 1928.
Stanley Mitchell to Fred Bell, 9 August 1927.

AC 00M/003:

H. Yamasaki to F.C. Bell, 14 March 1928.

H. Yamasaki to F.C. Bell, 1 May 1928.

Mitchell to Bell, 1 February 1928.

Mitchell to Bell, 2 March 1928.

Mitchell to Bell, 2 April 1928.

Mitchell to Bell, 12 April 1928.

AC 00M/004:

Mitchell to Moffat, 22 August 1928.

Mitchell to Moffat, 3 September 1928.

Moffat to Mitchell, 4 September 1928.

Mitchell to Moffat, 26 September 1928.

Mitchell to Moffat, 5 November 1928.

Moffat to Mitchell, 19 November 1928.

AC 00M/005:

Mitchell to Moffat, 8 December 1928.

Mitchell to Moffat, 14 March 1929.

Moffat to Mitchell, 18 March 1929.

Mitchell to Moffat, 21 March 1929.

AC 00M/006:

A.O. Wheeler to Parker, 6 May 1906.

A.O. Wheeler to William Whyte, 31 March 1910.

Mitchell to Moffat, 4 April 1929.

Mitchell to Moffat, 16 April 1929.

Mitchell to Moffat, 30 April 1929.

Mitchell to T.B. Moffat, 20 May 1929.

Mitchell to Moffat, 21 June 1929.

AC 00M/007:

Mitchell to Moffat, 16 September 1929.

Mitchell to Moffat, 10 October 1929.

Mitchell to Moffat, 4 December 1929.

Mitchell to Moffat, 27 December 1929.

Mitchell to Moffat, 21 January 1930.

AC 00M/008:

ACC Candidates for Election, n.d., c. March 1930.

Mitchell to Grassi, n.d., c. April 1930.

Mitchell to Moffat, 11 February 1930.

Mitchell to Moffat, 29 April 1930.

Tweedy to Moffat, 27 May 1930.

AC 00M/009:

Mitchell to Moffat, 18 July 1930.

Mt. Little Climb, 30 July 1930.

AC 00M/010:

Mitchell to Sampson, 18 October 1930.

Sampson to Tweedy, 26 August 1930.

Sampson to Tweedy, 3 October 1930.

AC 00M/011:

Sampson to Tweedy, 25 February 1931.

Sampson to Tweedy, 4 March 1931.

Tweedy to Sampson, 18 April 1931.

Tweedy to Sibbald, 26 May 1931.

AC 00M/012:

Sampson to Tweedy, 31 December 1931.

Sampson to Tweedy, 12 January 1932.

Tweedy to Sibbald, 12 January 1932.

AC 00M/013:

Stanley Mitchell to H.E. Sampson, 26 February 1932.

Tweedy to Sampson, 2 January 1931.

Tweedy to Sampson, 20 June 1932.

Tweedy to Sampson, 5 July 1932.

ACC 00M/015:

ACC Camp Costs Summary 1930–32.

McCoubrey to Tweedy, 5 May 1933.

McCoubrey to Management Committee, 31 May 1933.

McCoubrey to Management Committee, 5 June 1933.

McCoubrey to Tweedy, 17 April 1933.

McCoubrey to Tweedy, 5 May 1933.

Tweedy to McCoubrey, 26 May 1933.

AC 00M/016:

List of Members in Arrears, 1 October 1933.

McCoubrey to Tweedy, 20 July 1933.

McCoubrey to Tweedy, 1 December 1933.

McCoubrey to Tweedy, 8 December 1933.

Tweedy to McCoubrey, 20 July 1933.

Tweedy to McCoubrey, 25 July 1933.

Tweedy to McCoubrey, 30 August 1933.

AC 00M/017:

McCoubrey to Tweedy, 30 January 1934.

Tweedy to McCoubrey, 6 February 1934.

AC 00M/018:

Contract between Tweedy and ACC, 1 November 1932.

Jack Hargreaves to McCoubrey, 5 March 1934.

McCoubrey to Tweedy, 9 April 1934.

McCoubrey to Tweedy, 7 June 1934.

McCoubrey to Tweedy, 27 June 1934.

Osborne Scott to McCoubrey, 13 March 1934.

Tweedy to McCoubrey, 31 March 1934.

Tweedy to McCoubrey, 30 August 1933.

Tweedy to McCoubrey, 23 March 1934.

Tweedy to McCoubrey, 10 April 1934.

AC 00M/019:
Sibbald to Tweedy, 17 August 1934.

Tweedy to Sibbald, 28 December 1934.

AC 00M/020:
Tweedy to Sibbald, 12 May 1935.

AC 00M/021:
Sibbald to Tweedy, 11 June 1935.

AC 00M/022:
Tweedy to Sibbald, 17 April 1936.

Tweedy to Sibbald, 2 July 1936.

AC 00M/023:
Sibbald to Tweedy, 3 April 1937.

Tweedy to Sibbald, 18 March 1937.

Tweedy to Sibbald, 21 May 1937.

AC 00M/025:
Tweedy to Wates, 15 November 1938.

Tweedy to Wates, 6 January 1939.

Wates to Tweedy, 10 January 1939.

AC 00M/027:
Wates to Tweedy, 25 September 1939.

Tweedy to Wates, 20 November 1939.

Tweedy to Wates, 4 January 1940.

Tweedy to Wates, 7 March 1940.

AC 00M/0028:
Tweedy to Wates, 13 March 1940.

Tweedy to Wates, 21 March 1940.

AC 00M/029:
Gibson et al. to Executive Board, n.d. 1940.

Wates to Tweedy, 14 November 1940.

AC 00M/030:
Tweedy to Wates, 22 January 1940.

Tweedy to Wates, 8 March 1941.

AC 55-7:
Frank Freeborn Albums, 1911.

AC 90 F97-121
Membership Applications.

Cyndi Smith Fonds

S41/2 Sound Recording, Cassette Side 1, Interview Cyndi Smith with Margaret Fleming, c. 1980s.

David Fisher Papers, M200

M200/ACCN. 6375, BOX 3:

Eric Brooks to Dave Fisher, 6 May 1967.

David Fisher to Jean Chrétien, 2 March 1971.

David Fisher to J.R. Chalker, 27 July 1971.

David Fisher to Phyllis Munday, 13 February 1968.

David Ross to D.R. Fisher, 3 December 1968.

G.F. Delaney to D.R. Fisher, 1 December 1970.

Hodgson to Fisher, 2 December 1968.

Hodgson to Fisher, 14 September 1971.

J. Smith to D.R. Fisher, 4 August 1971.

Jean Alarie to D. Fisher, 9 August 1971.

L.J. Wallace to D. Fisher, 10 August 1971.

"A National Park in the Cumberland Peninsula of Baffin Island: A brief prepared by the Alpine Club of Canada, Ottawa, Ontario, January 25, 1972."

"A National Park in the Yukon: A brief submitted by the Conservation Committee to the Board of Management of the Alpine Club of Canada," Edmonton, Alberta, 18 January 1971.

P.B. Howard to D. Fisher, 4 August 1971.

"Ragged Range National Park: A Proposal to National and Historic Parks Branch, Department of Indian Affairs and Northern Development from The Alpine Club of Canada," David R. Fisher, President, n.d., draft version.

Yukon Territorial Government and the Alpine Club of Canada, et al., "Yukon Alpine Centennial Expedition: A Proposal for a Sporting and Mountain Exploration Activity among the Highest Mountains of Canada, The Icefield Ranges of the Saint Elias Mountains in Celebration of the Centennial of Confederation of Canada 1967," January 1966.

Lillian Gest Collection

ACC Camp in Paradise Valley 1933, (Gest, 1933), 16mm sil b&w film, no. 51421/NF-13.

▲ **Yukon Archives**

file 8, series 1, GOV 2274, John O. Livesey to H.J. Taylor, 24 May 1968.

Government of Canada Annual Reports (GCAR)

Department of Indian Affairs and Northern Development, 1959–60, 1969–70.

Department of the Interior, 1911–32.

Department of Mines, 1944–45.

Department of Mines and Resources, 1944–46.

Department of Northern Affairs and National Resources, 1959–60.

Department of Resources and Development, 1949–50, March 31, 1950.

Report of the Department of Mines and Resources March 31, 1945; March 31, 1946.

Secondary Literature

Abella, Irving M. *A Coat of Many Colours: Two Centuries of Jewish Life in Canada*. Toronto, ON: Key Porter Books, 1999.

Albright, Horace M. *The Birth of the National Parks Service: The Founding Years, 1913–33*. Salt Lake City, UT: Howe Bros., 1985.

Alford, Monty. *The Raven and the Mountaineer: Explorations of the St. Elias Mountains*. Surrey, BC: Hancock House, 2005.

———. "South Summit of Mount Vancouver ('Good Neighbour Peak')." *CAJ* 51 (1968): 37.

Allen, E. John B. "Sierra 'Ladies' on Skis in Gold Rush California." *Journal of Sport History* 17 (Winter 1990): 347–53.

Alpine Club of Canada. "Backcountry Huts." http://www.alpineclubofcanada.ca/facility/info.html. Accessed 9 November 2013.

———. "Brief to the Four Mountain Parks Planning Programme." Edmonton, AB: 30 May 1983. In "Letters and Briefs from Four Mountain Parks Planning Program 1983 Public Session." Calgary, AB: Parks Canada Western Regional Office, 1983.

———. *Red Book*. 1967.

Altmeyer, George. "Three Ideas of Nature in Canada, 1893–1914." *Journal of Canadian Studies* 11 (August 1976): 21–36.

Anderson, H. Allen. *The Chief: Ernest Thompson Seton and the Changing West*. College Station, TX: Texas A&M University Press, 1986.

Andrews, Mary. "Passport to Paradise: The Alpine Club of Canada Summer Camps." *B.C. Historical News* 24, 2 (Spring 1991): 19–27.

Andruschuk, Sue. *TransAlta Utilities: 75 Years of Progress*. Calgary, AB: TransAlta Utilities, 1986.

Appadurai, Ajun. *Modernity at Large*. Minneapolis, MN: University of Minnesota Press, 1996.

Arctic Institute of North America (AINA). "Exploring Baffin Island: The Baird Expeditions." http://www.ucalgary.ca/arcticexpedition/baffin. Accessed 17 November 2009.

———. "Northern Highlights of Centennial." http://pubs.aina.ucalgary.ca/arctic/Arctic204222.pdf. Accessed 7 May 2010.

Armstrong, Christopher, and H.V. Nelles. "Competition vs. Convenience: Federal Administration of Bow River Waterpowers, 1906–13." In *The Canadian West: Social Change and Economic Development*, edited by Henry C. Klassen. Calgary, AB: University of Calgary, Comprint Publishing, 1977.

———. *Monopoly's Moment: The Organization and Regulation of Canadian Utilities, 1830–1930*. Philadelphia, PA: Temple University Press, 1986.

Baldwin, John. "A History of Ski Mountaineering in the Coast Mountains." *CAJ* 66 (1983): 24–25.

Bale, John. "Human Geography and the Study of Sport." In *Handbook of Sport Studies*, edited by Jay J. Coakley and Eric Dunning. London: Sage, 2002.

———. *Landscapes of Modern Sport*. London: Leicester University Press, 1994.

———. "Space, Place and Body Culture: Yi-Fu Tuan and a Geography of Sport." *Geografiska Annaler, Series B, Human Geography* 78, 3 (1996): 163–71.

Barman, Jean. *Growing Up British in British Columbia: Boys in Private Schools*. Vancouver, BC: University of British Columbia Press, 1984.

Bayers, Peter L. *Imperial Ascent: Mountaineering, Masculinity and Empire*. Boulder, CO: University of Colorado Press, 2003.

BC Parks Kootenay District. *Management Plan for Bugaboo Provincial Park, March 1999*. Wasa, BC: British Columbia Ministry of Environment, Lands, and Parks.

Bell, Catherine. "'Performance' and other Analogies." In *The Performance Studies Reader*, edited by Henry Bial. London: Routledge, 2007.

Bella, Leslie. *Parks for Profit*. Montreal, QC: Harvest House, 1987.

Bella, Leslie, and Susan Markham. "Parks First: Patriotic Canadians from Coast to Coast in Support of National Parks." *Canadian Parks/Recreation Association* 42 (December 1984): 15–16.

Bennett, Russell H. "The Ski Ascent of Snow Dome." *CAJ* 19 (1931): 107–10.

Berg, Lawrence, Terry Fenge, and Philip Dearden. "The Role of Aboriginal Peoples in National Park Designation, Planning, and Management in Canada." In *Parks and Protected Areas in Canada: Planning and Management*, 225–55. Toronto, ON: Oxford University Press, 1993.

Berger, Carl. *Science, God, and Nature in Victorian Canada*. Toronto, ON: University of Toronto Press, 1985.

———. *The Sense of Power: Studies in the Ideas of Canadian Imperialism 1867–1914*. Toronto, ON: University of Toronto Press, 1976.

Betke, Carl. "Stewart, Charles." In *The Canadian Encyclopedia*. Edmonton, AB: Hurtig, 1988.

Binnema, Theodore, and Melanie Niemi, "'Let the Line Be Drawn Now': Wilderness, Conservation, and the Exclusion of Aboriginal People from Banff National Park in Canada." *Environmental History* 11, 4 (October 2006): 724–50.

Birkett, Bill, and Bill Peascod. *Women Climbing: 200 Years of Achievement*. Seattle, WA: The Mountaineers; London: A & C Black, 1989.

Blunt, Alison. *Travel, Gender, and Imperialism: Mary Kingsley and West Africa*. New York: Guilford Press, 1994.

Bold, Christine. *Selling the Wild West: Popular Western Fiction, 1860 to 1960*. Bloomington: Indiana University Press, 1987.

Boles, Glen. "Logan, Mount." In *The Canadian Encyclopedia*, 1st edition, edited by James H. Marsh. Edmonton, AB: Hurtig, 1985.

Boswell, Pat. "Clubhouse." *The Gazette* 82 (November 1973): 3.

Bothwell, Robert, and William Kilbourn. *C.D. Howe: A Biography*. Toronto, ON: McClelland & Stewart, 1980.

Bouchier, Nancy. *For the Love of the Game: Amateur Sport in Small-town Ontario, 1838–1895*. Montreal, QC: McGill-Queen's University Press, 2003.

Brendon, Piers. *Thomas Cook: 150 Years of Popular Tourism*. London: Secker & Warburg, 1991.

Bridgland, M.P. "Report, Yoho Camp." *CAJ* 1, 1 (1907): 171–73.

British Columbia Royal Commission on Forest Resources. *Report of the Commissioner, Gordon McG. Sloan, Relating to the Forest Resources of British Columbia*. Vols. 1 and 2. Victoria, BC: D. McDiarmid, 1956.

Broda, Fips. "Centennial Peak." *CAJ* 51 (1968) 42–49.

Brower, Jennifer. *Lost Tracks: National Buffalo Park, 1909–1939*. Edmonton, AB: Athabasca University Press, 2008.

Brown, Doug. "Fleshing-out Field Notes: Prosaic, Poetic and Picturesque Representations of Canadian Mountaineering, 1906–1940." *Journal of Sport History* 30, 3 (Fall 2003): 347–71.

Brown, Robert C. "The Doctrine of Usefulness." In *The Canadian National Parks: Today and Tomorrow*, edited by J.G. Nelson and R.C. Scace. Calgary, AB: University of Calgary Press, 1968.

———. "The Doctrine of Usefulness: Natural Resource and National Park Policy in Canada, 1887–1914." In *Canadian Parks in Perspective*, edited by J.G. Nelson. Montreal, QC: Harvest House, 1970.

Brown-John, C. Lloyd. "Canada's National Parks Policy: From Bureaucrats to Collaborative Managers." Paper presented at the Canadian Political Science Association Annual Conference, Toronto, ON, 1–3 June 2006. http://www.cpsa-acsp.ca/template_e. cfm?folder=conference&page_name=agm-papers-2006.htm. Accessed 28 November 2008.

Browne, Belmore. *The Conquest of Mount McKinley*. Boston, MA: Houghton Mifflin, 1956.

Bruce, C.G. *The Assault on Mount Everest, 1922*. London: Edward Arnold, 1923.

Butling, Helen. "Mt. Saskatchewan." *The Kootenay Karabiner* (Fall 1967): 10, 16.

Calcaterra, Paul. "Ode to a Mountain Stove." *CAJ* (1957): 81.

The Calgary Albertan. "Alpine Club Denies." 30 August 1930, 4.

———. "Alpine Club Has Wide Objective—Members Point Out That it is Not Close Limited in Scope." 30 August 1930, 3.

———. "Making Themselves Ridiculous." 25 August 1930, 4.

Calgary Daily Herald. "Amateur Climbers Battle Storms and Extreme Cold to Scale Mount Logan: Canadian Leads Climbers to Logan Peak." 14 July 1925, 1.

———. "Colonization Must Keep Pace With Construction of Irrigation Projects." 7 March 1922.

———. "Influx of Settlers from Western States is Plainly Forecast." 4 March 1922, 1.

———. "Irrigation Projects in Alberta are Enumerated." 8 March 1922.

———. "Legislation Aiming to Aid Colonization Where Irrigation is Proposed." 9 March 1922.

———. "Many Problems Face the Future of Irrigation." 4 March 1922, 7.

———. "Minnewanka Dam Discussed." 22 August 1930, 13.

———. "Province Will Back MacLeod Irrigation Plan." 4 March 1922, 1.

The Calgary Herald. "W.J. Selby Walker, Sanctuary Founder Dies." 22 July 1952, 1–2.

Cameron, Meghan Elizabeth. "'How the Dominion Heard the Cry': The Early History of the Canadian Save the Children Fund, 1922–1946." MA thesis, University of Guelph, 2001.

Cameron, Ross D. "Tom Thomson, Anti-Modernism, and the Ideal of Manhood." *Journal of Canadian Historical Association* 10 (1999): 185–208.

Campbell, Claire Elizabeth. *Shaped by the West Wind: Nature and History in Georgian Bay*. Vancouver, BC: University of British Columbia Press, 2005.

Campbell, James. *This is the Beat Generation: New York, San Francisco, Paris*. Berkeley, CA: University of California Press, 2001.

Campbell, Sheila. "Branding the Last Best West: Regionalism, Tourism, and the Construction of the Tourist Gaze in Alberta, 1905–1940." MA thesis, University of Alberta, 2005.

Canada. *In Trust for Tomorrow: A Management Framework for Four Mountain Parks*. Ottawa, ON: 1988.

_____. National and Historic Sites Branch. *Preliminary Report of the Public Meeting on Banff, Jasper, Yoho, and Kootenay National Parks at Golden, British Columbia, May 10, 1971*. Ottawa, ON: National Historic Parks and Sites Branch, Department of Indian Affairs and Northern Development, 1971.

_____. *Transcript of Proceedings of Public Hearings on Banff, Jasper, Yoho, and Kootenay National Parks, April 19 to 26, 1971, at Calgary, Edmonton and Vancouver*. Vols. I–V. Ottawa, ON: National Historic Parks and Sites Branch, 1971.

_____. Office of the Auditor General. *Report of the Auditor General to the House of Commons for the Year Ended 1928*.

_____. Office of the Auditor General. *Report of the Auditor General to the House of Commons for the Year 1931-32*.

_____. *House of Commons Debates*, 1 June 1923. 3442.

_____. *House of Commons Debates*, 14 June 1923. 3939–3940.

_____. *House of Commons Debates*, 10 April 1924. 1259–1260.

"Canada's Past Matters." http://www.canadaspastmatters.ca/. Accessed 29 March 2013.

Canadian Alpine Journal (*CAJ*). "ACC Annual General Meeting, 1968." 52 (1969): 108–21.

_____. "Banff to Mt. Assiniboine, A Walking or Riding Tour for Outdoorspeople, 1924." Advertisement (1923): n.p.

_____. "Albert H. MacCarthy." 40 (1957): 64–65.

_____. "Alexander Addison McCoubrey." (1941): 120–26.

_____. "Alpine Climbing Camps." 59 (1976): 151.

_____. "Alpine Equipment," 32 (1949): 140d.

_____. "Andrew S. Sibbald," 29, 2 (1945): 274–77.

_____. "Annual Meeting 1926," 16 (1926–1927): 247–48.

_____. "Arthur Oliver Wheeler." 27 (1940): 205–12.

_____. "Arthur Oliver Wheeler, 1860–1945." 29, 1 (1944–1945): 140–46.

_____. "Arthur Philemon Coleman." 26 (1938): 131–32.

_____. "Banff to Mt. Assiniboine: A Walking or Riding Tour for Outdoorspeople, 1924." 13 (1923): 274d.

_____. "Brigadier Sir Edward Oliver Wheeler." 45 (1962): 160–63.

_____. "Christian Häsler, 1889–1940." 27, 1 (1939): 231–34.

_____. "Club Proceedings." 31 (1948): 241–44.

_____. "Club Proceedings." 29, 1 (1944): 165–68.

_____. "Club Proceedings and Club News." 18 (1929): 129.

_____. "Club Proceedings and Club News." 23 (1934–1935): 118–20.

_____. "The Columbia Icefields Camp." 26 (1938): 145–47.

_____. "Constitution." 1, 1 (1907): 178–81.

_____. "Cyril Geoffrey Wates, 1884–1946." 29, 2 (1946): 277–81.

_____. "David Henry Laird." 36 (1953): 129.

_____. "Edna Caroline Kelley." 36 (1953): 130–31.

_____. "Edouard Gaston Deville." 14 (1924): 131–33.

_____. "Elizabeth Parker." 29, 1 (1944): 122–27.

_____. "Emmie Brooks." 73 (1990): 92.

_____. "Fred Brigden." 40 (1957): 66–67.

_____. "Frederick William Godsal." 23 (1934–1935): 90–93.

_____. "General Mountaineering Camps." 59 (1976): 150.

_____. "Graduating Members," 1, 1 (1907): 193–96.

_____. "Interim Report of the Ski Committee." 22 (1933): 240.

_____. "James Outram." (1925): 127-28.

_____. "John Brett." 66 (1983): 53.

_____. "John L. Dudra." 42 (1959): 92.

_____. "List of Members." 1, 1 (1907): 182-92.

_____. "Local Section Officers." 40 (1957): vii.

_____. "Local Sections." 51 (1968): v.

_____. "Major W.J. Selby Walker." 36 (1953): 128.

_____. "Members on War Service." (1944 and 1945): 175-76.

_____. "Mt. Assiniboine Camp." 36 (1953): 173-74.

_____. "Mount Eisenhower." 29, 2 (1945): 305-06.

_____. "Mrs. A.L. Yeigh." 44 (1961): 135.

_____. "Peyto Lake Camp." 32 (1949): 138-39.

_____. "Phyllis Munday." 74 (1991): 98-99.

_____. "Post-war Development of National Parks." 29, 1 (1944): 168-74.

_____. "Report of the 1910 Camp." 3 (1911): 189-95.

_____. "Report of the 1911 Camp." 4 (1912): 145-47.

_____. "Report of the 1912 Camp." 5 (1913): 130-37.

_____. "Report of the Secretary." 1, 1 (1907): 164-66.

_____. "Report of the Secretary." 1, 2 (1908): 320-23.

_____. "Report Yoho Camp." 1, 1 (1907): 169-70.

_____. "Ski Camps." 59 (1976): 151.

_____. "Stanley Hamilton Mitchell." 27, 1 (1939): 101-06.

_____. "Statement of Treasurer." 3 (1911): 197-98.

_____. "Viking Nylon Climbing Rope." 36 (1953): 174f.

_____. "Wharton Richard Tweedy." 48 (1965): 208-10.

_____. "Where to Meet in 1925." 13 (1923): 275.

_____. "World of Your Own." 36 (1953): n.p.

_____. "Yoho Camp Circular Issued," 1, 1 (1907): 170.

_____. "Yukon Alpine Centennial Expedition Team Members for Centennial Climb." 50 (1967): 1.

Canadian Hostelling Association. *Fifty Years of Canadian Hostelling.* Calgary, AB: Detselig Enterprises, 1988.

Canadian Parks Council. *Aboriginal Peoples and Canada's Parks and Protected Areas, Case Studies* (n.d.): 91-94.

Canadian Wildlife Service. *Some Ecological Considerations Relating to the Provisional Master Plans for Jasper and Banff National Parks, Alberta and Kootenay and Yoho National Parks, British Columbia.* Edmonton, AB: Canadian Wildlife Service, April 1969.

Carpé, Allen. "The Mount Logan Adventure." *American Alpine Journal* 2 (1933): 85-86.

_____. "Observations." *CAJ* 15 (1925): 82.

Cavell, Edward. *Legacy in Ice: The Vaux Family and the Canadian Alps.* Banff, AB: Whyte Foundation, 1983.

CBC News. "Syncrude to Pay $3M Penalty for Duck Deaths." 22 October 2010, http://www. cbc.ca/news/canada/edmonton/syncrude-guilty-in-alberta-duck-deaths-1.882380. Accessed 4 December 2013.

"Chasing Ice." http://www.chasingice.com/about-the-film/credits/. Accessed 3 December 2013.

Clark, Douglas A., Shaun Fluker, and Lee Risby. "Deconstructing Ecological Integrity Policy in Canadian National Parks." In *Transforming Parks and Protected Areas: Policy and Governance in a Changing World*, edited by Kevin S. Hanna, Douglas A. Clark, and D. Scott Slocombe. New York: Routledge, 2008.

Clark, Ronald W. *Men, Myths and Mountains*. New York: Thomas Y. Crowell, 1976.

Cleare, John. *Collins Guide to Mountains and Mountaineering*. London: Collins, 1979.

Coates, Ken. *Land of the Midnight Sun: A History of the Yukon*. Montreal, QC: McGill-Queen's University Press, 2005.

Cohen, Michael P. *The History of the Sierra Club 1892–1970*. San Francisco, CA: Sierra Club, 1988.

Cole, C.L., Michael D. Giardina, and David L. Andrews. "Michel Foucault: Studies of Power and Sport." In *Sport and Modern Social Theorists*, edited by Richard Giulianotti. New York: Palgrave Macmillan, 2004.

Coleman, Annie Gilbert. *Ski Style: Sport and Culture in the Rockies*. Lawrence, KS: University Press of Kansas, 2004.

Cook, Ramsay. *The Regenerators: Social Criticism in Late Victorian English Canada*. Toronto, ON: University of Toronto Press, 1985.

Council of Yukon First Nations. "Champagne and Aishihik First Nation." http://www.cyfn.ca/ournationscafn?noCache=302:1240334101. Accessed 21 April 2009.

———. "Kluane First Nation." http://www.cyfn.ca/ournationskfn?noCache=509:1240334271. Accessed 21 April 2009.

Cowell, Doug. "The Old Lady of Sulphur Mountain: A History of the Alpine Club Banff Clubhouse." *Banff Crag and Canyon*, 24 December 1975.

Crag and Canyon. "Making Themselves Ridiculous." 29 August 1930, 4.

———. "Advisory Council Receive Letter on Lake Minnewanka Dam." 6 December 1940.

Craighead, Charles, and Bonnie Kreps. *Arctic Dreams: The Mardy Murie Story*. Portland, OR: Graphic Arts Center Publishing, 2002.

Crawford, Mary E. "Mountain Climbing for Women." *CAJ* (1909): 86.

Crawshaw, Carol, and John Urry. "Tourism and the Photographic Eye." In *Touring Cultures: Transformations of Travel and Theory*, edited by Chris Rojek and John Urry. London: Routledge, 1997.

Cronon, William. "The Trouble with Wilderness: Or, Getting Back to the Wrong Nature." *Environmental History* 1, 1 (1996): 7–28.

Cruikshank, Julie. *Do Glaciers Listen? Local Knowledge, Colonial Encounters, and Social Imagination*. Vancouver, BC: University of British Columbia Press, 2005.

Culbert, Dick. "Book Reviews: *Expedition Yukon*." *CAJ* 55 (1972): 58.

Cuthbertson, R.J. "Alpine Club Activities: A Description of Chrome Lake Camp in the Eremite Valley." *The Royal Bank Magazine* 158 (May 1935): 4.

Daly, Tom (director). *Ordeal by Ice*. National Film Board of Canada, 1945. http://www.nfb.ca/film/ordeal_by_ice. Accessed 18 January 2010.

Davies, Helen. "The Politics of Participation: A Study of Canada's Centennial Celebration." PHD dissertation, University of Manitoba, 1999.

d'Egville, A.H. "Ski-mountaineering." *CAJ* 19 (1931): 96–99.

de la Barre, Suzanne. "Place Identity, Guides, and Sustainable Tourism in Canada's Yukon Territory." PHD dissertation, University of Alberta, 2009.

Dean, Misao. "The Centennial Voyageur Canoe Pageant as Historical Re-enactment." *Journal of Canadian Studies* 40, 3 (Fall 2006): 43–67.

Dearden Philip, and Rick Rollins. "The Times They Are Still A-Changin'." In *Parks and Protected Areas in Canada: Planning and Management*, 2nd Edition, edited by Philip Dearden and Rick Rollins. Toronto, ON: Oxford University Press, 2002.

Deloria, Philip. *Playing Indian*. New Haven, CT: Yale University Press, 1998.

Denis, Leo G., and J.B. Challies. *Water Powers of Manitoba, Saskatchewan, and Alberta*. Ottawa, ON: Commission of Conservation Canada, Committee on Waters and Water Powers, 1916.

Dick, Lyle. "Epilogue." In *A Century of Parks Canada, 1911–2011*, edited by Claire Elizabeth Campbell. Calgary, AB: University of Calgary Press, 2011.

Donnelly, Peter. "The Invention of Tradition and the (Re) Invention of Mountaineering." In *Method and Methodology in Sport and Cultural History*, edited by Kevin Wamsley. Dubuque, IA: Brown and Benchmark Publishers, 1995.

———. "The Paradox of Parks: Politics of Recreational Land Use Before and After the Mass Trespasses." *Leisure Studies* 5 (1986): 189–99.

———. "Playing with Gravity: Mountains and Mountaineering." In *Sites of Sport: Space, Place, Experience*, edited by Patricia Vertinsky and John Bale. London: Routledge, 2004.

Dudra, J.L. "In Defence of a Piton." *CAJ* 37 (1953): 150–51.

Duffy, Pat. "Climbing over the Ottawa." *CAJ* 40 (1957): 81–84.

Dummit, Chris. "Finding a Place for Father: Selling the Barbeque in Postwar Canada." *Journal of the Canadian Historical Association* 9, 1 (1998): 209–23.

———. "Risk on the Rocks: Modernity, Manhood, and Mountaineering in Postwar British Columbia." *BC Studies*, 141 (Spring 2004): 3–29.

Dunnell, Basil. "The First Steele Glacier Camp, 1967." *CAJ* 51 (1968): 104–12.

EcoJustice.ca. "Environmentalists Spur Government to Prosecute Over Duck Deaths in Tar Sands: Province and Feds Take Over Charges Against Syncrude." 18 January 2010, http://www.ecojustice.ca/media-centre/press-releases/environmentalists-spur-government-to-prosecute-over-duck-deaths-in-the-tar-sands/?searchterm=sierra. Accessed 4 December 2013.

Ellis, Reuben. *Vertical Margins: Mountaineering and the Landscapes of Neo-imperialism*. Madison, WI: University of Wisconsin Press, 2001.

Engel, Claire Eliane. *A History of Mountaineering in the Alps*. Westport, CT: Greenwood Press, 1950.

Fee, Everett J. "Manitobans in the Mountains: Fifty Years of Ski Mountaineering." *CAJ* 66 (1983): 19–20.

Fentress, James, and Chris Wickham. *Social Memory*. Cambridge, MA: Blackwell, 1992.

Finkel, Alvin. *The Social Credit Phenomenon in Alberta*. Toronto, ON: University of Toronto Press, 1989.

Finkelstein, Max. *National Parks System Plan*. Hull, QC: Environment Canada, Parks Service, 1990.

Finlay, J.L., and D.N. Sprague. *The Structure of Canadian History*. Scarborough, ON: Prentice Hall Canada, 1984.

Fisher, D.R. "Report on Yukon Alpine Centennial Expedition." *CAJ* 51 (1968): 252–55.

———. "Summary of Climbs from the General Camp." *CAJ* 51 (1968): 129–36.

———. "Summary of the Centennial Climbs." *CAJ* 51 (1968): 97–103.

_____. "Yukon Alpine Centennial Expedition." *CAJ* 51 (1968): 1–33.

Fisher, Marnie, ed. *Expedition Yukon*. Don Mills, ON: Thomas Nelson and Sons, 1971.

Fisher Marnie, and R.W. Sandford, eds. *Expedition Yukon: The 30th Anniversary Celebration*. Canmore, AB: Alpine Club of Canada, 1997.

Foran, Max. *Calgary: An Illustrated History*. Toronto, ON: Lorimer, National Museums of Canada, 1978.

Ford, A.L., and G.H. Whyte. *Hydrometric Surveys in the Provinces of Alberta and Saskatchewan*. Ottawa, ON: Department of the Interior, Reclamation Service, 1921.

Foster, W.W. "Mt. Robson, 1913." *CAJ* 6 (1914–15): 11–28.

_____. "The Story of the Expedition." *CAJ* 15 (1925): 47–58.

_____. "Strathcona Park." *CAJ* 5 (1913): 96–99.

Foucault, Michel. *Discipline and Punish: The Birth of the Prison*. Translated by Alan Sheridan. London: Allen Lane, Penguin Books, 1977.

_____. "The Subject and Power." *Critical Inquiry* 8, 4 (Summer 1982): 777–95.

Fox, Stephen R. *The American Conservation Movement: John Muir and his Legacy*. Madison, WI: University of Wisconsin Press, 1985.

Francis, R. Douglas, and Donald B. Smith, eds. *Destinies: Canadian History Since Confederation*. Toronto, ON: Holt, Rinehart and Winston, 1988.

Fraser, Esther. *Wheeler*. Banff, AB: Summerthought, 1978.

Fuller, Carleton P. "Fortieth Anniversary Camp." *CAJ* 30 (1947): 149–52.

Gampo Abbey. "Death of Harry Habgood." http://www.gampoabbey.org/life/harry-habgood.htm. Accessed 7 March 2010.

Gampo Abbey. "The Fortunate Life of Ani Migme." http://www.gampoabbey.org/newsletter/Lions_Roar_08.pdf. Accessed 7 March 2010.

Garner, Andrew. "Living History: Trees and Metaphors of Identity in an English Forest." *Journal of Material Culture* 9, 1 (March 2004): 87–100.

The Gazette (Alpine Club of Canada newsletter). "1943 Summer Camp." (January 1943): 2.

_____. "1970 Clubhouse Operations." 76 (November 1970): 2.

_____. "Alpine Club Huts." 70 (February 1968): 2.

_____. "Annual Meeting, 1922." (December 1922): 17–18.

_____. "Annual Meeting, 1923." (December 1923): 17–22.

_____. "Annual Meeting, 1926." (1926 and 1927): 248.

_____. "Annual Meeting, 1930." (October 1930): 12.

_____. "The Annual Meeting, 1931." 18 (October 1931): 7.

_____. "The Annual Meeting, 1933." 22 (October 1933): 7.

_____. The Annual Meeting, 1934." 24 (October 1934): 8.

_____. "The Annual Meeting, 1935." (October 1935): 18.

_____. "The Annual Meeting, 1936." 28 (October 1936): 5–6.

_____. "The Annual Meeting, 1937." 30 (October 1937): 7.

_____. "The Annual Meeting, 1938." 32 (November 1938): 12.

_____. "Auditor's Report and Balance Sheet." 17 (June 1931): 20.

_____. "Business Arising." (November 1939): 5.

_____. "Canadian National Parks Association." (December 1923): 8.

_____. "Club and Other Huts." 63 (November 1965): 5.

_____. "Clubhouse." 76 (November 1970): 2.

_____. "Clubhouse." 78 (November 1971): 14.

_____. "Clubhouse Ballot." 75 (May 1970): 1.

———. "Conrad Kain Hut–Bugaboos." 73 (February 1969): 2.

———. "Conservation." 76 (November 1970): 11–12.

———. "Conservation." 80 (November 1972): 16.

———. "Conservation Committee." 74 (November 1969): 3–4.

———. "Conservation Committee." 77 (May 1971): 4.

———. "Contributions to Mt. Logan Expedition." (January 1926): 24.

———. "E.C. Brooks takes the Chair." (January 1942): 14.

———. "Edmonton." 29 (May 1937): 7–8.

———. "Edmonton." 60 (November 1964): 28.

———. "Honourary President's Address." (November 1940): 7.

———. "Honourary President's Address." (November 1943): 6–7.

———. "Hut Committee." (October 1936): 12.

———. "The Hut Committee Report." (October 1935): 20.

———. "Larch Valley Camp, 1923." (December 1923): 14.

———. "A Letter from the President." (January 1942): 14.

———. "A Letter from the President." (November 1944): 3.

———. "Mountain Manners." 79 (May 1972): 6.

———. "Notes from the Sections." (June 1923): 20–21.

———. "Notes from Sections." 31 (June 1938): 12.

———. "President's Message." 77 (May 1971): 1.

———. "Questionnaire Results." 72 (November 1968): 2.

———. "Report of Auditor." 27 (May 1936): 16–17.

———. "Report of Auditor." (June 1938): 19–21.

———. "Report of Auditor." 33 (June 1939): 15–17.

———. "Report of the Hut Fund Committee." 11 (June 1926): 13–14.

———. "Resolution re. Lake Minnewanka." (October 1930): 20–21.

———. "Roger Neave to Members and Associate Members." (May 1968).

———. "Schedules and Report of Auditors." (June 1934): 20–23.

———. "Schedules and Report of Auditors." 25 (June 1935): 13–15, 18.

———. "The Stanley Mitchell Hut." (November 1938): 8.

———. "Stanley Mitchell Hut Fund." (June 1938): 13.

———. "Stanley Mitchell Hut Fund." (November 1938): 26.

———. "Statement of Income and Expenditure." (November 1949): 27.

Geddes, M.D. "The Call of the Alpine." In *Songs of Canadian Climbers*, edited by C.G.
   Wates. Edmonton, AB: Alpine Club of Canada, c. 1922.

Geismar, Haidy, and Heather A. Horst. "Materializing Ethnography." *Journal of Material
   Culture* 9, 1: 6.

Gerson, Jen. "Mountain of Change in Store as Canada's National Parks Aim to Attract
   Mass-Tourism." *National Post*, 31 May 2013, http://news.nationalpost.com/2013/05/31/
   mountain-of-change-in-store-as-canadas-national-parks-aim-to-attract-mass-tourism/.
   Accessed 5 December 2013.

Getty, Ian A.L. "A History of the Human Settlement at Waterton Lakes National Park,
   1800–1937." MA thesis, University of Calgary, March 1971.

Getty, Ian. *A History of Human Settlement at Waterton Lakes National Park, 1800–1937*.
   Ottawa, ON: National Parks Branch, Department of Indian Affairs and Northern
   Development, 1971.

Gibson, E.R. "A Jubilee Message." *CAJ* 39 (1956): 1.

_____. "A Winter Ascent of Mt. Resplendent." *CAJ* 19 (1931): 111–13.

Gibson, R.A. "Department of Mines and Resources Ottawa." *CAJ* 29, 1 (1944): 174.

Gibson, Rex. "Climbs in the Main Bugaboo Group." *CAJ* 30 (1947): 153–60.

_____. "The Saskatchewan Glacier Hut." *CAJ* 29, 2 (1945): 202–03.

_____. "Troop Training in the Rockies." *CAJ* 29, 2 (1945): 177–91.

Gietschier, Steve. "The International Bowling Museum and Hall of Fame." *Journal of Sport History* 31, 2 (Summer 2004): 246–48.

Grant, Shelagh. "Arctic Wilderness—and Other Mythologies." *Journal of Canadian Studies* 32, 2 (1998): 27–42.

Graves, H.J. "Little Yoho Valley Military Camp." *CAJ* 28, 2 (1943): 230–46.

_____. "Ski Climbing." *The Gazette* (June 1930): 5–7.

Gray, James H. *R.B. Bennett: The Calgary Years.* Toronto, ON: University of Toronto Press, 1991.

Great Plains Research Consultants (GPRC). *Banff National Park, 1792–1965: A History.* Ottawa, ON: Parks Canada, 1984. Microfiche Report Series 196.

Green, William Spotswood. *Among the Selkirk Glaciers: Being an Account of a Rough Survey in the Rocky Mountain Regions of British Columbia.* London: Macmillan, 1890.

Greene, B.M., ed. *Who's Who in Canada.* Toronto, ON: International Press, 1936–37.

Greer, Edna H. "The Elizabeth Parker Cabin, Lake O'Hara." *CAJ* 19 (1931): 159–61.

Griffiths, Alison, and Gerry Wingenbach. *Mountain Climbing Guides in Canada: The Early Years.* Unpublished manuscript, Parks Canada, 1977.

Gruff, Andrew. "Editorial." *CAJ* 53 (1970): 45.

Gruneau, Richard S. "Modernization or Hegemony: Two Views on Sport and Social Development." In *Not Just a Game: Essays in Canadian Sport Sociology*, edited by Jean Harvey and Hart Cantelon. Ottawa, ON: University of Ottawa Press, 1988.

Haberl, Keith. *Alpine Huts: A Guide to the Facilities of the Alpine Club of Canada.* Canmore, AB: Alpine Club of Canada, 1995.

Habgood, Harry. "Preservation vs. Use in the National Parks." *CAJ* 55 (1972): 67–68.

_____. "Swan Song from the Conservation Chairman." *The Gazette* 83 (May 1974): 5.

Habgood, Henry Walter. "Dielectric Polarization of Propane, the Butanes, and the Pentanes." PHD dissertation, University of Michigan, 1952.

Hall, M. Ann. *The Girl and the Game: A History of Women's Sport in Canada.* Peterborough, ON: Broadview Press, 2002.

Hancock House Publishers. "Monty Alford." http://www.hancockhouse.com/products/pdfs/RavMou_author%20bio.pdf. Accessed 1 February 2008.

Hansen, Peter H. "Albert Smith, the Alpine Club, and the Invention of Mountaineering in Mid-Victorian Britain." *Journal of British Studies* 34 (July 1995): 300–24.

_____. "Vertical Boundaries, National Identities: British Mountaineering on the Frontiers of Europe and the Empire, 1868–1914." *The Journal of Imperial and Commonwealth History* 24, 1 (January 1996): 48–71.

Hardin, G. "We Must Earn for Ourselves What We Have Inherited." In *Wilderness at the Edge of Knowledge*, edited by M.E. McCloskey. San Francisco, CA: Sierra Club, 1970.

Hargreaves, Jennifer. *Physical Culture, Power, and the Body.* New York: Routledge, 2006.

Harkin, J.B. *The History and Meaning of the National Parks of Canada.* Saskatoon, SK: H.R. Larson, 1957.

Harmon, Carole, ed. *Byron Harmon, Mountain Photographer.* Banff, AB: Altitude, 1992.

Harmon Photography. "Aileen Harmon: Photographer." Banff, AB: n.d. http://www.
wildelementsart.com/wearts/hp.asp?page=Aileen. Accessed 10 March 2008.

Hart, E.J. *Diamond Hitch: The Early Outfitters and Guides of Banff and Jasper*. Banff, AB:
Summerthought, 1989.

———. *J.B. Harkin: Father of Canada's National Parks*. Edmonton, AB: University of Alberta
Press, 2010.

———. *The Selling of Canada: The CPR and the Beginnings of Tourism*. Banff, AB: Altitude,
1983.

Hawkins, W.E. *Electrifying Calgary: A Century of Public and Private Power*. Calgary, AB:
University of Calgary Press, 1987.

Hayter, Roger. *Flexible Crossroads: The Restructuring of British Columbia's Forest Economy*.
Vancouver, BC: University of British Columbia Press, 2000.

Heine, Michael K., and Kevin B. Wamsley, "'Kickfest at Dawson City': Native Peoples and
the Sports of the Klondike Gold Rush." *Sport History Review* 27 (1996): 72–86.

Henderson, Gavin. "James Bernard Harkin: The Father of Canadian National Parks."
Borealis 5, 2 (Fall 1994): 28–33.

Henderson, Stuart. "'While there is Still Time…': J. Murray Gibbon and the Spectacle of
Difference in Three CPR Folk Festivals, 1928–1931." *Journal of Canadian Studies* 39
(Winter 2005): 139–74.

Hessing, Melody, Rebecca Raglon, and Catriona Sandilands. *This Elusive Land: Women
and the Canadian Environment*. Vancouver, BC: University of British Columbia Press,
2005.

Heuer, Karsten. "Wake-up Call." *Alberta Views* (September 2013): 18.

Hickman, M., C.E. Schweger, and T. Habgood, "Lake Wabamun, Alta.: A
Paleoenvironmental Study." *Canadian Journal of Botany* 62 (1984): 1438–65.

Hiebler, Toni. "The Evolution of Karabiners in Alpine History." *Alpine Journal* 74 (1969):
320–23.

Hind, R.C. "E. Rex Gibson, 1892–1957." *CAJ* 41 (1958): 111–14.

Hobsbawm, Eric. "Introduction: Inventing Traditions." In *The Invention of Tradition*, edited
by Eric Hobsbawm and Terence Ranger. Cambridge, UK: Cambridge University Press,
1993.

———. "Mass-Producing Traditions: Europe, 1870–1914." In *The Invention of Tradition*, edited
by Eric Hobsbawm and Terence Ranger. Cambridge, UK: Cambridge University Press,
1993.

Höbusch, H. "Germany's 'Mountain of Destiny': Nanga Parbat and National Self-
Representation." *The International Journal of Sport History* 19, 4 (1 December 2002):
137–68.

Hodgins, Bruce W., and Bernadine Dodge, eds. *Using Wilderness: Essays on the Evolution of
Youth Camping in Ontario*. Peterborough, ON: The Frost Centre, 1992.

"Hon. James M. Morton, Junior," *National Associations of Referees in Bankruptcy*, October
1940, http://heinonline.org/HOL/LandingPage?collection=journals&handle=hein.
journals/ambank15&div=18&id=&page=. Accessed 29 September 2013.

Howard-Bury, C.K. *Mount Everest: The Reconnaissance, 1921*. London: Edward Arnold, 1922.

Howell, Colin. *Blood, Sweat and Cheers: Sport and the Making of Modern Canada*. Toronto,
ON: University of Toronto Press, 2001.

_____. "Borderlands, Baselines, and Bearhunters: Conceptualizing the Northeast as a Sporting Region in the Interwar Period." *Journal of Sport History* 29 (Summer 2002): 251–70.

_____. *Northern Sandlots: A Social History of Maritime Baseball*. Toronto, ON: University of Toronto Press, 1995.

Huel, Raymond. "The CPR and the Promotion of Tourism in Western Canada: Edward Whymper in the Crowsnest Pass." *Prairie Forum* 11, 1 (Spring 1986): 21–32.

_____. "Edward Whymper in the Rockies." Pts. 1 and 2. *Alberta History* 29, 4 (Autumn 1981): 6–17; 30, 1 (Winter 1982): 28–29.

Hunter, Dave. "The Descendants of Robert Orr and Janet Lyle." http://www.islandregister.com/orr1.html. Accessed 21 June 2005.

Hutchinson, Ralph. "Roger Neave." *CAJ* 75 (1992): 117–18.

Irving, R.L.G. "Trends in Mountaineering." *CAJ* 40 (1957): 53–63.

Isaac, Sean. "Editorial: Relevance, Elitism and Cover Shots." *CAJ* 92 (2009): 5.

Jackson Lears, T.J. *No Place for Grace: Antimodernism and the Transformation of American Culture 1880–1920*. New York: Pantheon Books, 1981.

Jasen, Patricia. *Wild Things: Nature, Culture, and Tourism in Ontario, 1790–1914*. Toronto, ON: University of Toronto Press, 1995.

Jessup, Lynda. "The Group of Seven and the Tourist Landscape in Western Canada, or The More Things Change..." *Journal of Canadian Studies* 37, 1 (Spring 2002): 144–79.

_____, ed. *Antimodernism and Artistic Experience: Policing the Boundaries of Modernity*. Toronto, ON: University of Toronto Press, 2001.

Johnston, Margaret E. "Diffusion and Difference: The Subcultural Framework for Mountain Climbing in New Zealand." *Tourism Recreation Research* 18, 1 (1993): 41–43.

Johnston, Margaret, and John Marsh. "The Alpine Club of Canada, Conservation and Parks, 1906 to 1930." *CAJ* 69 (1986): 16–19.

Jones, Chris. *Climbing in North America*. Berkeley, CA: University of California Press, American Alpine Club, 1976.

Jones, Holway R. *John Muir and the Sierra Club: The Battle for Yosemite*. San Francisco, CA: Sierra Club, 1965.

Kain, Conrad. "The First Ascent of Mt. Robson." In *The Canadian Mountaineering Anthology*, edited by Bruce Fairley. Edmonton, AB: Lone Pine Publishing, 1994.

_____. *Where the Clouds Can Go*. Boston, MA: Charles T. Branford, 1954.

Kariel, Herbert, and Pat Kariel. *Alpine Huts in the Rockies, Selkirks and Purcells*. Banff, AB: Alpine Club of Canada, 1986.

Kauffman, Andrew J., and William L. Putnam. *The Guiding Spirit*. Revelstoke, BC: Footprint Publishing, 1986.

Keenleyside, Francis. *Peaks and Pioneers: The Story of Mountaineering*. London: Paul Elek, 1976.

Kelly, Caralyn J. "'Thrilling and Marvelous Experiences': Place and Subjectivity in Canadian Climbing Narratives, 1885–1925." PHD dissertation, University of Waterloo, 2000.

Kelsey, Michael R. *Climbers and Hikers Guide to the World's Mountains*. Springville, UT: Kelsey, 1984.

Kerouac, Jack. *Dharma Bums*. New York: Viking Press, 1958.

Kidd, Bruce. *The Struggle for Canadian Sport*. Toronto, ON: University of Toronto Press, 1996.

Killan, Gerald. *Protected Places: A History of Ontario's Provincial Parks System*. Toronto, ON: Dundurn Press, 1993.

Kines, Gary Bret. "Chief Man-of-Many-Sides: John Murray Gibbon and His Contribution to the Development of Tourism and the Arts in Canada." MA thesis, Carleton University, 1988.

Kingman, Henry S. "Ski Climbs at Skoki." *CAJ* 19 (1931): 114–16.

Kjeldsen, Jim. *The Mountaineers: A History*. Seattle, WA: The Mountaineers, 1998.

Klaszus, Jeremy. "Trouble in the Fields." *Alberta Views*, 9, 8 (October 2006): 28–33.

Kopas, Paul. *Taking the Air: Ideas and Change in Canada's National Parks*. Vancouver, BC: University of British Columbia Press, 2007.

Kruszyna, Robert, and William L. Putnam. *The Rocky Mountains of Canada North*. New York: American Alpine Club; Banff, AB: Alpine Club of Canada, 1985.

LaForce, Gina. "The Alpine Club of Canada, 1906–1929: Modernization, Canadian Nationalism, and Anglo-Saxon Mountaineering." MA thesis, University of Toronto, 1978.

Laing, Hamilton M. "Wild Life of the Upper Chitina." *CAJ* 15 (1925): 99–114.

Lavallée, Claude. "Mont Québec." *CAJ* 51 (1968): 84.

Lawrence, Andrew. "Kluane National Park Reserve Climbing Summary: 1992." *CAJ* 76 (1993): 68–69.

Leighton, David, and Peggy Leighton. *Artists, Builders and Dreamers: 50 Years at the Banff School*. Toronto, ON: McClelland & Stewart, 1982.

Lenskyj, Helen. *Out of Bounds: Women, Sport and Sexuality*. Toronto, ON: Women's Press, 1986.

Leslie, Susan, ed. *In the Western Mountains: Early Mountaineering in British Columbia*. Victoria, BC: Provincial Archives of British Columbia, 1980.

Lethbridge Herald. "Finishing a Big Job." 7 January 1922, 10.

———. "Protest Against Big Reservoir at Waterton Lakes." 7 January 1922, 7.

———. "Thousands of Irrigation Farmers in Western States Ready to Come to Southern Alberta." 6 January 1922, 7.

Lewis, Gwyn. "Climbs in the Canadian Rockies." *CAJ* 35 (1952): 153–54.

Lewis, Neil. "The Climbing Body, Nature and the Experience of Modernity." In *Bodies of Nature*, edited by Phil Macnaghten and John Urry. London: Sage, 2001.

Longstaff, F.V. "The Story of the Swiss Guides in Canada." *CAJ* 28, 2 (1941–1942): 189–97.

Loo, Tina. "Of Moose and Men: Hunting for Masculinities in British Columbia, 1880–1939." *Western Historical Quarterly* 32, 3 (2001): 296–319.

———. *States of Nature: Conserving Canada's Wildlife in the Twentieth Century, 1867–1939*. Vancouver, BC: University of British Columbia Press, 2006.

Loonsberry, Loraine. "Wild West Shows and the Canadian West." In *Cowboys, Ranchers and the Cattle Business: Cross-Border Perspectives on Ranching History*, edited by Simon M. Evans, Sarah Carter, and Bill Yeo. Calgary, AB: University of Calgary Press, 2000.

Lothian, W.F. *A History of Canada's National Parks*, Vols. I–IV. Ottawa, ON: Parks Canada, 1977.

Louie, Siri Winona. "Gender in the Alpine Club of Canada, 1906–1940." MA thesis, University of Calgary, 1996.

Louv, Richard. *Last Child in the Woods: Saving our Children from Nature-Deficit Disorder*. Chapel Hill, NC: Algonquin Books of Chapel Hill, 2008.

Lower, J. Arthur. *Western Canada: An Outline History*. Vancouver, BC: Douglas & McIntyre, 1983.

Lumley, Elizabeth. "Thorsell, James Westvick." In *Canadian Who's Who: 2001*. Toronto, ON: University of Toronto Press, 2001.

Lund, Rolf Tonning. "A History of Skiing in Canada Prior to 1940." MA thesis, University of Alberta, 1971.

——. "Skiing in Canada: The Early Years." *The Beaver* (Winter 1977): 48–53.

MacAdam, David P. "Pat Baird: Recollection and an Appreciation." *CAJ* 68 (1985): 35.

MacCarthy, A.H. "The Climb." *CAJ* 15 (1925): 59–80.

——. "The First Ascent of Mt. Eon and Its Fatality." *CAJ* 12 (1922): 14–25.

MacDonald, Les. "Oh, Canada." *CAJ* 53 (1970): 2–3.

MacDonald, Robert H. *Sons of Empire*. Toronto, ON: University of Toronto Press, 2003.

MacEachern, Alan. *Natural Selections: National Parks in Atlantic Canada, 1935–1970*. Montreal, QC: McGill-Queen's University Press, 2001.

MacEwan, Grant. *Colonel James Walker: Man of the Western Frontier*. Saskatoon, SK: Western Producer Prairie Books, 1989.

MacGregor, James G. *A History of Alberta*. Edmonton, AB: Hurtig, 1972.

MacIntosh, A. "First Ascent of Peak Three." *CAJ* 30 (1947): 152–53.

Macintosh, Donald, with Tom Bedecki and C.E.S. Franks. *Sport and Politics in Canada: Federal Government Involvement since 1961*. Kingston, ON: McGill-Queen's University Press, 1987.

MacLaren, I.S., ed. *Culturing Wilderness in Jasper National Park: Studies in Two Centuries of Human History in the Upper Athabasca River Watershed*. Edmonton, AB: University of Alberta Press, 2007.

MacLaren, I.S., with Eric Higgs and Gabrielle Zezulka-Mailloux. *Mapper of Mountains: M.P. Bridgland in the Canadian Rockies, 1902–1930*. Edmonton, AB: University of Alberta Press, 2005.

Macoun, James M. "The Flora of Strathcona Park." *CAJ* 5 (1913): 62–70.

——. "List of the Birds Noted in Strathcona Park in July and August, 1912." *CAJ* 5 (1913): 71.

Manning, Harvey, ed. *Mountaineering: The Freedom of the Hills*. 2nd edition. Seattle, WA: Mountaineers Society, 1967.

Markham-Starr, Susan E. "W.J.S. Walker and the Canadian National Parks Association: Protectors of Canadian Leisure Interests." *Leisure/Loisir: Journal of the Canadian Association for Leisure Studies* 32, 2 (July 2008): 649–80. *SPORTDiscus with Full Text*, EBSCO*host*. Accessed 22 January 2010.

Markula, Pirkko, and Richard Pringle. *Foucault, Sport and Exercise: Power, Knowledge and Transforming the Self*. London: Routledge, 2006.

Marsh, James H., ed. *The Canadian Encyclopedia*. 2nd edition. "Calgary." Edmonton, AB: Hurtig, 1988.

Marsh, John. "Glacier National Park." *CAJ* 54 (1971): 39–40.

——. "A History of Backcountry Facilities in Glacier National Park." *CAJ* 55 (1972): 66–67.

Marty, Sid. *Headwaters*. Toronto, ON: McClelland & Stewart, 1973.

——. "Snows of Yesteryear." *Elsewhere*, Rocky Mountain Recording Studios, Calgary, AB, 2002.

McCandless, Robert G. *Yukon Wildlife: A Social History*. Edmonton, AB: University of Alberta Press, 1985.

McCarthy, Jeffrey. "A Theory of Place in North American Mountaineering." *Philosophy and Geography* 5, 2 (2002): 179–94.

McCoubrey, A.A. "A Contribution to the History of Winter Climbing, Ski-Mountaineering and Skiing in Canada." *CAJ* 28, 1 (1942): 116–19.

McCoubrey, A.A., Jr. "Skis in the Little Yoho." *CAJ* 22 (1933): 164–66.

McDowall, Duncan. *Quick to the Frontier: Canada's Royal Bank*. Toronto, ON: McClelland & Stewart, 1993.

McKillop, A.B. *Matters of the Mind: The University in Ontario, 1791–1951*. Toronto, ON: University of Toronto Press, 1991.

McManus, Sheila. "Mapping the Alberta–Montana Borderlands: Race, Ethnicity and Gender in the Late Nineteenth Century." *Journal of American Ethnic History* 20 (2001): 71–87.

Mears, R.P. "The Climbing Rope Defined." *CAJ* 34 (1951): 129–45.

Melville, Michael Leslie. *The Story of the Lovat Scouts 1900–1980*. Edinburgh: St. Andrews Press, 1981.

Merleau-Ponty, Maurice. *Phenomenology of Perception*. New York: Routledge, 1962.

Metcalfe, Alan. *Canada Learns to Play: The Emergence of Organized Sport, 1807–1914*. Toronto, ON: Oxford University Press, 1987.

Metcalfe, Bill. "Orchestra Travels to Kootenays to Play Requiem for Melting B.C. Glacier." *The Vancouver Sun*, 29 July 2013, http://www.vancouversun.com/entertainment/ Orchestra+travels+Kootenays+play+requiem+melting+glacier/8718868/story. html#ixzz2aVIikODH. Accessed 3 December 2013.

Miller, Daniel. *Material Culture and Mass Consumption*. Oxford, UK: Blackwell, 1987.

——. *Stuff*. Cambridge, UK: Polity Place, 2010.

Mitchinson, Wendy. *The Nature of Their Bodies: Women and Their Doctors in Victorian Canada*. Toronto, ON: University of Toronto Press, 1991.

Mitchner, E. Alyn. "The Development of Western Waters 1885–1930." Edmonton, AB: University of Alberta, Department of History, 1973.

——. "William Pearce and Federal Government Activity in the West, 1874–1904." *Canadian Public Administration* 10, 2 (June 1967): 235–43.

——. "William Pearce and Federal Government Activity in Western Canada 1882–1904." PHD dissertation, University of Alberta, 1971.

Mittelstadt, David. *Calgary Goes Skiing: A History of the Calgary Ski Club*. Victoria, BC: Rocky Mountain Books, 2005.

Morrow, Don, and Kevin B. Wamsley. *Sport in Canada: A History*. Toronto, ON: Oxford University Press, 2005.

Morton, Desmond. *1945: When Canada Won the War*. Ottawa, ON: Canadian Historical Association, 1995.

Morton, W.L. *The Progressive Party in Canada*. Toronto, ON: University of Toronto Press, 1950.

Mott, Morris. "One Solution to Urban Crisis: Manly Sports and Winnipeggers, 1900–1914." *Urban History Review* 12, 2 (October 1983): 57–70.

Mummery, A.F. *My Climbs in the Alps and Caucasus*. London: 1896.

Munday, Don. "Mountain Troops: A Lighter View." *CAJ* 30 (1947): 83–90.

——. "Seymour Hut of the Vancouver Section." *CAJ* 19 (1931): 117–19.

——. "A Ski Trip to Mt. Baker." *The Gazette* (June 1930): 7–10.

Murphy, J. Peter. "Homesteading the Athabasca Valley to 1910: An Interview with Edward Wilson Moberly, Prairie Creek, Alberta, 29 August 1980." In *Culturing Wilderness in Jasper National Park: Studies in Two Centuries of Human History in the Upper Athabasca River Watershed*, edited by I.S. MacLaren. Edmonton, AB: University of Alberta Press, 2007.

The National Parks Act, May 30, 1930, c. 33, s. 4.

Natural Resources Canada. "Hydro-electric Development in Canadian West: Great Activity in Prairie Provinces." December 1929.

———. "Mid-Season Review of Power Development in Canada." August 1928.

———. "Mid-Year Water-Power Review." August 1929.

———. "Power Development in Alberta: Rapid Progress Made with Construction of Ghost Plant on Bow River." May 1929.

Neave, Hugh. "The Second Steele Glacier Camp, 1967." *CAJ* 51 (1968): 115–20.

Neave, Ferris. "Spring Snows of the Yoho." *CAJ* 13 (1932): 122–27.

Neave, Roger. "The Yukon Alpine Centennial Expedition: Foreword." *CAJ* 51 (1968): xi–xii.

Nelson, J.G. "Canada's National Parks: Past, Present and Future." In *Recreational Land Use: Perspectives on Its Evolution in Canada*, edited by Geoffrey Wall and John S. Marsh. Ottawa, ON: Carleton University Press, 1982.

Nelson, J.G., with R.C. Scace, eds. *Canadian National Parks: Today and Tomorrow.* Proceedings of a conference organized by the National and Provincial Parks Association of Canada and the University of Calgary, 9–15 October 1968. Calgary, AB: University of Calgary Duplicating Services, 1968.

———. *Canadian Parks in Perspective: Based on the Conference The Canadian National Parks Today and Tomorrow, Calgary, October 1968*. Montreal, QC: Harvest House, 1970.

New York Times. "Mount Logan Scaled by Six Climbers; American in the Lead." 15 July 1925, 1.

New York Times (Jones Library Special Collections). "Mrs. Stone Resting in Mountain Camp." 30 July 1921.

Norton, E.F. *The Fight for Everest: 1924*. London: Edward Arnold, 1925.

O'Brien, M.E. "Monte Rosa from the South." *CAJ* 19 (1931): 100–06.

Oltmann, C. Ruth. *The Valley of Rumours...the Kananaskis*. Seebe, AB: Ribbon Creek Publishing, 1976.

Olton, Percy T., Jr. "The Bugaboos, 1938." *American Alpine Journal* 3, 3 (1939): 292–98.

Opp, James, and John C. Walsh, eds. *Placing Memory and Remembering Place in Canada*. Vancouver, BC: University of British Columbia Press, 2010.

Owram, Douglas. *Born at the Right Time: A History of the Baby Boom Generation*. Toronto, ON: University of Toronto Press, 1996.

Paris, Leslie. "Children's Nature: Summer Camps in New York State, 1919–1941." PHD dissertation, University of Michigan, 2000.

Park, Roberta J., J.A. Mangan, and Patricia Vertinsky. *Gender, Sport, Science: Selected Writings of Roberta J. Park*. London: Routledge, 2009.

Parker, Elizabeth. "The Alpine Club of Canada." *CAJ* 1 (1907): 3–8.

———. "The Approach to Organization." *CAJ* 26 (1938): 97.

———. "A Backward Look at a Midsummer Holiday." *Manitoba Free Press*, 30 September 1905, 21.

———. "The Canadian Rockies: A Joy to Mountaineers." *Manitoba Free Press*, 23 September 1905, 20.

———. "Clara Wheeler: An Appreciation." *CAJ* 23 (1923): 252–53.

_____. "Edward Whymper," *CAJ* 4 (1912): 126–35.

_____. "Frank Yeigh: An Appreciation." *CAJ* 24 (1936): 115–16.

_____. "Henry Bucknall Mitchell, 1857–1935." *CAJ* 23 (1934 and 1935): 87–90.

_____. "A Holiday Trip in the West." *Manitoba Free Press*, 16 September 1905, 21.

_____. "Mathew Arnold's Alpine Poetry." *CAJ* 8 (1910): 178–82.

_____. "Report of the Secretary." *CAJ* 1, 1 (1907): 164–66.

_____. "Report of the Secretary." *CAJ* (1908): 323.

_____. "Reviews: *The Rockies of Canada*, by Walter Dwight Wilcox." *CAJ* 3 (1909): 142–44.

_____. "Reviews: Two Notable Alpine Books." *CAJ* 2 (1910): 204.

_____. "The Selkirk Range." *Manitoba Free Press*, 25 November 1905, 23.

_____. "Some Memories of the Mountains." *CAJ* 17 (1929): 56–60.

Parker, Herschel C. "Conquering Mt. McKinley: The Parker-Browne Expedition of 1912."
       CAJ 5 (1913): 11–19.

Parkes, Fred H.H. "Commission Brief." *CAJ* 39 (1956): 125–28.

Parks Canada. "Rouge National Park Initiative." http://www.pc.gc.ca/progs/np-pn/cnpn-
       cnnp/rouge/index.aspx. Accessed 9 December 2013.

_____. "Time for Nature: Healing Broken Connections." http://www.pc.gc.ca/canada/pn-tfn/
       pdf/2007/2007-12-10_e.pdf. Accessed 17 November 2009.

_____. "Kluane National Park and Reserve, Cultural Heritage." http://www.pc.gc.ca/pn-np/
       yt/kluane/natcul/natcul2_e.asp. Accessed 21 April 2009.

Pedersen, Larry. "Allowable Annual Cuts in British Columbia: The Agony and the Ecstasy."
       UBC Faculty of Forestry Jubilee Lecture, March 20, 2003, http://www.for.gov.bc.ca/
       hts/pubs/jubilee_ubc.pdf. Accessed 16 March 2009.

Peepre, Juri, and Philip Dearden. "The Role of Aboriginal Peoples." In *Parks and Protected
       Areas in Canada: Planning and Management*, edited by Philip Dearden and Rick
       Rollins. Toronto, ON: Oxford University Press, 2002.

Phelps, Dan. "Conservation, Preservation: Same Thing." *CAJ* 54 (1971): 58–59.

Pilley, Dorothy. *Climbing Days*. London: G. Bell & Sons, 1935.

Pilley Richards, Dorothy. "Club Proceedings Lake O'Hara Camp, 1943." *CAJ* 28, 2 (1943):
       277–81.

Potyandi, Barry. *Where the Rivers Meet: A History of the Upper Oldman River Basin to 1939*.
       Lethbridge, AB: Robins Southern Printing, 1990.

Prentice, Alison, Paula Bourne, Gail Cuthbert Brandt, and Beth Light. *Canadian Women: A
       History*. Toronto, ON: Harcourt Brace, 1988.

Pronger, Brian. *Body Fascism: Salvation in the Technology of Physical Fitness*. Toronto, ON:
       University of Toronto Press, 2002.

Prosper, Lisa. "Wherein Lies the Heritage Value? Rethinking the Heritage Value of Cultural
       Landscapes from an Aboriginal Perspective." *The George Wright Forum*, 24, 2 (2007):
       117–24.

Rak, Julie. "Social Climbing on Annapurna: Gender in High-altitude Mountaineering
       Narratives." *English Studies in Canada*, 33, 1–2 (2007): 109–46.

Ramshaw, Gregory. "The Construction of Sport Heritage Attractions." PHD dissertation,
       University of Alberta, 2009.

Rankin, Andrea J. "Climbs from Prairie Camp." In *Expedition Yukon: The 30th Anniversary
       Celebration*, edited by Marnie Fisher and R.W. Sandford. Canmore, AB: Alpine Club of
       Canada, 1997.

Regehr, T.D. *The Beauharnois Scandal: A Story of Canadian Entrepreneurship and Politics.* Toronto, ON: University of Toronto Press, 1990.

R. v. Syncrude Canada Ltd. 2010 ABPC 229 (CanLII). 2010-06-25, Provincial Court. Alberta.

Reichwein, PearlAnn, "Elizabeth Parker." In *Biographical dictionary of American and Canadian Naturalists and Environmentalists,* edited by Keir B. Sterling, Richard P. Harmond, George A. Cevasco, and Lorne F. Hammond. Westport, CT: Greenwood Press, 1997.

——. "Holiday at the Banff School of Fine Arts: The Cinematic Production of Culture, Nature, and Nation in the Canadian Rockies, 1945–1952." *Journal of Canadian Studies* 39, 1 (Winter 2005): 49–73.

——. "Expedition Yukon 1967: Canada's Centennial and the Politics of Mountaineering in Kluane." Canadian Historical Review 92, 3 (September 2011): 481–514.

Reichwein, PearlAnn, and Karen Fox. "Margaret Fleming and the Alpine Club of Canada: A Woman's Place in Mountain Leisure and Literature, 1932–1952." *Journal of Canadian Studies* 36, 3 (Fall 2001): 35.

——, eds. *Mountain Diaries: The Alpine Adventures of Margaret Fleming, 1929–1980.* Calgary, AB: Historical Society of Alberta, 2004.

Reichwein, PearlAnn, and Lisa McDermott. "Opening the Secret Garden: Mary Schäffer, Jasper Park Conservation, and the Survey of Maligne Lake, 1911." In *Culturing Wilderness in Jasper National Park: Studies in Two Centuries of Human History in the Upper Athabasca River Watershed,* edited by I.S. MacLaren. Edmonton, AB: University of Alberta Press, 2007.

Richards, John, and Larry Pratt. *Prairie Capitalism: Power and Influence in the New West.* Toronto, ON: McClelland & Stewart, 1981.

Robbins, David. "Sport, Hegemony and the Middle Class: The Victorian Mountaineers." *Theory, Culture & Society* 4, 3 (1987): 579–601.

Robinson, Zac. *A Family for the Outfit: Harrisons and the General Mountaineering Camp.* Canmore, AB: The Alpine Club of Canada, 2008.

——. "The Golden Years of Canadian Mountaineering: Asserted Ethics, Form, and Style, 1886–1925." *Sport History Review* 35 (2004): 1–19.

——. "Selected Alpine Climbs." PHD dissertation, University of Alberta, 2006.

——. "Storming the Heights: Canadian Frontier Nationalism and the Making of Manhood in the Conquest of Mount Robson, 1906–13." *International Journal of Sport History* 22, 3 (May 2005): 415–33.

Robinson, Zac, and PearlAnn Reichwein, "Canada's Everest? Rethinking the First Ascent of Mt. Logan and the Politics of Nationhood, 1925." *Sport History Review* 35 (November 2004): 95–121.

Rosenbaum, Stan. "A Photographic Essay about the Climb." In *Proudly Canadian, Expo 67 in Montreal, a Photo Collection about Canada's Centennial Celebration.* http://expo67. ncf.ca/centennial_peak_p2.html. Accessed 18 January 2008.

——. "President's Message." *The Gazette* 81 (May 1973): 1.

Routledge, Karen. "'Being a Girl Without Being a Girl': Gender and Mountaineering on Mount Waddington, 1926–36." *BC Studies* 141 (Spring 2004): 31–58.

Rowe, Stan. *Home Places: Essays on Ecology.* Edmonton, AB: NeWest Press, 2002.

Runte, Alfred. *National Parks: The American Experience.* Lincoln, NE: University of Nebraska Press, 1979.

Russell, Mary. *The Blessings of a Good Thick Skirt: Women Travellers and Their World.* London: Flamingo, 1994.

Rutherdale, Myra, and Jim Miller, "'It's Our Country': First Nations' Participation in the Indian Pavilion at Expo '67." *Journal of the Canadian Historical Association* 17, 2 (2006): 148–73.

Ryden, Kent C. *Mapping the Invisible Landscape: Folklore, Writing, and the Sense of Place.* Iowa City: University of Iowa Press, 1993.

Sandlos, John. *Hunters at the Margin: Native People and Wildlife Conservation in the Northwest Territories.* Vancouver, BC: University of British Columbia Press, 2007.

Saskatoon Star Phoenix. "Industry in National Parks." 20 August 1930, 13.

Schäffer, Mary M. "Breaking the Way." *Rod and Gun in Canada* 6, 3 (1904): 111–12, cited in *This Wild Spirit: Women in the Rocky Mountains of Canada,* edited by Colleen Skidmore. Edmonton, AB: University of Alberta Press, 2006.

Schama, Simon. *Landscape and Memory.* New York: A.A. Knopf, 1995.

Schindler, David. "Climate Unchanged." *Alberta Views* (September 2013): 19.

Schintz, Mike. *High Walls and Close Calls and other Tales from the Warden Service.* Calgary, AB: Rocky Mountain Books, 2005.

Schneider, Steven. *High Technology.* Chicago, IL: Contemporary Books, 1980.

Scott, Chic. *Powder Pioneers: Ski Stories from the Canadian Rockies and Columbia Mountains.* Calgary, AB: Rocky Mountain Books, 2005.

———. *Pushing the Limits: The Story of Canadian Mountaineering.* Calgary, AB: Rocky Mountain Books, 2000.

Selters, Andy. *Ways to the Sky: A Historical Guide to North American Mountaineering.* Golden, CO: American Alpine Club Press, 2004.

Sheppard, H., N. Woledge, O. Hermanrude, R. Wood, and W. Vroom. *Backcountry Management Plan for the Four Contiguous Mountain National Parks, 1973.* Field, BC: Indian and Northern Affairs, 25 September 1973.

Sherman, Paddy. "Mount Manitoba." *CAJ* 51 (1968): 55–58.

Shokoples, Cyril. "Harrisons." *CAJ* 81 (1998): 61–62.

Silversides, Brock V. *Waiting for the Light: Early Mountain Photography in British Columbia and Alberta, 1865–1939.* Saskatoon, SK: Fifth House, 1995.

Sissons, C.B., and E.O. Wheeler. "Morrison P. Bridgland." *CAJ* 31 (1948): 218–22.

Skidmore, Colleen, ed. *This Wild Spirit: Women in the Rocky Mountains of Canada.* Edmonton, AB: University of Alberta Press, 2006.

Slemon, Stephen. "Climbing Mount Everest: Postcolonialism in the Culture of Ascent." *Canadian Literature* 158 (Autumn 1998): 15–41.

Sloan, Gordon McGregor. *Report of the Commissioner Relating to the Forest Resources of British Columbia.* Victoria, BC: C.F. Banfield, Printer to the King, 1945.

Smith, Cyndi. *Jasper Park Lodge in the Heart of the Canadian Rockies.* Jasper, AB: Cyndi Smith, 1985.

———. *Off the Beaten Track: Women Adventurers and Mountaineers in Western Canada.* Jasper, AB: Coyote Books; 1989.

Smith, D.W., R.K. Guest, C.P. Svrcek, and K. Farahbakhsh. "Public Health Evaluation of Drinking Water Systems for First Nations in Alberta, Canada." *Journal of Environmental Engineering and Science* 5 (2006): S1–S17. http://article.pubs.nrc-cnrc.gc.ca/RPAS/rpv?hm=HInit&afpf=s06-023.pdf&journal=jees&volume=5. Accessed 10 September 2009.

Smith, Gertrude. "Mount Saskatchewan." *CAJ* 51 (1968): 87–88.

Smith Maguire, Jennifer. "Michel Foucault: Sport, Power, Technologies and Governmentality." In *Theory, Sport and Society*, edited by Joseph Maguire and Kevin Young. Oxford, UK: Elsevier Science, 2002.

Synder, Gary. *No Nature: New and Selected Poems*. New York: Pantheon Books, 1992.

Stewart, Gordon T. "The British Reaction to the Conquest of Everest." *Journal of Sport History* 7 (Spring 1980): 21–39.

Strasdin, Kate. "'An Easy Day for a Lady...': The Dress of Early Women Mountaineers." *Costume* 38 (2004): 72–85.

Strong-Boag, Veronica, and Carole Gerson. *Paddling Her Own Canoe: The Times and Texts of E. Pauline Johnson (Tekahionwake)*. Toronto, ON: University of Toronto Press, 2000.

Strom, Erling. *Pioneers on Skis*. Central Valley, NY: Smith Clove Press, 1977.

Struck, Doug. "Canada Evacuates Indian Reserve Over Contaminated Water Supply." *The Washington Post*, 27 October 2005, A22.

Swinnerton, Guy. "The Alberta Park System: Policy and Planning." In *Parks and Protected Areas in Canada: Planning and Management*, edited by Philip Dearden and Rick Rollins. Toronto, ON: Oxford University Press, 1993.

Tallentire, Jenéa L. "Building a 'Shining Moment': Social Memory and Community Identity in the 1967 Centennial Projects." Unpublished paper presented at the Canadian Historical Association Conference, Quebec, 30 April 2001.

Taylor, C.J. "The Canadian National Parks Today and Tomorrow Conference of 1968 vs. Banff and Jasper National Parks." Canadian Parks for Tomorrow Conference, May 8–12, 2008, 40th Anniversary, CD-ROM, 1–11.

———. "The Changing Habitat of Jasper Tourism." In *Culturing Wilderness in Jasper National Park: Studies of Two Centuries of Human History in the Upper Athabasca River Watershed*, edited by I.S. MacLaren. Edmonton, AB: University of Alberta Press, 2007.

———. "Legislating Nature: The National Parks Act of 1930." In *To See Ourselves/To Save Ourselves: Ecology and Culture in Canada*, edited by Rowland Lorimer. Montreal, QC: Association for Canadian Studies, 1991.

———. *Negotiating the Past: The Making of Canada's National Historic Parks and Sites*. Montreal, QC: McGill-Queen's University Press, 1990.

Taylor, William C. *Highland Soldiers: The Story of a Mountain Regiment*. Canmore, AB: Coyote Books, 1994.

Tetarenko, Lorne, and Kim Tetarenko. *Ken Jones: Mountain Man*. Calgary, AB: Rocky Mountain Books, 2000.

Thorpe, F.J. "Historical Perspective on the 'Resources for Tomorrow' Conference." In *Resources for Tomorrow*. Ottawa, ON: Department of Northern Affairs and National Resources, 1961.

Thorsell, James W. *An Analysis of Mountaineering and Ski Touring Registrations, Banff National Park, 1966–67*. Ottawa, ON: National Parks Service, Planning, National and Historic Parks Branch, Department of Indian Affairs and Northern Development, 1967.

———. "On Planning Canada's Mountain National Parks." *CAJ* 54 (1971): 18–19.

Tilley, Christopher. "Identity, Place, Landscape and Heritage." *Journal of Material Culture* 11, 1 (March–July 2006): 7–32.

Tillotsen, Shirley. *The Public at Play: Gender and the Politics of Recreation in Post-War Ontario*. Toronto, ON: University of Toronto Press, 2000.

London Times. "Mt. Logan Climbed, Canadian Party's Exploit." 15 July 1925, 14.

Tippett, Maria. *Making Culture: English-Canadian Institutions and the Arts before the Massey Commission*. Toronto, ON: University of Toronto Press, 1990.

Toronto Daily Star. "Mt. Logan Has Been Climbed for First time: Party of Six Canadians Reported Back From Successful Climb, Americans Drop Out, Bitter Cold and Blinding Blizzard Was Fought by the Hardy Alpinists." 14 July 1925, 1.

———. "Writer and Churchman, Frank Yeigh buried to-day." 28 October 1935, 5.

Towner, John. "The Grand Tour: Sources and a Methodology for an Historical Study of Tourism." *Tourism Management* 5 (1984): 211–15.

Trottier, Garry C., and George W. Scotter. *A Survey of Backcountry Use and the Resulting Impact near Lake Louise, Banff National Park*. Edmonton, AB: Canadian Wildlife Service, 1973.

Tuan, Yi-Fu. *Dominance and Affection: The Making of Pets*. New Haven, CT: Yale University Press, 1984.

———. *Space and Place: The Perspective of Experience*. Minneapolis, MN: University of Minnesota Press, 1997.

———. *Topophilia: A Study of Environmental Perception, Attitudes, and Values*. New York: Columbia University Press, 1990.

Turner, James Morton. "From Woodcraft to 'Leave No Trace': Wilderness, Consumerism, and Environmentalism in Twentieth-Century America." *Environmental History* 7, 3 (July 2002): 462–84.

Underhill, Miriam O'Brien. "Manless Climbing." In *Leading Out*, edited by Rachel da Silva. Seattle, WA: Seal Press, 1992.

Underhill, Robert L.M. "Modern Ice Climbing Equipment." *CAJ* 22 (1933): 116–32.

———. "Modern Rock Climbing Equipment." *CAJ* 21 (1932): 165.

United Nations Educational, Scientific, and Cultural Organization, Intergovernmental Committee for the Protection of the World Natural and Cultural Heritage. *Operational Guidelines for the Implementation of the World Heritage Convention*. Paris: World Heritage Centre, January 2008.

United Nations Educational, Scientific, and Cultural Organization. "World Heritage, the List." http://whc.unesco.org/pg.cfm?cid=31&id_site=72. Accessed 15 June 2009.

University of Alberta. "University of Alberta: People, James Thorsell." http://www.ualbertacentennial.ca/people/displaybio.php?bio_id=168. Accessed 24 October 2008.

Unsworth, Walt. *Hold the Heights: The Foundations of Mountaineering*. Seattle, WA: Mountaineers, 1994.

———, ed. *Encyclopedia of Mountaineering*. London: Robert Hale, 1975.

Urry, John. *The Tourist Gaze: Leisure and Travel in Contemporary Societies*. San Francisco, CA: Sage, 1990.

Vamplew, Wray. "Taking a Gamble or a Racing Certainty: Sports Museums and Public Sports History." *Journal of Sport History* 31, 2 (Summer 2004): 177–88.

Van Tighem, Kevin. "Safeguarding the Source: How Alberta Can Heal its Headwaters—Before We Run Dry." *Alberta Views* (July/August 2013): 28–35.

———. "Waterton, Crown of the Continent." *Borealis* 2, 1 (May–July 1990): 24–30.

Vaux, George, Jr., and William S. Vaux. "Glacier Observations." *CAJ* 1, 1 (1907): 138.

Vertinsky, Patricia Anne. *The Eternally Wounded Woman: Women, Doctors, and Exercise in the Late Nineteenth Century*. Urbana, IL: University of Illinois Press, 1994.

——. "Locating a 'Sense of Place': Space, Place and Gender in the Gymnasium." In *Sites of Sport: Space, Place, Experience*, edited by Patricia Vertinsky and John Bale. London: Routledge, 2004.

Vertinsky, Patricia Anne, and John Bale, eds. *Sites of Sport: Space, Place, Experience*. London: Routledge, 2004.

Waiser, W.A. *Park Prisoners: The Untold Story of Western Canada's National Parks, 1915–1946*. Saskatoon, SK: Fifth House, 1995.

Wall, G., and R. Wallis. "Camping for Fun: A Brief History of Camping in North America." In *Recreational Land Use: Perspectives on Its Evolution in Canada*, edited by Geoffrey Wall and John S. Marsh. Ottawa, ON: Carleton University Press, 1982.

Wall, Geoffrey. "Recreational Lands." In *Historical Atlas of Canada Volume III: Addressing the Twentieth Century 1891–1961*, edited by Donald Kerr and Deryck W. Holdsworth. Toronto, ON: University of Toronto Press, 1990.

Wall, Karen. "Fort Edmonton Mall: Heritage, Community and Commerce." PHD dissertation, University of Alberta, 1998.

Wall, Sharon. *The Nature of Nurture*. Vancouver, BC: University of British Columbia Press, 2009.

——. "Totem Poles, Teepees, and Token Traditions: 'Playing Indian' at Ontario Summer Camps, 1920–1955." *Canadian Historical Review* 86, 3 (September 2005): 513–44.

Waterman, Jonathan. *Where Mountains are Nameless: Passion and Politics in the Arctic National Wildlife Refuge*. New York: W.W. Norton and Company, 2005.

Wates, Cyril G. "The Memorial Cabin on Penstock Creek." *CAJ* 19 (1930): 124–29.

——, ed. *Songs of Canadian Climbers*. Edmonton, AB: Alpine Club of Canada, c. 1922.

Wates, Cyril G., and E.R. Gibson, "The Eremite and Beyond." *CAJ* 22 (1933): 63–81.

——. "The Memorial Cabin in 1931." *CAJ* 20 (1931): 5–29.

Watson, G. Llewellyn. *Social Theory and Critical Understanding*. Washington, DC: University Press of America, 1982.

Weber, Bob. "Proposed Oil Sands Health Study Derailed After Aboriginal Band Pulls Support Over Cancer Rate Debate." *Financial Post*, 22 February 2013, http://business.financialpost.com/2013/02/22/oil-sands-health-survey-collapses-after-aboriginal-band-pulls-support/?__lsa=e169-0f63. Accessed 9 December 2013.

Weekend Picture Magazine. "High Mountain Holiday." 7 February 1953, 1–5.

Weekly Albertan. "Are We Irrigation Mad? Markets Great Problem." 11 March 1922, 20.

——. "Debate Tame on Question of Transfer of Resources." 9 March 1922, 1, 5.

——. "Dominion Will Keep Irrigation Surveys Going." 6 March 1922, 2.

——. "Farmers In Dry Belt Abandon Their Farms." 4 January 1922, 2.

. "Industries for the Irrigation Districts." 21 February 1922, 4.

——. "Interesting Comment on Survey Board Report." 9 March 1922, 4.

——. "An Irrigation Dam at Waterton Lakes." 16 March 1922, 6.

——. "King Offers Natural Resources to Prairie Provinces." 1 March 1922, 1.

——. "Legislators Will Talk over the Policy of the Resources." 7 March 1922, 1.

——. "Plan for Carrying Out Irrigation Legislation." 30 March 1922, 1.

——. "Take the Resources, Give Up Subsidies, Offer of Dominion." 2 March 1922, 1.

West, Roxroy. "Swiss Guides and the Village of Edelweiss." *The Beaver* (Summer 1979): 50–53.

Wheeler, Arthur O. "The Alpine Club of Canada." *Canadian Life and Resources* (March 1910): 7–12.

_____. "The Alpine Club of Canada in Strathcona Park." *CAJ* 5 (1913): 82–95.

_____. "The Alpine Club of Canada's Expedition to Jasper Park, Yellowhead Pass and Mount Robson Region, 1911." *CAJ* 4 (1912): 1–83.

_____. "In Memoriam: Elizabeth Parker." *CAJ* (1944–45): 125.

_____. "Memorandum." *The Gazette* (June 1922): 5.

_____. "National Parks Association." *The Gazette* (June 1923): 4–5.

_____. "Origin and Founding of the Alpine Club of Canada, 1906." *CAJ* 26 (1938): 82–95.

_____. "Recent Proposal to Exploit Lake Minnewanka." *Crag and Canyon*, 22 August 1930, 1.

_____. "Report of 1910 Camp." *CAJ* 3 (1911): 188–96.

Wheeler, A.O., and Elizabeth Parker. *The Selkirk Mountains: A Guide for Mountaineers and Pilgrims*. Winnipeg, MB: Stovel Company, 1912.

Wheeler, E.O. "Foreword." *CAJ* 37 (1954): 1–6.

_____. "Golden Jubilee." *CAJ* 39 (1956): 3–24.

_____. "Mount Elkhorn: Strathcona Park." *CAJ* 5 (1913): 44–48.

White, Jim. "The Freshfields: ACC General Mountaineering Camp, 1969." *CAJ* 53 (1970): 76.

Whymper, Edward. *Scrambles Amongst the Alps*. London: John Murray, 1954. First published 1871, John Murray.

Whyte, William. "Greetings." *CAJ* 1, 1 (1907): 1–2.

Wiessner, Fritz H. "The First Ascent of Mt. Waddington." *CAJ* 24 (1936): 18–24.

Wilbur, Richard. *The Bennett Administration, 1930–1935*. Ottawa, ON: Canadian Historical Association, 1969.

Williams, Chris. "'That Boundless Ocean Of Mountains': British Alpinists and the Appeal of the Canadian Rockies, 1885–1920." *The International Journal of the History of Sport* 22, 1 (January 2005): 70–87.

Williams, Raymond. *Marxism and Literature*. Oxford, UK: Oxford University Press, 1977.

Wilson, Alexander. *Culture of Nature: North American Landscape from Disney to the Exxon Valdez*. Toronto, ON: Between the Lines, 1991.

Wilson, J. Macartney. "The Camp in the Upper Yoho Valley (1914)." *CAJ* 6 (1915): 217–28.

Wilts, C.H. "Unusual Ice Climbing." *CAJ* 35 (1952): 160.

Winnipeg Free Press. "Mrs. Elizabeth Parker Dies In Her 88th Year." 27 October 1944, 11.

Wright, Jack. "Urban Open Space in Transition." In *Proceedings of the Third Canadian Congress on Leisure Research*, edited by Thomas L. Burton and Jan Taylor. Edmonton, AB: The University of Alberta, Canadian Association for Leisure Studies, 1983.

Yeigh, Frank. "Canada's First Alpine Club Camp." *CAJ* 1, 1 (1907): 47–57.

_____. *Through the Heart of Canada*. Toronto, ON: H. Frowde, 1910.

Yeo, William B. "Making Banff a Year-Round Park." In *Winter Sports in the West*, edited by E.A. Corbett and A.W. Rasporich. Calgary, AB: Historical Society of Alberta, 1990.

Yukon Daily News. "Alpine Dinner a Success." 20 July 1967, 1.

_____. "Climbers on Schedule." 5 July 1967, 1.

Zeller, Suzanne. *Inventing Canada: Early Victorian Science and the Idea of a Transcontinental Nation*. Toronto, ON: University of Toronto Press, 1987.

_____. "Logan, Sir William Edmond." In *The Canadian Encyclopedia*, 1st edition, edited by James H. Marsh. Edmonton, AB: Hurtig, 1985.

Zezulka-Mailloux, Gabrielle. "Laying the Tracks for Tourism: Paradoxical Promotions and the Development of Jasper National Park." In *Culturing Wilderness in Jasper*

National Park: Studies in Two Centuries of Human History in the Upper Athabasca River Watershed, edited by I.S. MacLaren. Edmonton, AB: University of Alberta Press, 2007.

Index

Mathews, Bill, 228

Maurice, Eileen, 80

McCaul, R.D., 125

McCoubrey, Alexander
    and ACC membership, 163, 164–65
    on admitting minors to camp, 83
    biography, 111
    as *CAJ* editor, 44
    at camp, **81**
    and fee paying, 167
    and CNPA, 143
    and skiing, 176, 178, 183

McDonald, Jean, **83**

Memorial Hut, 181

memory-making, 232–33, 241–42

Mendelson, Miss, 46–47

Merrill, Miss, 46

Minnewanka dam project, 137, 156–62

Mitchell, Stanley
    and ACC finances, 163, 165
    administration of summer camps, 67, 70
    on admitting minors to camp, 83
    biography, 68-**69**
    on Brewsters, 74, 75
    and *CAJ*, 27
    death, 199
    and discrimination, 46–47, 48–49
    on first ACC executive, 32
    as founding member, **24**
    as friend of W.R. Tweedy, 71–72
    on hiring cooks, 80
    view of ACC's distinctiveness, 173, 184
    work as secretary of ACC, 108, 110

Moat Lake, 209

Moberly, Edward, 73

Moffat, T.B.
    and ACC finances, 110, 165
    and ACC prejudice, 46, 47, 49
    on ACC's role in economic development, 185
    as climber, **94**
    as head of ACC Calgary section, 90
    and CNPA, **144**, 145
    and Waterton Lakes dam proposal, 134

Mondolfo, Lucio, 218

Mondolfo, Vicki, 218

Monod's Sports Shop, 222

Moore, Philip A., 74–75

Morgan, Robert, 54

Morton, Jr., Marcus, 127

mountaineering
    and *CAJ*, 27–28
    conservative style of ACC, 92–96, 185, 223, 233
    as core of ACC, 4
    end of Canadian golden era, 57–58
    framework for history of, 10–11
    history of women in, 38–39, 40–42
    as imperialist expansionism, 89–90
    importance of, 308–09
    and improved equipment, 220–23
    international trends in 1920s and 30s, 171–72
    as nationhood exercise, 233–34
    pre-Alpine Club years, 15–16
    seen as male domain, 37–38
    and sense of oneness with nature, 237–38, 251
    sense of place and ethic, 7–8, 10, 279–81, 293
    and technical climbing, 56–57, 96, 171, 172, 173–74, 216, 219–20
    versions of its history, xii–xiii
    in Yukon, 231
    see also Alpine Club of Canada (ACC)

Mount Alberta, 56

Mount Assiniboine Camp, 164

Mount Assiniboine Provincial Park, 86, **101**

Mount Assiniboine Walking and Riding Tour, 122–28, 138, 149

Mount Baker, **199**

Mount Eisenhower, **207**

Mount Logan, 50–55, 55–57

Mount Robson, 50, 90

Mount Robson Provincial Park, 204

Mount Sir Wilfrid Laurier, 298–300

Mumm, Arnold L., 84

Mummery (Blaeberry River), 209

Munday, Don, 40, 45, 176, 183, 188, 188-**89**, 190, 192

Munday, Edith, **45**

Munday, Phyllis, 40, 44, **45**, 78, 176, **191**, 244, 282, 300

Murphy, T.G., 162

Nahanni National Park, 249

Naiset Cabins, 218

National and Provincial Parks Association of Canada (NPPAC), 226, 263, 278

National Film Board of Canada, 194, 211

nationalism, 57, 223, 233–34, 235, 246, 251, 252

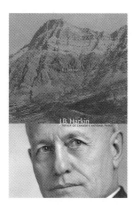

J.B. Harkin

Father of Canada's National Parks

E.J. (TED) HART

592 pages | 64 B&W photographs, index

Mountain Cairns: A series on the history and culture of the Canadian Rocky Mountains

978-0-88864-512-8 | $34.95 (T) paper

978-0-88864-761-0 | $27.99 (T) PDF

Canadian History/Biography

Conrad Kain

Letters from a Wandering Mountain Guide, 1906–1933

CONRAD KAIN

Edited with an Introduction by ZAC ROBINSON

MARIA KOCH & JOHN KOCH, *Translators*

CHIC SCOTT, *Foreword*

472 pages | 30 B&W photographs, 3 maps, notes, bibliography, index

Mountain Cairns: A series on the history and culture of the Canadian Rocky Mountains

978-1-77212-004-2 | $34.95 (T) paper

978-1-77212-016-5 | $27.99 (T) EPUB

978-1-77212-017-2 | $27.99 (T) Amazon Kindle

978-1-77212-018-9 | $27.99 (T) PDF

Letters/Mountaineering/Canadian Rockies

Culturing Wilderness in Jasper National Park

*Studies in Two Centuries of Human History in the
Upper Athabasca River Watershed*

I.S. MACLAREN, *Editor*

THE RT. HON. JEAN CHRÉTIEN, *Foreword*

400 pages | Colour throughout, introduction, foreword, maps, notes, bibliography, index

Mountain Cairns: A series on the history and culture of the Canadian Rocky Mountains

978-0-88864-483-1 | $45.00 (T) paper

978-0-88864-570-8 | $35.99 (T) PDF

History/Tourism/National Parks